Big Data Science in Finance

Big Data Science in Finance

By

Irene Aldridge
Marco Avellaneda

WILEY

Published by John Wiley & Sons, Inc., Hoboken, New Jersey.

Published simultaneously in Canada.

For general information on our other products and services or for technical support, please contact our Customer Care Department within the United States at (800) 762–2974, outside the United States at (317) 572–3993, or fax (317) 572–4002.

Wiley publishes in a variety of print and electronic formats and by print-on-demand. Some material included with standard print versions of this book may not be included in e-books or in print-on-demand. If this book refers to media such as a CD or DVD that is not included in the version you purchased, you may download this material at http://booksupport.wiley.com. For more information about Wiley products, visit www.wiley.com.

Library of Congress Cataloging-in-Publication Data is available:

ISBN 9781119602989 (Hardcover)
ISBN 9781119602996 (ePDF)
ISBN 9781119602972 (ePub)

Cover Design: Wiley
Cover Images: © Anton Khrupin anttoniart/Shutterstock, ©Sunward Art/Shutterstock

SKY10023471_122120

Contents

Preface

Financial technology has been advancing steadily through much of the last 100 years, and the last 50 or so years in particular. In the 1980s, for example, the problem of implementing technology in financial companies rested squarely with the prohibitively high cost of computers. Bloomberg and his peers helped usher in Fintech 1.0 by creating wide computer leasing networks that propelled data distribution, selected analytics, and more into trading rooms and research. The next break, Fintech 2.0, came in the 1990s: the Internet led the way in low-cost electronic trading, globalization of trading desks, a new frontier for data dissemination, and much more. Today, we find ourselves in the midst of Fintech 3.0: data and communications have been taken to the next level thanks to their pure volume and 5G connectivity, and Artificial Intelligence (AI) and Blockchain create meaningful advances in the way we do business.

To summarize, Fintech 3.0 spans the A, B, C, and D of modern finance:

A: Artificial Intelligence (AI)
B: Blockchain technology and its applications
C: Connectivity, including 5G
D: Data, including Alternative Data

Big Data Science in finance spans the A and the D of Fintech, while benefiting immensely from B and C.

The intersection of just these two areas, AI and Data, comprises the field of Big Data Science. When applied to finance, the field is brimming with possibilities. Unsupervised learning, for example, is capable of removing the researcher's bias by eliminating the need to specify a hypothesis. As discussed in the classic book, *How to Lie with Statistics* (Huff [1954] 1991), in the traditional statistical or econometric analysis, the outcome of a statistical experiment is only as good as the question posed. In the traditional environment, the researcher forms a hypothesis, and the data say "yes" or "no" to the researcher's ideas. The binary nature of the answer and the breadth of the researcher's question may contain all sorts of biases the researcher has.

As shown in this book, unsupervised learning, on the other hand, is hypothesis-free. You read that correctly: in unsupervised learning, the data are asked to produce their key drivers *themselves*. Such factorization enables us to abstract human biases and distill the true data story.

As an example, consider the case of minority lending. It is no secret that most traditional statisticians and econometricians are white males, and possibly carry their race- and gender-specific biases with them throughout their analyses. For instance, when one looks at the now, sadly, classic problem of lending in predominantly black neighborhoods, traditional modelers may pose hypotheses like "Is it worth investing our money there?," "Will the borrowers repay the loans?," and other yes/no questions biased from inception. Unsupervised learning, when given a sizable sample of the population, will deliver, in contrast, a set of individual characteristics within the population that the data deem important to lending without yes/no arbitration or implicit assumptions.

What if the data inputs are biased? What if the inputs are collected in a way to intentionally dupe the machines into providing false outcomes? What if critical data are missing or, worse, erased? The answer to this question often lies in the data quantity. As this book shows, if your sample is large enough, in human terms, numbering in millions of data points, even missing or intentionally distorted data are cast off by the unsupervised learning techniques, revealing simple data relationships unencumbered by anyone's opinion or influence.

While many rejoice in the knowledge of unbiased outcomes, some are understandably wary of the impact that artificial intelligence may have on jobs. Will AI replace humans? Is it capable of eliminating jobs? The answers to these questions may surprise. According to the Jevons paradox, when a new technology is convenient and simplifies daily tasks, its utilization does not replace jobs, but creates many new jobs instead, all utilizing this new invention. In finance, all previous Fintech innovations fit the bill: Bloomberg's terminals paved the way for the era of quants trained to work on structured data; the Internet brought in millions of individual investors. Similarly, advances in AI and proliferation of all kinds of data will usher in a generation of new finance practitioners. This book is offering a guide to the techniques that will realize the promise of this technology.

REFERENCE

Huff, D. ([1954] 1991). *How to Lie with Statistics*. New York: Penguin.

Chapter 1

Why Big Data?

Introduction

It is the year 2032, and with a wave of your arm, your embedded chip authenticates you to log into your trading portal. For years, Swedes have already been placing chips above their thumb to activate their train tickets or to store their medical records.[1] Privacy, Big Brother, and health concerns aside, the sheer volume of data collected by IDs from everything from nail salons through subway stations is staggering, yet needs to be analyzed in real time to draw competitive inferences about impending market activity.

Do you think this is an unlikely scenario? During World War II, a passive ID technology was developed to leave messages for one's compatriots inside practically any object. The messages were written in tin foil, but were virtually unnoticeable by one's enemy. They could last forever since they didn't contain a battery or any other energy source, and they were undetectable as they did not emit heat or radiation. The messages were only accessible by the specific radio frequency for which they were written – a radio scanner set to a specific wavelength could pick up the message from a few feet away, without holding or touching the object.

Today, the technology behind these messages has made its way into Radio-Frequency Identification devices, RFIDs. They are embedded into pretty much every product you can buy in any store. They are activated at checkout and at the exit, where giant scanners examine you for any unpaid merchandise in your possession. Most importantly, RFIDs

---

[1] NPR, October 22, 2018, "Thousands of Swedes Are Inserting Microchips Under Their Skin." *All Things Considered*. Available at: https://www.npr.org/2018/10/22/658808705/thousands-of-swedes-are-inserting-microchips-under-their-skin

are used to collect data about your shopping preferences, habits, tastes, and lifestyle. They know whether you prefer red to green, if you buy baby products, and if you drink organic orange juice. And did you know that nine out of every ten purchases you make end up as data transmitted through the Internet to someone's giant private database that is a potential source of returns for a hedge fund?

Welcome to the world of Big Data Finance (BDF), a world where all data have the potential of ending up in a hedge fund database generating extra uncorrelated returns. Data like aggregate demand for toothpaste may predict the near-term and long-term returns of toothpaste manufacturers such as Procter & Gamble. A strong trend toward gluten-free merchandise may affect the way wheat futures are traded. And retail stores are not alone in recording consumer shopping habits: people's activity at gas stations, hair salons, and golf resorts is diligently tracked by credit card companies in data that may all end up in a hedge fund manager's toolkit for generating extra returns. Just like that, a spike in demand for gas may influence short-term oil prices.

Moving past consumer activity, we enter the world of business-to-business (B2B) transactions, also conducted over the Internet. How many bricks are ordered from specific suppliers this spring may be a leading indicator of new housing stock in the North-East. And are you interested in your competitor's supply and demand? Many years ago, one would charter a private plane to fly over a competitor's manufacturing facility to count the number of trucks coming and going as a crude estimate of activity. Today, one can buy much less expensive satellite imagery and count the number of trucks without leaving one's office. Oh, wait, you can also write a computer program to do just that instead.

Many corporations, including financial organizations, are also sitting on data they don't even realize can be used in very productive ways. The inability to identify useful internal data and harness them productively may separate tomorrow's winners from losers.

Whether you like it or not, Big Data is influencing finance, and we are just scratching the surface. While the techniques for dealing with data are numerous, they are still applied to only a limited set of the available information. The possibilities to generate returns and reduce costs in the process are close to limitless. It is an ocean of data and whoever has the better compass may reap the rewards.

And Big Data does not stop on the periphery of financial services. The amount of data generated internally by financial institutions are at a record-setting number. For instance, take exchange data. Twenty years ago, the exchange data that were stored and distributed by the financial institutions comprised Open, High, Low, Close, and Daily Volume for each stock and commodity futures contract. In addition, newspapers printed the yield and price for government bonds, and occasionally, noon or daily closing rates for foreign exchange rates. These data sets are now widely available free of charge from companies like Google and Yahoo.

Today's exchanges record and distribute every single infinitesimal occurrence on their systems. An arrival of a limit order, a limit order cancellation, a hidden order update – all of these instances are meticulously timestamped and documented in maximum detail for posterity and analysis. The data generated for one day by just one exchange can measure in terabytes and petabytes. And the number of exchanges is growing every year. At the time this book was written, there were 23 SEC-registered or "lit" equity exchanges in the U.S. alone,[2] in addition to 57 alternative equity trading venues, including dark pools and order internalizers.[3] The latest exchange addition, the Silicon Valley-based Long Term Stock Exchange, was approved by the regulators on May 10, 2019.[4]

These data are huge and rich in observations, yet few portfolio managers today have the necessary skills to process so much information. To that extent, eFinancialCareers .com reported on April 6, 2017 that robots are taking over traditional portfolio management jobs, and as many as 90,000 of today's well-paid pension-fund, mutual-fund, and hedge-fund positions are bound to be lost over the next decade.[5] On the upside, the same article reported that investment management firms are expected to spend as much as $7 billion on various data sources, creating Big Data jobs geared at acquiring, processing, and deploying data for useful purposes.

Entirely new types of Big Data Finance professionals are expected to populate investment management firms. The estimated number of these new roles is 80 per every $3 billion of capital under management, according to eFinancialCareers. The employees under consideration will comprise:

1. Data scouts or data managers, whose job already is and will continue to be to seek the new data sources capable of delivering uncorrelated sources of revenues for the portfolio managers.
2. Data scientists, whose job will expand into creating meaningful models capable of grabbing the data under consideration and converting them into portfolio management signals.
3. Specialists, who will possess a deep understanding of the data in hand, say, what the particular shade of the wheat fields displayed in the satellite imagery means for the crop production and respective futures prices, or what the market microstructure patterns indicate about the health of the market.

And this trend is not something written in the sky, but is already implemented by a host of successful companies. In March 2017, for example, BlackRock made news when they announced the intent to automate most of their portfolio management function. Two Sigma deploys $45 billion, employing over 1,100 workers, many of whom have data

---

[2] U.S. Securities and Exchange Commission, Investor Information. Available at: https://www.sec.gov/fast-answers/divisionsmarketregmrexchangesshtml.html

[3] U.S. Securities and Exchange Commission, Alternative Trading System ("ATS") List, Alternative Trading Systems with Form ATS on File with the SEC as of November 30, 2019. Available at: https://www.sec .gov/foia/docs/atslist.htm

[4] "U.S. Regulators Approve New Silicon Valley Stock Exchange." Reuters, May 10, 2019. Available at: https://www.reuters.com/article/us-usa-sec-siliconvalley/u-s-regulators-approve-new-silicon-valley-stock-exchange-idUSKCN1SG21K

[5] EFinancialCareers, April 6, 2017. "The New Buy-Side Winners as Big Data Takes Over." Available at: http://news.efinancialcareers.com/uk-en/279725/the-new-buy-side-winners-as-big-data-takes-over/

science backgrounds. Traditional human-driven competition is, by comparison, suffering massive outflows and scrambling to find data talent to fill the void, the *Wall Street Journal* reports.

A recent *Vanity Fair* article by Bess Levin reported that when Steve Cohen, the veteran of the financial markets, reopened his hedge fund in January 2018, it was to be a leader in automation.[6] According to *Vanity Fair*, the fund is pursuing a project to automate trading "using analyst recommendations as an input, the effort involves examining the DNA of trades: the size of positions; the level of risk and leverage." This is one of the latest innovations in Steve Cohen's world, a fund manager whose previous shop, SAC in Connecticut, was one of the industry's top performers. And Cohen's efforts appear to be already paying off. On December 31, 2019, the *New York Post* called Steve Cohen "one of the few bright spots in the bad year for hedge funds" for beating out most peers in fund performance.[7]

Big Data Finance is not only opening doors to a select group of data scientists, but also an entire industry that is developing new approaches to harness these data sets and incorporate them into mainstream investment management. All of this change also creates a need for data-proficient lawyers, brokers, and others. For example, along with the increased volume and value of data come legal data battles. As another *Wall Street Journal* article reported, April 2017 witnessed a legal battle between the New York Stock Exchange (NYSE) and companies like Citigroup, KCG, and Goldman Sachs.[8] At issue was the ownership of order flow data submitted to NYSE: NYSE claims the data are fully theirs, while the companies that send their customers' orders to NYSE beg to differ. Competent lawyers, steeped in data issues, are required to resolve this conundrum. And the debates in the industry will only grow more numerous and complex as the industry develops.

The payouts of studying Big Data Finance are not just limited to guaranteed employment. Per eFinancialCareers, financial quants are falling increasingly out of favor while data scientists and those proficient in artificial intelligence are earning as much as $350,000 per year right out of school.[9]

Big Data scientists are in demand in hedge funds, banks, and other financial services companies. The number of firms paying attention to and looking to recruit Big Data specialists is growing every year, with pension funds and mutual funds realizing

---

[6] *Vanity Fair*, March 15, 2017. "Steve Cohen Ramping Up Effort to Replace Idiot Humans with Machines." Available at: http://www.vanityfair.com/news/2017/03/steve-cohen-ramping-up-effort-to-replace-idiot-humans-with-machines

[7] *New York Post*, December 31, 2019. "Steve Cohen One of Few Bright Spots in Bad Year for Hedge Funds." Available at: https://nypost.com/2019/12/31/steve-cohen-one-of-few-bright-spots-in-bad-year-for-hedge-funds/

[8] *Wall Street Journal*, April 6, 2017. "With 125 Ph.D.s in 15 Countries, a Quant 'Alpha Factory' Hunts for Investing Edge." Available at: https://www.wsj.com/articles/data-clash-heats-up-between-banks-and-new-york-stock-exchange-1491471000

[9] EFinancialCareers, March 23, 2017, "You Should've Studied Data Science." Available at: http://news.efinancialcareers.com/us-en/276387/the-buy-side-is-having-to-sweeten-offers-to-ai-experts-data-scientists-and-quants

the increasing importance of efficient Big Data operations. According to *Business Insider*, U.S. bank J.P. Morgan alone has spent nearly $10 billion dollars just in 2016 on new initiatives that include Big Data science.[10] Big Data science is a component of most of the bank's new initiatives, including end-to-end digital banking, digital investment services, electronic trading, and much more. Big Data analytics is also a serious new player in wealth management and investment banking. Perhaps the only area where J.P. Morgan is trying to limit its Big Data reach is in the exploitation of retail consumer information – the possibility of costly lawsuits is turning J.P. Morgan onto the righteous path of a champion of consumer data protection.

According to Marty Chafez, Goldman Sachs' Chief Financial Officer, Goldman Sachs is also reengineering itself as a series of automated products, each accessible to clients through an Automated Programming Interface (API). In addition, Goldman is centralizing all its information. Goldman's new internal "data lake" will store vast amounts of data, including market conditions, transaction data, investment research, all of the phone and email communication with clients, and, most importantly, client data and risk preferences. The data lake will enable Goldman to accurately anticipate which of its clients would like to acquire or to unload a particular source of risk in specific market conditions, and to make this risk trade happen. According to Chafez, data lake-enabled business is the future of Goldman, potentially replacing thousands of company jobs, including the previously robot-immune investment banking division.[11]

What compels companies like J.P. Morgan and Goldman Sachs to invest billions in financial technology and why now and not before? The answer to the question lies in the evolution of technology. Due to the changes in the technological landscape, previously unthinkable financial strategies across all sectors of the financial industry are now very feasible. Most importantly, due to a large market demand for technology, it is mass-produced and very inexpensive.

Take regular virtual reality video games as an example. The complexity of the 3-D simulation, aided by multiple data points and, increasingly, sensors from the player's body, requires simultaneous processing of trillions of data points. The technology is powerful, intricate, and well-defined, but also an active area of ever-improving research.

This research easily lends itself to the analytics of modern streaming financial data. Not processing the data leaves you akin to a helpless object in the virtual reality game happening around you – the virtual reality you cannot escape. Regardless of whether you are a large investor, a pension fund manager, or a small-savings individual, missing out on the latest innovations in the markets leaves you stuck in a bad scenario.

Why not revert to the old way of doing things: calmly monitoring daily or even monthly prices – doesn't the market just roll off long-term investors? The answer is

---

[10] *Business Insider*, April 7, 2017. "JP Morgan's Fintech Strategy." Available at: http://www.businessinsider .com/jpmorgans-fintech-strategy-2017-4

[11] *Business Insider*, April 6, 2017. "Goldman Sachs Wants to Become Google of Wall Street." Available at: http://www.businessinsider.com/goldman-sachs-wants-to-become-the-google-of-wall-street-2017-4

two-fold. First, as shown in this book, the new machine techniques are able to squeeze new, nonlinear profitability from the same old daily data, putting traditional researchers at a disadvantage. Second, as the market data show, the market no longer ebbs and flows around long-term investment decisions, and everyone, absolutely everyone, has a way of changing the course of the financial markets with a tiniest trading decision.

Most orders to buy and sell securities today come in the smallest sizes possible: 100 shares for equities, similar minimal amounts for futures, and even for foreign exchange. The markets are more sensitive than ever to the smallest deviations from the status quo: a new small order arrival, an order cancellation, even a temporary millisecond breakdown in data delivery. All of these fluctuations are processed in real time by a bastion of analytical artillery, collectively known as Big Data Finance. As in any skirmish, those with the latest ammunition win and those without it are lucky to be carried off the battlefield merely wounded.

With pension funds increasingly experiencing shortfalls due to poor performance and high fees incurred by their chosen sub-managers, many individual investors face non-trivial risks. Will the pension fund inflows from new younger workers be enough to cover the liabilities of pensioners? If not, what is one to do? At the current pace of withdrawals, many retirees may be forced to skip those long-planned vacations and, yes, invest in a much-more affordable virtual reality instead.

It turns out that the point of Big Data is not just about the size of the data that a company manages, although data are a prerequisite. Big Data comprises a set of analytical tools that are geared toward the processing of large data sets at high speed. "Meaningful" is an important keyword here: Big Data analytics are used to derive meaning from data, not just to shuffle the data from one database to another.

Big Data techniques are very different from traditional Finance, yet very complementary, allowing researchers to extend celebrated models into new lives and applications. To contrast traditional quant analysis with machine learning techniques, Breiman (2001) details the two "cultures" in statistical modeling. To reach conclusions about the relationships in the data, the first culture of *data modeling* assumes that the data are generated by a specific stochastic process. The other culture of *algorithmic modeling* lets the algorithmic models determine the underlying data relationships and does not make any a priori assumptions on the data distributions. As you may have guessed, the first culture is embedded in much of traditional finance and econometrics. The second culture, machine learning, developed largely outside of finance and even statistics, for that matter, and presents us *ex ante* with a much more diverse field of tools to solve problems using data.

The data observations we collect are often generated by a version of "nature's black box" – an opaque process that turns inputs x into outputs y (see Figure 1.1). All finance, econometrics, statistics and Big Data professionals are concerned with finding:

1. Prediction: responses y to future input variables x.
2. Information: the intrinsic associations of x and y delivered by nature.

While the two goals of the data modeling traditionalists and the machine learning scientists are the same, their approaches are drastically different as illustrated in Figure 1.2.

Figure 1.1   Natural data relationships: inputs x correspond to responses y.

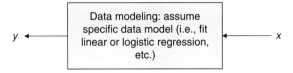

Panel a. Approach of traditional data modeling

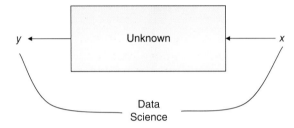

Panel b. Approach of Data Science.

Figure 1.2   Differences in data interpretation between traditional data modeling and data science per Breiman (2001).

The traditional data modeling assumes an a priori function of the relationship between inputs x and outputs y:

$$y = f(x, \textit{random noise } \varepsilon, \textit{parameters } \theta)$$

Following the brute-force fit of data into the chosen function, the performance of the data fit is evaluated via *model validation*: a yes–no using goodness-of-fit tests and examination of residuals.

The machine learning culture assumes that the relationships between x and y are complex and seeks to find a function $y = f(x)$, which is an algorithm that operates on x and predicts y. The performance of the algorithm is measured by predictive accuracy of the function on the data not used in the function estimation (the "out-of-sample" data set).

And what about artificial intelligence (AI), this beast that evokes images of cyborgs in Arnold Schwarzenegger's most famous movies? It turns out that AI is a direct byproduct of data science. The traditional statistical or econometric analysis is a "supervised" approach, requiring a researcher to form a "hypothesis" by asking whether a specific idea is true or false, given the data. The unfortunate side effect of the analysis has been that the output can only be as good as the input: a researcher incapable of dreaming up a hypothesis "outside the box" would be stuck on mundane inferences. The "unsupervised" Big Data approach clears these boundaries; it instead *guides* the researcher toward the key features and factors of the data. In this sense, the unsupervised Big Data approach explains all possible hypotheses to the researcher, without any preconceived notions. The new, expanded frontiers of inferences are making even the dullest accountant-type scientists into superstars capable of seeing the strangest events appear on their respective horizons. Artificial intelligence is the result of data scientists letting the data do the talking and the breathtaking results and business decisions this may bring. The Big Data applications discussed in this book include fast debt rating prediction, fast and optimal factorization, and other techniques that help risk managers, option traders, commodity futures analysts, corporate treasurers, and, of course, portfolio managers and other investment professionals, market makers, and prop traders make better and faster decisions in this rapidly evolving world.

Well-programmed machines have the ability to infer ideas and identify patterns and trends with or without human guidance. In a very basic scenario, an investment case for the S&P 500 Index futures could switch from a "trend following" or "momentum" approach to a "contrarian" or "market-making" approach. The first technique detects a "trend" and follows it. It works if large investors are buying substantial quantities of stocks, so that the algorithms could participate as prices increase or decrease. The second strategy simply buys when others sell and sells when others buy; it works when the market is volatile but has no "trend." One of the expectations of artificial intelligence and machine learning is that Big Data robots can "learn" how to detect trends, counter trends – as well as periods of no trend – attempting to make profitable trades in the different situations by nimbly switching from one strategy to another, or staying in cash when necessary.

Big Data science refers to computational inferences about the data set being used: the bigger the data, the better. The biggest sets of data, possibly spanning all the data available within an enterprise in loosely connected databases or data repositories, are known as *data lakes*, vast containers filled with information. The data may be *dark*, which is collected, yet unexplored and unused by the firm. The data may also be *structured*, fitting neatly into rows and columns of a table, for example, like numeric data. Data also can be *unstructured*, as in something requiring additional processing prior to fitting into a table. Examples of unstructured data may include recorded human speech, email messages, and the like.

The key issue surrounding the data, and, therefore, covered in this book, is data size, or dimensionality. In the case of unstructured data that are not presented in neat tables, how many columns would it take to accommodate all of the data's rich features? Traditional analyses were built for small data, often manageable with basic software, such as Excel. Big Data applications comprise much larger sets of data that are unwieldy and cannot even be opened in Excel-like software. Instead, Big Data applications require their own processing engines and algorithms, often written in Python.

Exactly what kinds of techniques do Big Data tools comprise? Neural networks, discussed in Chapter 2, have seen a spike of interest in Finance. Computationally intensive, but benefiting from the ever-plummeting costs of computing, neural networks allow researchers to select the most meaningful factors from a vast array of candidates and estimate non-linear relationships among them. Supervised and semi-supervised methods, discussed in Chapter 3 and 4, respectively, provide a range of additional data mining techniques that allow for a fast parametric and nonparametric estimation of relationships between variables. Unsupervised learning discussion begins in Chapter 5 and goes on through the end of the book, covering dimensionality reduction, separating signals from noise, portfolio optimization, optimal factor models, Big Data clustering and indexing, missing data optimization, Big Data in stochastic modeling, and much more.

All the techniques in this book are supported by theoretical models as well as practical applications and examples, all with extensive references, making it easy for researchers to dive independently into any specific topic. Best of all, all the chapters include Python code snippets in their Appendices and also online on the book's website, BigDataFinanceBook.com, making it a snap to pick a Big Data model, code it, test it, and put it into implementation.

Happy Big Data!

Appendix 1.A Coding Big Data in Python

This book contains practical ready-to-use coding examples built on publicly available data. All examples are programmed in Python, perhaps the most popular modeling language for data science at the time this book was written. Since Python's syntax is very similar to those of other major languages, such as C++, Java, etc., all the examples presented in this book can be readily adapted to your choice of language and architecture.

To begin coding in Python, first download the Python software. One of the great advantages of Python is that the software is *free*! To download and install Python, go to https://www.python.org/downloads/, select the operating system of the computer on which you are planning to install and run Python, and click "Download." Fair Warning: At the time this book was written, the latest Python software version was 3.7.2. Later versions of Python software may have different commands or syntax. The readers may experience some issues with different versions of the Python software.

After saving the installation file, and installing Python software, open the IDLE editor that comes with the package. The editor typically has a white icon that can be located in the Apps menu. The editor allows one to save Python modules as well as dynamically check for errors and run the modules in the shell with just a click of the "F5" button. In contrast, the black IDLE icon opens an old-school less-user-friendly Python shell without the ability to open an editor. Figure 1.A.1 shows the Apps menu with the white IDLE editor icon circled.

In the editor that opens, select "File -> New" to open a new instance of a Python module. You may choose to save the module right away to avoid accidental loss of your

Figure 1.A.1   Selecting the user-friendly Python editor upon installation.

code. To save the file, select "File -> Save As," navigate to your desired location, and enter the name of the file, for example, "NeuralNetworkSPY_101.py." By convention, all Python files have ".py" extension, similar to ".cpp" of C++ files or ".m" of Matlab files.

Opening a Data File in Python

The first step to a successful data analysis is opening a data file and correctly extracting the content. Here, we show step-by-step instructions to opening a Yahoo! Finance historical data file and loading the content into Python variables.

As a first exercise, we grab and open the entire Yahoo! Finance file for the S&P 500 ETF (NYSE:SPY) we downloaded previously. The file contains 10 years of daily data with the following fields:

- Date in YYYY–MM–DD format
- Daily open
- Daily high
- Daily low
- Daily close
- Daily adjusted close (accounting for dividends and share splits, where applicable)
- Daily cumulative trading volume recorded across all the U.S. exchanges.

The first ten lines of the input data (ten years of daily data for NYSE:SPY from Yahoo! Finance) are shown as in Figure 1.A.2.

We downloaded and saved the SPY data from Yahoo! Finance as SPY_Yahoo_2009-2019.csv in "C:/Users/A/Documents/Data" directory. Please note the forward slashes in the directory name. As with other computer languages, Python balks at the single backward slashes in strings, causing errors.

To open the file and display the first ten lines, type the Python code snippet shown in Figure 1.A.3 into the Python editor, remembering to replace the directory shown with your own directory name.

```
»
>

Date Open High Low Close Adj Close Volume
2009-03-30 79.800003 79.870003 77.959999 78.790001 64.419357 324108500
2009-03-31 79.559998 81.080002 79.050003 79.519997 65.016212 364238300
2009-04-01 78.529999 81.419998 78.330002 81.059998 66.275345 377018300
2009-04-02 83.080002 84.610001 81.129997 83.430000 68.213081 476230700
2009-04-03 83.489998 84.279999 82.669998 84.260002 68.891693 284646300
2009-04-06 83.339996 84.279999 82.290001 83.599998 68.352074 264866600
2009-04-07 82.250000 82.650002 81.510002 81.650002 66.757751 258947800
2009-04-08 82.059998 82.940002 81.540001 82.529999 67.477219 230402800
2009-04-09 84.669998 85.820000 84.330002 85.809998 70.158974 269653500
»
>
```

Figure 1.A.2 The first 10 lines of data input (ten years of daily data for NYSE:SPY from Yahoo! Finance).

```
import numpy as np

my_data = np.genfromtxt('C:/Users/A/Documents/Data/SPY_Yahoo_2009-2019
.csv', delimiter=',')
print(data[:10])
```

Figure 1.A.3 Python code opening a Yahoo! Finance daily history data and displaying the first ten rows.

Save the module by selecting "File -> Save" or pressing "Ctrl" and "S" keys at the same time. Now, you can run your Python module by pressing the "F5" key or selecting "Run -> Run Module" from the top bar menu.

If you have just installed Python and are using it for the first time, you may receive the following error:

```
ModuleNotFoundError: No module named 'numpy'
```

The error says that you need to install an add-on library called numpy. To do so:

1. Open a brand-new Python module (select File->New File in Python server). If you do not see the menu at the top of your Python server window, you are in the wrong application. Go back to the Python folder and select the first Python server application that appears there. Once you open a new module, please type the following commands inside the module and press F5 to run the commands to find the location of python.exe:

```
import sys; print(sys.executable)
```

    The location will appear in the server window and may be something like C:\Users\A\Programs\Python\Python37-32\pythonw.exe

2. Open a command prompt/shell. To do so in Microsoft Windows, search for "cmd."

3. Navigate to the directory where pythonw.exe is installed, as shown in step 1 above.

4. Run the following command: `python -m pip install numpy`. If you encounter errors again, you need to download an installing utility first: run `python -m ensurepip` to do so, then run `python -m pip install numpy`. You should be all set.

5. To execute other programs throughout this book, however, you will need to install additional libraries, namely, `random` for advanced number generation, `matplotlib` for plotting data, and `scipy` for scientific statistics functions like skewness. To do so, please run `python -m pip install random`, `python -m pip install matplotlib`, `python -m pip install scipy` and `python -m pip install pandas` from the command line.

Tip: during your Python programming, you may encounter the following error on the Python server: "Subprocess startup error: IDLE's subprocess didn't make a connection." Either IDLE can't start a subprocess or personal firewall software is blocking the connection. The error dialogue box is shown in Figure 1.A.4.

To fix the issue, simply close the existing instance of the server, but leave the Python module open. Then, press F5 on the existing module to run it again – a new server instance will open. This workaround is guaranteed to save you time in the programming process! The alternative of closing all the Python windows and then restarting the server from the start-up menu is too time-consuming.

When you run the module for the first time, a Python shell opens with potential errors and output of the module. In our case, the output looks like the text shown in Figure 1.A.5. Since numpy is configured to deal with numbers, the first row and the first columns are replaced by nan, while all other numbers are presented in scientific notation:

Let's examine our first program, shown in Figure 1.A.3. The first line directs us to `import numpy`, a Python library the name of which sounds like a cute animal, but

Figure 1.A.4   Error dialogue box.

```
[[         nan         nan         nan         nan         nan
           nan         nan]
 [         nan 7.9800003e+01 7.9870003e+01 7.7959999e+01 7.8790001e+01
  6.4419357e+01 3.2410850e+08]
 [         nan 7.9559998e+01 8.1080002e+01 7.9050003e+01 7.9519997e+01
  6.5016212e+01 3.6423830e+08]
 [         nan 7.8529999e+01 8.1419998e+01 7.8330002e+01 8.1059998e+01
  6.6275345e+01 3.7701830e+08]
 [         nan 8.3080002e+01 8.4610001e+01 8.1129997e+01 8.3430000e+01
  6.8213081e+01 4.7623070e+08]
 [         nan 8.3489998e+01 8.4279999e+01 8.2669998e+01 8.4260002e+01
  6.8891693e+01 2.8464630e+08]
 [         nan 8.3339996e+01 8.4279999e+01 8.2290001e+01 8.3599998e+01
  6.8352074e+01 2.6486660e+08]
 [         nan 8.2250000e+01 8.2650002e+01 8.1510002e+01 8.1650002e+01
  6.6757751e+01 2.5894780e+08]
 [         nan 8.2059998e+01 8.2940002e+01 8.1540001e+01 8.2529999e+01
  6.7477219e+01 2.3040280e+08]
 [         nan 8.4669998e+01 8.5820000e+01 8.4330002e+01 8.5809998e+01
  7.0158974e+01 2.6965350e+08]]
```

Figure 1.A.5   The output of the first Python program, the code for which is shown in Figure 1.A.3.

actually stands for NumPy – Python's numerical manipulation library. After importing the library and its component, the next line instructs Python to open our data file and store it in a variable called my_data. Next, we display exactly 10 rows of the data file and then exit the program. While 10 is an arbitrary number, the restriction on the total lines displayed is in place to prevent Python from using too many system resources. In particular, Python tends to struggle and "hang up" when asked to display large chunks of data.

If you come to Python from Java, C++, or Perl, you'll immediately notice numerous similarities as well as differences. On the differences front, the lines do not end in a semi-colon! Instead, the lines are terminated by a new line character. Variables are type-less, that is, the coder does not need to tell the compiler ahead of time whether the new variable is bound to be an integer or a string. Single-line comments are marked with # at the beginning of a commented-out line, and with " " at the beginning and the end of the comment block. On the similarity side, Python's structure and keywords largely follow preexisting languages' convention: keywords like "class," "break," and "for" are preserved as well as many other features, making the transition from most programming languages into Python fairly intuitive.

If you encounter any issues successfully running your first Python program of this book, Google is possibly your best bet as a solution finder. Just type any questions or error codes into the Google prompt, and you may be amazed at the quantity and quality of helpful material available online to assist you with your problem. Once our first program runs successfully, we will proceed with the more complicated task of actually building our first neural network.

While techniques discussed in this book are applicable across a wide range of applications, including credit risk rating and Natural Language Processing (NLP) of documents like financial statements, the main focus of this book remains portfolio management and trading. As such, most of the examples in the book will be focused on predictability of future realizations of prices, returns, and other metrics that help portfolio managers make educated investment decisions.

Reference

Breiman, L. (2001). Statistical modeling: The two cultures (with comments and a rejoinder by the author). *Statistical Science* 16(3): 199–231.

Chapter 2

Neural Networks in Finance

Introduction

Neural networks are an important tool for machine learning. Truly deep learning was originally designed to model the complexities of the human brain. Neural networks typically require intensive computer power but with technology costs now at their historic low and projected to decrease further, neural networks are a cost-efficient yet powerful methodology for discovering nonlinear relationships that can be useful inputs into predicting future results. Here, following our paper, Aldridge and Avellaneda (2019), we discuss the theoretical background and develop a step-by-step implementation of a toy model for a neural network using financial data. The paper show practical and potentially profitable application of machine learning. The Appendix provides discussion and actual coding blocks for building a simple financial neural network in Python.

This chapter's focus is on simple explanation and the core principles of the neural network's design. One class of models that has been popular across image recognition and social media applications is Generative Adversarial Networks (GANs). The advantage of GANs is that they introduce randomization to enable classification of variables, even if none was previously available. Thus, Chen, Pelger, and Zhu (2019) use a deep learning GAN framework for estimating the stochastic discount factors (SDF), the unobservable Rosetta Stone of all pricing engines. As Chen, Pelger, and Zhu point out, SDF indeed presents a perfect Big Data problem: SDF in theory reflects all available information, comprising very Big Data; the functional form of SDF is unknown and the key drivers of SDF are potentially not fully known; SDF may vary over time and have a complex dynamic structure; the available data may be highly noisy from the SDF estimation perspective. While simple neural networks can probably be applied to the SDF estimation as well, here we focus on the successful and novel application to the workhorse of financial data modeling: end-of-day stock price data.

Neural networks are relatively novel in finance since, in the past, the cost of creating a network well outweighed the benefits of doing so. The earliest neural networks and machine learning in general harken back to the 1950s Control Theory – a science of feedback loops and error minimization developed with the invention and proliferation of computer technology. In the mid-1980s, interest in machine learning led to neural networks as a more sophisticated, human-like technology.

A neural network is an advanced optimization tool that, by trial and error, models complex functional relationships between a set of observable inputs and outputs. Academic research on neural networks in Finance goes back at least 25 years (for a review, see Gallo 2005). Some early work in Finance in the 1990s concerned derivatives pricing with incomplete data (Avellaneda et al. 2000).

Neural network modeling and traditional forecasting and econometric modeling are different yet complementary approaches to quantitative modeling, not a beauty contest. In traditional statistics or econometrics, researchers make assumptions about data distributions ahead of the analysis. Unlike traditionalists, neural networks scientists make no assumptions about the data whatsoever and let the data (and computers) decide what fits best, often in a black-box construct. As discussed in Aldridge and Krawciw (2017), letting machines make autonomous decisions is a growing trend, rapidly expanding in Finance.

Even though neural networks are the cornerstone of machine learning, neural networks and machine learning are not perfectly synonymous. Gu, Kelly, and Xiu (2019), for example, define ML to encompass:

1. A wide-ranging collection of models for statistical prediction, including econometrics.
2. Methods for model selection and mitigation of overfit.
3. Efficient algorithms for searching among model specifications, i.e., neural networks.

Hastie et al. (2009) include the following topics in machine learning: linear regression, generalized linear models with penalization, dimension reduction via principal components regression (PCR), partial least squares (PLS) regression trees (including boosted trees and random forests), and, of course, neural networks. Other supervised machine learning methods are discussed in Chapter 3, semi-supervised learning addressed in Chapter 4, and the unsupervised methodologies are introduced in Chapter 5 and discussed throughout much of the book.

The key benefits of neural networks methodologies are:

1. In principle, the algorithms should be able to accommodate all available input data at once – no need to pick and choose the potential factors ahead of the analysis.
2. The algorithms account for nonlinear relationships and complex interactions among the variables – a superior prediction vis-à-vis traditional linearization of relationships in Finance.

To understand why neural networks are important in Finance, consider, for example, prepayments on mortgages. This is a situation when the borrower chooses to pay off the balance of the money owed ahead of schedule, potentially due to refinancing with another lender or another reason. This kind of event creates a significant risk to the lender or to the buyer or holder of pass-through Mortgage-Based Securities (MBS). The expected mortgage rate is often modeled as a function of the yield curve (linearly and nonlinearly), and modeling of prepayment rate is typically represented as an S-shape curve based on mortgage rate expectations (see Avellaneda and Ma, 2014). The Richard and Roll (1989) model, also known as DTCC/FICC model and a de-facto industry standard, relates refinance rate to monthly mortgage payments (Weighted Average Coupon, or WAC) and mortgage rates. As detailed in Avellaneda and Ma (2014), this industry standard for mortgage rates is determined as cointegration of 2-year and 10-year swap rates over a one-year window.

Numerous other studies linearize the relationship between the prepayment risk and other variables. For example, Campbell & Dietrich (1983) study variables like payment/income and loan/value ratios and unemployment rates, as well as age and the original loan/value ratio. Cunningham & Capone (1990) look at Caps, both periodic and lifetime; Curley & Guttentag (1974) consider loan maturity and policy year. Deng, Quigley & Van Order (2000) examine various factors in a proportional hazard model. Instead of linearizing the relationship between explanatory variables and the risk of prepayment, fitting an S-shaped curve produced better results (see Fabozzi 2016). Still, neural networks can identify dependencies that are an even tighter fit, as shown in Sirignano, Sadhwani, and Giesecke (2018).

Other potential applications of neural networks include index replication, where a neural network chooses the stocks that together best mimic the performance of a given index (Heaton, Polson, and Witte 2016). The strategy can also be applied to uncovering the composition of a given hedge fund strategy. In addition, Heaton, Polson, and Witte, (2016) show the neural network process for optimal nonlinear factor selection in asset pricing, as well as the estimation of default probabilities in a large-scale setting that takes creditworthiness, text data of corporate news and announcements, and accounting data as inputs. Heaton, Polson, and Witte also develop a neural network framework for hidden-factor event studies estimation.

In machine learning, neural networks may be referred to as *reinforcement learning*. As described in the next section, a neural network trains itself on the available data, reinforcing its own inferences in the process.

Neural Network Construction Methodology

While many variations of the neural networks exist, here we focus on the more traditional feedforward networks.

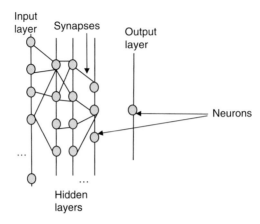

Figure 2.1 A sample neural network.

The three layers of a traditional neural network are:

1. Input layer of raw predictor inputs.
2. Hidden layer of predictor interaction and nonlinear transformation.
3. Output layer of outputs aggregated from the results of the hidden layer.

A sample neural network is shown in Figure 2.1. The layers are computational stages. In each layer, there are computational cells, known as neurons, which correspond to the inputs, or columns of data, coming into the computation at that stage. The number of neurons may or may not be the same in sequential layers. Typically, the number of neurons decreases from one layer to the next in the direction of output. The neural network thins out toward its end as various data columns, also known as features, drop out, due to their lack of predictive power. In the input layer, the number of neurons most often corresponds to the number of columns (features) in the original data set. Some neural network designers may add an additional input layer neuron to capture bias. Generally, however, once the shape of the data is known, the number of neurons in the input layer is uniquely determined.

The number of neurons in the output layer depends on the neural network's output configuration. Traditional networks can output either a continuous number (e.g., a price forecast), or a discrete classification (e.g., portfolio identifiers or yes/no answers). For example, in mortgage prepayment modeling, the output neurons may be the following states:

0 = current mortgage (up-to-date with payments)
1 = 30 days late
...
5 = paid off via prepayment
...

Following the human nervous system nomenclature, the connections between neurons in neighboring layers are referred to as "synapses." Each synapse corresponds to a numerical value, referred to as weight, that has to be estimated. As Figure 2.1 shows, the neurons in neighboring layers may or may not be connected.

The graph of the synapses between two layers with number of neurons N_1 and N_2 corresponds to a bipartite graph, which, if all links were allowed, would be a full graph with $N_1 \times N_2$ edges. Some links do not exist, and the resulting graphs may not be full. Each neuron also has an additional parameter known as the activation parameter or activation level, discussed in the next section, along with the synapse weight estimation.

The configuration of the neural network that returns a number is referred to as the "regression mode" while the configuration that returns a discrete value is known as the "machine mode." Correspondingly, the regression mode has only one output neuron containing the output number while the machine mode may have either a single output node returning a value or a node for each of the output "states."

The number of neurons in the hidden layer with the most neurons is referred to as the width of the neural network. The optimal width of the neural network, as well as the optimal number of hidden layers, is an active area of research. Most researchers agree that, as a rule of thumb, the optimal width of the hidden layers needs to fall between the width of the input layer and the width of the output layer.

While each neural network has exactly one input layer and one output layer, the number of hidden layers has varied. Intuitively, the number of hidden layers depends on how intertwined the input parameters are. If the inputs are linearly separable, the neural network does not need any hidden layers at all – in fact, the neural network itself is not needed as the problem can be estimated using basic linear regression.

The three-layer depth of neural networks, comprised of the input, output, and just one hidden layer, was a product of much research in the 1980s that showed that the three levels are optimal from a computational perspective. Specifically, the additional hidden layers were shown to add too much computational complexity for the machine power available at the time while contributing little additional value. However, more recently, computational power has experienced a significant drop in price. This ongoing trend is due to massive computing demands from all industries. In addition, researchers like Hinton, Osindero, and Teh (2006) have produced fast, greedy computational algorithms that make multi–hidden layer neural networks efficient and useful. Eldan and Shamir (2016) demonstrate that increases in depth are more valuable than increasing width in standard feedforward neural networks. He et al. (2016) derive an easy-to-train residual learning network, with as many as 152 layers.

Neural networks with a large number of hidden layers collectively form what is commonly called deep learning. Usually, subsequent hidden layers drop inputs to produce a narrowing input funnel toward the output. Different feedforward and backpropagation multi-layer methodologies exist to produce a spectrum of results. For instance, a GAN creates random features and feeds them into the neural network alongside real data to aid network training.

The Architecture of Neural Networks

A neural network is a form of a learning machine. Learning machines are designed to find a predictor $\widehat{Y}$ of an output Y, given input X. Thus, like most learning machines, a neural network is a mapping $Y = F(X)$, where $X = (X_1, X_2, \ldots X_p)$. The predictor is denoted $\widehat{Y}(X) := F(X)$.

Formally, a deep learning neural network architecture comprises $f_1, f_2, \ldots, f_L$ univariate activation functions for each of the L layers. For each layer l, we define a semi-affine *transformation rule* which defines exactly how the activation function transforms the data inputs at layer l:

$$f_l^{W,b} := f_l \left(\sum_{j=1}^{N_l} W_{lj} X_j + b_l \right) = f_l(W_l X_l + b_l), 1 \leq l \leq L \tag{2.1}$$

where W_l is the weight matrix at layer l estimated during the training phase below, and b_l is the threshold or activation level for layer l.

The *deep predictor* $\widehat{Y}(X)$ then becomes a composite map, a superposition of univariate semi-affine functions:

$$\widehat{Y}(X) := F(X) = (f_1^{W_1, b_1} \circ f_2^{W_2, b_2} \circ \ldots \circ f_L^{W_L, b_L})(X) \tag{2.2}$$

If $Z^{(l)}$ is the output of the lth layer, the hidden features or factors that the algorithm extracts at each layer l, then $Z^{(0)} = X$ is the input, and, recursively,

$$Z^{(1)} = f^{(1)}(W^{(0)} X + b^{(0)}) \tag{2.3}$$

$$Z^{(2)} = f^{(2)}(W^{(1)} Z^{(1)} + b^{(1)})$$

$$\ldots$$

$$Z^{(l)} = f^{(l)}(W^{(l-1)} Z^{(l-1)} + b^{(l-1)})$$

$$\ldots$$

$$Z^{(L)} = f^{(L)}(W^{(L-1)} Z^{(L-1)} + b^{(L-1)})$$

$$\widehat{Y}(X) = Z^{(L+1)} = W^{(L)} Z^{(L)} + b^{(L)} \tag{2.4}$$

To obtain the desired output, a prediction, the input data are passed through hidden layers of abstraction. In each layer, the algorithm extracts data features into factors. A given level's factors become the next level's features.

In general, in a neural network with L hidden layers, layer $l = 0$ is the input layer X, layer $l = L + 1$ is the output forecast layer $\widehat{Y}$, and each hidden layer $l \in [1, \ldots, L]$ is a nonlinear transformation applied to the previous layer $l - 1$. The number of hidden layers, $|$, is known as the depth of the neural network architecture.

Each layer l contains N_l "neurons," features or, simply, columns of data. A layer may choose to drop a data feature (data column) based on analysis, and this feature will not be available in the later layers of analysis. N_l needs to be explicitly specified for each layer l by the neural network's architect. Each layer is a nonlinear univariate transformation that uses as inputs the outputs of the previous layer. Thus, layer l takes output of layer $l - 1$ as input.

The nonlinear transformation f_l that occurs at every level l is known as the activation function. When neural networks are referred to as reinforcement learning, activation functions are often called *reward functions*. If there are L layers with N neurons on each layer, there are $N \times N$ transformations from one layer to the next, as each neuron or datum i in layer l connects to every neuron j in layer $l + 1$. The resulting weight matrix W has dimensions of $N_l \times N_{l-1}$. Activation functions are nonlinear univariate transformations of weighted input data, where the weight matrices $W_l \in R^{N_l \times N_{l-1}}$ are adjusted during the training process described in the next section. In neural network computation, commonly used activation functions are sigmoidal (e.g., $1/(1 + \exp(-x))$, $\cosh(x)$, $\tanh(x)$) and indicator functions $I(x > 0)$. Functions like $max\{x, 0\}$ are known to lead to rapid dimension reduction.

In mathematical summary, a neural network is an iteration of affine vector-valued maps. Each neural network has a certain, usually large, number of unknown parameters. The total approximate number of unknown parameters in a neural network is of order $N \times N \times L$ and the complexity reaches $N \times N \times L + N \times L$. In principle, any function in the world can be approximated to great accuracy by a neural network. In reality, the computing time and power are still an issue, and the neural network approximation is usually restricted by the realities of computing technology.

Choosing the Activation Function

In finance, activation functions can be simple or complex, depending on the underlying application. Avellaneda et al. (2020) chose linear function for modeling VIX futures changes. Ritter (2017) used a quadratic activation function corresponding to the classic utility maximization problem of a risk-averse agent in an asset-pricing framework. Specifically, here, we show that the tanh(x) function may work best for leptokurtic security returns, we consider the following activation functions:

- sigmoid, or logistic, function
- hyperbolic tangent, tanh
- Rectifier Linear Unit (ReLU)
- linear

The choice of the activation function depends on the fit of the functional output to the distribution of data. Does the output range from 0 to 1, as it would in a binary (yes/no) classifier? An example of a binary output may be the answer to the question "is the market in a recession?" Does the output accommodate negative numbers, which would be suitable for financial returns? The objective of the activation function is also to be taken into account: is its output to be used to construct trading strategies with a buy vs sell vs hold recommendation, or is the output to create point forecasts for returns?

Sigmoid or Logistic Function

The sigmoid or logistic function

$$\sigma(x) = 1/(1 + exp(-x)) \tag{2.5}$$

has a first derivative of

$$\frac{d\sigma}{dx} = \frac{-exp(-x)}{(1 + exp(-x))^2} = -\sigma^2(x)\left(\frac{1 - \sigma(x)}{\sigma(x)}\right) = \sigma(x)(1 - \sigma(x)) \tag{2.6}$$

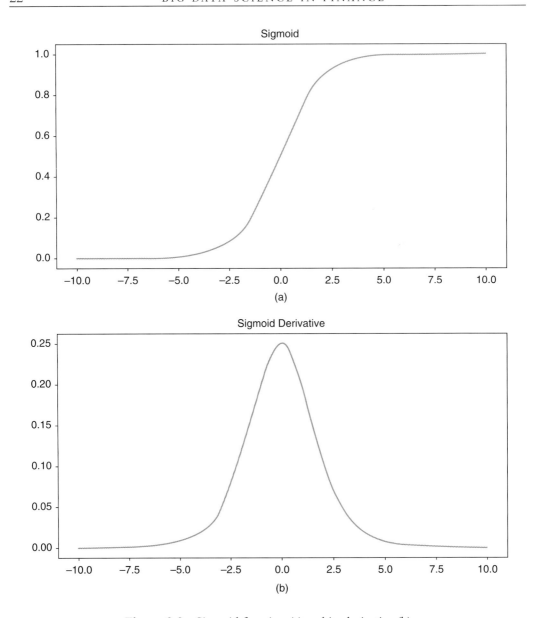

Figure 2.2   Sigmoid function (a) and its derivative (b).

The sigmoid, shown in Figure 2.2, varies from 0 to 1 and has large derivatives in the middle and relatively slow changes at either end. As a result, the sigmoid is a great tool for binary "yes/no" classification, allowing for fast segmentation of objects into the "one or the other" categories. Sigmoids are non-negative, and are, therefore, ill-suited for modeling returns. In addition, sigmoids suffer from the "vanishing gradient" problem – when the function plateaus, the converging rates halt to nearly zero, which is often undesirable.

Rectifier Linear Unit Function (ReLU)

The rectifier linear unit function (ReLU) is

$$ReLU(x) = max(x, 0) \tag{2.7}$$

On the other hand, ReLU has become the most popular first-pass function for neural networks. Originally developed for "rectifying" electric current, they are simple with a fast derivative:

$$\frac{\partial[ReLU(x)]}{\partial x} = I_{x>0} \qquad (2.8)$$

Rectifier functions also provide "model sparsity": they activate selectively, saving computational time and power. Still, rectifiers like sigmoids are non-negative and are poor choices for financial returns. A plot of ReLU is shown in Figure 2.3. ReLU output ranges from 0 to infinity. Its shape is a shoe-in for pricing call options and, when appropriate or used in combinations, other options on financial instruments.

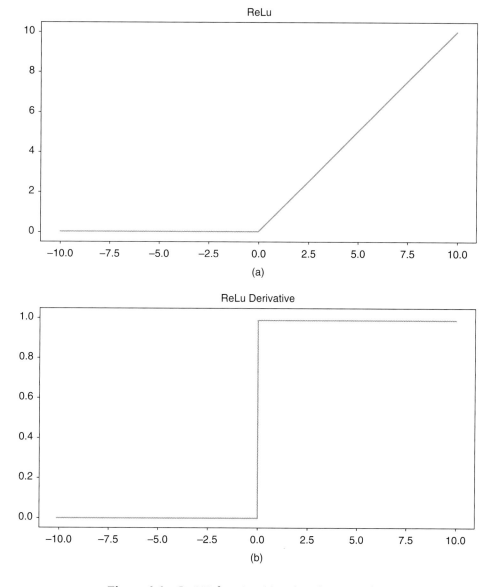

Figure 2.3 ReLU function (a) and its derivative (b).

Hyperbolic tangent, tanh

The tanh function varies from –1 to 1 and presents a viable choice for return modeling. The derivative of tanh is

$$\frac{\partial[tanh(x)]}{\partial x} = 1 - tanh^2(x) \tag{2.9}$$

A plot of tanh is shown in Figure 2.4. As Figure 2.4 shows, tanh is very similar to sigmoid, except its output extends from –1 to 1, making it more suitable for modeling financial returns than sigmoid, since tanh can accommodate negative returns. The –1 to +1 restriction works particularly well in shorter-term returns where these boundaries are unlikely to be breached. In a longer term return, most financial instruments can breach

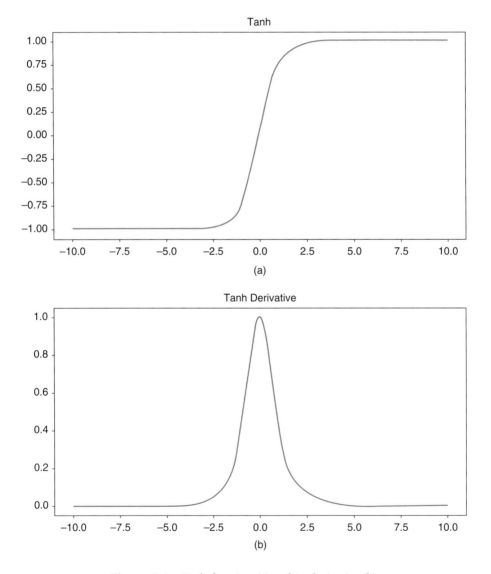

Figure 2.4   Tanh function (a) and its derivative (b).

100% upside limit. On the downside, the loss may extend beyond 100% in currencies and short-sale strategies, a possibility not captured by tanh. In equities, however, -1 is the maximum loss corresponding to the complete loss of one's investment: 100% in the case of a stock-issuer's bankruptcy.

Linear function

Linear function, $f(x) = x$, also known as identity function, turns a neural network into a good old linear regression, making it a great tool to assess the usefulness of the neural network modeling. With a simple derivative $\frac{df}{dx} = 1$, the linear function is easy to program and assess. The linear activation function and its derivative are illustrated in Figure 2.5.

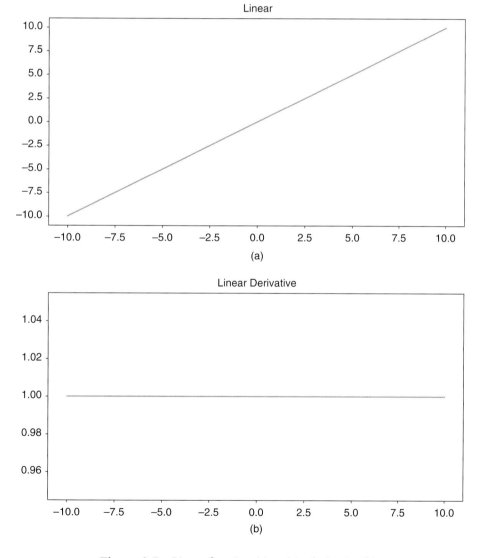

Figure 2.5   Linear function (a) and its derivative (b).

The sample prediction output $\widehat{Y}$ generated by the neural network is known as the *feedforward* operation. For a basic three-layer network with just one hidden layer, weights W_1 transform the inputs into the hidden layer, and weights W_2 operate on the hidden layer to derive the output. Each layer transforms the previous layer's output with the corresponding weights and the chosen activation function. Thus, the output of our first layer is $\widehat{y}_1 = \sigma(W_1 x + b_1)$, where W_1 and b_1 are the weights and bias of the first (and, so far, the only) hidden layer, and $\sigma(z)$ is the chosen function, in our case, sigmoid. The output of the hidden layer model is the input of the final output layer, so $\widehat{Y} = \sigma(W_2 \widehat{y}_1 + b_2) = \sigma(W_2 \sigma(W_1 x + b_1) + b_2)$. For a general neural network with k total layers (k-2 hidden layers),

$$\widehat{Y} = \sigma(W_{k-1}\widehat{y}_{k-2} + b_{k-1}) = \sigma(W_{k-1}\sigma(W_{k-2}\widehat{y}_{k-3} + b_{k-2}) + b_{k-1})$$

$$= \sigma(W_{k-1}\sigma(W_{k-2}\sigma(W_{k-3}\widehat{y}_{k-4} + b_{k-3}) + b_{k-2}) + b_{k-1})$$

and so on, until we reach $\widehat{y}_1 = x$ in the model.

During the first iteration, it is common to guess the weights and biases, and often even to pick them at random. To determine the correctly fitting weights and biases, the resulting feedforward prediction $\widehat{Y}$ is compared with its target or actual value Y in a process called *backpropagation*. In backpropagation, the difference between the prediction $\widehat{Y}$ and the actual value Y is computed in what is known as the *loss function*. The loss function can be as simple as a squared error:

$$L = (\widehat{Y} - Y)^2 \tag{2.10}$$

Once the loss with the latest set of weights and biases is computed, the loss is backpropagated to the beginning of the network and parameters are adjusted to minimize the loss. The loss function is then recalculated in a recursive procedure and the weights are adjusted again. The process repeats itself until some target error criterion is reached.

A common way to adjust the weights and biases is to rely on the derivative of the loss function with respect to weights and biases to guide the direction of the required adjustment. The derivative of the loss function is the slope of the loss function observed in response to minute changes in parameters. Since we are looking to find the minimum or minima of the loss function, we will seek to adjust the parameters in the direction that makes the loss function smaller. This technique may be familiar to many readers as *gradient descent*.

For a sigmoid

$$\sigma(x) = 1/(1 + exp(-x)) \tag{2.11}$$

$$\frac{\partial L}{\partial W} = \frac{\partial L}{\partial \widehat{Y}} \frac{\partial Y}{\partial x} \frac{\partial x}{\partial W} = 2(\widehat{Y} - Y)(\sigma(x)(1 - \sigma(x)))x \tag{2.12}$$

$$\frac{\partial L}{\partial b} = \frac{\partial L}{\partial \widehat{Y}} \frac{\partial Y}{\partial x} \frac{\partial x}{\partial b} = 2(\widehat{Y} - Y)(\sigma(x)(1 - \sigma(x)))1 \tag{2.13}$$

One piece still missing from our optimal trading neural network is the actual realized output, given inputs X arising from downloaded daily data. In many neural networks, Y

is the observed output of the natural system given inputs X. In the case of a trading or a portfolio management system, Y is not given, but must be selected by a researcher. The following section discusses possible choices for the model output.

Construction and Training of Neural Networks

Similar to traditional data modeling techniques, construction and training of deep learning algorithms are conducted on three distinct data sets split from the original data into (1) training, (2) validation, and (3) testing.

The training set is used to adjust the weights of the network. The validation set is used to minimize the overfitting of data. Finally, the testing data set is used to measure the predictive power of the constructed neural network.

Training

The objective of the training stage of the neural network design is to maximize its performance. Performance of a neural network is measured by the residual *loss function*, the difference between the *deep learning predictor*, $\widehat{Y}$, and the realized output Y. Better performance corresponds to a tighter fit, or smaller loss function. Our objective, therefore, is to design a neural network with the minimum residual loss function. If a loss function is denoted as $L(Y, \widehat{Y})$, the training problem comprises finding parameters (weights $\widehat{W} = (\widehat{W}_0, \widehat{W}_1, \dots \widehat{W}_L)$ and activation thresholds $\widehat{b} = (\widehat{b}_0, \widehat{b}_1, \dots \widehat{b}_L)$) that minimize the loss function on the training data set of input–output pairs $D = \{Y^{(i)}, X^{(i)}\}_{i=1}^T$. Thus, the training problem can be written as:

$$arg\ min_{W,b} \frac{1}{T} \sum_{i=1}^T L(Y_i, \widehat{Y}^{W,b}(X_i)) \tag{2.14}$$

The most basic loss function is the ordinary least squares (OLS) L_2-norm, mean-squared error (MSE) of estimation over the training data set $D = \{Y^{(i)}, X^{(i)}\}_{i=1}^T$:

$$L(Y_i, \widehat{Y}(X_i)) = ||Y_i - \widehat{Y}(X_i)||_2^2 \tag{2.15}$$

If the output Y can be considered to be a random variable generated by the probability model $p(Y|Y^{\widehat{W},b}(X))$, the corresponding probabilistic loss function can then be a negative log likelihood:

$$L(Y_i, \widehat{Y}(X_i)) = -logp(Y|Y^{\widehat{W},\widehat{b}}(X)) \tag{2.16}$$

The main drawback of machine learning has always been its computational complexity. To accurately map or fit a function transforming inputs, X, into outputs, Y, computer programs necessitated millions of iterations. The iterative nature of machine learning resulted in two major issues: overfitting and (relatively) slow processing. Overfitting refers to the situation where the output function fits the observable data X and Y closely, but, perhaps, has little to do with the "true" relationship between X and Y, with many observations not yet available. The overfitting problem has been plaguing industries like Finance, where the data used traditionally were collected on a daily basis and, as a result, expensive to generate and use: just 750 daily trading observations amount to three full years of financial data!

Different models penalize fitting X to Y too closely, leaving room for the models "to breathe" – to allow for a potential modeling error and more successful application to the data yet unseen. Still, pure machine learning has had adoption challenges, mostly due to the cost and inefficiency of heavy-duty processing required by an iterative approach taken when testing these algorithms. The number of times a machine learning program needs to run to generate a solid nonlinear prediction can number in hundreds of thousands, which can cost a lot in terms of time and processing power required.

The processing power conundrum has been largely solved by the computing industry via cloud technology (outsourced computation on distant and cheap server farms) and generally, ever decreasing costs of computers due to the insatiable demand for technology from people in all walks of life.

To avoid overfitting and to stabilize the predictive rule, it is common to add a *regularization penalty* $\phi(W, b)$. The additional parameter λ then determines the overall level of regularization, with the minimization problem becoming:

$$arg\ min_{W,b} \frac{1}{T} \sum_{i=1}^{T} L(Y_i, \widehat{Y}^{W,b}(X_i)) + \lambda\phi(W, b) \qquad (2.17)$$

Too little regularization λ leads to overfitting and poor out-of-sample performance.

The regularization penalty may take many functional forms, from separable $\phi(W, b) = \phi(W) + \phi(b)$ to ridge L^2-norm $\phi(W) = ||W||_2^2 = \sum_{i=1}^{T} W_i^T W_i$ to LASSO L^1-norm.

The ridge L^2-norm regularization penalty is useful when the overall level of regularization, λ, needs to be determined. LASSO L^1-norm helps induce sparsity in the weights W and offsets b.

In the probabilistic models where the output is a random variable generated by $P(Y|Y^{\widehat{W,b}}(X))$, the regularization term $\lambda\phi(W, b)$ can be thought of as a negative log-prior distribution over parameters, corresponding to the Bayes learning with the deep predictor $\widehat{Y}$ a regularized maximum a posteriori (MAP) estimator:

$$\lambda\phi(W, b) = -log\ p(\phi(W, b)) \qquad (2.18)$$

$$p(\phi(W, b)) = C\ exp(\lambda\phi(W, b)) \qquad (2.19)$$

Using Bayes rule, we obtain:

$$p(W, b|D) \propto p(Y|Y^{W,b}(X))p(W, b) \qquad (2.20)$$

and

$$p(W, b|D) \propto exp(-log\ p(Y|Y^{W,b}(X)) - log(p(W, b))) \qquad (2.21)$$

Thus, the deep learning predictor $\widehat{Y}$ is:

$$\widehat{Y}:=Y^{\widehat{W},\widehat{b}}(X) \text{ where } (\widehat{W},\widehat{b}):=arg\ min_{W,b}\ log\ p\ (W,b|D) \tag{2.22}$$

Then, the log-posterior distribution over parameters given the training data $D = \{\,Y^{(i)}, X^{(i)}\,\}_{i=1}^{T}$ is

$$-log\ p(W,b|D) = \sum_{i=1}^{T} L(Y^{(i)}, Y^{W,b}(X^{(i)})) + \lambda\phi(W,b) \tag{2.23}$$

Validation

In the design of neural networks, validation boils down to identifying:

1. The levels of regularization, λ, that lead to the optimal prediction in a variance vs. bias tradeoff.
2. The depth of the neural network (number of hidden layers), L.
3. The size of the hidden layers (number of neurons: data features or fields to keep at each layer), $N_l, 1 \leq l \leq L$.

An efficient validation technique designed to reduce overfitting and increase out-of-sample performance is known as cross-validation. Cross-validation involves splitting the training data into complementary subsets, potentially of equal length, and then producing comparative validation on diverse sets.

In particular, when dealing with financial time series, it may make sense to split training data into disjoint time periods of identical length. This is particularly useful when data are expensive to obtain and the models have to be tested extensively.

Model Selection via Dropout

When we start a neural network with many inputs, it may be desirable to reduce the size of the inputs used in a given layer in order to do the following:

- Retain only the most significant data parameters.
- Prevent overfitting – a condition when the network appears to work in sample due to a too-close fitting nonlinear regression, and then fails to work out-of-sample.

A popular technique for selecting features is called *dropout*. In a dropout, a given hidden layer retains p fraction of inputs at random and drops off the fraction $(1-p)$ of inputs to a given layer. The technique then processes the neural network to see if the loss function has increased or decreased. The random dropout is then repeated with another set of randomly selected p fraction of inputs. The process is repeated until the minimum-loss input selection is achieved. The fraction p is known as the *dropout threshold* and is usually set by the neural network designer, and can be a number like 0.7 or 0.9. With the dropout threshold of 0.9, for instance, 90% of inputs are retained while 10% are dropped off in a given layer. The actual inputs or features that are retained or dropped off are decided upon at random by the neural network itself. The only human input is the value of the dropout threshold and the layers to which the dropout threshold applies.

Dropout works because it trains the neural network not to rely significantly on any particular input, since that input may be removed in the next iteration. As a result, instead of assigning higher weights to certain features, the neural network will instead try to spread the weights across many features, delivering better network stability out-of-sample in the process. Still, even though the weights across many features will be smaller, some, most significant, features may stand out with higher weights.

Econometricians may recognize dropout as a version of classic bootstrapping. Similar to bootstrapping, dropout techniques repeatedly sample the regression dependent variables, now known as inputs, in an effort to develop stable coefficients for all the data inputs. Dropout is also a version of the machine-learning technique called boosting.

With h inputs, a neural network may contain up to 2^{h-1} permutations of inputs, based on a binary calculation of whether a given input is included in the system and retaining at least one input in each layer. With so many permutations, dropout requires a lot of iterations. However, due to the smaller number of inputs in a given layer, the processing time required for each iteration is substantially shorter than without the dropout.

The impact of dropout selection on the neural network's performance can be quantified *a priori*. Heaton, Polson, and Witte (2016) quantify the impact of the dropout on the neural network's loss minimization function by noting that the dropout layer selection follows a Bernoulli distribution:

$$D_i^{(l)} \sim Ber(p) \tag{2.24}$$

Then, for the MSE minimization function, $L(Y_i, \widehat{Y}(X_i)) = ||Y_i - \widehat{Y}(X_i)||_2^2$, the objective function becomes

$$L(Y_i, \widehat{Y}_D(X_i)) = arg\ min_W E_{D \sim Ber(p)} ||Y - W(X * D)|| \tag{2.25}$$

where $*$ is the element-wise product and D is a matrix of independent Bernoulli $D \sim Ber(p)$ distributed random variables. Equation (2.25) is equivalent to:

$$L(Y_i, \widehat{Y}_D(X_i)) = arg\ min_W ||Y - pWX||_2^2 + p(1-p)||\Gamma W||_2^2 \tag{2.26}$$

where $\Gamma = (diag(X^T X))^{1/2}$.

Overfitting

Overfitting is a blanket term that explains why a model that worked well in-sample does not work out-of-sample. Has a trading model worked and then stopped working? Some blame overfitting.

The main idea of overfitting is that in a static population, if we have enough data, we can accurately match inputs and outputs via nonlinear regressions in a neural network. If the out-of-sample data do not work in given parameters determined in-sample, under the overfitting hypothesis, the neural network has a high variance and cannot yet "generalize" to the new out-of-sample data set. Under one solution, a researcher can use even more data in an attempt to model the population even better. In another solution, the researcher prevents the neural network from too tight a fit, measured by a loss function, by adding a regularization penalty.

Regularization is usually accomplished in one of two ways:

- The loss function is artificially decreased by the "regularization parameter." Such a parameter may be a simple coefficient $\lambda = 0.9$ that is multiplied with the loss calculated by the neural network. The artificially lower loss function results in faster convergence and, as a result, in more straightforward functionals, avoiding too much nonlinear complexity in the neural network.
- Feature dropout reduces the number of input parameters once again to simplify the complexity of the network.

In reality, overfitting may not really be the culprit for the non-working data. Instead, the neural networks may stop working because the underlying data distributions change. Known as nonstationary, these distributions have long been studied in statistics and econometrics. No matter how much data we have, the environment around us evolves with time and neural networks trained on historical data may cease to provide meaningful answers, overfitting or not.

Adding Complexity

So far, we have discussed the most basic network using multinomial nonlinear regression with gradient descent on backpropagation, first developed by LeCun et al. (1989). A more complex neural network is designed following Krizhevsky et al. (2012) as a multinomial logistic regression using mini-batch gradient descent based on backpropagation (LeCun et al. 1989) with momentum. Parameters like the batch size can be set to a power of 2 to speed up computation and the momentum can be set to 0.9 to ensure a reasonable convergence.

Big Data in Machine Learning

Much of the above discussion on neural networks has focused on pure machine learning – an iterative algorithmic approach to solving problems. The fun of data science comes in at this point to dramatically speed up the machine learning computation, making it efficient with a dramatic size of inputs and a large number of neurons at each of the numerous hidden layers. For instance, market data used for high-frequency trading are so voluminous that they require special techniques that are far beyond basic neural networks (Aldridge 2013). Various data science methodologies deliver improvements in computational performance of loss functions used to parameterize neural networks (Aldridge and Avellaneda 2019).

A geometric representation of a loss function is known as a *loss surface*. In general, loss surfaces of dynamic neural networks can be not at all convex and depend on thousands of parameters. At the time this chapter was written, the loss surfaces were an active area of research in data science. The Big Data studies of loss surfaces tend to approach the problems of loss surface modeling from two angles:

1. Finding the local structure of minima, typically using the Stochastic Gradient Descent methodology (SGD).
2. Examining the global loss structure.

The local structure of minima of the loss surface allows researchers to distinguish sharp and wide local minima, found by using large and small batch sizes during the neural network training. Wide local minima are thought to deliver productive generalizations (Hochreiter and Schmidhuber 1997; Keskar et al. 2017). However, the local minima methodology has come under criticism from Dinh et al. (2017) for its lack of intuitiveness.

Studies of global loss structure seek to overcome poor local minima found by the SGD. For example, Lee et al. (2016) showed that under mild conditions gradient descent almost surely converges to a local minimizer. Freeman and Bruna (2017) theoretically show that local minima of a neural network are connected with a curve along which the loss is upper-bounded by a constant that depends on the number of parameters of the network and the smoothness of the data. Garipov et al. (2018) further show that the optima of the loss functions are connected by curves over which the training and test accuracy are nearly constant. The researchers then use the property to develop a high-performing training method that outperforms other existing methodologies. Garipov et al. (2018) dub this methodology *Fast Geometric Ensembling* (FGE).

Coding a Simple Neural Network for One Instrument from Daily Data

For an example of a very basic neural network, intended as an academic example to illustrate the technique in view of investment management applications, consider the S&P 500 ETF (NYSE:SPY). Using data from Yahoo! Finance for 10 years of SPY from 3/28/2009 through 3/29/2019, we construct a neural network for modeling the next day's return given the previously available data. As we demonstrate, the simplest neural network on a commonly traded S&P 500 ETF is able to produce 15% per year with a Sharpe ratio of about 1.0.

Our objective is to create a neural network in the simplest way to model the next period's returns in a way similar to that of technical analysts: using the previous returns' data only. We are not yet accounting for transaction costs or other potential "trading frictions," such as potential inability to execute a large transaction at the end-of-the-day price due to liquidity constraints.[1]

To create the basic neural network, we will utilize all the available data for SPY that Yahoo! Finance provides: Date, Open, High, Low, Close, Adj.Close and Volume. While

---

[1] In such cases, execution managers tend to rely on slightly earlier execution at potentially worse prices.

Close and Adj.Close features are very similar, we will let the neural network decide which of the two time series to keep and which to discard.

As discussed in the overview of neural network theory, our example neural network will consist of the following items:

- "Layers" comprise input X, output $\hat{Y}$, and potentially multiple hidden layers. For simplicity of exposition, we will start our programming example with just one hidden layer. Likewise, to keep things simple, the input X will comprise just one variable, the closing price for each day.
- Weights and biases, W and b, connecting each pair of successive layers.
- "Activation function" σ for each layer.

Defining Target Outputs

One of the critical aspects of neural networks and machine learning in general is the specification of the output of the system, Y. This is the problem that stumps many alternative-data-hungry fund managers: once the alternative data are purchased and stored on our servers, what's next? In the case of our simple neural network, we will define the output as the next day's return.

If we predict the return correctly, we can trade on the strategy in the following two ways:

1. Long-only: If today the neural network expects tomorrow's return to be positive, we liquidate all prior positions, and buy the instrument at close today with the intention of selling it at close tomorrow. If the neural network expects tomorrow's return to be negative, we liquidate all yesterday's positions and do nothing, or zero if the price next day goes down. Our expected trading strategy return then can be written as:

$$ER_{max,t} = max(EP_t/P_{t-1} - 1, 0)$$

2. Long-short: If today the neural network expects tomorrow's return to be positive (negative), we liquidate all prior positions, and buy (sell) the instrument at close today with the intention of selling (buying) it at close tomorrow. If the neural network expects tomorrow's return to be negative, we liquidate all yesterday's positions and do nothing, or zero if the price next day goes down. Our expected trading strategy return then can be written as:

$$ER_{max,t} = |EP_t/P_{t-1} - 1|$$

Testing Performance

How does the neural network's prediction stack up against realized out-of-sample returns? To test this, we create a rolling window estimator with 1-day-ahead forecasts. The forecasts are then compared with the 1-day returns immediately following the neural network's estimation period, yet not used in the neural network computation. We compare the results as point estimates of returns and as directional forecasts.

The point estimates compare the values of realized 1-day returns with the neural network's out-of-sample prediction for the same date:

$$e_{point,t} = R_t - E[R_t|R_{t-1} \ldots R_{t-1-k}] \tag{2.27}$$

The directional forecasts of the same neural network place less emphasis on the actual value of the forecast, instead considering the accuracy of the forecast direction. Thus, if the neural network's one-day-ahead forecast predicted a positive (negative) return and the realized out-of-sample return was indeed positive (negative), the error was recorded as an absolute value of the realized return. However, if the neural network's one-day-ahead forecast predicted a positive (negative) return and the realized out-of-sample return was indeed negative (positive), the error was recorded as the negative of the absolute value of the realized return:

$$e_{directional,t} = R_t * \text{sign}(E[R_t|R_{t-1} \ldots R_{t-1-k}]) \tag{2.28}$$

Next, we translate the results into a trading strategy and test performance. To evaluate the neural network modeling tool we have just created, we will proceed in the following way:

1. Calculate the neural network's "next day" prediction using a rolling window of training data.
2. If the prediction is positive, "buy" S&P 500 ETF, otherwise, "sell" S&P 500 ETF.
3. Use the next day's actual returns to calculate the profit and loss of the strategy generated in point 2.

The initial weights connecting the layers are first selected at random. The weights are then adjusted with each subsequent iteration based on gradient descent. As a result of the initial randomization, several consecutive neural network analyses on the same sets of data may produce slightly varying results.

We begin with a single hidden layer, single-input, single-output system: SPY returns predicting 1-day-ahead returns of SPY. SPY is one of the most liquid and widely held financial instruments in the world, and accurate prediction of its prices can be critical to a broad swath of portfolio management and all sorts of investors.

One of the key metrics of single instrument predictability is the system's performance versus long-established time-series analyses, such as technical indicators. Specifically, indicators such as moving average (MA) crossovers have been used by generations of technical analysts to determine the impending direction of the prices. While different configurations of neural networks deviate in various directions from the MA crossovers, sometimes outperforming and sometimes underperforming the technical indicator, in many cases the SPY vs SPY neural network matches MA crossover quite closely, as shown in Figure 2.6.

Neural networks have proven successful in identifying features in an image: given a set of inputs (matrices containing images) and corresponding outputs (classifiers, "dog,"

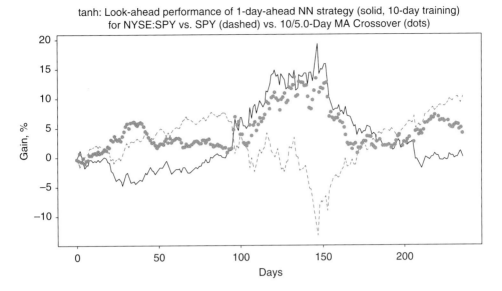

Figure 2.6 Performance of the neural network with one hidden layer, tanh activation function, SPY returns as inputs, SPY returns as outputs, and 10-day training period, from May 7, 2018, through May 6, 2019. The neural network performance (solid line) closely traces the performance of the 10-5 MA crossover (dots) in the period of high volatility, yet both NN and MA crossovers end up underperforming the SPY (dashed line).

"cat," etc.), a neural network can successfully recognize image features and use those in future assessment of yet-unprocessed, out-of-sample images. The trading strategy analogue would determine, on the basis of recent history, whether the next day's, week's or month's returns are likely to be positive or negative, and with what magnitude.

While the neural network results may incorporate known factors, as specified by a researcher, a simple neural network is hardly a tool for factor identification. As a nonlinear regression, the neural network creates a better fit of inputs to outputs, yet it fails to independently identify the relevant factors from the range presented, at least in its simplest iterations.

To illustrate the limitations of a neural network, consider, for example, a neural network training SPY returns on just one previous day of SPY returns. Figure 2.7 plots the time series of the W1 and W2 weights from May 7, 2018, through May 6, 2019. As Figure 2.7 shows, the weights move around quite a bit between 0 and 1. Further research into the weights' dynamics seems warranted to uncover the dependencies of the weights on other factors. Figures 2.8 and 2.9 show the rolling out-of-sample performance of the corresponding trading strategy: if the neural network predicts a positive return, the system buys SPY at that day's close and sells at the next day's close. If the neural network predicts a non-positive return, the system sells at close and closes the position at the next day's close.

As shown in Figures 2.8 and 2.9, the neural network–based strategy significantly underperforms the passive buy-and-hold in SPY. One improvement may be to expand

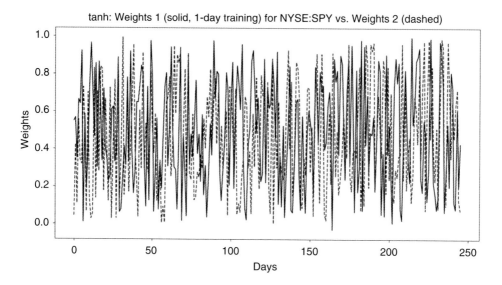

Figure 2.7   Weights W1 and W2 from the one-day-ahead SPY return NN prediction with a single input of the previous day's SPY return. Activation function: tanh.

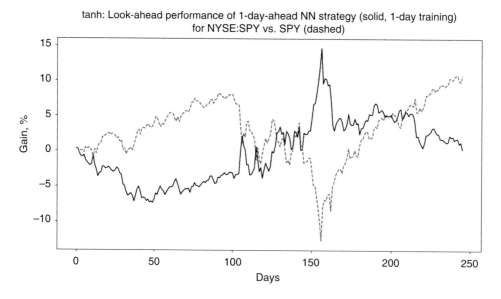

Figure 2.8   Predictability of the SPY return based on the previous day's SPY return with a single hidden layer neural network with activation function tanh, 2018-19.

the number of inputs. For instance, adding monthly changes in the SPY trading volume as an input in addition to the SPY return to predict the direction of the next month's SPY return produces the following performance shown in Figure 2.10.

As Figure 2.11 illustrates, the choice of the activation function matters. Thus, Figure 2.11 uses a linear activation function, and all the advantages developed in the

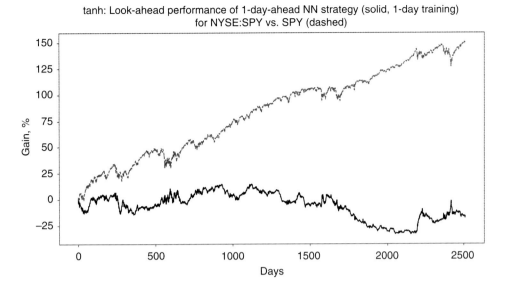

Figure 2.9 Predictability of the SPY return based on the previous day's SPY return with a single hidden layer neural network with activation function tanh, 2009-19.

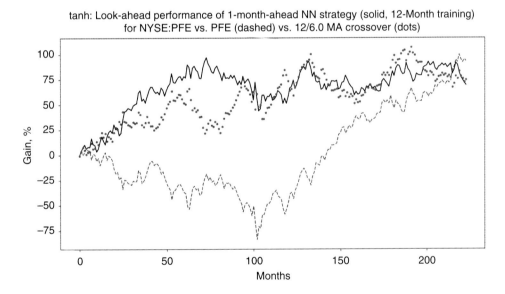

Figure 2.10 A monthly neural network strategy on NYSE:PFE with input variables of PFE returns and SPY returns; a training period of 12 months produces average annualized returns of 3.7% and a Sharpe ratio of 0.20. The neural network prediction closely tracks 12/6 month MA crossover for PFE. The neural network strategy "buys" ("sells") at the end of each month if the predicted next-month return is positive (negative) and then liquidates the position at the end of the following month.

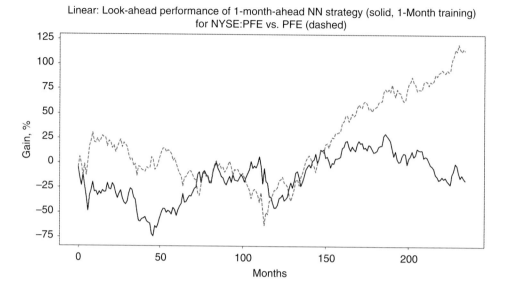

Figure 2.11   A monthly neural network strategy with linear activation function on NYSE:PFE with input variables comprising PFE and SPY returns, training period of 1 month. The strategy is significantly underperforming simple passive buy-and-hold investment in PFE from May 1999 through May 2019.

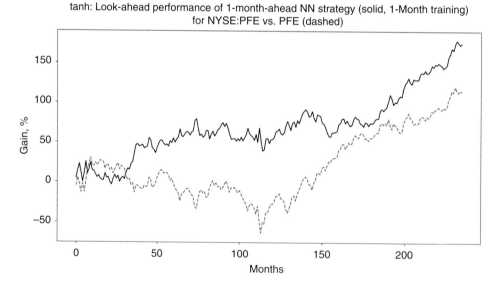

Figure 2.12   A monthly neural network strategy with tanh activation function on NYSE:PFE with input variables comprising PFE and SPY returns, training period of 1 month. The strategy produces annualized returns of 9.478% and a Sharpe ratio of 0.48 from May 1999 through May 2019.

tanh–activated neural network (Figure 2.12) evaporate. As Figures 2.13 and 2.15 show, the monthly tanh neural network delivers results on other major stocks as well. Similarly, Figure 2.14 shows that the linear activation function still underperforms when other instruments are considered.

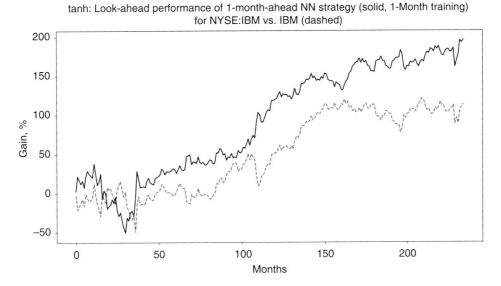

Figure 2.13 A monthly neural network strategy with tanh activation function on NYSE:IBM with input variables comprising IBM and SPY returns, training period of 1 month. The strategy produces annualized returns of 9.987% and a Sharpe ratio of 0.396 from May 1999 through May 2019.

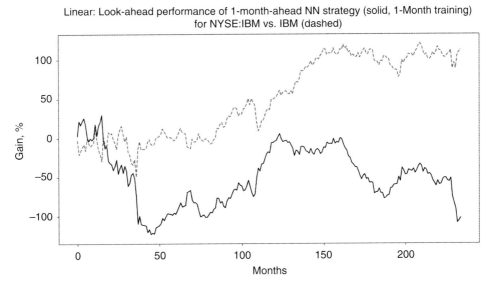

Figure 2.14 A monthly neural network strategy with linear activation function on NYSE:IBM with input variables comprising IBM and SPY returns, training period of 1 month. The strategy is significantly underperforming simple passive buy-and-hold investment in IBM from May 1999 through May 2019.

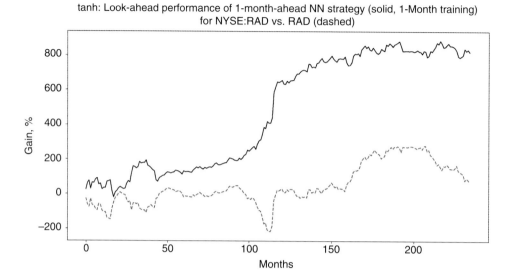

Figure 2.15 A monthly neural network strategy with tanh activation function on NYSE:RAD with input variables comprising RAD and SPY monthly returns, training period of 1 month. The strategy produces annualized returns of 41.81% and a Sharpe ratio of 0.628 from May 1999 through May 2019.

To prevent overfitting, the training is "regularized" by weight decay – the loss function is assigned a penalty, where the penalty multiplier is set to something like $5 \cdot 10^{-4}$. In addition, the dropout regularization can be applied to the first few layers to ensure that the number of parameters does shrink considerably. The dropout ratio can be set to 0.5.

A separate parameter, known as the learning rate, can be set to 10^{-2}, and then decreased by a factor of 10 when the validation set accuracy stops improving.

Adding Activation Levels

Activation levels are intercepts b in the nonlinear regressions of the neural networks. As such, the intercepts move the given layer's output up or down on the output vertical axis. While potentially improving the results of linear regressions or ReLu by offsetting the graph away from 0, the presence of activation levels often produces worse results with sigmoid or tanh regressions by shifting the output.

Convergence

Figure 2.16 shows the convergence of a loss function of a simple return neural network with one hidden layer and sigmoid activation function on the S&P 500 ETF (NYSE:SPY) using data from April 2009 through August 2009. The input of the neural

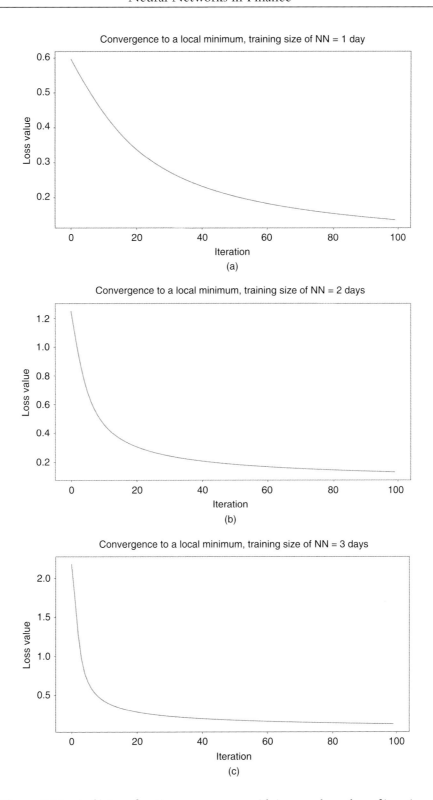

Figure 2.16 (a–k) Loss function convergence with increased number of iterations.

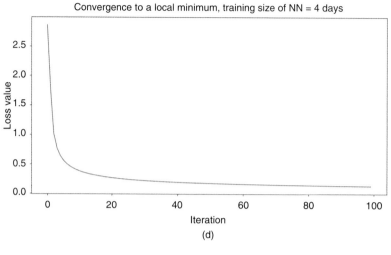

(d)

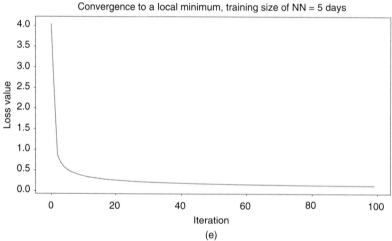

(e)

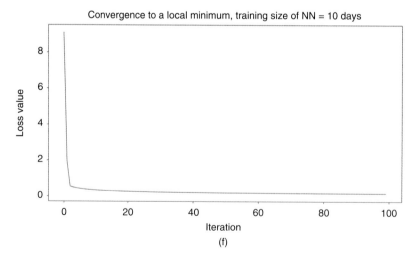

(f)

Figure 2.16   (*Continued*)

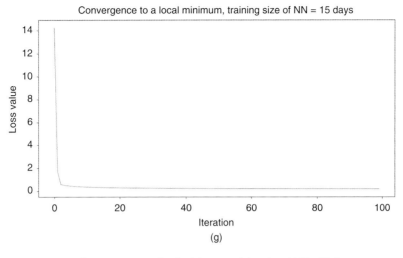

(g)

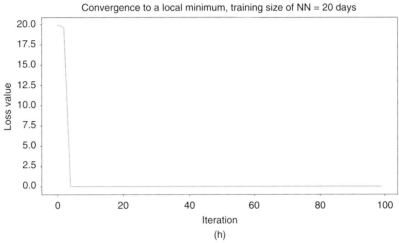

(h)

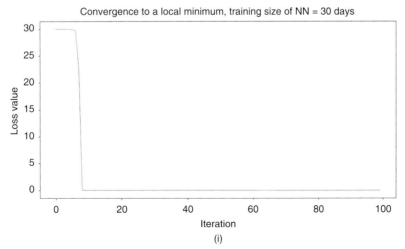

(i)

Figure 2.16   (*Continued*)

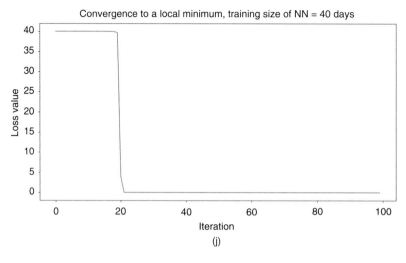

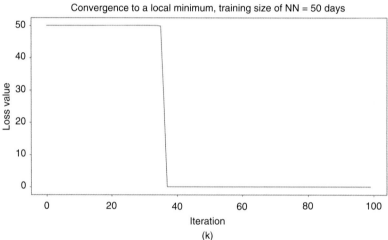

Figure 2.16   (*Continued*)

network is a vector of simple daily returns $X = \{R_t\}$ based on adjusted close prices: $R_t = P_t/P_{t-1} - 1$. The output is a one-day-ahead return for long-only strategies: $X = \{R_{t+1}\}$, where $R_{t+1} = P_{t+1}/P_t - 1$. Convergence speeds up when the number of elements in X and Y increases to about 10, and then gradually starts plateauing in the first 10–20 iterations before converging. Changing the time period within the 2009–2019 date range still produces similar results.

Due to the random starting point of the weights in the neural network, subsequent iterations on the same data with the same parameterization deliver different investment decisions and results. Overall, however, the results stay in the same range, fostering confidence in the methodology and showing its applicability.

Choosing Input Variables

The success of the neural networks in Figures 2.13 and 2.15 shares an important common factor: returns of the S&P 500 ETF (NYSE:SPY). The presence of SPY as a dependent variable, of course, is quite familiar to finance professionals as a good old Capital Asset Pricing Model (CAPM), due to Sharpe (1964) and Lintner (1965). While the linear version of CAPM appears to have run its course due to its popularity in investing as demonstrated in Figure 2.16, the nonlinear configuration we identify by the neural network in this chapter is still very much alive.

Similar reasoning potentially applies to other model factors previously identified as successful predictors of outcomes under consideration. Whether it is a quick ratio in the loan pricing model per Altman (1968), the three factors of Fama and French (Fama and French 1992, 1993) or other predictors, nonlinear structure of neural networks may help identify new ways to analyze the financial data.

Conclusion

Machine learning and neural networks are powerful tools for identifying complex non-linear dependencies in financial data. In many cases, the techniques serve as play-dough modeling tools for data scientists. While the neural networks help identify patterns, many of the patterns are already known to researchers. The nonlinear functionals produced by the neural networks, however, deepen the typically linear relationships like monthly momentum and market return dependency discussed in this chapter, and help design systems that exploit more market inefficiencies.

Appendix 2.A Building a Neural Network in Python

Python is a versatile programming language with a wide selection of libraries that allow researchers to easily program a number of tasks. Programming a neural network in Python is also easy. Here, we will consider an approach that leverages the powerful built-in Python library Keras, which in turn contains well-regarded libraries Theano and TensorFlow.

For an example here, we will start with a fully connected neural network, a model where each node in one layer is connected with every node in the next layer. Such models are known as dense. We will further add layers sequentially until our model reaches the desired levels of predictability. To do so, our Python code will require the following imports:

```
from keras.models import Sequential
from keras.layers import Dense
```

In Keras, we programmatically add layers one at a time as follows:

```
model = Sequential()
model.add(Dense(5, input_dim=13, activation='sigmoid'))
model.add(Dense(3, activation='sigmoid'))
model.add(Dense(1, activation='sigmoid'))
```

The first hidden layer takes 13 inputs (variables summarized in columns) and outputs 5 using sigmoid activation function. The next hidden layer converts the 5 outputs of layer 1 into 3 outputs, also using sigmoid. The final layer converts the data into the final output for each row of data.

Next, the Keras model needs to be compiled:

```
model.compile(loss='binary_crossentropy', optimizer='adam', metrics=['accuracy'])
```

In the compilation function above, we need to specify a loss function, here, specific to our binary outputs, `'binary_crossentropy'`, a gradient descent optimizer "adam," and the prediction accuracy as the target evaluation metric.

Next, after loading our input variables into a matrix X and output variables into a matrix Y, we fit the neural network over 300 iterations as follows:

```
model.fit(X, y, epochs=300)
```

For each epoch, the model will print out the achieved loss and in-sample accuracy.

Making out-of-sample predictions with Keras is equally easy. For a new, unused sample of data X_new, the model can predict the out-of-sample outcomes with just one additional line of code:

```
predicted_y = model.predict(X)
```

Comparing the predicted y with the realized y delivers the out-of-sample performance evaluation for the neural network.

For specific code examples, please visit https://www.BigDataFinanceBook.com, and register with password *Neural* (case-sensitive).

References

Aldridge, I. (2013). *High-Frequency Trading: A Practical Guide to Algorithmic Strategies and Trading Systems*, 2nd ed. Hoboken, NJ: Wiley.

Aldridge, I. and Avellaneda, M. (2019). Neural networks in finance: design and performance. *The Journal of Financial Data Science* 1(4): 39–62.

Aldridge, I. and Krawciw, S. (2017). *Real-Time Risk: What Investors Should Know About Fintech, High-Frequency Trading and Flash Crashes*. Hoboken, NJ: Wiley.

Altman, E.I. (1968). Financial ratios, discriminant analysis and the prediction of corporate bankruptcy. *Journal of Finance* 23(4): 189–209.

Avellaneda, M., Li, T. N., Papanicolaou, A., and Wang, G. (2020). Trade Signals In VIX Futures. Working Paper, Courant Institute, New York University.

Avellaneda, M., and Ma, T. (2014). Risk Models for Agency Residential Mortgage-Backed Securities (RMBS). Working Paper, Courant Institute for Mathematical Sciences, New York University.

Avellaneda, M., Carelli, A., and Stella, F. (2000). A Bayesian approach for constructing implied volatility surfaces through neural networks. *Journal of Computational Finance* 4(1): 83–107.

Campbell, T. and J. Dietrich (1983). The determinants of default on insured conventional residential mortgage loans, *Journal of Finance* 38: 1569–1581.

Chen, L., Pelger, M., and Zhu, J. (2019). Deep learning in asset pricing. Working paper, Stanford University, CA.

Cunningham, D. F. and Capone, C. A. (1990). The relative termination experience of adjustable to fixed-rate mortgages. *The Journal of Finance* 45(5): 1687–1703.

Curley, A., and Guttentag, J. (1974). The yield on insured residential mortgages. *Explorations in Economic Research* 1: 114–161.

Deng, Y., Quigley, J., and Van Order, R. (2000). Mortgage terminations, heterogeneity, and the exercise of mortgage options. *Econometrica* 68(2): 275–307.

Dinh, L., Pascanu, R., Bengio, S., and Bengio, Y. (2017). "Sharp Minima Can Generalize For Deep Nets." *Proceedings of the 34th International Conference on Machine Learning*, Sydney, Australia.

Eldan, R. and Shamir, O. (2016). The power of depth for feedforward neural networks. In: *29th Annual Conference on Learning Theory,* vol. *49* of *Proceedings of Machine Learning Research (PMLR)* (ed. V. Feldman, A. Rakhlin, and O. Shamir), 907–940. New York: Columbia University Press.

Fabozzi, F.J. (2016). *The Handbook of Mortgage-Backed Securities*, 7th edn. Oxford: Oxford University Press.

Fama, E.F. and French, K.R. (1992). The cross-section of expected stock returns. *The Journal of Finance* 47(2): 427–465.

Fama, E.F. and French, K.R. (1993). Common risk factors in the returns on stocks and bonds. *Journal of Financial Economics* 33: 3–56.

Freeman, C.D. and Bruna, J. (2017). Topology and geometry of half-rectified network optimization. International Conference on Learning Representations.

Gallo, C. (2005). Artificial Neural networks in finance modelling. Experimental 0509002, University Library of Munich, Germany.

Garipov, T., Pavel, I., Podoprikhin, D., Vetrov, D., and Wilson, A.G. (2018). Loss surfaces, mode connectivity, and fast ensembling of DNNs. 32nd Conference on Neural Information Processing Systems (NIPS 2018), Montreal, Canada.

Gu, S., Kelly, B., and Xiu, D. (2019). Empirical asset pricing via machine learning. University of Chicago Booth School of Business working paper.

Hastie, T., Tibshirani, R., and Friedman, J. (2009). *The Elements of Statistical Learning: Data Mining, Inference, and Prediction*. New York: Springer.

He, K., Zhang, X., Ren, S., and Sun, J. (2016). Identity Mappings in Deep Residual Networks. European Conference on Computer Vision - ECCV 2016: 630–645.

Heaton, J.B., Polson, N.G., and Witte, J.H. (2016). Deep learning in finance. arXiv preprint arXiv:1602.06561.

Hinton, G.E., Osindero, S., and Teh, Y-W. (2006). A fast learning algorithm for deep belief nets. *Neural Computation* 18: 1527–1554.

Hochreiter, S. and Schmidhuber, J. (1997). Flat minima. *Neural Computation* 9(1): 1–42.

Keskar, N.S., Mudigere, D., Nocedal, J., et al. (2017). On large-batch training for deep learning: generalization gap and sharp minima. *International Conference on Learning Representations*.

Krizhevsky, A., Sutskever, I. and Hinton, G.E. (2012). ImageNet classification with deep convolutional neural networks. *Advances in Neural Information Processing Systems* 25(2): 1097–1105.

LeCun, Y., Boser, B., Denker, J.S., et al. (1989). Backpropagation applied to handwritten zip code recognition. *Neural Computation* 1: 541–551.

Lee, J.D., Simchowitz, M., Jordan, M.I., and Recht, B. (2016). Gradient descent only converges to minimizers. *Conference on Learning Theory*, pp. 1246–1257.

Lintner, J. 1965. The valuation of risk assets and the selection of risky investments in stock portfolios and capital budgets. *Review of Economics and Statistics* 47(1): 13–37.

Richard, S.F. and R. Roll. (1989) Prepayments on Fixed-Rate Mortgage-Backed Securities, *Journal of Portfolio Management*, 73–82.

Ritter, G. (2017). Machine Learning for Trading. In *Big Data and Machine Learning in Quantitative Investment*, Tony Guida ed., 225–250.

Sharpe, W.F. 1964. Capital asset prices: A theory of market equilibrium under conditions of risk. *Journal of Finance* 19(3): 425–442.

Sirignano, J., Sadhwani, A., and Giesecke, K. (2018). Deep learning for mortgage risk. Available at: SSRN 2799443.

Chapter 3

Supervised Learning

Introduction

Neural networks, discussed in Chapter 2, may fall into supervised, semi-supervised, or unsupervised categories, depending on their design and, thus, required researcher involvement. In this chapter, we discuss other, non-neural, supervised models and their applications.

Supervised learning (SL) is most akin to econometrics. As such, SL models tend to work with perfectly cleaned and organized data. Of course, financial data rarely come to the analyst in a format perfect for econometrics. Figure 3.1 shows a snippet of trading data logs from a BATS equities exchange. The information shown is neither neat nor accessible, save only with the help of a thick instruction manual.

As a result, legions of quants with their advanced degrees costing billions have been deployed in banks and funds to scrub, polish, and organize data in order to make it presentable to their econometrics-trained portfolio managers. Companies like Bloomberg and Reuters amassed fortunes greater than those of many sovereign funds by processing and reselling financial data in econometrics-friendly formats to hedge funds, pension funds, banks, and endowments.

Cleaning and organizing data are traditional pre-processing tasks required to make decisions based on the data. The use of indexing and structured databases speeds up algorithms that search various database languages and, increasingly, Python.

Data science evolved from a different origin than econometrics. Its appetite for capturing and making sense of every available data point, however dirty or imprecise, is characteristic of the discipline. While the raw data may be voluminous, the data columns,

S.A1T1KT90000LYB000100AAPL   0001680100Y

Figure 3.1   Raw equity data sample. The data record a limit buy order for 100 shares of Apple (NYSE:AAPL) at 168.01.

also known as data *features*, are often not well-defined and some values may be missing altogether. Known as *unstructured*, the raw data do not typically fit into any specific format. Such unstructured data are the opposite of *structured data*, parsed, scrubbed, and organized data neatly presented in rows and columns. Driven by companies that unintentionally created vast amounts of data, such as Google and Facebook, data scientists seek to minimize the costs of cleaning and handling data while maximizing the quality of the output. This is a business model that will prove to be competitive in the present environment, where margins have been compressing for several years.

Fully structured or "labeled" data lend themselves easily to "supervised learning," a more traditional set of methodologies discussed in this chapter. Supervised learning (SL) uses fully labeled data to teach the computer to classify objects or to predict continuous values from a given data set. SL generates a function over variables in the data set. SL can also be thought of as the classic analysis of hypotheses, where the researcher postulates an idea and then asks whether the idea can be supported by the data.

By contrast, in completely unsupervised learning (UL), the computer does not have a guide for the relationships among variables. The machine has to autonomously determine the relationships among data points. In unsupervised learning, the computer has to learn the structure of the data to fully understand relationships embedded in the data. In unsupervised learning, the researcher does not create a priori hypotheses about the information in the data set; instead, the researcher asks the computer to provide the researcher with key themes embedded in the data. Unsupervised models are discussed throughout much of this book, beginning with Chapter 5.

Semi-supervised learning (SSL), as its name implies, is a hybrid between the supervised and unsupervised methods. In the semi-supervised setup, the computer deploys techniques involving regressions and data structure methods. In SSL, a researcher may label a portion of the data set, and then ask the computer to complete the labeling of the entire data set given the example the researcher has provided and the structure of the data. Presently, most common uses for SSL relate to processing documents such as earnings reports, sentiment analysis of news articles, and the like. Whereas a traditional researcher reading and analyzing corporate reports may take two weeks to classify a report into a positive or a negative predictor of corporate health, the semi-supervised approach can often accomplish the same in an hour or less. Such a speed improvement grants the technology-enabled investors a leg up over the traditional competition, the ability of the early bird to catch the worm in short-term trading and long-term investing alike. Semi-supervised learning is detailed in Chapter 4.

While the importance of structured data is not likely to change, the unsupervised models discussed in Chapter 5 and later throughout this book suggest approaches that involve less data structuring. Until these latter techniques become commonplace, the costs of perfecting data structures are ultimately passed on in the form of fees charged by hedge funds, mutual funds, ETFs, etc. Algorithms for cleaning the data and inferring, or imputing, missing values traditionally discarded in econometric modeling are a well-defined area of data science and are presented in Chapter 7 of this book.

Supervised Learning

Supervised learning techniques seek a data model that fits the relationships between data inputs and outputs as closely as possible. To do so, most supervised learning algorithms employ the optimization of the loss function, where loss is defined as the squared error between model prediction $\hat{Y}$ and the realized data Y:

$$L = \sum_{i=1}^{N} (\hat{Y}_i - Y_i)^2 \tag{3.1}$$

For example, if predicting stock returns, $\hat{Y}$ will serve as the returns prediction generated by the model while Y is the realized value of the returns. The loss function is then a measure of the goodness of fit of the model vis-à-vis the realized values. Of course, when there is too close a fit, there may be a resulting "overfitting problem," as introduced in Chapter 2. This is a machine learning problem where the model fits closely to the intricacies of past data but does not represent the future. In many cases, an overfitting penalty is applied to mitigate the problem. For example, LASSO and ridge regressions, discussed in this chapter, explicitly incorporate an overfitting penalty in the model optimization function.

Supervised learning tackles both regression and classification. In a *regression*, the output is continuous. In other words, the data estimate produced by the regression is a variable that is a real number, for example, a return or correlation. In a classification, the output is discrete. Classification output can be binary, answering whether a question about the data is true or false, for example, "Is a given financial instrument an ETF?" Classification output can also be enumerated, outputting, for example, the best match of the given k classes as the best fit for an object at hand. An example question that a classification problem seeks to answer is "What kind of financial instrument is this? 0 Equity, 1 Fixed Income, 2 Commodity, … " In the context of finding missing values, both regression and classification frameworks may be of use, depending on the content of the missing and partially missing data.

A basic linear regression is a tried-and-true method for classification and regression. In addition to predicting future continuous values based on the past data in the classic regression scenario, a linear regression can help separate the data into clear binary "yes/no" classifications. This linear classifier draws the line through the data with the majority of "yes" points falling on one side of the line and the majority of "no" hitting the other side. However, linear regression has many known shortcomings. For example, it does not work well on data that are best modeled by a nonlinear function. The following techniques, jointly referred to as supervised machine learning, have been created over the years to improve upon the basic linear regression setup, are used by practitioners today, and are covered in this chapter along with their applications in finance that were developed by the time this book was written:

- *Penalized least square regressions*, including *ridge regression*, its close cousin *LASSO*, and their combination, known as *elastic net*
- *K nearest neighbors (K-NN)*
- *Random decision forests* and their variation, known as extra trees
- *Support Vector Machines (SVMs)*.

These items are described hereafter in detail.

Ridge Regression, LASSO, and Elastic Nets

Ridge regression, LASSO, and elastic nets are extensions of linear regressions with built-in regularization designed to prevent overfitting, and they deal with flawed data sets. Specifically, the techniques estimate parameters in data that are (i) small in length (small sample) in comparison with the number of data features or columns, or (ii) contain correlated data features or columns, i.e., exhibit a high degree of collinearity.

A traditional linear regression, also known as Ordinary Least Squares (OLS), finds a line that minimizes the squared distances from the data points in the data set at hand. OLS can act as a regression predictor, estimating future values of a variable Y, or as a classifier by separating two kinds of data points with a single line. To find the line, OLS optimizes

$$Y = \beta X + \varepsilon \tag{3.2}$$

where X is the set of data features and Y is the dependent variable, changes in which we seek to explain with X, and β are the resulting regression coefficients or parameters that relate X to Y. The OLS optimization finds β by minimizing the loss function of Eq (3.1), equivalent to:

$$\hat{\beta} = argmin_\beta \sum (Y - X\beta)^2 \tag{3.3}$$

When the data are small in length relative to the number of columns of X, or the columns of X are correlated, the resulting inferences may not be predictive as the β may falsely identify the flawed relationships. The traditional approach for dealing with the collinearity in OLS is to test the columns for correlation, and remove one or more correlated columns, discarding potentially useful data.

The ridge regression, LASSO, and elastic nets help use every piece of flawed data by adding an extra term to the loss function. The extra term, known as the regularization penalty, is directly dependent on the regression coefficients β. The optimization then seeks to minimize not just the loss function itself, but the β as well. Then, in the presence of collinearity, smaller βs have less importance in determining future values of Y, thus improving the estimates.

The ridge regression, LASSO, and elastic nets differ in their regularization specification. The ridge regression, due to Hoerl, Kannard, and Baldwin (1974), adds a penalty in the form of the squared sum of the regression coefficients multiplied by a regularization parameter, λ_{Ridge}:

$$L = \sum (\hat{Y}_i - Y_i)^2 + \lambda_{Ridge} \sum \beta^2 \qquad (3.4)$$

or

$$\hat{\beta} = arg\,min_\beta \left[\sum (Y - X\beta)^2 + \lambda_{Ridge} \sum \beta^2 \right] \qquad (3.5)$$

Essentially, the ridge regression mandates that the betas are lower, but not necessarily 0, that is, the fit is not as close as it would be without the penalty.

It is interesting to note that the ridge regression penalty shrinks not only betas, but also the eigenvalues of predicted data. However, while ridge regression is convex, it does not promote degree reduction, known as *sparsity*, among its coefficients. Sparsity is desirable in many financial applications, including portfolio optimization.

Least Absolute Shrinkage and Selection Operator (LASSO), due to Tibshirani (1996), is very similar to a ridge regression, but adds a penalty based on the sum of absolute values of the regression coefficients β:

$$L = \sum (\hat{Y}_i - Y_i)^2 + \lambda_{LASSO} \sum |\beta| \qquad (3.6)$$

or

$$\hat{\beta} = arg\,min_\beta \left[\sum (Y - X\beta)^2 + \lambda_{LASSO} \sum |\beta| \right] \qquad (3.7)$$

While accomplishing the same thing as the ridge regression, LASSO is perhaps more intuitive but may be harder to compute due to its lack of immediate differentiability.

While the ridge and LASSO techniques help deal with collinearity, issues persist. For example, LASSO tends to select just one data feature out of the correlated set. To address these concerns, elastic net linearly combines regularization imposed by ridge regression and LASSO as follows:

$$L = \sum (\hat{Y}_i - Y_i)^2 + \lambda_{Ridge} \sum \beta^2 + \lambda_{LASSO} \sum |\beta| \qquad (3.8)$$

Pereira, Basto, and Ferreira da Silva (2015) use logistic LASSO and ridge regressions to predict corporate bankruptcies in the hospitality industry. LASSO is the darling tool of many a portfolio manager who seeks to minimize extreme weights in Markowitz optimization, avoiding high turnover and transaction costs, all the while satisfying regulatory and short-selling constraints. Examples of LASSO in portfolio management include Jagannathan and Ma (2003), Ledoit and Wolf (2008), Brodie et al. (2009), DeMiguel et al. (2009), Fan et al. (2012), and Kolm, Tütüncü, and Fabozzi (2014). Carrasco and Noumon (2012) show that ridge regression does *not* work in portfolio optimization as it leads to portfolios with an undesirably large number of positions. Kozak, Nagel, and Santosh (2019) use elastic nets on the U.S. stock data and economic indicators to shrink the contributions of low-variance principal components of candidate factors. The resulting approach selects factors that explain variation and mean returns.

In portfolio management, the classic Markowitz (1952) framework optimizes mean-variance tradeoff of a portfolio of financial instruments. For a full survey of models, see Brandt (2004) and Kolm, Tütüncü, and Fabozzi (2014). For N risky assets with random returns vector R_{t+1} and a risk-free rate R_t^f, the excess return is defined as $r_{t+1} = R_{t+1} - R_t^f$ with conditional means μ and covariance Σ. An investor allocates fraction w of his wealth to the risky assets and the rest $(1 - 1_N'w)$ to the risk-free asset, such as government-issued fixed income debt. Here, 1_N is an $N \times 1$ vector of ones. The total portfolio return is then $w\, r_{t+1} + R_t^f$. The mean-variance problem is then minimizing the variance of the portfolio subject to a target portfolio return μ_p:

$$\min_w \frac{1}{2} Var[r_{p,t+1}] = w'\Sigma w \qquad (3.9)$$

$$\text{s.t. } E[r_{p,t+1}] = w'\mu = \mu_p \qquad (3.10)$$

The optimal solution is then

$$w^* = \frac{\mu_p}{\mu'\Sigma^{-1}\mu}\Sigma^{-1}\mu \qquad (3.11)$$

Most investors, at the time this book was written, measured their investment performance via a Sharpe ratio, after Sharpe (1966):

$$SR = E[r_{p,t+1}]/\sigma[r_{p,t+1}] = \sqrt{\mu'\Sigma^{-1}\mu} \qquad (3.12)$$

that corresponds to $\mu_{SR} = \mu'\Sigma^{-1}\mu/1_N\ \Sigma^{-1}\mu$ and optimal weight

$$w_{SR}^* = \Sigma^{-1}\mu/1_N\ \Sigma^{-1}\mu \qquad (3.13)$$

Jobson and Korkie (1983) and Britten-Jones (1999) showed that the optimal allocation of Eq (3.13) can be expressed as

$$\widehat{w}^* = \widehat{\beta}/1_N'\widehat{\beta} \qquad (3.14)$$

where $\widehat{\beta}$ is the OLS estimate of β in the regression

$$1 = \beta'r_{t+1} + u_{t+1} \qquad (3.15)$$

If R is a $T \times N$ matrix composed of r_t', then Eq (3.15) can be rewritten as

$$1_T = R\beta + u \qquad (3.16)$$

and then β can be found as a solution to the following OLS regression:

$$R\beta = 1_T \qquad (3.17)$$

The optimal weights can often be extreme, especially in problems with insufficient or highly correlated data that generate highly correlated or singular covariance matrices.

The solutions minimizing extreme weights have also been found using supervised regularization, such as ridge regression and LASSO.

Here, however, we'll focus on finding the weights in a supervised OLS framework, known as penalized least squares regression. The penalization term can be interpreted as the transaction cost associated with portfolio reallocation.

Using $\Sigma = E(r_t' r_t) - \mu\mu'$, we can rewrite Eq (3.9) as

$$w^* = arg\ min_x E\left[|\mu_p - w'r_t|^2\right] \tag{3.18}$$

$$\text{s.t. } w'\mu = \mu_p$$

With ridge regression penalization, the optimal weights of Eq (3.18) become:

$$w^* = arg\ min_x |\mu_p 1_T - Rw|^2 + \lambda_{Ridge}|w|^2 \tag{3.19}$$

$$\text{s.t. } w'\mu = \mu_p$$

With LASSO, Eq (3.18) can be rewritten as:

$$w^* = arg\ min_x |\mu_p 1_T - Rw|^2 + \lambda_{Ridge}|w|^2 + \lambda_{LASSO}|w| \tag{3.20}$$

$$\text{s.t. } w'\mu = \mu_p$$

And with the elastic net, Eq (3.18) becomes:

$$w^* = arg\ min_x |\mu_p 1_T - Rw|^2 + \lambda_{Ridge}|w|^2 + \lambda_{LASSO}|w| \tag{3.21}$$

$$\text{s.t. } w'\mu = \mu_p$$

The solution is then found by using standard optimization techniques.

As an example, consider an application of the ridge regression, LASSO, and elastic net to predict U.S. Daily Treasury rates. The data used in this example are taken from the U.S. Department of Treasury. According to the Department's website (https://www.treasury.gov/resource-center/data-chart-center/interest-rates/pages/Text View.aspx?data=yieldYear&year=2020), "The Treasury yield curve is estimated daily using a cubic spline model. Inputs to the model are primarily indicative of bid-side yields for on-the-run Treasury securities. Treasury reserves the option to make changes to the yield curve as appropriate and in its sole discretion."

By cubic spline construction, the daily changes in the Treasury yields are highly correlated. In fact, over the 2018–2019 period, the correlation between the daily changes in the yields of the 3-Month and 6-Month T-bills was 57.01%, the correlation between the daily changes in the yields of the 1-Year and 2-Year T-bonds was 75.57%, and the correlation between the daily changes in the yields of the 2-Year and 3-Year T-bonds was 95.52%. Table 3.1 displays the complete correlation structure of daily changes of the U.S. Treasury yields.

Table 3.1   Correlations of daily changes of selected U.S. Treasuries.

	3 Mos	6 Mos	1 Year	2 Year	3 Year	5 Year	7 Year	10 Year
3 Mos	1.000	0.570	0.368	0.271	0.243	0.231	0.215	0.190
6 Mos	0.570	1.000	0.632	0.506	0.472	0.453	0.426	0.384
1 Year	0.368	0.632	1.000	0.755	0.745	0.721	0.689	0.638
2 Year	0.271	0.506	0.755	1.000	0.952	0.926	0.889	0.842
3 Year	0.243	0.472	0.745	0.952	1.000	0.966	0.942	0.903
5 Year	0.231	0.453	0.721	0.926	0.966	1.000	0.977	0.951
7 Year	0.215	0.426	0.689	0.889	0.942	0.977	1.000	0.976
10 Year	0.190	0.384	0.638	0.842	0.903	0.951	0.976	1.000

Here, we seek to train the models on the two years of data, 2018–2019, and predict out-of-sample the changes in the 20-Year U.S. Treasury rates using the 2018–2019 rates for 3-Month, 6-Month, 1-Year, 2-Year, 3-Year, 5-Year, 7-Year, and 10-Year T-bonds. First, the parameters β are calculated on the 2018–2019 training set, and then they are applied to the January 1-10, 2020. data to predict out-of-sample $t+1$ values. Figure 3.2 illustrates the performance of different forecasts vis-à-vis the realized out-of-sample 20-Year rates (x axis), ridge, LASSO, and elastic net using regularization $\lambda = 0.1$. As Figure 3.2 shows, linear regression and ridge regression outperform LASSO and elastic net in the current forecasting problem. In fact, LASSO and elastic net forecast 0% changes in the 20-Year rates, resulting in the goodness of fit measured by R^2 of -1.74% for both. In comparison, ridge regression delivers R^2 of 49.45%, and linear regression produces the best R^2 of 55.37% in predicting the bond yields. When January 2018–October 2019 training data were used to find parameters and then predict $t+1$ daily changes in November 2019–January 2020 20-Year T-bonds, the linear regression R^2 hit 83.6% while ridge R^2 was 78.1% and LASSO and elastic net were still approximately 0. The out-of-sample predicted vs. realized changes in the 20-year T-bonds for November 2019–January 2020 are shown in Figure 3.3.

The penalized OLS regressions are known to be very sensitive to the regularization parameter λ. In the Treasury example, when regularization decreased to $\lambda = 0.01$, the ridge regression sprang into life and outperformed linear regression in the prediction of the 20-Year rates. When January 2018–October 2019 training data were used to find parameters and then predict $t+1$ daily changes in November 2019–January 2020 20-Year T-bonds, the linear regression R^2 was 83.6% as before while ridge regression–produced R^2 was 85.7% and LASSO and elastic net were still approximately 0. Table 3.2 displays the resulting coefficients and Figure 3.4 shows the predicted values vs. realized (x-axis).

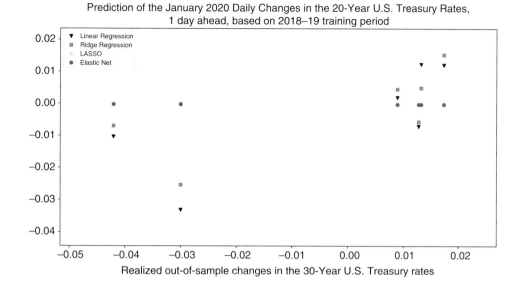

Figure 3.2 Out-of-sample t + 1 prediction of 20-Year U.S. Treasury rates with linear regression, ridge regression, LASSO, and elastic net for January 1-10, 2020.

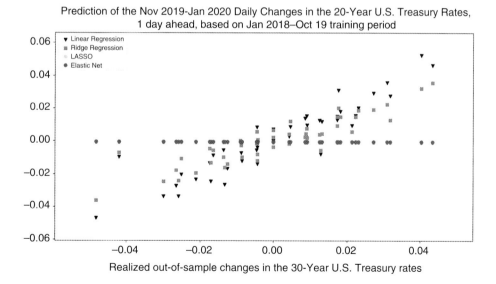

Figure 3.3 Out-of-sample t + 1 prediction of 20-Year U.S. Treasury rates with linear regression, ridge regression, LASSO, and elastic net for November 1, 2019–January 10, 2020. Regularization $\lambda = 0.1$.

Table 3.2   Coefficients determined by linear regression, ridge regression, LASSO, and elastic net.

	3 Mos	6 Mos	1 Year	2 Year	3 Year	5 Year	7 Year	10 Year
Linear	0.036	−0.023	0.016	−0.083	−0.090	−0.265	0.142	1.063
Ridge	0.029	−0.023	−0.027	−0.111	−0.067	0.040	0.275	0.569
LASSO	0.	0.	0.	0.	0.	0.	0.	0.
Elastic net	0.	0.	0.	0.	0.	0.	0.	0.

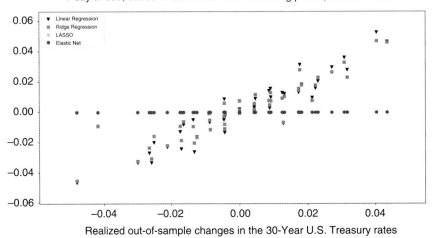

Figure 3.4   Out-of-sample $t + 1$ prediction of 20-Year U.S. Treasury rates with linear regression, ridge regression, LASSO, and Elastic Net for November 1, 2019–January 10, 2020. Regularization $\lambda = 0.01$.

K Nearest Neighbors (K-NN)

In the K Nearest Neighbors (K-NN) algorithm, first developed by Fix and Hodges (1951), the computer assumes that data points located close to each other along some dimension evolve similarly. The algorithm then extends the properties of points based on their proximity to each other. The algorithm is known as a "lazy algorithm": it assumes nothing about the data and requires no extensive training, making it suitable for real-time applications. It is also very easy to implement, particularly with built-in Python functionality. However, the algorithm works best with a limited number of data features, as extensive amounts of data make K-NN computation overly complex.

K-NN is a classic data mining algorithm that assumes that historical patterns recur, as in Technical Analysis. In time series estimation, the algorithm forecasts a future data value, given the latest pattern of data. To do so, the algorithm searches historical data for K patterns that are closest to the one at hand. For each of the K historical patterns, the algorithm records their respective future values already realized in the past. Finally, the algorithm aggregates the future values of past patterns to deliver the future value for the most recent pattern.

As an illustration of K-NN in time series, say, daily stock returns on a single stock, consider the following example for K = 2.

Latest pattern of returns: +0.02, −0.04, −0.13, ?

where the question mark? stands for next day's return we are trying to predict.

Suppose that in the historical data, K = 2 closest patterns and their respective future values are:

+0.02, −0.04, −0.12, +0.01

+0.01, −0.04, −0.13, −0.05

The future value of interest in the most primitive version of K-NN is then the average of the past patterns' future values, +0.01 and −0.05. The resulting answer is −0.02.

In identifying the most similar patterns in K-NN, researchers often pick patterns related to the minimum square distance between their respective points. The square distance is known as Euclidean distance:

$$d_{ij}^2 = \|x_i - x_j\|_2^2 \tag{3.22}$$

The above example shows that K-NN is a technical analyst's dream come true: an algorithm that automatically sifts historical data for chart patterns.

K-NN has been successfully applied to a variety of financial problems. Meade (2002) used K-NN to predict foreign exchange rates. Ban, Pang, Zhang, and Sarrafzadeh (2013) apply K-NN to financial time series prediction. Yu, Sorjamaa, Miche, Séverin, and Lendasse (2008) combine K-NN with neural networks to also make predictions for financial time series. Alkhatib, Najadat, Hmeidi, and Shatnawi (2013) and Shi (2016) use K-NN to predict daily closing prices. Teixeira and De Oliveira (2010) develop a stock trading system using technical analysis and K-NN. In addition, K-NN has often been used for consumer credit scoring (see, e.g., Henley and Hand (1996), Paleologo, Elisseeff, and Antonini (2010)). Mukid, Widiharih, Rusgiyono, and Prahutama (2018) apply Weighted K-NN (WKNN) to predict borrowers' default on Indonesian banks personal loan data.

A simple intraday example on the S&P 500 stocks illustrates the nonparametric power of the K-NN. Consider the 30-second data recorded on January 30, 2015. We seek to build a trading strategy by correctly predicting the next 30-second direction of one stock, in this case, Abbott Laboratories, NYSE:ABT, based on prior (not contemporaneous) 30-second realizations of the stocks in the S&P 500. We first separate the sample into in-sample (80% of data) and out-of-sample elements to ensure objective testing.

For in-sample, we first determine the optimal value of K. One way of doing so is running the K-NN regression for various values of K and measuring the Root Mean Squared Error (RMSE), the square root of the loss function in Eq (3.1). Typically, RMSE is high for the first few Ks when the K closest neighbors patterns are not numerous enough to be representative of the data evolution at large, then drops for several Ks, and then rises again as the number of Ks becomes unmanageable. Figure 3.5 illustrates the in-sample RMSE for the 30-second intraday data for the S&P 500.

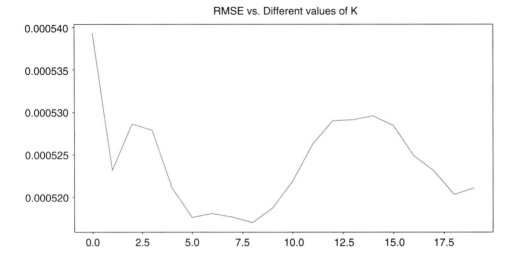

Figure 3.5   In-sample Root Mean Squared Error (RMSE) for 30-second NYSE:ABT price prediction using K-NN for different values of K.

As Figure 3.5 shows, the best value of K in-sample is 8. We next apply this value of K to the out-of-sample data and build the strategy based on the predicted sign of the next 30-second price change of NYSE:ABT. Specifically, if the algorithm predicts the next 30-second price change in ABT to be positive, the system executes a paper buy order and nets out the position 30 seconds later. If, instead, the algorithm predicts the next 30-second price change in ABT to be negative, the system short sells the ABT stock and buys it back 30 seconds later. Using K = 8, we obtain the out-of-sample performance of over 1.2% with relatively little volatility in just 160 30-second intervals, or 80 minutes, shown in Figure 3.6. The performance shown does not subtract costs, but can still be optimal for market makers and institutional investors facing low commissions. In contrast, a model with K = 12 delivers less optimal performance, as shown in Figure 3.7.

In addition to the basic historical time series patterns, K-NN can be used in most settings by relying on the idea of referential next neighbors (RNN): closest neighbors along a specific chosen axis. For example, Ban et al. (2013) determine RNNs based on ρ_{ij}, the simple daily return correlation between each pair of financial instruments i and j under consideration measured over the previous t consecutive trading days. Then, the researchers determine the distance between any two instruments as

$$D(x_i, x_j) = 1 - \rho_{ij}^2 \qquad (3.23)$$

The K instruments with the closest correlation values to the target instrument x_i become the referential nearest neighbors (RNNs). Next, the RNNs' historical data are examined for return patterns that most closely match the latest returns sequence of the target instrument x_i. Finally, the next day's price prediction is obtained as a simple average of "future values" following just identified patterns in the histories of RNNs.

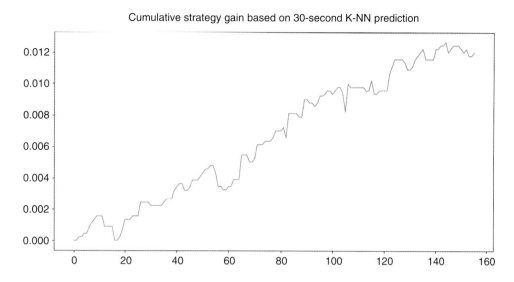

Figure 3.6 Out-of-sample performance of K-NN on intraday S&P 500 data forecasting 30-second changes in NYSE:ABT with K=8.

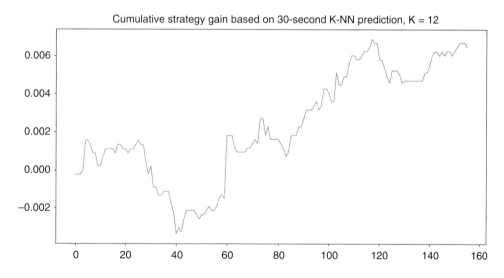

Figure 3.7 Out-of-sample performance of K-NN on intraday S&P 500 data forecasting 30-second changes in NYSE:ABT with K=12.

How well does K-NN work overall? Indyk (2004) and Pestov (2013) show that K-NN suffers from the "curse of dimensionality" and becomes biased as the data size increases. However, other studies like Andrada-Félix et al. (2003) and Lin, Shang, Feng, and Zhong (2012) praise K-NN for its seamless operation in high-dimensional and possibly incomplete data.

Decision Trees, Random Decision Forests, and Extra Trees

Decision trees, random decision forests, and extra trees are nonparametric prediction techniques. A decision tree is a way to classify variables based on a sequence of yes/no or greater/less questions (see, e.g., Rada and Wimmer 2017). Has the S&P 500 increased by more than 2% in the last 5 days? If yes, then the price of a stock like AT&T (NYSE:T) is likely to increase as well since NYSE:T exhibits strong correlation with the market. Has the company issued a press release in the last month? If no, the company is likely to stay under the radar for retail investors and not experience an unexpected bump in prices. Questions like these guide typical decision tree methodologies to estimate the final classification, albeit without human justification and explanation. Decision trees ask binary yes/no questions of the features or columns of the dataset to make path predictions for the variable of interest.

A decision tree methodology differs from a classical regression in that a regression finds coefficients, also known as parameters. The coefficients are then used to predict future values of variables based on the continuous values of the predictors. As a result, regressions are known as parametric approaches. By contrast, a decision tree does not operate over the entire possible continuum of predictors, instead organizing the data provided in a map-like fashion, with one or few major changes or "path turns" for each feature in the dataset. At these turns, also known as *split nodes*, the decision trees split into binary paths, each leading to another split node or a terminal node, known as a *leaf*. A leaf can be a classification, such as "this financial instrument behaves like a commodity" or "the price of this financial instrument is likely to go up."

The decision tree methodology traces back to Quinlan (1986). Originally called an Iterative Dichotomizer 3 (ID3), the algorithm measures the information gain (IG) of each feature or data column. The information gain is computed as the difference of the entropy before the split less the average entropy after the split, where entropy is computed as follows:

$$H = - \sum_{i=1}^{m} p_i \log_2(p_i) \tag{3.24}$$

where p_i is the proportion of time class i appears in the data set. The feature with the highest information gain becomes the split at the given node.

An alternative approach to IG uses the probability of wrongly classifying a given object, known as *GINI Impurity*, as a measure of split. The lower the GINI impurity following the split in the given feature, the more valuable is the split.

To illustrate the construction of a decision tree based on IG, we take a "bag" of daily foreign exchange rates spanning from January 1, 2015, through 31 December, 2019. The rates comprise 31 major currencies, all referencing EUR. In other words, EUR is the "denominator" currency against which all the 31 currencies are priced. The currencies are:

- Canadian Dollar, CAD
- Hong Kong Dollar, HKD

- Singapore Dollar, SGD
- Philippine Peso, PHP
- Danish Krone, DKK
- Hungarian Forint, HU
- Czech Koruna, CZK
- Australian Dollar, AUD
- Romanian Leu, RON
- Swedish Krona, SEK
- Indonesian Rupiah, IDR
- Indian Rupee, INR
- Brazilian Real, BRL
- Russian Ruble, RUB
- Croatian Kuna, HRK
- Japanese Yen, JPY
- Thai Baht, THB
- Swiss Franc, CHF
- Polish Zloty, PLN
- Bulgarian Lev, BGN
- Turkish Lira, TRY
- Chinese Yuan, CNY
- Norwegian Krone, NOK
- New Zealand Dollar, NZD
- South African Rand, ZAR
- U.S. Dollar, USD
- Mexican Peso, MXN
- Israeli Shekel, ILS
- British Pound, GBP
- Korean Won, KRW
- Malaysian Ringgit, MYR

If we are classifying the Australian Dollar–U.S. Dollar foreign exchange rate, AUD/EUR, into positive and negative daily changes, and AUD/EUR falls for 559 days out of 1,266 daily observations, then the AUD/EUR has p_1 of falling 44.2% and p_2 of rising or staying the same is 55.8% in our dataset, and the total entropy of the direction of the daily changes is:

$$H_{AUD/EUR} = -0.442 \log_2(0.442) - 0.558 \log_2(0.558) = 0.990$$

Entropy, in physics, is a measure of uncertainty or disorder. The objective of a decision tree is to bring as much certainty and order into the data set as possible. To understand how splitting the data along another variable or feature can help us reduce disorder, we deploy the Information Gain (IG) metric that measures the informational "value-added" of having variable X in prediction or classification of variable Y:

$$IG = H(Y) - H(Y|X) \qquad (3.25)$$

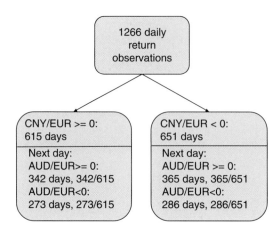

Figure 3.8 A simple decision tree illustrating predictability of AUD/EUR given the return of the CNY/EUR on the previous trading day.

IG measures the reduction in uncertainty from using X as a predictor for organizing data for Y. A valuable feature or predictor helps increase IG and reduce entropy H of the dataset.

To see if the AUD/EUR exchange rate is dependent, for example, on the previous trading day's return on the Chinese Yuan, CNY/EUR, we calculate the IG per Eq (3.25). Then we construct a simple decision tree. In this tree, we split the CNY/EUR daily returns into two groups, say, those that fall below 0 and those that rise or stay flat, as shown in Figure 3.8. Next, we calculate the number of down and up-or-flat AUD/EUR returns in the days immediately *following* down and up-and-flat return "buckets" for CNY/EUR and compute information gain based on conditional entropy:

$$H(AUD/EUR_t \mid CNY/EUR_{t-1} >= 0)$$

$$= -\left(\frac{342}{615}\right)\log_2\left(\frac{342}{615}\right) - \left(\frac{273}{615}\right)\log_2\left(\frac{273}{615}\right) = 0.702$$

$$H(AUD/EUR_t \mid CNY/EUR_{t-1} < 0)$$

$$= -\left(\frac{286}{651}\right)\log_2\left(\frac{286}{651}\right)$$

$$-\left(\frac{365}{651}\right)\log_2\left(\frac{365}{651}\right) = 0.691$$

Next, the average of entropy weighted by the total number of AUD/EUR returns in each CNY/EUR "bucket" is:

$$\underline{H}(AUD/EUR_t \mid CNY/EUR_{t-1}) = \frac{615}{1266} H(AUD/EUR_t \mid CNY/EUR_{t-1} >= 0) +$$

$$\frac{651}{1266} H(AUD/EUR_t \mid CNY/EUR_{t-1} < 0)$$

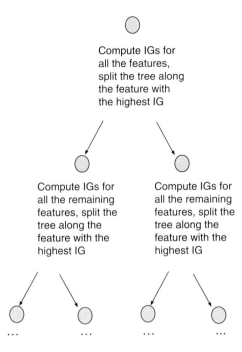

Figure 3.9   Single decision tree process.

$$\underline{H}(AUD/EUR_t \mid CNY/EUR_{t-1}) = 0.485 * 0.702 + 0.514 * 0.691 = 0.696$$

The information gain from adding CNY/EUR direction as a predictor to AUD/EUR returns is then

$$IG = H(AUD/EUR) - \underline{H}(AUD/EUR \mid CNY/EUR) = 0.990 - 0.696 = 0.294$$

At each decision point, known as a node, the tree is split along the feature that delivers the highest information gain, as illustrated in Figure 3.9. Once all the obtained information gains are the same or within a certain stopping criterion, the decision tree stops splitting. The decision trees can be tested out-of-sample by reserving a portion of the data for out-of-sample testing.

The main disadvantage of decision trees is their reliance on the dataset being used as a true representation of the population of data. With one decision tree per dataset, the binary questions or the rules are usually created to closely fit the data into various categories. As a result, decision trees are notoriously prone to overfitting, that is, establishing the partitions that are too close to the training data set and not representative of the out-of-sample data (see, e.g., Dietterich and Kong (1995), Breiman (1996a) and Friedman (1997), and Lopez de Prado (2018)).

To reduce decision tree overfitting, a technique known as *random decision forests* randomly features columns from the decision tree data set. Importantly, this method allows for each decision forest to draw on the full set of columns. By allowing for replacement in the process of building many decision trees, the method is similar to the econometric

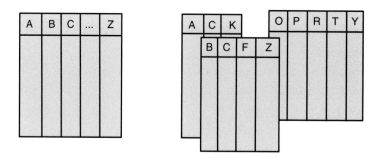

Figure 3.10 Single decision tree (left) vs. random decision forest, an illustration.

bootstrapping technique. First proposed by Mingers (1989), and extended by Ho (1998), random forests emulate the extended population of decision trees, and then average the outcomes, thus reducing overfitting of the data. Like decision trees, random forests are used for both classification and inference and are a form of machine learning.

In finance, random forests have been successfully used in predicting impending price direction in the U.S. equities by Khaidem, Saha, and Dey (2016). Tan, Yan, and Zhu (2019) obtain Sharpe ratios of 2.5–5 by applying random forests to investing in Chinese stocks. Creamer (2009) uses random forests to predict the performance of Latin American ADRS and banks. Liu et al. (2015) use random forests to detect financial fraud. Kim and Giles (2016) use random forests to automatically link records for the same financial entity across different databases. Hunt (2018) applies random forests to predict upcoming earnings numbers.

Having evolved from the decision tree methodology, random decision forests extend the concept of the decision tree with an injection of stochastic procedures, as shown in Figure 3.10. While a basic decision tree features just one tree that closely fits the data and, as a result, poorly predicts out-of-sample outcomes, the random forest creates many decision trees from random subsamples of the data. Thus, while the one and only traditional decision tree considers all the features of a given data set, each tree in the random forest takes into consideration just a handful of randomly selected features in order to determine the features most useful for inclusion in the final output. The random forest trees are constructed from data sets drawn from the original data with replacement, that is, multiple trees may contain the same data. The splits in the random forests' decision trees are deterministic, performed on the "best" node that displays the most variance and depends on the subset of the data at hand. As shown by Wehenkel (1997), Geurts and Wehenkel (2000), and Geurts (2002), the selection of the "best" cut-point may still induce significant overfitting as it fitted too closely to the random sample modeled by the tree.

To further tighten the random forests around the true data population, researchers proposed Bayesian averaging to reduce variance (Buntine and Weigend 1991; Buntine 1992), Stacking and boosting to reduce bias and variance (Wolpert 1992; Freund and Schapire 1995), and bagging (Breiman 1996b) to further randomize tree selection and then average the outcomes to reduce variance and bias. Collectively, by using multiple trees to make predictions, stacking, boosting, and bagging techniques are often referred to as *ensemble methods.*

Bagging, short for bootstrap aggregation, is a procedure whereby a new tree is created with data randomly sampled from the original dataset with a replacement, resulting in a forest of randomly different trees. The individual tree inferences are then aggregated (often, averaged) to create much more robust inferences. As a classical bootstrapping, this technique helps create inferences from limited data samples.

Boosting is a form of gradient descent where each tree (model) gets added into the optimization framework sequentially. The process helps avoid the optimizer getting stuck in a local minimum. Each subsequent model helps improve the accuracy of the optimization.

Stacking is another ensemble method, whereby the predictions of two or more trees serve as an input to another tree or a layer of trees. Stacking is also often referred to as blending because the output is a blended version of various models used in the process.

In practice, random forests not only provide a simple classification tool, but they also present an easy nonparametric identification of key drivers or factors underlying changes in a specific variable. Unlike unsupervised methods, discussed in Chapter 4 and onwards, random forests fall short of combining various variables into optimal factors.

As an example, we deploy the random forests methodology using code from a Python library (as described in Appendix 3.A) to predict drivers of foreign exchange rates. To predict CAD/EUR exchange one day ahead, we convert all of the currency time series into returns, and use their lagged values (lag $= 1$ only for simplicity) as variables to train our random decision trees. The random forests model deems the following variables to be most important to the next day's CAD/EUR prediction: Indonesian Rupiah, IDR, South African Rand, ZAR, and the U.S. Dollar, USD.

The U.S. Dollar presents an obvious choice as several studies have shown that the U.S. Dollar is a major macro driver for global currencies (see, for example, Haberler 1972; Genberg and Swoboda 1977; Ross 1983; McMichael 1996; McKinnon and Schnabl 2003; Devereux, Shi, and Xu 2007; Chunwei 2008; Bracke and Bunda 2011). Dooley, Folkerts-Landau, and Garber (2004) even go as far as to consider the U.S. as the central country for the international monetary system. Ehrmann, Fratzscher, and Rigobon (2011) emphasize

> the dominance of US markets as the main driver of global financial markets, an illustration of which is that the US financial markets explain, on average, more than 25% of movements in euro area financial markets, whereas euro area markets account only for about 8% of US asset price changes.

The importance of the Indonesian Rupiah and South African Rand in pricing CAD/EUR may seem like a complete surprise. Upon closer examination, however, we notice that the South African Rand and the Canadian Dollar have long been considered "commodity currencies," often along with Australian Dollar, AUD. These are

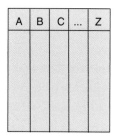
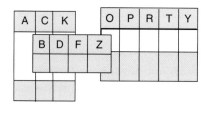

Figure 3.11   Single decision tree (left) vs. Extra Trees, an illustration.

OECD countries where primary commodities constitute a meaningful share of their exports (see, e.g., Chen and Rogoff 2003). Such commodity currencies are often subject to identical commodity shocks and move together as a result. Recent research on Indonesian Rupiah (see, e.g., Putra and Robiyanto 2019) also designates the Rupiah as the commodity currency, subject to fluctuations driven by commodity prices in many cases.

However, other currencies are driven by a different set of factors. According to the random forest analysis, the Japanese Yen/Euro exchange rate, JPY/EUR, for example, is best predicted by past Japanese Yen realizations followed by those of Korean Won vs. Euro (KRW/EUR) and Czech Koruna (CZK/EUR). Danish Krone (DKK/EUR) is best predicted by the Czech Koruna (CZK/EUR) followed by the Danish Krone (DKK/EUR) itself. While little research into the importance of the Czech Koruna (CZK/EUR) had been done at the time this book was written, one may speculate that, located in the middle of the European Union, the Czech Republic best proxies for regional variations in the European economy.

Extra Trees, short for Extremely Randomized Trees, first proposed by Geurts, Ernst, and Wehenkel (2006), take the concept of random forests further by randomizing the splits of the decision trees and limiting repetition of the data used in the samples: Extra Trees sample from the original data set without replacement, creating less overfitting than random forests and reducing bias. In essence, Extra Trees sample smaller subsets of data not only by randomly selecting features, but also by selecting only a portion of the data within each sample of features, as shown in Figure 3.11.

With traditional decision trees, the splitting of a tree into branches of different parameters is based on the largest-variance parameter. That is, a parameter with the largest variation is picked as the decision node. This process alone drives a high variance of outcomes in the predicted values. In the Extra Trees model, the cuts are randomized by construction and, thus, reduce the variance of the estimates.

Support Vector Machines (SVMs)

Support Vector Machines (SVMs) are a set of models often used for classification. Originally developed by Cortes and Vapnik (1995), Vapnik (1995), Vapnik (1998a; 1998b),

SVMs quickly became popular across a variety of applications and disciplines. For example, Fletcher, Hussain, and Shawe-Taylor (2013) use SVMs to predict intraday price direction in foreign exchange. Similarly, Kercheval and Zhang (2015) apply SVMs to intraday U.S. equities data to successfully classify impending mid-price direction into {upward, downward or stationary}. Over the years, SVMs have been deployed to forecast financial time series by Van Gestel et al. (2001), Tay and Cao (2001; 2002), Cao (2003) and Kim (2003). Perez-Cruz et al. (2003) find SVM useful in GARCH model estimation. Huang, Nakamori, and Wang (2005) forecast the direction of the stock market with SVM. Hazarika and Taylor (2002) predict bond returns. Nikolaev, Tino, and Yao (2005) predict volatility. Min and Lee (2005) apply SVMs to predict corporate bankruptcies. Huang and Wu (2008) add wavelet-based feature extractions with relevance vector machines to forecast stock indexes. Ullrich (2009) forecasts and hedges in forex with SVM.

Dai and Zhang (2013) use 3M Stock data from 9 January, 2008 to 8 November, 2013 (1,471 data points). Multiple algorithms were chosen to train the prediction system. These algorithms include Logistic Regression, Quadratic Discriminant Analysis, and SVM. These algorithms were applied to predict the stock price on the next trading day as well as over the next n days. The next-day prediction model produced accuracy results ranging from 44.52% to 58.2%. However, the long-term prediction worked better, particularly for n around 44, or two trading months. Using SVM, the accuracy of 2-month-ahead out-of-sample return prediction was reported as 79.3%.

The theory of SVM is discussed after the following example showcasing the performance of a SVM on intraday 30-second return data for the S&P 500. In the example, the returns are calculated as a 30-second difference in last trade prices. If the last trade price remained unchanged in the last 30 seconds, or if there simply were no trades in that time period, the corresponding 30-second return is recorded as 0, resulting in sparse data matrix. Next, the SVM is trained on 1-hour, or 120 30-second returns, for the entire S&P 500 to predict the direction of the next 30-second return for each of the S&P 500 stocks. The prediction is accomplished through classification. As in Kercheval and Zhang (2015), our SVM predicts that the impending return of each of the S&P 500 stocks will fall into one of the following three classes: {negative, 0, or positive}. Figure 3.12 shows the out-of-sample rolling window performance of individual S&P 500 stocks on January 30, 2015, traded in the following strategy:

- The SVM is trained on the previous 1-hour data, comprising 120 30-second price changes, for all the S&P 500 stocks.
- Based on the training, an out-of-sample SVM prediction is generated for the next 30 seconds for each of the S&P 500 stocks.
- If the prediction for a given stock is positive, the stock is bought immediately, held for 30 seconds, then sold.
- Otherwise, if the prediction for the stock is negative, the stock is (short) sold immediately and bought back 30 seconds later.
- If the prediction is 0, no action is taken.

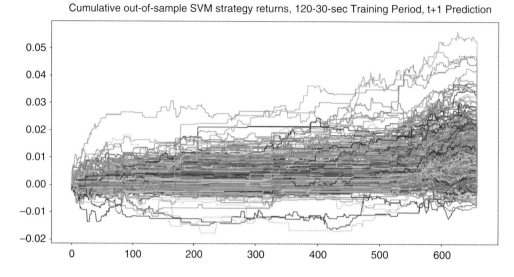

Figure 3.12 Cumulative performance paths for the S&P 500 constituents following the SVM classification trading strategy described in this chapter.

This analysis shown in Figure 3.12 was obtained with a rolling window that moves forward 30 seconds after each estimation, ensuring extensive out-of-sample prediction. Figure 3.13 shows the distribution of the cumulative out-of-sample returns obtained at 4:00 PM. As both Figures 3.12 and 3.13 show, the strategy is quite successful, delivering on average 1.116% return for each of the S&P 500 stocks for January 30, 2015, gross of investment costs. Similarly positive results were obtained throughout January 2015.

Is an SVM prediction perfect? Figure 3.14 displays the histograms of predictions as compared with their realized returns for one 30-second interval obtained on January 30, 2015, from 3:55:00 PM to 3:55:30 PM. As Figure 3.14 shows, the majority of both predicted (top panel) and realized (middle panel) returns are 0, which is consistent with the asynchronous nature of the intraday trading. As the bottom panel of Figure 3.14 shows, however, the prediction does not always line up with the realized returns. Figure 3.15 plots cumulative loss computed following Eq (3.1) for each constituent of the S&P 500 by estimating and predicting the direction of the next 30-second return via a rolling window over the entire trading day of January 30, 2015, from 10:30 AM to 4:00 PM. As Figure 3.14 illustrates, the sum of squared prediction errors can be quite high, yet the predicted classification can still deliver significant results in trading and market-making as shown in Figures 3.12 and 3.13.

To classify, SVMs work with a "feature space," a finite-dimensional vector space where each dimension is a feature of the subject of classification. In financial time series, the features can be any and all financial variables. In the 30-second trading example presented above, the features are lagged 30-second trade returns for all the S&P 500 stocks. However, there are no limitations on what kind of features can be deployed in the analysis. For example, the features used by Kercheval and Zhang (2015) are:

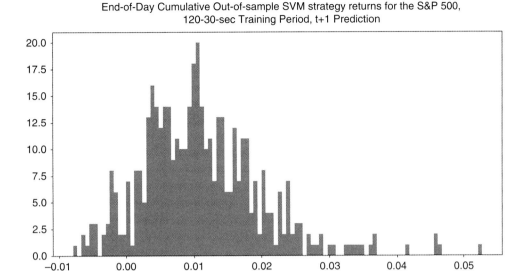

Figure 3.13 Distribution of cumulative end-of-day returns for the S&P 500 recorded at 4:00 PM ET on January 30, 2015, the paths of which are shown in Figure 3.12. The average end-of-day gross of trading costs return for the S&P 500 stocks was 1.116%.

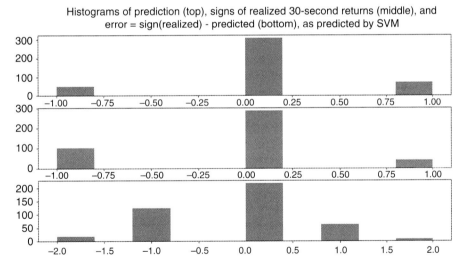

Figure 3.14 Prediction of 30-second returns of the S&P 500 stocks using SVM. The top panel shows the predicted return signs {-1, 0, 1}, the middle panel shows realized out-of-sample signs of returns for the same 30 seconds {-1, 0, 1}, and the bottom panel shows the difference between the sign of the realized and the sign of the predicted return {-2, -1, 0, 1, 2}.

- Last quote for both bid and ask, at the best bid/ask and for different ticks away from the best bid/ask up to 10 ticks, $P_{bid,t,i}$, $P_{ask,t,i}$, where $i \in [0, 9]$ is the number of ticks

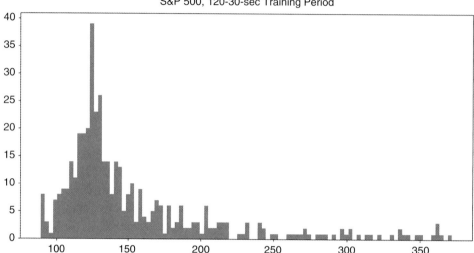

Figure 3.15 Cumulative error computed by Eq (3.1) for each constituent of the S&P 500 by estimating and predicting the direction of the next 30-second return via a rolling window over the entire trading day of January 30, 2015, from 10:30 AM to 4:00 PM. The distribution shown is that of the sum of squared errors for each S&P 500 stock. Each error was computed as the difference between actual realized return, a continuous variable, and SVM prediction falling in $\{-1, 0, 1\}$ classification corresponding to negative, 0, and positive predicted return direction.

away from the best bid and ask. Last quotes are drawn from snapshots of the limit order book every 1 second.

- Last quote size for both bid and ask, at the best bid/ask and for different ticks away from the best bid/ask up to 10 ticks, $S_{bid,t,i}$, $S_{ask,t,i}$, where $i \in [0, 9]$ is the number of ticks away from the best bid and ask. Last quote sizes are also drawn from snapshots of the limit order book every 1 second.
- Changes in quote price and quote size over the most recent 1 second, that is, "derivatives" with respect to time: $\{dP_{bid,t,i}/dt, dP_{ask,t,i}/dt, dS_{bid,t,i}/dt, dS_{ask,t,i}/dt\}$.
- Average rates of arrival of limit order additions, cancellations, and executions, computed over the past second, separated by bid and ask, and expressed as Poisson intensities (see Cont, Stoikov, and Talreja, 2010, for more details): $\{\lambda_{ask,a}, \lambda_{bid,a}, \lambda_{ask,c}, \lambda_{bid,c}, \lambda_{ask,e}, \lambda_{bid,e}\}$.
- "Accelerations" or change of rates of order arrival: $\{d\lambda_{ask,a}/dt, d\lambda_{bid,a}/dt, d\lambda_{ask,c}/dt, d\lambda_{bid,c}/dt, d\lambda_{ask,e}/dt, d\lambda_{bid,e}/dt\}$.
- Others.

SVMs classify inputs on the basis of features alone. In this respect, an SVM is a non-probabilistic classifier. In the case of email spam determination, the SVM performs binary classification (spam/not spam). In other applications the classification may be more complex. Kercheval and Zhang (2015), for example, classify the impending market movements into three categories: $\{up, down, no\ change\}$. In general, SVMs help classify inputs $\{x_k\} \in R^N$ on the basis of known labeled input–output pairs $\{y_k, x_k\}_{k=1}^N$. To extend classification to multiple end-states, kernel functions, discussed next, are used to create nonlinear boundaries among data point sets.

A sample SVM that classifies outputs $\{y_k\}$ into $\{-1, 0, +1\}$ set consumes a training set of N input–output data point pairs, $\{y_k, x_k\}_{k=1}^N$, where $x_k \in R^N$ is the kth input pattern and $y_k \in R$ is the kth output pattern. Given the training data, the SVM constructs a classifier of the form

$$y(x) = sign\left[\sum_{k=1}^N a_k\, y_k\, \psi(x, x_k) + b\right] \qquad (3.26)$$

where a_k and b are real and a_k is positive. The separation model of the SVM is specified by $\psi(., .)$. It can be, among other models,

- linear, with $\psi(x, x_k) = x_k^T x$
- polynomial of degree d, $\psi(x, x_k) = (x_k^T x + 1)^d$
- Radial Basis Function (RBF) $\psi(x, x_k) = exp(-\|x - x_k\|_2^2/\sigma^2)$ where σ is a constant
- even two-layer neural with $\psi(x, x_k) = tan[c\, x_k^T x + \theta]$ where c and θ are constants.

Unlike the universal spectral clustering, discussed in Chapter 7, the choice of the SVM function often depends on the underlying structure of data and the classification objective. For example, concentric circles are best detected with RBF and SVM.

Having constructed the "rule engine" for training data, Eq (3.26), we next construct a "classification engine" for untrained data as follows:

$$y_k[w^T \varphi(x_k) + b] \geq 1, k = 1, 2, \ldots, N \qquad (3.27)$$

where $\varphi(x)^T \varphi(x_k) = \psi(x, x_k)$. Equation (3.27) ensures that the points $y_k = 1$ and $y_k = -1$ end up on the same side of the hyperplane and at least a distance M away from the hyperplane. In other words, we require $y_k = 1$ when $w^T \varphi(x_k) + b = 1$, and $y_k = -1$ when $w^T \varphi(x_k) + b = -1$.

To prevent overfitting, we now introduce the classifier of "soft margin of error," $(1 - \xi_k)$, a margin multiplier that allows the points to fall in the region close to the hyperplane without classifying them and hence avoiding overfitting. All the slack variables ξ_k are subject to the following "budget" constraint:

$$\sum_{k=1}^n \xi_k \leq C \qquad (3.28)$$

where $C \geq 0$ is a tuning parameter, the maximum allowed total slack across all dimensions of data to avoid hard classification into –1 or 1. Now, Eq (3.27) can be rewritten as:

$$y_k[w^T \varphi(x_k) + b] \geq (1 - \xi_k)\, k = 1, 2, \ldots, N \qquad (3.29)$$

Going back to our classification example, and letting $y_k = 0$ fall into the margin between $y_k = -1$ and $y_k = 1$, we use the simplest linear kernel $\varphi(x)^T \varphi(x_k) = \psi(x, x_k) = x_k^T x$.

The optimization function then reduces to:

$$min_{w, \xi_k} \frac{1}{2} w^T w + c \sum_{k=1}^{N} \xi_k \qquad (3.30)$$

The solution is then obtained via Lagrangian.

Most variations of SVMs are already built into Python libraries, making it very easy to implement the models, as discussed in Appendix 3.A.

Supervised Learning Model Comparison

Several researchers have compared supervised models against each other to measure their relative performance. For example, Kanas (2003) pitches a standard regime-switching model and a Markov regime-switching model against K nearest neighbors (K-NN) and a neural network (NN) model on the U.S. stock returns from 1872 through 1999. Kanas found that the Markov switching model and NN outperformed vanilla regime switching and K-NN.

Kim and Swanson (2014) compare the performance of various supervised models on 144 U.S. macroeconomic time series for the period 1960:01–2009:5, including statistics such as the unemployment rate, personal income less transfer payments, the 10-year Treasury bond yield, the consumer price index, the producer price index, non-farm payroll employment, housing starts, industrial production, M2, the S&P 500 index, and gross domestic product. Kim and Swanson find that while the models do not necessarily dominate, using the models in tandem by feeding outputs of one model as inputs to another increases performance.

Gu, Kelly, and Xiu (2019) also compare the performance of various methods, in this case, to compare various machine learning methods' ability to estimate risk premia. The results from Gu, Kelly, and Xiu's research favor neural networks and trees-based methods for their ability to model nonlinearities.

Conclusion

Supervised learning spans both parametric and nonparametric estimation and can uncover many variable relationships in finance that previously did not stand out with linear modeling. Whether on a longer or shorter time scale, supervised learning provides many quantitative researchers with a brand-new toolkit for new discoveries and automation. The findings may immediately translate into investing gains, better risk management, and lower costs of doing business.

Appendix 3.A Python for Supervised Models

Python libraries for supervised models are also extensive. A library known as scikit-learn alone provides built-in tools for model selection, validation, and testing of a range of supervised learning models. In Python code, the library is referred to as sklearn. Since this library is voluminous, researchers tend to import only the necessary components in order to speed up processing, such as:

```
from sklearn.model_selection import train_test_split
```

The train_test_split functionality provides a built-in selector for the in-sample and out-of-sample data. The core advantage of the train_test_split utility is in its default configuration: the X and Y data rows are split into the train (in-sample) and test (out-of-sample) subsets at random, and are reshuffled in the process to create robust inferences. The only parameter that is required from the researcher is the proportion of data rows that are to be allocated to the in-sample testing, say, 0.33:

```
X_train, X_test, y_train, y_test = train_test_split(X, y, test_size=0.33)
```

At the same time, train_test_split can also be configured to create replicable subsets that avoid randomization, if desired.

The scikit-learn library further provides built-in functions for most supervised learning algorithms. To use the random forest classifier, for example, one would write the following code:

```
from sklearn.ensemble import RandomForestClassifier
clf=RandomForestClassifier(n_estimators=100)
clf.fit(X_train,y_train)
y_pred=clf.predict(X_test)
```

where y_pred is the out-of-sample prediction based on X_test inputs, given the model is trained on the in-sample data X_train and the corresponding y_train.

The scikit-learn library also provides convenient model prediction accuracy functionality to measure how the model output stacks up against the realized values. For example, the following code outputs the accuracy of the prediction for model-generated y_pred as compared to the out-of-sample y_test:

```
from sklearn import metrics
print("Accuracy:",metrics.accuracy_score(y_test, y_pred))
```

The implementation is fast, seamless, and even fun!

For specific code examples, please visit https://www.BigDataFinanceBook.com, and register with password *Supervised* (case-sensitive).

References

Alkhatib, K., Najadat, H., Hmeidi, I., and Shatnawi, M.K.A. (2013). Stock price prediction using K-nearest neighbor (kNN) algorithm. *International Journal of Business, Humanities and Technology* 3(3).

Andrada-Félix, J., Fernadez-Rodriguez, F., Garcia-Artiles, M.-D., and Sosvilla-Rivero, S. (2003). An empirical evaluation of non-linear trading rules. *Studies in Nonlinear Dynamics & Econometrics* 7(3).

Ban, T., Pang, S., Zhang, R., and Sarrafzadeh, A. (2013). Referential kNN regression for financial time series forecasting. Neural Information Processing: 20th International Conference, ICONIP 2013, Daegu, Korea, November 3–7, 2013. Proceedings, Part I, pp. 601–608.

Bracke, T. and Bunda, I. (2011). Exchange rate anchoring: Is there still a de facto US dollar standard? ECB Working Paper No. 1353.

Brandt, W. (2004). Portfolio choice problems, http://home.uchicago.edu/ lhansen/handbook.htm

Breiman, L. (1996a). Arcing classifiers. University of California, Department of Statistics, technical report.

Breiman, L. (1996b). Bagging predictors. *Machine Learning* 24(2): 123–140.

Britten-Jones, M. (1999). The sampling error in estimates of mean-variance efficient portfolio weights. *Journal of Finance* 54: 655–671.

Brodie, J., Daubechies, I., DeMol, C., Giannone, D., and Loris, D. (2009). Sparse and stable Markowitz portfolios. *Proceedings of the National Academy of Science* 106(30): 12267–12272.

Buntine, W. (1992). Learning classification trees. *Statistics and Computing* 2: 63–73.

Buntine, W. and Weigend, A. (1991). Bayesian back-propagation. *Complex Systems* 5: 603–643.

Cao, L.J. (2003). Support vector machines experts for time series forecasting. *Neurocomputing* 51: 321–339.

Carrasco, M. and Noumon, N. (2012). Optimal portfolio selection using regularization. University of Montreal, working paper. http://www.unc.edu/maguilar/metrics/carrasco.pdf.

Chen, Y-C. and Rogoff, K. (2003). Commodity currencies. *Journal of International Economics* 60: 133–160.

Chunwei, Z. (2008). Dollar standard, dollar circumfluence and dollar trap [J]. *Studies of International Finance* 6(1).

Cont, R., Stoikov, S., and Talreja, R. (2010). A stochastic model for order book dynamics. *Operations Research* 58(3): 549–563.

Cortes, C. and Vapnik, V. (1995). Support vector networks. *Machine Learning* 20(3): 273.

Creamer, G. (2009). Using random forests and logistic regression for performance prediction of Latin American ADRS and banks. *Journal of Centrum Cathedra* 2(1): 24–36.

Dai, Y. and Zhang, Y. (2013). Machine learning in stock price trend forecasting. Stanford University, working paper.

DeMiguel, V., Garlappi, L., Nogales, F., and Uppal, R. (2009). A generalized approach to portfolio optimization: Improving performance by constraining portfolio norm. *Management Science* 55: 798–812.

Devereux, M.B., Shi, K., and Xu, J. (2007). Global monetary policy under a dollar standard. *Journal of International Economics* 71(1): 113–132.

Dietterich, T. and Kong, E. (1995). Machine learning bias, statistical bias, and statistical variance of decision tree algorithms. Department of Computer Science, Oregon State University, technical report.

Dooley, M.P., Folkerts-Landau, D., and Garber, P. (2004). The revived Bretton Woods system. *International Journal of Finance & Economics* 9(4): 307–313.

Ehrmann, M., Fratzscher, M., and Rigobon, R. (2011). Stocks, bonds, money markets and exchange rates: Measuring international financial transmission. *Journal of Applied Econometrics* 26(6): 948–974.

Fan, J., Zhang, J., and You, K. (2012). Vast portfolio selection with gross-exposure constraint. *Journal of the American Statistical Association* 107(498): 592–606.

Fix, E. and Hodges, J. L. (1951). Discriminatory analysis nonparametric discrimination: Consistency properties. USAF School of Aviation Medicine, Randolph Field, TX, Technical Report TR4.

Fletcher, T., Hussain, Z., and Shawe-Taylor, J. (2013). Multiple kernel learning with sher kernels for high frequency currency prediction. *Computational Economics* 42(2): 217–240.

Freund, Y. and Schapire, R. (1995). A decision-theoretic generalization of on-line learning and an application to boosting. In: *Proceedings of the 2nd European Conference on Computational Learning Theory*, 23–27.

Friedman, J. (1997). On bias, variance, 0/1-loss, and the curse-of-dimensionality. *Data Mining and Knowledge Discovery* 1: 55–77.

Genberg, H. and Swoboda, A. K. (1977). Worldwide inflation under the dollar standard. Institut universitaire de hautes études internationales.

Geurts, P. (2002). Contributions to decision tree induction: Bias/variance tradeoff and time series classification. PhD thesis, University of Liege.

Geurts, P., Ernst, D., and Wehenkel, L. (2006). Extremely randomized trees. *Machine Learning* 36(1): 3–42.

Geurts, P. and Wehenkel, L. (2000). Investigation and reduction of discretization variance in decision tree induction. In: *Proceedings of the 11th European Conference on Machine Learning*, 162–170.

Gu, S., Kelly, B., and Xiu, D. (2019). Empirical asset pricing via machine learning. University of Chicago Booth School of Business, working paper.

Haberler, G. (1972). Prospects for the dollar standard. American Enterprise Institute.

Hazarika, N. and Taylor, J.G. (2002). *Predicting Bonds Using the Linear Relevance Vector Machine*. New York: Springer-Verlag, 145–155.

Henley, W.E. and Hand D.J. (1996). A k nearest-neighbour classifier assessing consumer credit risk. *The Statistician* 45(1): 77–95.

Ho, T. (1998). The Random subspace method for constructing decision forests. *IEEE Transactions on Pattern Analysis and Machine Intelligence* 20(8): 832–844.

Hoerl, A.E., Kannard, R.W., and Baldwin, K.F. (1974). Ridge regression: Some simulations. *Communications in Statistics* 4(2): 105–123.

Huang, S-C. and Wu, T-K. (2008). Combining wavelet-based feature extractions with relevance vector machines for stock index forecasting. *Expert Systems* 25: 133–149.

Huang, W., Nakamori, Y., and Wang, S-Y. (2005). Forecasting stock market movement direction with support vector machine. *Computers & Operations Research* 32(10): 2513–2522.

Hunt, J. (2018). Predicting changes in earnings: A walk through a random forest. PhD thesis, University of Arkansas, Fayetteville.

Indyk, P. (2004). Nearest neighbors in high-dimensional spaces. In: *Proceedings of the 17th ACM Symposium on Computational Geometry*.

Jagannathan, R. and Ma, T. (2003). Risk reduction in large portfolios: Why imposing the wrong constraints helps. *The Journal of Finance* 58(4): 1651–1683.

Jobson, J.D. and Korkie, B. (1983). Statistical inference in two-parameter portfolio theory with multiple regression software. *Journal of Financial and Quantitative Analysis* 18: 189–197.

Kanas, A. (2003). Non-linear forecasts of stock returns. *Journal of Forecasting* 22(4): 299–315.

Kercheval, A.N. and Zhang, Y. (2015). Modelling high-frequency limit order book dynamics with support vector machines. *Quantitative Finance* 15(8): 1315–1329.

Khaidem, L., Saha, S., and Dey, S.R. (2016). Predicting the direction of stock market prices using random forest. *Applied Mathematical Finance April, 1–21*.

Kim, H.H. and Swanson, N.R. (2014). Forecasting financial and macroeconomic variables using data reduction methods: New empirical evidence. *Journal of Econometrics* 178(2): 352–367.

Kim, K. (2003). Financial time series forecasting using support vector machines. *Neurocomputing* 55: 307–319.

Kim, K. and Giles, C.L. (2016). Financial entity record linkage with random forests. DSMM'16.

Kolm, P., Tütüncü, R., and Fabozzi, F.J. (2014). 60 years of portfolio optimization: practical challenges and current trends. *European Journal of Operational Research* (2): 356–371.

Kozak, S., Nagel, S., and Santosh, S. (2019). Shrinking the cross section. *Journal of Financial Economics* 135(2): 271–292.

Ledoit, O. and Wolf, M. (2008) Robust performance hypothesis testing with the Sharpe ratio. *Journal of Empirical Finance* 15(5): 850–859.

Lin, A., Shang, P., Feng, G., and Zhong, B. (2012). Application of empirical mode decomposition combined with K-nearest neighbors approach in financial time series forecasting. *Fluctuation and Noise Letters* 11(2).

Lopez de Prado, M. (2018). *Advances in Financial Machine Learning*. Hoboken, NJ: Wiley.

Markowitz, H.M. (1952). Portfolio selection, *The Journal of Finance* 7(1): 77–91.

McKinnon, R. and Schnabl, G. (2003). The East Asian dollar standard, fear of floating, and original sin. HKIMR Working Paper No. 11/2003.

McMichael, P. (1996). Globalization: Myths and realities. *Rural Sociology* 61(1): 25–55.

Meade, N. (2002). A comparison of the accuracy of short term foreign exchange forecasting methods. *International Journal of Forecasting* 18(1): 67–83.

Min, J.H., and Lee, Y.C. (2005). Bankruptcy prediction using support vector machine with optimal choice of kernel function parameters. *Expert Systems with Applications* 28(4): 603–614.

Mingers, J. (1989). An empirical comparison of selection measures for decision-tree induction. *Machine Learning* 3: 319–342.

Mukid, M.A., Widiharih, T., Rusgiyono, A., and Prahutama, A. (2018). Credit scoring analysis using weighted k nearest neighbor. *IOP Conference Series: Journal of Physics* Conference Series 1025.

Nigam, K.P. (2001). Using unlabeled data to improve text classification. PhD thesis, Carnegie Mellon University, USA. CMU-CS-01-126.

Nikolaev, N., Tino, P., and Yao, X. (2005). Volatility forecasting with sparse Bayesian kernel models. In: *Proceedings of 4th International Conference on Computational Intelligence in Economics and Finance, Salt Lake City, UT*, 1150–1153.

Paleologo, G., Elisseeff, A., and Antonini, G. (2010). Subagging for credit scoring models. *European Journal of Operational Research* 201: 490-499.

Pereira, J.M., Basto, M., and Ferreira da Silva, A., (2016).The logistic LASSO and ridge regression in predicting corporate failure. *Procedia Economics and Finance* 39: 634–641.

Perez-Cruz, F., Alfonso-Rodriguez, J., and Giner, J. (2003). Estimating Garch models using support vector machines. *Quantitative Finance* 3(3): 163–172.

Pestov, V. (2013). Is the K-NN classifier in high dimensions affected by the curse of dimensionality? *Computers & Mathematics with Applications* 65(10): 1427–1437.

Putra, A. and Robiyanto, R. (2019). The effect of commodity price changes and USD/IDR exchange rate on Indonesian mining companies' stock return. *Jurnal Keuangan dan Perbankan*.

Quinlan, J.R. (1986). Induction of decision trees. *Machine Learning* 1(1): 81–106.

Rada, R. and Wimmer, H. (2017). Decision trees and financial variables. *International Journal of Decision Support System Technology* 9: 1–15.

Ross, M.H. (1983). Currency substitution and instability in the world dollar standard: Comment. *American Economic Review* 73(3).

Sharpe, W. (1966). Security prices, risk and maximal gains from diversification: reply. *Journal of Finance* 21(4): 743–744.

Shi, Y. (2016). KNN predictability analysis of stock and share closing prices. PhD thesis, University of Leicester.

Tan, Z., Yan, Z., and Zhu, G. (2019). Stock selection with random forest: an exploitation of excess return in the Chinese stock market. *Heliyon* 5(8).

Tay, F.E.H. and Cao. L.J. (2001). Application of support vector machines in financial time series forecasting. *Omega* 29: 309–317.

Tay F.E.H. and Cao L.J. (2002). Modified support vector machines in financial time series forecasting. *Neurocomputing* 48: 847–861.

Teixeira, L.A. and De Oliveira, A.L.I. (2010). A method for automatic stock trading combining technical analysis and nearest neighbor classification. *Expert Systems with Applications* 37(10): 6885–6890.

Tibshirani, R. (1996). Regression shrinkage and selection via the LASSO. *Journal of the Royal Statistical Society, Series B* (methodological) 58(1): 267–88.

Ullrich, C. (2009). *Forecasting and Hedging in the Foreign Exchange Markets*. New York: Springer.

Van Gestel, T., Suykens, J.A.K., Baestaens, D., et al. (2001). Financial time series prediction using least squares support vector machines within the evidence framework. *IEEE Transactions on Neural Networks*, 809–821.

Vapnik, V. (1995). *The Nature of Statistical Learning Theory*. New York: Springer-Verlag

Vapnik, V. (1998a). *Statistical Learning Theory*. New York: John Wiley & Sons, Inc.

Vapnik, V. (1998b). The support vector method of function estimation. In: *Nonlinear Modeling: Advanced Black-Box Techniques* (ed. J.A.K. Suykens and J. Vandewalle), 55–85. Boston: Kluwer Academic Publishers.

Wehenkel, L. (1997). Discretization of continuous attributes for supervised learning: variance evaluation and variance reduction. In: *Proceedings of the International Fuzzy Systems Association World Congress*, 381–388.

Wolpert, D. (1992). Stacked generalization. *Neural Networks* 5: 241–259.

Yu, Q., Sorjamaa, A., Miche, Y., Séverin, E., and Lendasse, A. (2008). OP-KNN for Financial regression problems. Helsinki University of Technology, working paper.

Chapter 4

Modeling Human Behavior with Semi-Supervised Learning

Introduction

One of the main challenges of data science is translating the human capital and know-how of expert professionals into computer models, often referred to as *artificial intelligence* programming applications. For example, a master trader may have a record-winning strategy, but is about to retire. How do you copy his decision-making? Alternatively, an industry analyst may have a successful ability to predict the content of upcoming earnings announcements. How do you immortalize his brain in a computer program? Is that even possible?

Supervised frameworks discussed in Chapter 3 covered models that used structured data neatly organized into rows in columns. An example of such data may be the corporate financials such as the figures in quarterly and annual regulatory filings, required and published by the U.S. Securities and Exchange Commission (SEC). By contrast, most of the data and news consumed by humans arrive as text. For example, news articles, social commentary, and regulatory updates that may directly affect asset prices comprise textual items. Traditionally, the text was read and interpreted by trained analysts, who collected and thought about various press releases and news articles about a specific firm and industry, alongside product and competitor information. Analysts next wrote and published opinion pieces on the upcoming changes in the given stock or bond price, industry forecasts, or the direction of the market as a whole. The process of evaluating a single company could take several weeks or more, and the industry reports were typically published quarterly.

Analysis historically required an enormous human input: a person had to sit for hours, days, weeks, and sometimes months and years, poring over images, news articles, and other information to reach conclusions that were later added to a table as a single word or a number. For example, a qualitative financial analyst would spend years developing core sector or industry expertise, studying all the players and their strengths and weaknesses, analyzing all the relevant news, in order to issue a brief statement on which label a given stock should be assigned, with labels comprising the following set: "buy," "strong buy," "hold," "sell," and "strong sell," or equivalently, "buy," "outperform," "hold," "underperform," and "sell." In the Big Data lingo, the analyst took volumes of raw unstructured data and *labeled it, assigning crisp buy/hold/sell monikers to piles of information.*

Semi-supervised learning (SSL) is great for structuring data, that is, converting the raw text or images into neat tables, with quantitative representation of data ready for computerized evaluation. SSL gives us a toolkit of fast computer techniques built to derive meaning from voluminous data like text.

How does one build an SSL algorithm? Observing human activity with its requisite inputs and outputs is a good place to start. For example, many master traders watch the observable market movements, discern specific intraday quote patterns in their brains (unobservable to bystanders), and then make buy and sell decisions which are observable in the traders' immediate surroundings such as the trading floor.

Another example is financial analysis, the focus of this chapter. Many financial analysts developing stock buy/hold/sell recommendations may do so in the following stages:

1. The analyst reads the latest news articles related to the stock under consideration.
2. The analyst summarizes the news. Does the article talk about a higher volume of sales? Has the company launched new products? Is there a new competitor to the company? A seasoned analyst classifies each news article based on such and many other questions.
3. Based on the news summaries, the analyst next makes an assessment of the impending changes to the quarterly revenue forecast.

A good and thorough analyst may be hard to find, he may be overloaded with assignments, or may just be too expensive for investors. With semi-supervised learning, the computer can be tasked with replicating the analyst's process based on the small sample of the analyst's work.

SSL is perhaps best understood in contrast to supervised learning, discussed in Chapter 3. Supervised learning comprises a class of models on well-defined data. An ordinary least squares (OLS) regression is a classic example of supervised learning: all inferences are drawn from clean, perfectly organized data. The trusted OLS suffers from many well-known flaws: potential model misspecification, limited inferences, particularly in small data samples, and the like. Semi-supervised learning helps relax the restrictions of the supervised learning by deriving inferences from much larger unstructured data sources, collectively known as unlabeled data.

What kind of data are we talking about? Unlabeled data may include unprocessed tick data logs, corporate CEO interview videos, news articles, and much more. Master traders, for example, make their decisions by observing the market movements. Some analysts parse over related economic, financial, and other qualitative and quantitative data points to determine a prognosis for the company's future quarterly revenues, and, therefore, stock price. Still others interpret aerial images of corporate warehouses to count the number of trucks and thus estimate business activity.

Unlabeled data can occur naturally or be human-created, but contain no useful explanation for each piece. Labeled data refer to processed unlabeled data that add a meaningful "tag," "label," or "class" to each piece of data. Labels for the raw tick data may include measurement of market volume, price changes, and much more. The audio recording labeling may involve transcription – information on the words the recording contains. Classification of a news article may deliver the topic of the news as well as the overall sentiment of the story. Labels for data are often obtained by extensive modeling; however, these are significantly more expensive to obtain than the raw unlabeled data. Semi-supervised learning combines unlabeled and labeled data into models from which future labeling can be devised in a Bayesian-like fashion. In comparison, deep neural networks and unsupervised learning are areas of research that attempt to build models of the unlabeled data alone, and then apply information from the labels to the interesting parts of the models.

To put it another way, SSL is a set of techniques that attempt to replicate human decision-making. To approximate the human decision-making process, SSL takes in:

1. A few of the human-generated decisions, such as buy/sell recommendations for a given company, referred to as *target* or *labels*.
2. Raw data, from which the analyst generates his forecast, such as company-specific news, referred to as *labeled data*.
3. Raw data for which the computer is requested to produce a human-like decision. This extra set of data can be much larger than the set in 2. These data are known as *unlabeled data*.

Labeled data, also sometimes referred to as the model's dictionary, are ready for traditional econometric analysis in that they have an outcome Y associated with every data feature or property, also known as covariate, X. For example, in the simplest case of an OLS regression, $Y = \alpha + \beta X$ or, formally, $m(x) = E(Y|X = x)$. On the other hand, unlabeled data refer to more voluminous data that contain only covariates X, without the Y required in most econometric modeling. Semi-supervised learning allows one to bridge the gap and use the full set of X to expand and improve the modeling of Y, bypassing the usually small-sample limitations of labeled data. Unlabeled data alone may yield random classification because there is no information about the class label (Castelli and Cover 1995). Applied together with samples of the labeled data, however, unlabeled data often contribute to a high degree of accuracy attained at a much lower processing cost compared to utilization of labeled data alone.

Our objective is to use computing horsepower to automatically label untouched data in the third point above in the same way an expert human would do it. Overall, SSL allows us to use unlabeled data that are numerous and cheap in place of the expensive data that are labeled. In the process, the much larger total volume of both labeled and unlabeled data allows for much stronger inferences.

The importance of the brilliant analyst cannot be overemphasized here. The semi-supervised learning process attempts to reproduce the thought process of the star human, given the observable inputs and the limited observable outputs. Top-quality outputs are required for the semi-supervised learning to create valuable approximations of the analyst's work. To put it another way, following the engineering truism "Garbage in, garbage out," poor modeling examples will not deliver solid semi-supervised learning predictions.

The discussion presented in this chapter by no means seeks to minimize the work and the importance of human analysis. In fact, a great financial analyst has a brilliant mind, works extremely hard to educate himself on the latest developments, and makes superior forecasts. The challenge is that the great analyst's time may be fully occupied, his stock coverage may be insufficient for the investment task at hand, or he may simply be prohibitively expensive to employ on a given project.

One may go even farther to suggest that the cost of quality financial analysis has been a big hurdle for masses of smaller investors. The best analysts have always been prized hires of the top banks and hedge funds, who then walled off the analysts' predictions and allowed access only to a select few investors, the latter typically already in the 99.99% wealth percentile. The ability to extend the star analyst's work by approximating his thinking with machine learning is bound to democratize the investment process, allowing smaller players to benefit from the traditionally inaccessible big-money information.

Besides allowing wide access to previously paywall-sequestered information resources and a lower cost, the SSL approximation of human decision-making process has several advantages. First, the SSL process delivers consistency. The SSL follows a computer script and sticks with it while a human star analyst's decision-making process may be a complete black box and subject to unforeseen influences, illnesses, etc. Second, SSL is reliable, replicable, and can be deployed on hundreds of computers to ensure a fail-safe environment with 24-hours a day, 7-days a week data processing, something too much to ask of even the most dedicated human. Third, the output from SSL can even be a nice starting point for star financial analysts – enabling them to benchmark their research and save time by seeing the keywords that drive the ratings of other contemporary analysts. Finally, the SSL process is easy to understand, unlike its neural network and some other machine-learning models.

Since its early versions, SSL has been researched in a number of concepts, first, as a technique for separating a mixture of distributions before finally settling into its most common application: parsing natural language and classifying text. The pioneering research in this area was produced by Yarowsky (1995), Blum and Mitchell (1998), Collins and Singer (1999), Joachims (1999), Nigam et al. (2000), and others.

Most semi-supervised learning techniques deploy the knowledge of probability distribution of raw input data, $p(x)$, to help infer probability of output data, given input, $p(y|x)$. For semi-supervised learning to be successful, the input data on x should carry information that is useful for determining the output, conditional on input, $p(y|x)$. This condition is summarized in the assumption required for the SSL to work: the *smoothness assumption*. Under the smoothness assumption, two points x_1 and x_2 in a high-density region should correspond to outputs y_1 and y_2 that are also close. If the points x_1 and x_2 are separated by a low-density region, then their points do not need to be close.

The semi-supervised learning solutions proposed up to the time this book was written fall into several categories:

1. Generative models by Nigam et al. (2000) and Nigam (2001).
2. The graph-based nonparametric approach by Zhu (2005) and Belkin, Niyogi, and Sindhwani (2006).
3. Discriminative models by Lawrence and Jordan (2006) and Balcan and Blum (2010).
4. Adaptive estimators by Kawakita and Kanamori (2013) and Chakrabortty (2016).

This chapter focuses on the generative models and discriminative models. Graph-based nonparametric clustering aligns better with unsupervised learning, and is therefore discussed in detail in Chapter 9.

The SSL experiment presented here attempts to replicate the stock-rating methodology deployed by financial analysts. To do so, the model described in this chapter takes a few available analyst ratings for selected companies, conditions them on a vast number of preceding news, and delivers a forecasting model for ratings for other stocks, previously untouched by the analysis. Similar techniques can be applied to generate portfolio strategies for illiquid instruments, i.e., the stocks that have missing data points due to irregular trading. Mizumoto, Yanagimoto, and Yoshioka (2012), for example, apply semi-supervised learning to sentiment analysis on the stock market news. As discussed in Aldridge and Krawciw (2017), sentiment of news has become a popular data input into many trading strategies. Sentiment analysis involved a human who manually mapped common words to their sentiment or polarity score, a mapping from words to sentiment. The polarity scores of all the words in the document are later aggregated to determine the sentiment of the entire news document. Mizumoto, Yanagimoto, and Yoshioka (2012) use semi-supervised learning to construct a polarity dictionary. The dictionary can then update itself automatically when it encounters new words.

As shown in Chapter 7, SSL techniques can also be used when data are incomplete or missing. For instance, when there is simply not enough data to estimate the full covariance matrix, SSL provides a way to fill in the missing data. The data may be missing due to suspended trading in certain instruments, server outage that resulted in a failure to capture the trading data, or simply because the data were not collected. As this book shows, semi-supervised learning is one of the techniques that allows the researchers to utilize the available data to their fullest capacity.

Additional studies on semi-supervised learning can be found in Chapelle, Scholkopf, and Zien (2006) and Zhu (2008), who provide comprehensive summaries of SSL literature. Before diving into the gritty details of SSL, we briefly discuss a popular set of machine-learning techniques designed to reduce overfitting in situations with limited data, like SSL. These techniques are collectively referred to as cross-validation and are presented in the next section.

Performance Evaluation via Cross-Validation

By design, semi-supervised learning models rely on a small sample of data. As a result, SSL models are prime candidates for overfitting – creating tight parameters fitting snugly to the available data that do not hold up out-of-sample. To avoid overfitting and the associated bias, researchers have devised techniques to intelligently sample and reuse the available data.

In the traditional econometric model testing, the complete data set is divided into two parts: the training set and the testing set. The parameters of the model are first developed on the training set. Next, the parameters are validated on the clean testing set, creating an "out-of-sample" verification.

In semi-supervised learning and other applications with small data, there may simply not be enough data to do unbiased out-of-sample testing. As a result, semi-supervised learning techniques rely extensively on a methodology for resampling the limited data known as *cross-validation* (Geisser 1975; Efron 1983; Kohavi 1995). To generate meaningful, population-appropriate outcomes, the cross-validation works as follows:

- Shuffle the rows of the data set randomly.
- Split the data set into k groups.
- For each unique group:
  - Take that group as a hold-out or test data set.
  - Take the remaining groups as a training data set.
  - Fit a model on the training set and evaluate it on the test set.
  - Keep the evaluation score for comparison with performance of other test groups as well as performance of other models.
- Summarize the skill of the model using the sample of model evaluation scores. The summary often delivers the mean, the standard deviation of the evaluation scores along with the aggregate score.

The above process is referred to as k-fold cross-validation. It is also known as *rotation estimation*. The number k can be chosen to make groups large enough to be representative of the entire sample, as shown in Figure 4.1. Alternatively, k may be chosen to equal the number of rows, so that each group contains just one row; such cross-validation is

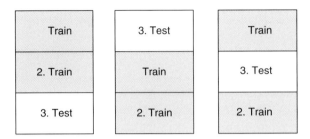

Figure 4.1 An illustration of 3-fold cross-validation. During each of the $k = 3$ stages, all but one of the partitions are used to train the model on the data while the hold-out partition is used to test the model.

known as *leave-one-out-cross-validation* (LOOCV). Another common "indecisive" k can be selected to be a number around 10.

The folds themselves can be equal in size or proportional to another aspect of data. For example, the k groups can be selected so that each target label, categorization, or cluster is represented proportionally in each group. Such a split is known as *stratification*. Alternatively, the k groups may be randomly shuffled after each k-fold cycle completion and repeated again n times; such a process is known as *repeated k-fold cross-validation*.

K-fold cross-validation has been shown to reduce look-ahead or data-snooping bias documented in Finance by Lo and McKinlay (1990), Sullivan et al. (1999), and White (2000), among others. At the time this book was written, cross-validation was accepted in the data mining and machine learning community as a standard procedure for performance estimation and model selection (Refaeilzadeh, Tang, and Liu 2007). Despite its ability to accurately estimate model performance, k-fold cross-validation is disadvantaged by small samples of performance estimation; overlapped training data; elevated Type I error for comparison; underestimated performance variance, or overestimated degree of freedom for comparison (for detailed studies, see Kohavi (1995), Salzberg (1997), and Dietterich (1998)).

Generative Models

Generative models, as their name suggests, generate extra data in order to improve their overall forecasting power. Generative models focus on developing a joint distribution of X and Y from the observations where Y is available, and then using the joint distribution to generate inferences for X and Y when Y is missing. Generative models are Bayesian in nature as they rely heavily rely on Bayes' theorem:

$$p(Y|X) = p(X|Y)p(Y) / \left[\int_Y p(X|Y)p(Y)dY \right] \qquad (4.1)$$

where $p(X|Y)p(Y) = p(X, Y)$ is the joint density of data from which pairs (x_i, y_i) are generated.

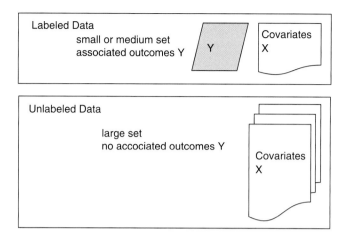

Figure 4.2   Semi-supervised learning. Source: Adapted from Chakrabortty (2016).

How does semi-supervised learning work? Semi-supervised learning takes the labeled data set L, with neat outcomes Y directly corresponding to covariates X, and the much larger unlabeled data set U, containing only covariates X. The unlabeled data set U, given its size, produces P_X, a population distribution of X. Figure 4.2 from Chakrabortty (2016) illustrates the idea behind semi-supervised learning. The goal of SSL is to find the conditional distribution of Y, given X, $P_{Y|X}$.

For convenience, it is common to assume that the labeled data comprise the first n data points of X, $X_l := (x_1, x_2, \ldots x_n)$, for which labels $Y_l := (y_1, y_2, \ldots y_n)$ are provided. The unlabeled data then are found in points $n + 1$ through N, $X_u := (x_{n+1}, x_{n+2}, \ldots x_N)$. The function of interest is $m(x) = E(Y|X = x)$. While such a setup has become a standard in Big Data, AI, and machine learning, other forms of partial supervision exist, distinguished primarily by their constraints.

Generative models have evolved from *self-learning* algorithms. Self-learning algorithms were the earliest SSL methods, due to Scudder (1965), Fralick (1967), Agrawala (1970), and others. Self-learning algorithms are also known as self-training, self-labeling, and decision-directed learning methods. These methods work as follows:

1. Train via a supervised technique on labeled data only, obtain predictions.
2. Incorporate a portion of the predictions in the training data.
3. Repeat from 1 above with the new data set expanded by predictions in 2.

This approach is successful only if the *generative model*, the conditional distribution for labeled and unlabeled data, is correct. When the Bayes generative model is highly correlated with the classification accuracy, then the model above works sufficiently well. When the Bayes generative model is not correlated with the output accuracy, a better generative model needs to be developed.

Generative models do so by recursively:

1. Applying a chosen variation of supervised learning, such as a regression, random forests, or other method to the raw data and their expert-generated labeling.
2. Using the parameters obtained in 1 for out-of-sample prediction on reserved data, generating machine-labeled data, known as *pseudo-labeled data*.
3. Sampling selected raw data: pseudo-labeled data pairs from the out-of-sample raw values and the corresponding predicted values in 2.
4. Adding these artificially or *pseudo-labeled* data to the original data set.
5. Finally, returning to 1 and applying the same variation of supervised learning as before.

The algorithm stops when it reaches the desired convergence levels. The result delivers enhanced precision in estimation. Nigam et al. (2000) show that using unlabeled data significantly improves data classification while reducing demand for labeled data. For example, to label text with 70% classification accuracy, a traditional supervised learning algorithm requires 2,000 labeled examples. The generative semi-supervised algorithm of Nigam et al. (2000) takes advantage of 10,000 unlabeled examples and requires only 600 labeled examples to achieve the same accuracy. This reduces the need for labeled training examples by more than a factor of three, lowering the associated costs of labeled data by the same factor.

Here, we follow Nigam et al.'s (2000) generative methodology to approximate financial analyst ratings for U.S. stocks, given wide-range news (unlabeled data) and limited analyst recommendations on other stocks (labeled data). As such, we develop an iterative expectation-maximization (EM) framework that maximizes the likelihood of a correct prediction. The term "correct" cannot be emphasized enough. A generative model that does not model the relationship between the labeled and unlabeled data correctly can significantly worsen the performance relative to a basic supervised model.

As in Nigam et al. (2000), we treat the missing classification of news by financial analysts as a latent variable. Our objective is to develop a model that takes in large amounts of unlabeled data and develops a more probable model for the latent variable.

Our task here is to develop a generative model that correctly classifies human-authored texts into the average ratings. The ratings are compiled from human financial analysts' classifications assigned to the texts. Nigam et al. (2000) believe that due to its complexity, human-authored text is very difficult to completely parameterize in a true generative model. Instead, Nigam et al. and many practitioners use a simple model like naïve Bayes. Using naïve Bayes, each news article is represented as a bag of words. The approach does away with any and all word ordering information, punctuation, and even word capitalization. In this setup, phrases like "Physics of young stars" (astronomy) and "Young Stars in Physics" (promising future star physicists) appear the same to the model, as do phrases like "men in white-collared shirts paid for laundering dirty money" and "men paid money for laundering dirty white-collared shirts."

The generative model that results from the naïve Bayes approach supposes that all the news articles are essentially created by drawing words from a multinomial distribution conditional on analyst ratings. This view dramatically oversimplifies the authorship of news articles. However, as Nigam et al. (2000) show, such an approach is appropriate for semi-supervised text classification whenever the following two conditions hold:

1. Probabilities produced by the selected generative model are correlated with the observed values of the latent variable, in our case, mean analyst ratings.
2. The EM optimization hits the global maximum instead of being trapped in a local one.

Even when the probabilities from the generative model are not well correlated with the desired output, a generative model may result in a better prediction than a supervised alternative. Furthermore, as discussed in this chapter, techniques such as deterministic annealing help reliably to find the global maximum. As Nigam et al. (2000) show, a bumpy expectation function is inevitable in sparse models with a very large number of parameters in domains like text classification. EM only guarantees discovery of a local maximum. Deterministic annealing helps overcome this issue.

Generative Models for Text Processing

The model deployed in our analysis is a naïve Bayes generative model that follows Lewis (1998), McCallum and Nigam (1998), and Nigam et al. (2000). The key assumption of the model is that all the news articles are generated by a mixture of multinomials, where each mixture component corresponds to one class. In our example, each class is a mean analyst rating for the given stock on a given day. Given M analyst rating classes and vocabulary of size $| X |$, each news article i falling into a class $c_m, m \in M$ has $| x_i |$ words. Each word is represented as a column in the vocabulary matrix X. Each news article may or may not possess a specific word w_j from the vocabulary X; when a given word j is not present in the news article i, $x_{it} = 0$. If a word j occurs in the news article i exactly once, $x_{ij} = 1$. Of course, the words may repeat, so the word matrix X may contain $x_{ij} > 1$. The total length of each news article in terms of its word count is then $| x_i | = \sum_{j=1}^{|X|} x_{ij}$. Each news article known to belong to class c_i is labeled x_i.

We further assume that each news article is generated according to a probability distribution defined by the parameters θ of the mixture model. Thus, for the sake of modeling, we reverse the process of news article creation. Specifically, we assume that each news article, prior to being written, is first assigned a certain length, the number of words $| x_i |$. Next, each article is assigned to a specific analyst rating class $c_m, m \in M$ that is dependent on the parameters θ. Thus, each new article originates from a chosen mixture component $P(c_m|\theta)$. Next, the selected mixture component generates its own news article according to the parameters θ with word distribution $P(x_i| c_m, \theta)$.

Nigam et al. (2000) intuitively explain the idea behind such a news article–generating model as a sequence of dice rolls. First, we randomly pick a number of words that go into the article. Next, we roll an M-sided dice, biased by parameters θ, to determine the class of the news article, c_m. We obtain each mixture component c_m with probability $P(c_m|\theta)$. Next, we roll an $| X |$-sided dice to pick the words that go into the news article "bag of words" given the class c_m and parameters θ. The resulting news article occurs with $P(x_i|c_m, \theta)$. The ensuing likelihood of seeing the document x_i is the sum of all $P(x_i|c_m, \theta)$ over all the classes c_m:

$$P(x_i|\theta) = \sum_{m \in M} P(c_m|\theta) P(x_i|c_m, \theta) \tag{4.2}$$

Since each mixture component corresponds to exactly one class by our original assumptions, we can now assign a label y_k to each mixture component c_m:

$$P(x_i|\theta) = \sum_{m \in M} P(y_m|\theta) P(x_i|y_m, \theta) \tag{4.3}$$

Under the naïve Bayes assumption, the words in each news article are conditionally independent of other words in the same document, given the class label. The probability of generating a given news article in terms of words and the article length is then:

$$P(x_i|y_m, \theta) \propto P(|x_i|) \prod_{w_j \in X} P(w_j|y_m, \theta)^{x_{ij}} \tag{4.4}$$

The parameters that define the multinomial distribution over a collection of word probabilities, $\theta_{w_j|c_m}$, are:

$$\theta_{w_j|c_m} \equiv P(w_j|c_m, \theta) \tag{4.5}$$

and

$$\sum_j \theta_{w_j|c_m} = \sum_j P(w_j|c_m, \theta) = 1 \tag{4.6}$$

The parameters that define the class selection are:

$$\theta_{c_j} \equiv P(c_j|\theta) \tag{4.7}$$

The full generative model then can be written as:

$$P(x_i|y_m, \theta) \propto P(|x_i|) \sum_{m \in M} P(y_m|\theta) \prod_{w_j \in X} P(w_j|y_m, \theta)^{x_{ij}} \tag{4.8}$$

The set of word counts x_{ij} is hence a sufficient statistic for classification of a given news article if we pick the right model to link the word counts with the financial analyst classifications.

Semi-Supervised Estimation of the Generative Model

To classify the unlabeled news articles, we first find the model that best classifies the word counts into the analysts' ratings. To do so, we perform supervised learning using a variety of parametric and nonparametric models discussed in Chapter 3 on the labeled news articles we have available. We choose the model that does best in the supervised setting.

Next, a naïve Bayes classifier is built from the selected supervised model, i.e., we determine the probabilities of each class given the words present in each news article. The naïve Bayes classifier is then put to work, classifying a random selection of unlabeled training data. The previously unlabeled news articles newly labeled with naïve Bayes probabilities are known as *pseudo-labeled* data. The pseudo-labeled data are then added to the pool of the training data. The pseudo labels, the estimated class probabilities, are now used as true labels. The process is then repeated with a new naïve Bayes classifier built over the expanded data set until the process converges to a stable classifier and a set of labels.

From the perspective of semi-supervised learning, the work of the financial analyst entails reading and then labeling the latest news for a given stock into one of the five categories: buy, strong buy, hold, sell, and strong sell. Each of the labels comprises a trading signal relied upon by many practitioners. The analysts' forecasts are issued by banks' research departments, specialized research firms, and others. Various data firms like Bloomberg often aggregate and redistribute the forecasts.

In our analysis, we deploy the analyst forecasts' summary from Zacks Analyst Research. Zacks collects analyst recommendations from various analysts, aggregates them each day, and distributes their data on Quandl, where a limited sample of Zacks data is offered free of charge. Those free data, updated daily, include the analyst ratings for the following stocks: AAPL, AXP, GE, BA, CSCO, DOW, DIS, GE, IBM, JNJ, KO, MCD, MMM, MRK, MSFT, PFE, PG, and UA. Zacks analyst ratings are in the "strong buy, buy, hold, sell, and strong sell" formats and are aggregated into cumulative by rating and overall mean scores. The ratings are encoded as follows:

1. represents "strong buy" recommendation
2. represents "buy"
3. represents "hold"
4. represents "sell"
5. represents "strong sell"

Zacks analyst ratings provide convenient human-generated labels to test the SSL. The limited data available from Zacks without charge are a perfect application of SSL. Research analysts update their ratings independently of each other, and, as a result, the aggregate rating, such as the rating mean, may change every day. Figure 4.3 shows the raw number of news announcements recorded for each mean analyst rating in the Zacks sample from February 1 through 12, 2020. The mean ratings are reported with 2-decimal precision in the range from 1 ("strong buy") to 5 ("strong sell"), inclusive, resulting in 401 potential mean ratings or classes in the model.

Financial analysts' ratings can be highly subjective. In addition to the mean ratings, Zacks reports the number of financial analysts who classified a given stock into each of the ratings categories. For example, during January–February 2020, the number of "strong buy" recommendations for Apple, Inc. (AAPL) reported by Zacks ranged between 14 and 16, "buys" held steady at 4, "holds" ranged from 7 to 9, there were no "sells" and only one "strong sell" position, showing a relative diversity of opinions. Mean ratings

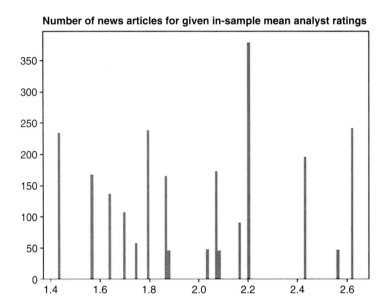

Figure 4.3   Raw number of news announcements recorded for each mean analyst rating in the Zacks sample from February 1 through 12, 2020. The ratings are encoded as follows: '1' = "strong buy," '2' = "buy," '3' = "hold," '4' = "sell," '5' = "strong sell."

aggregated from scores of several analysts can be even less predictable, given the range of opinions of the analysts. The task of correctly predicting the mean score ratings, therefore, is very difficult, even for a top-notch human analyst.

While the analysts' stock recommendations are the labels, the unlabeled data are the news. We obtain daily news in plain text from various sources. Online, the news articles are searchable by stock symbol, so we can select the news pertaining to each stock. The news articles can also be sorted by popularity and other factors. We select the news for each stock symbol from one month prior to the analyst ratings to the day before each analyst rating. All articles are used in their entirety and include the author's name and the publication venue.

First, the news articles are cleaned. All special characters and html tags are removed to retain just text. A cleaned article from *Business Insider* that appeared in the search for news on Microsoft (NYSE:MSFT) looks like this:

> *{id business insider name business insider} author antonio villas boas title microsofts newest internet browser is fast and finally does the things that makes googles chrome so popular \u2014 heres how to get it msft description microsoft released on wednesday its new edge web browser that lets users install extensions from the google chrome web store in some important ways the new edge is just google chrome dressed in microsoft clothing \u2014 its based on the same open […]*

A separate cleaned article from TechCrunch discussing changes in IBM leadership was pulled up by NewsApi in the search for news related to 3M Corporation (NYSE:MMM), a competitor of IBM:

{id techcrunch name techcrunch} author ron miller title arvind krishna will replace ginni rometty as ibm ceo in april description ibm announced today that the board of directors has elected ibm senior vice president for cloud and cognitive software arvind krishna to replace current ceo ginni rometty he will take over on april 6th after a couple of months of transition time rometty wil\u2026 url http techcrunchcom 2020 01 30 arvind krishna will replace ginni rometty as ibm ceo in april urltoimage https techcrunchcom wp content uploads 2017 10 gettyimages 503702216jpgw=548 publishedat 2020 01 30t215509z content ibm announced today that the board of directors has elected ibm senior vice president for cloud and cognitive software arvind krishna to replace current ceo ginni rometty he will take over on april 6th after a couple of months of transition time rometty […]

Still another excerpt from a cleaned news article that is indexed as related to Coca-Cola (NYSE:KO) stock looked like this:

{id business insider name business insider} author alan dawson title conor mcgregor has adjusted his training as hes learned from the mistakes made before during and after his spectacular failure against khabib nurmagomedov description conor mcgregor has learned from the mistakes he made before during and after his spectacular failure against khabib nurmagomedov […]

In the above news snippet, our news search most likely misclassifies the boxing term knock-out with the abbreviation "KO" for Coca-Cola stock symbol. As the last news example illustrates, the news provider's classification is not always perfect. However, under the Law of Large Numbers, even erroneous news classifications, when included in a large pool of news, will not do significant damage to the final output. A more thorough approach might involve the researcher reading and then manually classifying several dozen news articles before applying SSL to classify the rest of available news text.

After the news is cleaned from html tags and special characters, the news is *vectorized*: each news article is converted into a row in a news matrix where each word has its own column. Each element of the news matrix counts the number of times the corresponding word was mentioned in the news article. Just for the month of January 2020, the summaries of the most popular articles mentioning each of the 11 first stocks in the list contained 15,047 different words. The vectorized news matrix is naturally sparse as some words only appear in selected documents once. For the 11 stocks we chose to use in training, AAPL, AXP, GE, BA, CSCO, DOW, DIS, GE, IBM, JNJ, and KO, there were 5,685 rows in the news matrix for just 7 days of analyst ratings.

Following vectorization, the news data matrix was matched with the desired output: the average numerical rating produced by financial analysts and recorded on the day following the month of news items. In other words, all news articles from January 2 through February 1 had a corresponding target label of the average financial returns updated on February 2. This way, the algorithm accounted for the time it took a human analyst to read and process the news and to summarize the news in the buy/strong buy/hold/sell/strong sell recommendation. We are assuming that the analyst included the most popular news for the month preceding his recommendation and up to 1 day before his recommendation was published.

Table 4.1 Average and standard deviation of RMSE scores deployed in optimal model selection for news/analyst ratings pairings.

Model	Average of negative MSE (supervised learning, no output sampling/ bootstrapping/boosting) (%)	SD of negative MSE (supervised learning, no output sampling/ bootstrapping/boosting) (%)
Linear regression	26	3
Ridge regression	28	2
Bayesian ridge regression	28	1
Elastic net	37	1
Random forests	26	1
Extra trees	32	2
K nearest neighbors	39	4

Next, the algorithm split the data into the training and testing partitions, reserving 75% of rows for training and the rest for out-of-sample testing. The training data were next further split into k-folds for model cross-validation. To keep things simple, k was set to 3.

In the following step, the optimal supervised model was selected as a base for the generative model. To do so, a simple supervised analysis was executed with the $k = 3$ cross-validation framework. The average RMSE scores and their standard deviations are shown in Table 4.1. To ensure fair comparison of scores among different models, the negative MSE scoring methodology was deployed for each model.

Performance of the Generative Mechanism. The generative model was created to "grow" or generate extra training samples from prediction data. At each of the 10 iterations, the algorithm sampled values predicted by the model in the previous iteration. The sampling occurred at random. Each time, a sample of $c \in [0, 1]$ of the predicted values was retained and added to the new iteration's training data set. The sampling was performed with replacement to ensure that the test set does not shrink.

Figure 4.4 shows the resulting cross-validation RMSE scores for a ridge regression model with various sampling rates. As Figure 4.4 shows, iterative sampling to generate additional training samples considerably improves the performance of the algorithm, albeit increasing concerns of overfitting. As the number of iterations increases, the training pool of data becomes increasingly saturated by inferences from what would be out-of-sample observations. As a result, while the model has more observations to draw conclusions, the observations become more and more mired in their own predictive ability, potentially destroying their original predictive power. To allay these concerns, we next run the model on the reserved test data for extra stock tickers we have not used to date.

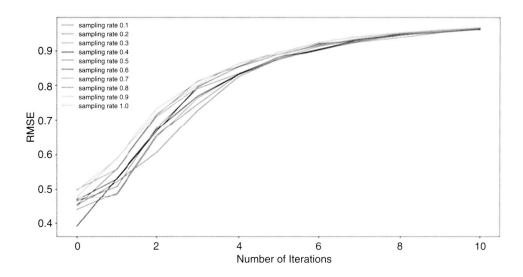

Figure 4.4 SSL with ridge regression, estimation performance with various sampling rates and number of iterations.

Out-of-Sample Performance of Generative Models

Figure 4.5 shows out-of-sample prediction of the generative SSL with ridge regression model on previously reserved names: MCD, MMM, MRK, MSFT, PFE, PG, and UA. The model was trained on news and ratings of AAPL, AXP, GE, BA, CSCO, DOW,

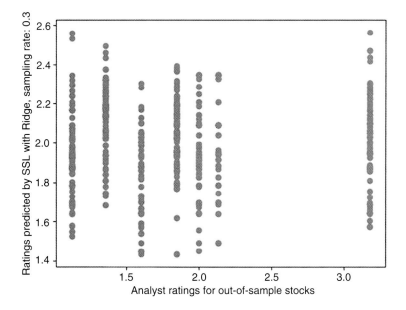

Figure 4.5 Out-of-sample prediction of analysts' forecasts using previous month's stock-specific news in a generative SSL with ridge regression, sampling rate of 30%, and 5 iterations.

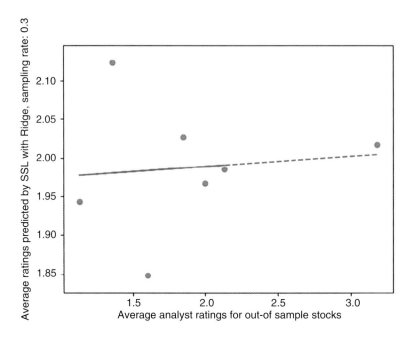

Figure 4.6 Average predictions of analysts' forecasts based on stock–specific news developed using generative SSL with ridge regression (30% sampling rate, 5 iterations) vs. realized means of analysts' forecasts.

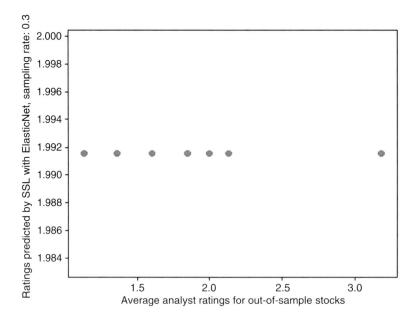

Figure 4.7 SSL ratings forecast for seven out–of–sample stocks produced by vanilla elastic net algorithm (pure supervised learning).

DIS, GE, IBM, JNJ, and KO. The forecasts were estimated by applying the model trained on the previous month's news articles with a sampling rate of 30% and 5 iterations to the previous month's news about a fresh subset of stocks. As in real life, different news articles produce different interpretations of the corporate future, resulting in a spectrum of ratings.

As Figure 4.6 shows, the SSL-generated forecasts (y-axis) are universally lower than those produced by human analysts (x-axis). This observation may be due to a well-documented analysts' optimism bias (see, for example, O'Brien, McNichols and Hsiou-Nei 2005), whereby analysts are often pressured for various reasons to deliver better-than-warranted forecasts. The SSL may actually turn out to be more objective, but additional research is required to ascertain this hypothesis.

The models underlying SSL analysis may significantly differ in their performance. Figure 4.7, for example, shows the performance of pure supervised elastic net in predicting future analyst forecasts. As Figure 4.7 shows, the elastic net SSL assigns nearly identical ratings to all the test stocks, pulling them toward the neutral "hold" rating encoded as 2.

Curiously, the words in the news articles that SSL deemed contributed most positively to the analyst reviews were "corporation," "good," "everyone," "streaming," "data," and "urltoimage," the latter suggesting that human analysts potentially prefer articles with images or that articles bearing good news were more likely to include images. The words that SSL deemed most decreased analyst ratings were "capital," "bancshares," "company," "transcribing," and "articles."

Introducing Market News. Much of modern Finance asserts (and later part of this book proves) that the fluctuation of prices of individual stocks is inevitably driven by the changes in the aggregate securities market. As such, news affecting ratings of individual corporations is not just limited to that of companies themselves and their competition. Instead, market-wide news may also significantly factor into the analysts' forecasts.

To test this hypothesis, we add news by searching for "SPY," a stock symbol for the widely traded electronically traded fund (ETF) that proxies the S&P 500 index. Our dictionary now expands to 48,350 words, and there are 10,507 news/ratings pairs in the labeled training data and 6,063 news/ratings data points in the testing sample. As before, we train our generative SSL model using ridge regression with a 30% sampling rate in 5 iterations. As before, the training is performed on news and analysts' ratings covering AAPL, AXP, GE, BA, CSCO, DOW, DIS, GE, IBM, JNJ, and KO, with the addition of the previous month's news for NYSE:SPY as input for each stocks' labeling mechanism. Also, as previously, the out-of-sample testing was performed by applying the parameterized model to reserved symbols: MCD, MMM, MRK, MSFT, PFE, PG, and UA. The resulting forecasts from inclusion of market-wide news, shown in Figures 4.8 and 4.9, performed better than the model without the market news (Figures 4.5 and 4.6).

To verify the findings on a completely clean sample, we reverse the sets of tickers. We first train the model on the seven stocks previously used in out-of-sample forecasting,

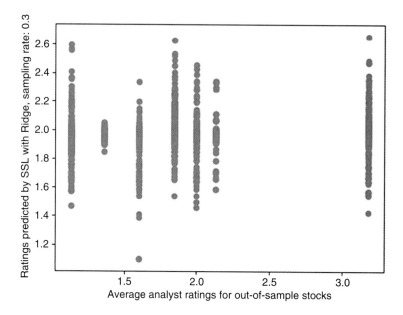

Figure 4.8   Out-of-sample prediction of analysts' forecasts using previous month's stock-specific and market news in a generative SSL with ridge regression, sampling rate of 30%, and 5 iterations.

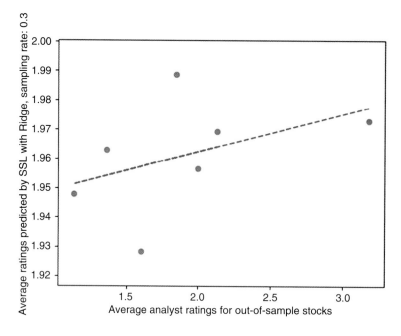

Figure 4.9   Average predictions of analysts' forecasts based on stock-specific and market news developed using generative SSL with ridge regression (30% sampling rate, 5 iterations) vs. realized means of analysts' forecasts.

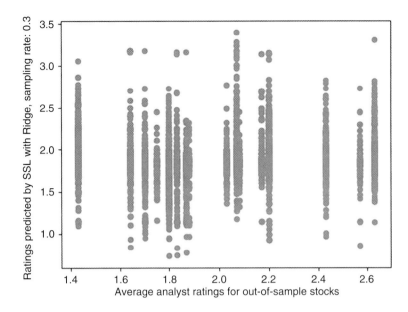

Figure 4.10 SSL with Ridge regression, out-of-sample predictions of ratings based on individual news articles vs. actual mean ratings for AAPL, AXP, GE, BA, CSCO, DOW, DIS, GE, IBM, JNJ, and KO with the model trained on news and financial ratings of MCD, MMM, MRK, MSFT, PFE, PG, and UA.

and then test the model on the stocks that were previously deployed in training. Thus, we train our generative model on MCD, MMM, MRK, MSFT, PFE, PG, and UA and test the model on AAPL, AXP, GE, BA, CSCO, DOW, DIS, GE, IBM, JNJ, and KO. Figures 4.10 and 4.11 show the results of modeling.

As Figures 4.10 and 4.11 illustrate, generative models deliver plausible out-of-sample predictions, positively correlated with the realized ratings.

For data spanning February 1, 2020, through March 14, 2020, out-of-sample predictions for the analyst recommendations have improved further. Top positive words changed to: "MMM," "Costco," "Liquidity," "Train," and "Baby," while the words with the most negative impact have become: "Covid," "stocks," "Francisco," as in "San Francisco," "Tech," and "Value." The key words seemed to reflect the reality of the emerging Coronavirus or COVID-19 crisis and its impact, including minimized impact on children and babies, a sell-out period at Costco, and desire for high-liquidity stocks.

Improvements to Generative Modeling

One of the potential pitfalls of SSL is its search for the optimal solution may turn up the local optimum only, which may significantly distort results. To overcome this issue, Rose, Gurewitz, and Fox (1990; 1992) proposed a technique where the optimization frontier is first approximated by a smooth convex function with an easy-to-find global maximum.

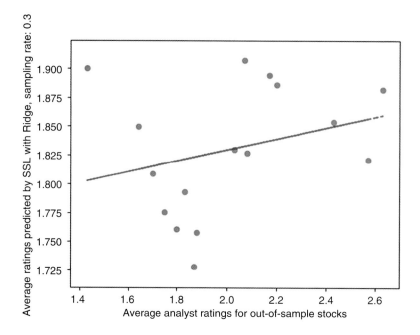

Figure 4.11 Average predictions of analysts; forecasts based on stock–specific and market news developed using generative SSL with ridge regression (30% sampling rate, 5 iterations) vs. realized means of analysts' forecasts. The out-of-sample predictions for AAPL, AXP, GE, BA, CSCO, DOW, DIS, GE, IBM, JNJ, and KO of ratings were based on one month of individual stock news articles and market news preceding the ratings. The model was trained on news for each given stock and the market only and financial ratings of MCD, MMM, MRK, MSFT, PFE, PG, and UA.

Next, in what is known as *deterministic annealing*, the process is changed to become more bumpy, with lots of local minima, to resemble the actual probability surface. With such an approach, the global maximum of the probability can be successfully found.

To further enhance generative inferences, one may use other variables within the labeled/unlabeled data set in a process referred to as *co-training*. For example, ratings provided by Zacks include mean rating on each day, but also daily sums of ratings by category: strong buy, buy, hold, sell, and strong sell. Associating raw news text with the additional variable, the sum of ratings per category, adds an additional parameter in the Bayesian estimation and thus strengthens the inferences. The additional variables $X = (x^{(1)}, x^{(2)}, \ldots)$ are referred to as *views* on the data, and the parameters or binary classifiers $\Theta = (\theta^{(1)}, \theta^{(2)}, \ldots)$ are known as *concepts*. If a data subset $A \subset X$, concepts Θ are compatible with A if $\theta^{(1)}x^{(1)} = \theta^{(2)}x^{(2)} = \ldots$ for all $X = (x^{(1)}, x^{(2)}, \ldots)$ that belong to A. Co-training is the process of jointly modeling two or more views due to Blum and Mitchell (1998). In essence, co-training is a Bayesian inference with conditional priors encoding the compatibility assumptions.

Zelikovitz and Hirsh (2000) proposed a refinement to the Bayes estimation in the spirit of K-nearest-neighbors (KNN) algorithm. To find a label for a document m_i, Zelikovitz and Hirsh seek to find the labeled document m_z whose k nearest neighbors are most similar to x_i. Using the inherent unlabeled data structure as a background for estimating the distribution can generate more sound inferences than using pure matching of m_z to the closest m_i.

Other SSL Models and Enhancements

Discriminative models and graph-based models were the top alternatives to generative modeling at the time this book was written. These models are discussed in this section.

Discriminative Models

In SSL, generative models contrast *discriminative* models. Generative models develop and use joint distribution for X and Y, while discriminative models deploy extreme conditional distributions: specifically, Y conditional on X, when $p(Y|X)$ is greater than a certain number, say, 0.5. Discriminative models are often used in support vector machines (SVMs), discussed in Chapter 3. While SVMs are strictly supervised methods, a variation called Semi-Supervised SVMs (S3VMs) relies on partially labeled data. In Generative Adversarial Networks (GANs), a popular class of neural networks at the time this book was written, generative and discriminative models work together with the discriminative part validating data produced by the generative part.

Discriminative models can be Bayesian or non-Bayesian. Non-Bayesian models include kernel regressions (e.g., Belkin et al. 2006), support vector machines (SVMs) discussed in Chapter 3, and AdaBoost (Shawe-Taylor and Cristianini 2004). In a kernel regression-based approach, Belkin, Niyogi, and Sindhwani (2006), for example, examine the geometry of the marginal distribution of $p(Y|X)$. In a nonparametric approach known as *manifold regularization*, Belkin et al. (2006) use a standard kernel regression, a locally constant estimator, and minimize the so-called regularized empirical risk functional, $R_\gamma(m)$:

$$\widehat{m}(x) = arg\ min_{m(x)} R_\gamma(m)$$

The locally constant estimate $\widehat{m}(x)$ depends on both labeled and unlabeled data:

$$R_\gamma(m) = \sum_{i=1}^{N}\sum_{j=1}^{n} K_H(X_iX_j)(Y_j - m(X_i))^2 + \gamma \sum_{i=1}^{N}\sum_{j=1}^{n} K_H(X_iX_j)(m(X_j) - m(X_i))^2$$

where K_H is a symmetric kernel, e.g., a heat kernel, depending on a matrix of bandwidths H and $K_H(X_iX_j) = K(H^{-1/2}(X_i - X_j))$.

This estimator, described by Sindhwani et al. (2005), Belkin et al. (2006), and Tsang and Kwok (2006), is also often used in support-vector machines (SVMs), a supervised learning classifier of data discussed in Chapter 3.

Here, we focus on Bayesian approaches to the discriminative SSL. Generative models form posterior probabilities $p(y_i|x_i)$ using Bayes' rule from class-conditional densities $p(x_i|\ y_i = c_m)$ and class prior probabilities $p(y_i = c_m)$. In contrast, Bayesian discriminative models focus on modeling the posterior probability $p(y_i|x_i)$.

To model $p(y_i|x_i)$, Lawrence and Jordan (2006) and Lafferty and Wasserman (2007) describe the data as $(x_1, y, r_1), \dots, (x_N, y_N, r_N)$ where $r_i \in \{0, 1\}$ is an indicator of whether y_i is observed: $r_i = 1$ if y_i is observed and 0 otherwise. Then, the labeled data set is $L = \{(x_i y_i), r_i = 1\}$ and the unlabeled data set is $U = \{(x_i y_i), r_i = 0\}$. The variable R_i is, of course, readily observable.

Next, Lawrence and Jordan (2006) follow the SVM-like construct and place the class decision boundary in a low-density region. To do so, Lawrence and Jordan construct a *null category*, a class for which no data is ever observed. The null category model can be thought of as a probabilistic version of the margin region in SVM.

Lawrence and Jordan introduce a latent process variable f_i that allows us to decompose the model into a *noise model*, $p(y_i|f_i)$, and a *process model*, $p(f_i|x_i)$, as follows:

$$p(y_i|x_i) = \int p(y_i|f_i)\, p(f_i|x_i)\, df_i$$

The null-category noise model $p(y_i|f_i)$ is next derived from the ordered categorical models (see, e.g., Agresti 2002). If we are looking to classify the labels into just two categories, for example, "buy" and "sell" (aggregating strong buy and buy, ignoring hold, and joining sell and strong sell), then the null-category model will look like this:

- For $y_i = 1$, $p(y_i|f_i) = \Phi\left(-\left(f_i + \frac{a}{2}\right)\right)$
- For $y_i = 0$, $p(y_i|f_i) = \Phi\left(f_i + \frac{a}{2}\right) - \Phi\left(f_i - \frac{a}{2}\right)$
- For $y_i = -1$, $p(y_i|f_i) = \Phi\left(f_i - \frac{a}{2}\right)$

where $\Phi(x)$ is the cumulative Gaussian distribution function, $\Phi(x) = \int_{-\infty}^{x} N(z|0, 1)\, dz$, and a is a parameter defining the width of the class $y_i = 0$. Using the instrument variable r_i that is 1 when the variable is present and 0 when it is missing, we can impose the following constraint: a data point cannot be from the $y_i = 0$ category as we created that category specifically to have no data points. In other words, the probability of observing a data point in class $y_i = 0$ is 0:

$$p(r_i = 1|\, y_i = 0) = 0$$

Next, Lawrence and Jordan (2006) estimate the probit model and use it to successfully estimate out-of-sample entries.

As an alternative to probit estimation, we consider the following formulation. First, the ratings data are discretized further into a $\{0, 1\}$ framework, where 1 is the negative rating of "sell" or "strong sell." Such discretization may be useful if we consider which securities we should remove from our portfolios. Unlike generative models, 0 now may denote a "buy," "strong buy," "hold," or, most importantly, "missing data." The key idea here is that the information on whether the data are present or missing also comprises a valuable part of the model. The output is essentially a product of the binary rating and the instrumental variable showing whether the data are available or missing.

Next, the chosen supervised model is then fit with the entire set of training data comprising both available and missing ratings data. The predictions on the out-of-sample

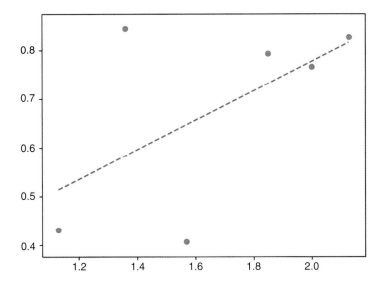

Figure 4.12 Discriminant analysis using ridge regression with output in $\{0,1\}$, where 1 denotes "sell" and "strong sell" while 0 stands for "buy," "strong buy," "hold," or "missing data."

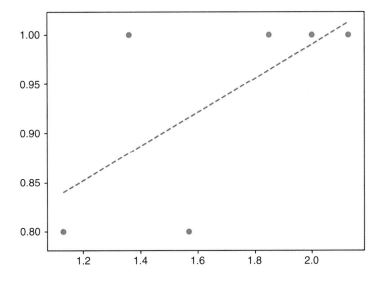

Figure 4.13 Discriminant analysis using K-nearest neighbors with output in $\{0,1\}$, where 1 denotes "sell" and "strong sell" while 0 stands for "buy," "strong buy," "hold," or "missing data."

stocks are next made from this formulation, with the results using ridge regression and K-nearest neighbors shown in Figures 4.12 and 4.13.

Graph-based Models

Graph-based models emerged from the image classification and are typically variants of the unsupervised models discussed later in this book. The models further help to fine-tune the sampling process by effectively representing a distribution over several variables. Specifically, graph-based models represent random variables as nodes. Directed edges exist between nodes only if there is a functional relationship between the parent and the child node. The resulting graph encodes conditional independence constraints that hold for the distribution. Once all the parents of the child are known, the child node can be sampled. Graph-based models are discussed in the context of clustering detail in Chapter 9.

Conclusion

Semi-supervised learning encompasses several models that fit on a wide spectrum between supervised models discussed in Chapter 3 of this book and unsupervised models discussed from Chapters 5 onwards. While the models diverge in their spirit and execution, they all help achieve an otherwise expensive task of classification by attempting to mimic limited human-generated examples.

Appendix 4.A Python for Semi-Supervised Models

Semi-supervised models are extensively developed in scikit-learn. Here, we will use semi-supervised models to classify reports.

First, about the measurement of quality of our predictions. To evaluate the accuracy of the models, we will use confusion matrices, also built-in in scikit-learn. A confusion matrix is a matrix C where each element $C_{i,j}$ corresponds to the number of observations known to be in the group i, but predicted to be in the group j. The confusion matrix conveniently delivers the counts of true positives, true negatives, false positives, and false negatives. For example, in a binary classification with only two states, 0 and 1, $C_{0,0}$ counts true negatives, $C_{1,1}$ represents the number of true positives, $C_{1,0}$ counts false negatives, and $C_{0,1}$ shows false positives.

Using the scikit-learn confusion matrix is easy. The following code snippet generates a confusion matrix C from the out-of-sample prediction y_pred determined based on X_test and the corresponding true realized values of y_test:

```
from sklearn.metrics import confusion_matrix
C = confusion_matrix(y_test, y_pred)
```

Armed with confusion matrices, we can optimize the parameters to minimize errors and improve fit.

Now, to the semi-supervised models themselves. A scikit-learn sub-library `sklearn.semi_supervised` contains out-of-the-box semi-supervised learning algorithms accessible with simple function calls. The following example uses the "Label Spreading" algorithm that follows the analyst rating process described in this chapter:

```
from sklearn.semi_supervised import LabelSpreading
lp_model = LabelSpreading()
```

```
lp_model.fit(X_train, y_train)
y_pred = lp_model.predict(y_test)
```

Calculating the confusion matrix and iterating over the label spreading model to minimize confusion helps build a robust semi-supervised framework even in the presence of significant noise.

For specific code examples, please visit https://www.BigDataFinanceBook.com, and register with password *SSL* (case-sensitive).

References

Agrawala, A.K. (1970). Learning with a probabilistic teacher. *IEEE Transactions on Information Theory* 16: 373–379.

Agresti, A. (2002). *Categorical Data Analysis*. Hoboken, NJ: Wiley.

Aldridge, I. and Krawciw, S. (2017). *Real-Time Risk: What Investors Should Know About Fintech, High-Frequency Trading and Flash Crashes*. Hoboken, NJ: Wiley.

Balcan, M.F. and Blum, A. (2010). A discriminative model for semi-supervised learning. *Journal of the ACM* 57(3).

Belkin, M., Niyogi, P., and Sindhwani, V. (2006). Manifold regularization: A geometric framework for learning from labeled and unlabeled examples. *The Journal of Machine Learning Research* 7: 2399–2434.

Blum, A. and Mitchell, T. (1998). Combining labeled and unlabeled data with co-training. In: *Proceedings of the Eleventh Annual Conference on Computational Learning Theory*, 92–100.

Castelli, V. and Cover, T.M. (1995). On the exponential value of labeled samples. *Pattern Recognition Letters* 16(1): 105–111.

Chakrabortty, A. (2016). Robust semi-parametric inference in semi-supervised settings. PhD thesis, Harvard University.

Chapelle, O., Scholkopf, B., and Zien, A. (2006). *Semi-Supervised Learning*. Cambridge, MA: MIT Press.

Collins, M. and Singer, Y. (1999). Unsupervised models for named entity classification. In: *Proceedings of the Joint SIGDAT Conference on Empirical Methods in Natural Language Processing and Very Large Corpora*, 189–196.

Dietterich, T.G. (1998). Approximate statistical tests for comparing supervised classification learning algorithms. *Neural Computing* 10(7): 1895–1923.

Efron, B. (1983). Estimating the error rate of a prediction rule: Improvement on cross-validation. *Journal of the American Statistical Association* 78: 316–331.

Fralick, S.C. (1967). Learning to recognize patterns without a teacher. *IEEE Transactions on Information Theory* 13: 57–64.

Geisser, S. (1975). The predictive sample reuse method with applications. *Journal of the American Statistical Association* 70(350): 320–328.

Joachims, T. (1999). Transductive inference for text classification using support vector machines. In: *Proceedings of the Sixteenth International Conference on Machine Learning,* 200–209, Bled, Slovenia. http://www-ai.cs.uni-dortmund.de/DOKUMENTE/joachims_99c.ps.gz.

Kawakita, M. and Kanamori, T. (2013). Semi-supervised learning with density-ratio estimation. *Machine Learning* 91: 189–209.

Kohavi, R. (1995). *A study of cross-validation and bootstrap for accuracy estimation and model selection*. In: *Proceedings of International Joint Conference on AI*, 1137–1145. http://citeseer.ist.psu.edu/kohavi95study .html.

Lafferty, J.D. and Wasserman, L. (2007). Statistical analysis of semi-supervised regression. *Advances in Neural Information Processing Systems* 20: 801–808.

Lawrence, N.D. and Jordan, M.I. (2006). Gaussian processes and the null-category noise model. In: *Semi-Supervised Learning* (ed. O. Chapelle, B. Scholkopf, and A. Zien). Cambridge, MA: The MIT Press.

Lewis, D.D. (1998). Naive (Bayes) at forty: The independence assumption in information retrieval. In: *Tenth European Conference on Machine Learning*, 4–15.

Lo, A.W. and McKinlay, A.C. (1990). Data-snooping biases in tests of financial asset pricing models, *Review of Financial Studies* 3(3): 431–467.

McCallum, A. and Nigam, K. (1998). A comparison of event models for naive Bayes text classification. In: *Learning for Text Categorization: Papers from the AAAI Workshop,* 41–48. AAAI Press.

Mizumoto, K., Yanagimoto, H., and Yoshioka, M. (2012). Sentiment analysis of stock market news with semi-supervised learning. 2012 IEEE/ACIS 11th International Conference on Computer and Information Science.

Nigam, K. (2001). Using unlabeled data to improve text classification. PhD Thesis, Carnegie Mellon University.

Nigam, K., McCallum, A.K., Thrun, S., and Mitchell, T. (2000). Text classification from labeled and unlabeled documents using EM. *Machine Learning* 39: 103–134.

O'Brien, P.C., McNichols, M.F., and Hsiou-Nei, L. (2005). Analyst impartiality and investment banking relationships. *Journal of Accounting Research* 43(4).

Refaeilzadeh, P., Tang, L., and Liu, H. (2007). On comparison of feature selection algorithms. AAAI-07 Workshop on Evaluation Methods in Machine Learning II.

Rose, K., Gurewitz, E., and Fox. G. (1990). A deterministic annealing approach to clustering. *Pattern Recognition Letters* 11(9): 589–594.

Rose, K., Gurewitz, E., and Fox. G. (1992). Vector quantization by deterministic annealing. *IEEE Transactions on Information Theory* 38(4): 1249–1257.

Salzberg, S. (1997). On comparing classifiers: pitfalls to avoid and a recommended approach. *Data Mining and Knowledge Discovery* 1(3): 317–328.

Scudder, H.J. (1965). Probability of error of some adaptive pattern-recognition machines. *IEEE Transactions on Information Theory* 11: 363–371.

Shawe-Taylor, J. and Cristianini, N. (2004). *Kernel Methods for Pattern Analysis*. Cambridge: Cambridge University Press.

Sindhwani, V., Niyogi, P., Belkin, M., and Keerthi, S. (2005). Linear manifold regularization for large-scale semi-supervised learning. In: *Proceedings of the 22nd ICML Workshop on Learning with Partially Classified Training Data*.

Sullivan, R., Timmermann, A., and White, H. (1999). Data-snooping, technical trading rule performance, and the bootstrap. *The Journal of Finance* 54: 1647–1691.

Tsang, I. and Kwok, J. (2006). Large-scale sparsified manifold regularization. *Advances in Neural Information Processing Systems (NIPS)* 19.

White, H. (2000). A reality check for data snooping. *Econometrica* 68: 1097–1126.

Yarowsky, D. (1995). Unsupervised word sense disambiguation rivaling supervised methods. In: *Meeting of the Association for Computational Linguistics*, 189–196.

Zelikovitz, S. and H. Hirsh (2000). Improving short text classification using unlabeled background knowledge to assess document similarity. In Proceedings of the Seventeenth International Conference on Machine Learning: 1183–1190.

Zhu, X. (2005). Semi-supervised learning through graphs. Ph.D. thesis, Carnegie Mellon University, USA. CMU-LTI-05-192.

Zhu, X. (2008). Semi-supervised learning literature survey. Computer Sciences, University of Wisconsin-Madison, USA, technical report no. 1530.

Chapter 5

Letting the Data Speak with Unsupervised Learning

Introduction

The supervised learning discussed in Chapter 3 typically requires a hypothesis and a neatly matching set of inputs and outputs. The semi-supervised learning covered in Chapter 4 relaxes some assumptions about data. The unsupervised learning (UL) discussed here and in the rest of this book does away with hypotheses, instead allowing the data to drive the analytical process.

In econometrics, a researcher dreams up a question to ask the data. The resulting question may be subjective, incomplete, outright irrelevant, or even severely biased by the researcher's own prejudice. Unsupervised learning eliminates the trickling of the researcher's personal opinions and beliefs into the analysis. Instead of waiting for the researcher's question, unsupervised learning tells the researcher what the data know. Specifically, unsupervised methods explain to the researcher the major trends in the data, the main factors driving observed behavior and the like, all at the stroke of a key on a computer keyboard.

UL is taking the industry by storm. Traditional disciplines like risk management can be improved by switching to a fast hypothesis-less environment, trusting the data to speak for themselves.

UL also comes with computational benefits: unsupervised techniques deliver results of complex mathematical analyses in a flash, all with existing computing power. The implementation of UL can reach most areas, saving corporations millions of dollars in the process. For example, one application that is waiting to benefit from unsupervised learning is modern risk management, where at present most financial decisions are made with at least a few days of risk horizon. Such a view ignores short-term risk events. The classic 10-day value at risk (VAR), a standard for banks, for example, misses many short-term risk events that end up costing financial institutions a pretty penny. The duration of the traditional risk measures was chosen as a balance between the application and the computational complexity. Many traditional models require extensive Monte-Carlo simulations that may take a very long time. This chapter and the following chapters in this book discuss the details of implementation of the fast hypothesis-less paradigm in Big Data Science.

The core unsupervised learning techniques have existed for over a century. However, most were shelved as toy models until the technology became powerful yet inexpensive. The advances in technology, however, are only part of the story of UL development. The state-of-the art improvements in data science are due to developments in mathematical aspects of computation. Most of the newest approaches are still waiting to be implemented in Finance. This book provides brand-new groundbreaking examples of the application of the latest techniques to facilitate financial strategies.

How does unsupervised learning work? From a high-level viewpoint, UL deploys a set of techniques known as principal component analysis (PCA) or singular value decomposition (SVD). These techniques identify the core characteristics of the data at hand. The characteristics can often be summarized by what has long been known as *characteristic values*, or alternatively, *singular values*, *eigenvalues* from German, or *principal components*. These data descriptors capture statistical properties of the data in a succinct and computer-friendly way, elucidating the key drivers of data in the process. Armed with the key drivers or factors, the researchers' problem data set shrinks instantly into a manageable smaller-scale optimization problem. Best of all, the characteristic values are able to capture the "feel" of the entire data population, mathematically stretching beyond the observable X and Y. State-of-the-art inferences emerge.

What kinds of inferences are we talking about? Inferences that made billions of dollars for companies like Google and Facebook, of course! And while Google and Facebook focused on modeling of online human behavior, the data of other industries, and especially in Finance, can bring their own pots of gold to the capable hands.

We can loosely separate all data into three categories: Small, Medium, and Big:

• Small Data possess low dimensionality. Small Data have their own advantages: the computation is transparent and inexpensive and often can be done by hand. On the other hand, Small Data may not at all be descriptive of the actual phenomenon they are trying to summarize – a sample may not represent the broader data population.
• Big Data are described by high dimensionality. An example of high-dimensional data may be a table with thousands, if not millions, of columns, and even more rows. Big Data are leveraging their size to their full potential. Large data size is great for describing the entire universe of events, taking into consideration inherent randomness

and statistical properties of the Law of Large Numbers and measuring concentration to deliver solid inferences about events.
• Medium Data have neither the advantage of Small Data nor of Big Data.

The Law of Large Numbers, one of the pillars of statistics, states that as the data sample increases in size, the data overcome potentially inherent noise and distortions to converge on the true data distribution. In other words, to obtain truly descriptive inferences about the world, one does not need to have every single point of the data in the world, although taking as large a sample of data as possible definitely helps make inferences more precise. Big Data help achieve stable inferences by taking into account large data populations.

Concentration of measure is another critical concept that states that a measured variable that depends on many independent variables, and not too much on any one variable in particular, is stable. Specifically, the measured variable's distribution concentrates around its median, hence the term "concentration of measure." Big Data provide sought-after measure concentration for output variables by considering massive dependencies.

Dimensionality Reduction in Finance

Fan, Fan, and Lv (2008) show that dimensionality reduction, in any form, significantly reduces the error of the estimation. Fan, Fan and Lv's main argument is that the amount of daily data in Finance is just insufficient to meaningfully draw inferences about things like covariance matrices. To overcome the problem, they expand the number of available observations by considering multiple factors in a Ross-like decomposition (Ross 1976; 1977):

$$Y_i = b_{i1}f_1 + b_{i2}f_2 + \ldots + b_{iK}f_K + \varepsilon_i, i = 1, \ldots, p$$

where Y_i is the decomposed variable, most often the excess return of a financial instrument i over the risk-free rate, $f_1, \ldots, f_K$ are the excessive returns of K factors relative to their means, b_{ij} are factor loadings ($i = 1, \ldots, p, j = 1, \ldots, K$), and $\varepsilon_1, \ldots, \varepsilon_p$ are p idiosyncratic errors uncorrelated given the excessive returns of K factors $f_1, \ldots, f_K$.

Fan, Fan, and Lv (2008) begin by examining covariance matrices with and without factor decomposition of the underlying instruments. Thus, in a data sample comprising p stocks, a sample covariance matrix without any factorization has $p(p + 1)/2$ parameters to be estimated. When all p stocks are factorized using the famous Fama-French three-factor model (Fama and French 1992; 1993), then the number of parameters to be estimated reduces to just $4p$, as each stock return is now correlated with the factor return instead of other stock returns, as shown in Tables 5.1 and 5.2. An example of a three-factor model is the Fama-French model (Fama and French 1992; 1993).

The factors in the Fama-French model are contemporaneous returns on three portfolios:

• A market portfolio in excess of the risk-free rate: $f_1 = R_m - r_f$.

Table 5.1 Traditional covariance matrix of security returns.

	R_1	R_2	...	R_p
R_1	σ_{11}	$\sigma_{12} = \sigma_{21}$	...	$\sigma_{1p} = \sigma_{p1}$
R_2	σ_{21}	σ_{22}	...	$\sigma_{p2} = \sigma_{2p}$
...				
R_p	σ_{p1}	σ_{p2}	...	σ_{pp}

Table 5.2 Factorized covariance matrix of security returns.

	f_1	f_2	f_3	R_i
R_1	σ_{11}	σ_{12}	σ_{13}	σ_1^2
R_2	σ_{21}	σ_{22}	σ_{23}	σ_2^2
...	...	...	...	...
R_p	σ_{p1}	σ_{p2}	σ_{p3}	σ_p^2

- A "size" portfolio, also known as "small minus big" stock returns, that subtracts large-cap stock returns from small-cap returns, recognizing small-cap ability to outperform large cap: $f_2 = R_{Small-Cap} - R_{Large-Cap}$. The "cap" is the capitalization of the company as reflected in its total market valuation (number of stocks issued × price of each stock). Small-cap stocks have historically outperformed large-cap stocks.
- A "book-to-market" portfolio, also known as "High Minus Low" in reference to the return difference between high book-to-market stocks versus low book-to-market stocks: $f_3 = R_{High\ Book\ to\ Market} - R_{Low\ Book\ to\ Market}$. The book-to-market ratio is calculated as the fraction of accounting value to market value, the latter measured by the stock valuation. Higher book-to-market stocks have been shown to outperform lower book-to-market stocks.

To construct the size and book-to-market portfolios, Fama and French (1992, 1993) sort all the stocks into deciles based on size and book-to-market, respectively. Then, Fama and French create equally weighted size portfolios adding long positions in the smallest by capitalization decile of stocks and shorting the largest decile by capitalization. Similarly, they create the book-to-market portfolios by going long on the highest decile of book-to-market stocks and shorting the lowest decile.

Factorized covariances à la Fan, Fan, and Lv (2008) provide immediate reduction in dimensionality, making the sample covariance matrices suitable for modeling those of the population. Further inversion of factorized, low-dimensional, covariance matrices delivers a sound alternative to the unstable high-dimensional covariance matrices.

Fan, Fan, and Lv's factors are known and may or may not be fully uncorrelated, i.e., orthogonal. In contrast, as shown later in this book, SVD and PCA deliver fully orthogonal factors that arise from the data. These factors, however, may or may not be known to the researchers.

Dimensionality Reduction with Unsupervised Learning

The methodology of Fan, Fan, and Lv (2008) calls on the researchers to determine the factors that are then used to create appropriate portfolios. The resulting factors may not at all represent the optimal factorization. For one, working with large data sets can be very time-consuming. Next, vast computing power may be required to handle the challenge of analyzing all possible factor combinations.

Advances in data processing technology help a bit. For example, researchers may rent powerful servers operated in parallel, hosted in remote locations and accessible online, collectively referred to as being located in a *cloud* and *cloud computing*. The servers in a cloud may be organized into interdependent and interoperating groups known as *clusters*. Each cluster may contain several independent processing *nodes* (servers, server partitions, or even just processes) capable of handling specific loads. *Cluster management* systems then may allow the computing load to be dynamically distributed among several nodes, all the while appearing seamless to the end user.

Still, even when equipped with state-of-the-art computing, manually searching for orthogonal factors explaining the data can be a daunting task taking weeks, months, and even years. For example, the best-known factor in Finance, such as Sharpe's (1964) and Lintner's (1965) CAPM, took years to develop and was even awarded a Nobel Memorial Prize in Economics!

UL techniques offer the promise of a fast factor development independent of the researchers. Armed with the latest technology, the factor selection becomes almost instantaneous.

What does UL actually do? By identifying key structural dependencies in the data, unsupervised learning techniques identify latent, unspecified, or previously unknown factors, or combinations of thereof. Furthermore, the factors presented by the UL are orthogonal to each other by construction, freeing the researchers' time from verification of the factors. Further still, the UL factors come ordered from the most globally significant to the least, simplifying the researchers' work even further.

The factors are known as principal components, characteristic values, eigenvalues, or singular values. The corresponding process of distilling the factors is known as principal component analysis (PCA), or singular value decomposition (SVD). Both PCA and SVD work with purely numerical data. Any data containing other-than-numeric values, say, text, have to be converted to the numeric format prior to the analysis.

The key idea behind factorization in either PCA or SVD is to find the dimensions of the data along which the data vary the most and the least. The factors that account for most variation in the data are typically critical to the reconstruction of the entire data set while the factors along which the data vary the least are the ones providing the final touches of detail, and, quite often, noise.

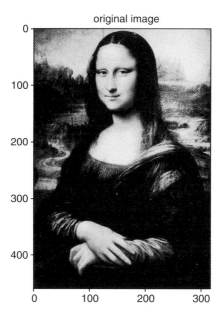

Figure 5.1 Original sample image.

Unsupervised Learning: Intuition via Image Factorization

Many Big Data techniques, such as spectral decomposition, first appeared in the eighteenth century when researchers grappled with solutions to differential equations in the context of wave mechanics and vibration physics. Fourier furthered the field of eigenvalue applications extensively with partial differential equations and other work.

At the heart of many Big Data models is the idea that the properties of every data set can be uniquely summarized by a set of values, called eigenvalues. An eigenvalue is a total amount of variance in the data set explained by the common factor. The bigger the eigenvalue, the higher the proportion of the data set dynamics that eigenvalue captures.

Eigenvalues are obtained via one of the techniques, principal component analysis (PCA) or singular value decomposition (SVD), discussed below. The eigenvalues and related eigenvectors describe and optimize the composition of the data set, perhaps best illustrated with an example of an image.

The intuition on which the technique is based is illustrated with the example from image processing. Consider the black-and-white image shown in Figure 5.1. It is a set of data points, "pixels" in computer lingo, whereby each data point describes the color of that point on a 0–255 scale, where 0 corresponds to pure black, 255 to pure white, and all other shades of gray lie in between. This particular image contains 460 rows and 318 columns.

To perform spectral decomposition on the image, we utilize SVD, a technique originally developed by Beltrami in 1873. For a detailed history of SVD, see Stewart (1993). Principal component analysis (PCA) is a related technique that produces eigenvalues and eigenvectors identical to those produced by SVD, when PCA eigenvalues are normalized. Raw, non-normalized, PCA eigenvalues can be negative as well as positive and do not equal the singular values produced by SVD. For the purposes of the analysis presented here, we assume that all the eigenvalues are normalized and equal to singular values. Later in this chapter, we show why and how PCA and SVD are related and can be converted from one to another.

Singular Value Decomposition

In SVD, a matrix X is decomposed into three matrices: U, S, and V,

$$X = USV'$$ (5.1)

where

X is the original n x m matrix;

S is an $m \times m$ diagonal matrix of singular values or eigenvalues sorted from the highest to the lowest on the diagonal;

V' is the transpose of the m x m matrix of so-called singular vectors, sorted according to the sorting of S;

U is an $n \times n$ "user" matrix containing characteristics of rows vis-à-vis singular values.

SVD delivers singular values sorted from the largest to the smallest. The plot of the singular values corresponding to the image in Figure 5.1 is shown in Figure 5.2. The plot of singular values is known as a "scree plot" since it resembles a real-life scree, a rocky mountain slope.

A scree plot is a simple line segment plot that shows the fraction of total variance in the data as explained or represented by each singular value (eigenvalue). The singular values are ordered and assigned a number label, by decreasing order of contribution to total variance.

To reduce the dimensionality of a data set, we select k singular values. If we were to use the most significant of the singular values, typically containing macro information common to the data set, we would select the first k values. However, in applications involving idiosyncratic data details, we may be interested in the last k values, for example, when we need to evaluate the noise in the system. A rule of thumb dictates breaking the eigenvalues into sets before the "elbow" and after the elbow sets in the scree plot.

What is the perfect number of singular values to keep in the image of Figure 5.1? An experiment presented in Figures 5.3–5.9 shows the evolution of the data with varying numbers of eigenvalues included. The eigenvalues and the corresponding eigenvectors comprised of linear combinations of the original data create new "dimensions" of data. As Figures 5.3–5.9 show, as few as 10 eigenvalues allow the human eye to identify the content of the image, effectively reducing dimensionality of the image from 318 columns to 10.

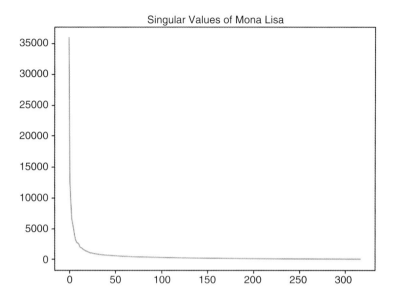

Figure 5.2   Scree plot corresponding to the image in Figure 5.1.

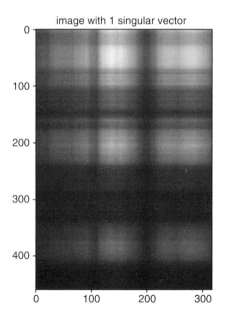

Figure 5.3   Reconstruction of the image of Figure 5.1 with just the first singular value.

However, the guesswork is not at all needed, as numerous methods of selecting the right cut-off value for the eigenvalues have already been researched. Chapter 7 discusses the methodologies for optimal scree plot "elbow" selection using the Marcenko-Pastur theorem.

To create the reduced data set, we restrict the number of columns in the S and V matrices to k by selecting k first elements, determined by the spectral cut-off method.

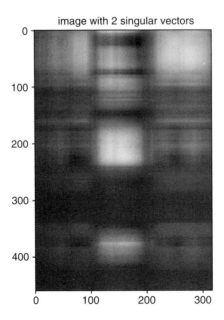

Figure 5.4 Reconstruction of the image in Figure 5.1 with the first 2 singular values.

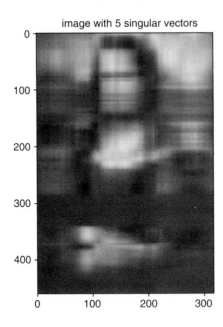

Figure 5.5 Reconstruction of the image of Figure 5.1 with the first 5 singular values. The outlines of the figure are beginning to appear.

The resulting matrix $X_{reduced}$ has dimensions n rows and k columns, where

$$X_{\text{reduced}, n \times k} = U_{n \times n} \, S_{n \times k} \, V^T_{k \times k} \tag{5.2}$$

and the unwanted or "cut-off" eigenvalues are replaced by zeros on the diagonal of the $S_{n \times k}$ matrix.

image with 10 singular vectors

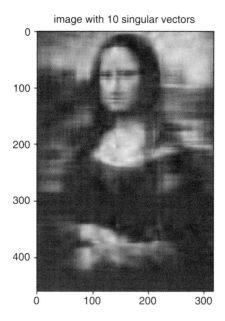

Figure 5.6 Reconstruction of the image in Figure 5.1 with the first 10 singular values.

image with 20 singular vectors

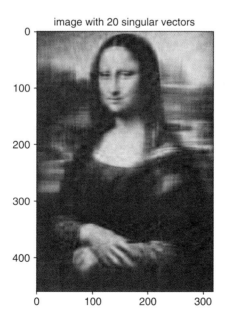

Figure 5.7 Reconstruction of the image in Figure 5.1 with the first 20 singular values.

The process of reducing the dimensionality of data by essentially wiping out a portion of eigenvalues and the associated eigenvectors is referred to as "whitening."

As the images above illustrated, Big Data techniques like SVD and PCA masterfully reduce the dimension of the data without sacrificing data quality and the following inferences.

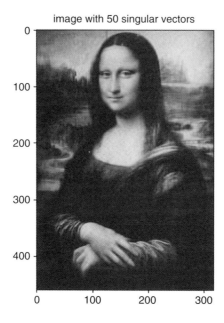

Figure 5.8   Reconstruction of the image in Figure 5.1 with the first 50 singular values.

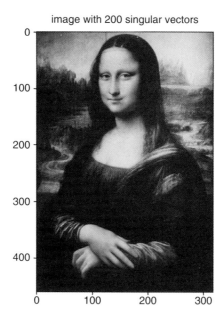

Figure 5.9   Reconstruction of the image in Figure 5.1 with the first 200 singular values.

Why reduce dimensions? Why not use the entire data set available? Many financial applications use daily data. Daily data suffer from relatively small sample size. Take three years of data and you are already counting 750 daily observations, corresponding to

750 rows in a matrix. If you are dealing with, say, 10 or even 50 stocks in portfolio allocation, organized in columns, then traditional covariance-based models will work just fine. However, if your mandate is to optimize a portfolio of the instruments comprising the S&P 500, S&P 1500, Russell 3000, or the entire trading universe, the covariance computation fails. Seminal studies like Johnstone (2001) showed that when the data dimensionality (the number of columns) approaches, not to mention exceeds, the sample size (the number of rows), the sample covariance matrix suffers considerably and is no longer a good estimator for the true population covariance.

Dimensionality reduction, however obvious and easy to grasp an application, is only a small subset of applications of SVD discussed in this book along with applications of PCA and other Big Data tools. Understanding the mechanics of SVD, therefore, is desirable and allows researchers to produce new innovative ideas. SVD, PCA, and several other key tools, like norms, are discussed in detail in the rest of this chapter.

Deconstructing Financial Returns

What do the U, S, and V matrices represent in practice? Consider the case of financial returns.

UL techniques distill the data down to a spectrum of influencing factors. The resulting factors are dependent on the specifics of the problem under consideration. Some of the frequent factors can be movements of the larger markets, others are characteristics of the financial instruments under consideration, and some may even turn out to be returns of other securities.

To determine significant factors driving the data, we rely on a technique known as *principal component regression*. In a principal component regression, the dependent variable is regressed not on other variables in the data set, but on linear combinations of these variables as determined by top eigenvalues and eigenvectors. Eigenvalues and eigenvectors can be thought of as the core representation of the data, or its most important characteristics. The motivation behind the principal component regression then is to elucidate the dependent variable's characteristics vis-à-vis these powerful singular value-driven factors.

What drives the U.S. equities markets? Here we present a toy example of dimensionality reduction for portfolio allocation and illustrate its performance. To assess, we start with the entire U.S. equities and Electronically Traded Funds (ETFs) universe, which on February 1, 2020, comprised 8,315 names, according to NASDAQ. To ensure a multi-year analysis, we restrict the sample to securities with a three-year or longer history, even though doing so potentially induces a survivorship bias *à la* Brown, Goetzmann, Ibbotson, and Ross (1992). Removing the names with less than three years of daily data left a sample of 5,983 observations.

Breaking up the sample into 100-stock groups, we perform an in-sample decomposition of returns via SVD on each group over the entire 2018, comprising 251 daily observations. The returns for each security i are computed as simple daily returns, $R_{i,t} = P_{i,t}/P_{i,t-1} - 1$, where $P_{i,t}$ is a closing price for a stock i on day t. The returns for every 100 stocks are arranged in an $n \times m$ matrix with $n = 251$ days in rows and $m = 100$ stocks in columns.

Each 251×100 matrix, representing a group of 251 daily returns for 100 stocks, was decomposed using SVD into matrices $U_{251 \times 251}$, $S_{251 \times 100}$, and $V_{100 \times 100}$. The matrix S is diagonal, that is, it is zeros everywhere except on the diagonal. The diagonal of S contains the singular values of the matrix, ordered from the largest to the smallest. The 100×1 vectors comprising the V matrix are known as the singular vectors and are the factors driving each given set of returns. All the columns of V, the singular vectors, are completely uncorrelated with each other, or orthogonal to each other, by construction, as discussed later in this chapter. The singular vectors, like their corresponding singular values, are ordered from the most impactful on the global return scale to the least impactful. The least important singular vectors are often considered to represent the qualities pertaining to the individual stocks, known as idiosyncratic properties.

The first singular vector is the most impactful across all the securities in the group. It is a linear combination of the returns series in the original returns matrix. Each value of the 100 within the first singular vector corresponds to the coefficient with which the given stock's returns vector is included in the singular vector. To illustrate the output of SVD, Table 5.3 shows the most positive and the most negative return contributions, as determined by SVD, in a portfolio composed from the first 100 stocks.

It is interesting to note that ETFs and pharmaceutical companies dominate the positive and the negative ends of the first singular vector. Similar results can be observed in the other 100-share groups. For example, Table 5.3 shows the most common securities that appeared as the top influencers in the singular value decomposition when all the traded securities were randomly drawn into groups of 200 with replacement. Here, the process of random 200-stock portfolio construction was repeated 1,000 times.

What are the top drivers of the random portfolios? Table 5.4 shows the names of securities that appeared at least twice as the highest coefficient in the first singular vector in 1,000 randomly picked portfolios. The portfolios were chosen randomly with replacement from the universe of all the securities traded in the United States over the 2018–2019 period.

As Table 5.4 shows, 12 out of 31 security names that appear at least in two portfolios as the top influencer in the top singular vector are ETFs or ETNs. In other words, even in a perfectly random portfolio, we have a decent chance of finding an ETF that well represents the underlying returns.

Why is this significant? As shown in Avellaneda and Lee (2010), in times of downward volatility, many investors would like to sell their portfolio holdings at the same time. In many cases, this results in severe liquidity shortages. To overcome the issue, investors sell the most liquid security available, such as NYSE:SPY. Next, the investors gradually rebalance their portfolios to buy back the liquid security and sell their actual portfolio holdings. The resulting approach allows investors to lock in the effects of the downward volatility and mitigate their losses. As Aldridge (2016) shows, the approach has been growing in popularity, as demonstrated by the ever increasing correlations between downward volatility and traded volume of NYSE:SPY (Figure 5.10). Identifying the

Table 5.3 Proportions of individual stock returns in the A-AEF Group (100 stocks) included in the first singular vector, as determined by SVD.

Stock symbol	Description	Proportion in the first singular vector
	Most positive	
ACWI	The iShares MSCI ACWI ETF seeks to track the investment results of an index composed of large and mid-capitalization developed and emerging market equities	0.3718
ACRX	AcelRx Pharmaceuticals, Inc., a specialty manufacturer of treatments for acute pain	0.3367
ADME	Aptus Drawdown Managed Equity ETF, that seeks out US stocks exhibiting strong yield plus growth characteristics, and includes market hedges	0.2706
ADMP	Adamis Pharmaceuticals Corporation, a specialty manufacturer of treatments for respiratory disease and allergies	0.2076
ACNB	ACNB Corporation, a parent holding company for Russell Insurance Group, Inc., ACNB Bank, Bankersre Insurance Group, Spc	0.2034
ACRS	Aclaris Therapeutics, Inc., manufacturer of specialty treatments in dermatology, both medical and aesthetic, and immunology	0.1116
ADSK	Autodesk, Inc., a maker of software for the architecture, engineering, construction, manufacturing, media, education, and entertainment industries	0.1107
ACN	Accenture plc, a Fortune 500 professional services company that provides services in strategy, consulting, digital, technology, and operations.	0.1013
ACSI	American Customer Satisfaction ETF, that seeks to track the performance, before fees and expenses, of the American Customer Satisfaction Investable Index	0.0987
ACU	Acme United Corporation, a supplier of cutting, measuring, and safety products for the school, home, office, hardware, and industrial markets	0.0972
	Most negative	
ACST	Acasti Pharma, a specialty manufacturer of cardiovascular treatments	-0.3473
ACT	AdvisorShares Vice ETF, tracking select alcohol and tobacco companies	-0.2409
ADMS	Adamas Pharmaceuticals, a specialty manufacturer of treatment for chronic neurological diseases	-0.2226
ACOR	Acorda Therapeutics, Inc., a specialty manufacturer of neurology therapies for Parkinson's disease, migraine, and multiple sclerosis	-0.2057
ACWX	iShares MSCI ACWI ex U.S. ETF, tracking large and mid-cap equities outside of the U.S.	-0.1903

Table 5.3   continued

Stock symbol	Description	Proportion in the first singular vector
ADES	Advanced Emissions Solutions, Inc., a holding company for a family of companies that provide emissions solutions to customers in the coal-fired power generation, industrial boiler, and cement industries	-0.1485
ADNT	Adient PLC, a manufacturer of automotive seating for customers worldwide	-0.1368
ACH	Aluminum Corporation of China Limited, the world's second-largest alumina producer and third-largest primary aluminum producer at the time this book was written	-0.1331
ACP	Aberdeen Income Credit Strategies Fund, a non-diversified, closed-end management investment company	-0.1265
ADRE	Invesco BLDRS Emerging Markets 50 ADR Index Fund	-0.1054

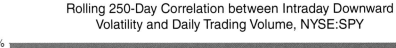

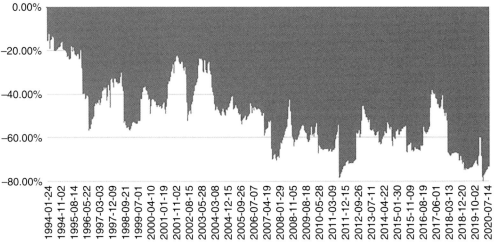

Figure 5.10   Rolling 250-day correlations between intraday downward volatility and volume of NYSE:SPY. Based on Aldridge (2016).

exact ETF driving the portfolio may deliver more precise outcomes in times of downward volatility than a blanket sell-off of NYSE:SPY.

For instance, in the initial days of the COVID-19 crisis emergence in the United States, investment professionals struggled to unload investments quickly in a rapidly declining market. The example below illustrates a practical way to hedge the sell-off by selecting and selling the most appropriate ETF, and then gradually rebalancing the portfolio to their desired composition.

Table 5.4 The most common top positive factors in the first singular value out of 10,000 portfolios of 200 stocks each selected randomly with replacement from the entire universe of securities traded in the U.S. for the 2018 calendar year.

Symbol	Name	Sector
ICOL	iShares MSCI Colombia ETF (ICOL)	ETF
CHD	Church & Dwight Co., Inc. (CHD)	Consumer Defensive, Household & Personal Products
DJP	iPath Bloomberg Commodity Index Total Return (SM) ETN (DJP)	ETN
AGEN	Agenus, Inc. (AGEN)	Healthcare, Biotechnology
EDU	New Oriental Education & Technology Group, Inc. (EDU)	Consumer Defensive, Education & Training Services
VER	VEREIT, Inc. (VER)	Real Estate, REIT—Diversified
ECH	iShares MSCI Chile Capped ETF (ECH)	ETF
KEP	Korea Electric Power Corporation (KEP)	Utilities, Utilities—Regulated Electric
NEOS	Neos Therapeutics, Inc. (NEOS)	Healthcare, Drug Manufacturers—Specialty & Generic
XWEB	SPDR S&P Internet ETF (XWEB)	ETF
EEMV	iShares Edge MSCI Min Vol Emerging Markets ETF (EEMV)	ETF
PSMB	Invesco Balanced Multi-Asset Allocation ETF (PSMB)	ETF
TDW	Tidewater, Inc. (TDW)	Energy, Oil & Gas Equipment & Services
OII	iPath Series B S&P GSCI Crude Oil Total Return Index ETN (OIL)	ETN
DLX	Deluxe Corporation (DLX)	Communication Services, Advertising Agencies
ADRO	Aduro BioTech, Inc. (ADRO)	Healthcare, Biotechnology
PNI	PIMCO New York Municipal Income Fund II (PNI)	ETF
MPB	Mid Penn Bancorp, Inc. (MPB)	Financial Services, Banks—Regional
NAT	Nordic American Tankers Limited (NAT)	Industrials, Marine Shipping
FLTR	VanEck Vectors Investment Grade Floating Rate ETF (FLTR)	ETF
BKI	Black Knight, Inc. (BKI)	Technology, Software—Infrastructure
NMRK	Newmark Group, Inc. (NMRK)	Real Estate, Real Estate Services
VRTV	Veritiv Corporation (VRTV)	Industrials, Business Equipment & Supplies
JAN	JanOne, Inc. (JAN)	Industrials, Waste Management
IAT	iShares U.S. Regional Banks ETF (IAT)	ETF
DCP	DCP Midstream, LP (DCP)	Energy, Oil & Gas Midstream
DEUR	Citigroup ETNs linked to the VelocityShares Daily 4X Long USD vs. EUR Index (DEUR)	ETN
ZEUS	Olympic Steel, Inc. (ZEUS)	Basic Materials, Steel
BOXL	Boxlight Corporation (BOXL)	Technology, Communication Equipment
REDU	RISE Education Cayman Ltd (REDU)	Consumer Defensive, Education & Training Services
RVRS	Reverse Cap Weighted U.S. Large Cap ETF (RVRS)	ETF

Table 5.5 Correlation of the top-ten eigenvectors of the Russell 3000 stocks with ETFs (highest and lowest ETF correlation shown) and Fama-French factors in 2018 (Fama and French 1992, 1993).

# Eigenvector	Maximum Correlation ETF (%)	Minimum Correlation ETF (%)	Correlation with Excess Market R (%)	Correlation with SMB (%)	Correlation with HML (%)
1	18.1, ACH	−19.1, AACG	6.6	−2.2	2.4
2	44.0, AFB	−25.1, ABEV	12.8	1.2	−1.5
3	21.0, AGG	−49.4, ADRA	−11.6	0.0	−1.7
4	58.5, AGGE	−47.7, AGT	−2.0	−3.0	2.5
5	24.4, AGZ	−24.0, AZUL	2.9	15.3	−5.9
6	17.1, BSCM	−20.6, EDEN	2.3	7.9	1.3
7	25.6, GDO	−19.7, EZT	4.9	5.0	4.2
8	15.6, AB	−18.2, WPP	1.1	−1.3	−1.8
9	22.5, ABEV	−21.2, AACG	7.8	−8.3	−2.8
10	26.8, ACT	−24.5, AAXJ	4.6	2.9	−2.6

Why is selection of the best-fit ETF a problem warranting its own solution? As discussed earlier in this chapter, selling SPY in times of downward volatility has become a go-to strategy for portfolio managers. In times of crises, when most of the investors rush over to short SPY, doing so becomes unreasonably expensive. Separately, the number of ETFs has exploded in recent years. As of January 2020, for example, the Boston Stock Exchange has traded 5,179 stocks and 4,176 non-stock issues, including ETFs, electronically-traded notes (ETNs), and American Depository Receipts (ADRs), the latter being proxies for the foreign-traded shares. With the number of non-corporate securities rapidly approaching and even threatening to exceed the number of publicly traded shares, there may be a reasonably-priced SPY alternative for pretty much most equity portfolios!

As Table 5.5 shows, ETFs dominated Russell 3000 in 2018. Returns on certain ETFs like AGGE, ADRA, and AGT were highly positively and negatively correlated with returns composed of eigenvector allocations based on dimensionality reduction of Russell 3000 returns. The highest positive correlation was due to AGGE (IQ Enhanced Core Bond U.S. ETF that ceased trading on February 4, 2020, according to ET.com), followed by AFB (AllianceBernstein National Municipal Income Fund). AGGE showed 58.5% correlation with the fourth eigenvector-portfolio of Russell 3000 returns in 2018 while AFB registered 44% correlation with the second eigenvector of the Russell 3000 returns. The funds most negatively correlated with the Russell 3000 eigenvectors were ADRA (Invesco BLDRS Asia 50 ADR Index Fund, ceased trading on February 14, 2020) and AGT (iShares MSCI Argentina and Global Exposure ETF). ADRA showed -49.4% correlation with the third eigenvector of Russell 3000, and AGT delivered -47.7% with the fourth eigenvector.

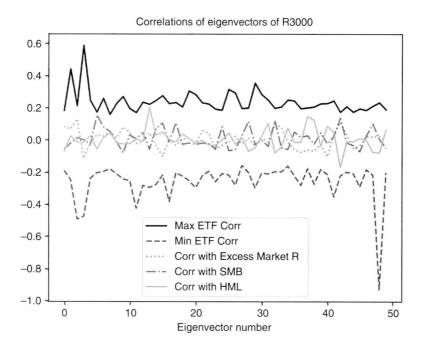

Figure 5.11 2018 returns' eigenvectors' correlation with contemporaneous Fama-French factors and all contemporaneous ETFs.

To benchmark the factor correlations, we compare that with the correlations of the Fama and French factors. According to the Fama and French classic three-factor model (Fama and French 1992, 1993), financial returns can be explained by:

- excess market return (Rm – Rf)
- growth: HML ("High Book-to-Value Minus Low Book-to-Value" portfolio returns)
- size: SML ("Small Minus Large" portfolio returns).

As shown in Table 5.5 and Figure 5.11, the highest Fama-French factor correlations were reached by the excess market return with the second eigenvector portfolio of the Russell 3000 returns (12.8%), SMB with the fifth eigenvector portfolio (15.3%), and HML with the seventh eigenvector portfolio (just 4.2%). Potentially, the dominance of ETFs can explain the increasingly poor performance of the Fama-French factors, documented on the Kenneth French website (https://mba.tuck.dartmouth.edu/pages/faculty/ken.french/data_library.html).

Why did AGGE and ADRA shut down? The coronavirus COVID-19 crisis was sweeping the world in February 2020. AGGE and ADRA perhaps wisely stopped operating to avoid catastrophic losses. However, AFB only lost 22% while the S&P 500 was down 33% of its pre-crisis high. AGT, on the other hand, lost 45% of value in a span of a few days. Also, while the sell-off in SPY and AGT began on February 20, 2020, AFB held strong through March 6. All three securities reached the bottom on March 23, 2020.

Table 5.5 further compares COVID-crisis performance of the top-five ETFs most positively and negatively correlated with the top eigenvectors of the Russell 3000 index. As Table 5.5 shows, the most positively correlated ETFs have largely retained their value

Table 5.6   Covid crisis performance of the ETFs most correlated with the top-ten eigenvectors of the Russell 3000.

# Eigenvector	Maximum Correlation ETF	Minimum Correlation ETF
1	ACH Jan. 6–Mar. 26, 2020, -48.05%	AACG Oct. 2019–Mar. 23, 2020, -60.0%
2	AFB Mar. 6–Mar. 23, 2020, -23%	ABEV Jan. 2–Mar. 16, 2020, -55.39%
3	AGG March 9–18, 2020, -8.6%	ADRA Stopped trading Feb. 14, 2020
4	AGGE Stopped trading Feb. 4, 2020	AGT Feb. 20–Mar. 20, 2020, -45.08%
5	AGZ Feb. 6–Mar. 9, 2020, +4.3%	AZUL Feb. 5–Mar. 18, 2020, -86.16%

through the crisis while the most negatively correlated ETFs lost an extreme proportion of their equity, often way in excess of the -32.10% drop in the S&P 500 over Feb. 20–Mar. 23, 2020. It is likely that the top positively correlated ETFs indeed will capture the core structure of the Russell 3000 and retain a higher proportion of their values in crises.

Interestingly, the top positively correlated issue was an ADR for Aluminum Corporation of China Limited (ACH), which understandably performed poorly due to the economic devastation in China. At the same time, the next top issues were all bond funds: AllianceBernstein National Municipal Income Fund (AFB), iShares Core U.S. Aggregate Bond ETF (AGG), IQ Enhanced Core Bond U.S. ETF (AGGE), and iShares Agency Bond ETF (AGZ).

On the negative correlation side, the top funds covered emerging markets, in a sense, the antithesis of Russell 3000: ATA Creativity Global (AACG), a Chinese education company, Ambev S.A. (ABEV), a Brazilian beverage manufacturer, Invesco BLDRS Asia 50 ADR Index Fund (ADRA), iShares MSCI Argentina and Global Exposure ETF (AGT), and Azul S.A. (AZUL), a Brazilian airline. Figures illustrate the performance of the top issues positively correlated ("good") and negatively correlated ("bad") with the top-five eigenvectors of the Russell 3000 returns (Table 5.6) (Figures 5.12 and 5.13).

The application of the principal component regression presented here illustrates an investment strategy that dives into the "surrogate" core structure issues of financial data. Instead of investing in the Russell 3000 itself, we consider the proxies for the drivers of the Russell 3000 returns. Investing in the core drivers delivered relative stability in the COVID-19 crisis. Overall, issues like China Aluminum have delivered growth (until the crash) while the bond funds buoyed the portfolio. Avoiding issues negatively correlated with the top eigenvectors helps to further bullet-proof the portfolio against the crises.

Figures 5.14 and 5.15 further show performance of the "good" and "bad" ETFs selected based on 2018 data through 2019 and the COVID crisis. As Figures 5.14 and 5.15 show, ACH indeed led SPY throughout 2019 and early 2020.

Using Singular Vectors as Portfolio Weights

Since singular vectors represent the core of the data, it is natural to ask whether they can be used in portfolio construction. Can the weights of the individual securities forming the first singular vector or vectors in proxying their respective 100-stock groups be used

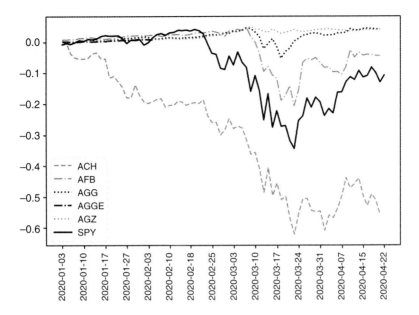

Figure 5.12 January–April 2020 Performance of the issues most positively correlated with the top-five eigenvectors of the Russell 3000. Except for Aluminum Corporation of China Limited (ACH), most outperformed the S&P 500 during the COVID crisis.

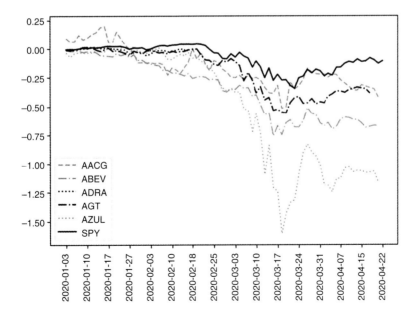

Figure 5.13 January–April 2020 Performance of the issues most negatively correlated with the top-five eigenvectors of the Russell 3000. All underperformed the S&P 500 during the COVID crisis.

to form portfolios of stocks that outperform the market? Since these weights represent the dominant drivers of the returns of the 100 stocks, shouldn't the portfolio with these weights outperform the equally weighted portfolio?

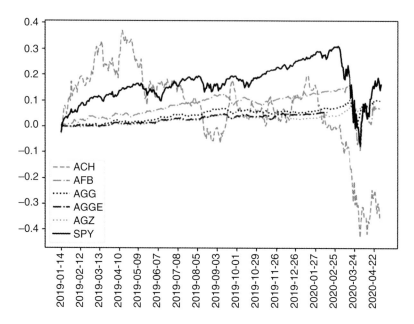

Figure 5.14 January 2019-April 2020 Performance of the issues most positively correlated with the top five eigenvectors of the Russell 3000.

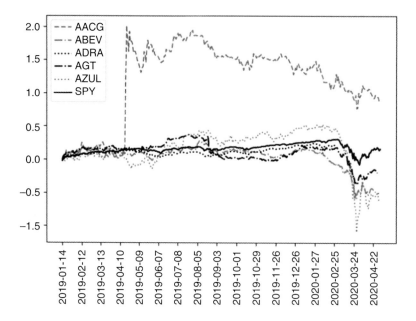

Figure 5.15 January 2019-April 2020 Performance of the issues most negatively correlated with the top five eigenvectors of the Russell 3000.

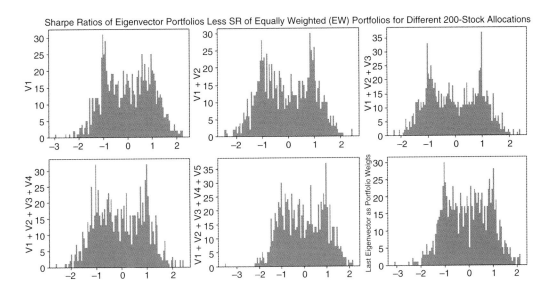

Figure 5.16 Distribution of Excess Sharpe ratios (SR of Portfolio less SR of the Equally Weighted Portfolio) of 1,000 random portfolios allocated according to the coefficients of their returns' first 5 singular vectors and the very last singular vector. All the portfolio Sharpe ratios are adjusted by their Equally Weighted Sharpe ratio.

As Figure 5.16 shows, the portfolios based on top singular vectors of their returns have a bimodal distribution and do not necessarily outperform equally weighted allocation on the respective securities. Specifically, portfolios in Figures 5.10–5.13 were constructed by drawing 200 random names from the entire universe of securities traded in the United States. The instruments that were not traded for the entire 2018–2019 span were next removed from the portfolios. For each of the resulting portfolios, the singular vectors were calculated over the 2018 returns. The performance shown was determined in-sample over the 2018 data, with the weights of the top-5 singular vectors as well as the very last singular vector serving as the weights of the portfolios under consideration.

As Figures 5.17 and 5.18 show, positive and negative singular vectors deliver portfolios that are positively and negatively correlated with the benchmarks, such as the equally weighted portfolio. Long-only portfolios consisting of just positive elements of the first 5 and the very last singular vectors are positively correlated with the equally weighted portfolios made up of the same elements. Short-only portfolios that include just negative elements of the first 5 and the last singular vectors are negatively correlated with the equally weighted portfolios.

Factorized portfolios show that, as the number of singular vectors comprising the portfolios increases, the average returns decrease. At the same time, the return variances decrease as well, resulting in stable, slightly positive Sharpe ratios (Figure 5.19).

Of course, the classic portfolio management theory relates the optimal portfolio construction to the covariance and correlations of returns, not returns themselves. The technique of eigenportfolios, discussed in detail in Chapter 6, applies dimensionality reduction to large correlation matrices. The key idea there is that the correlation data may not be driven by all the correlations in the matrices. Preserving the most important

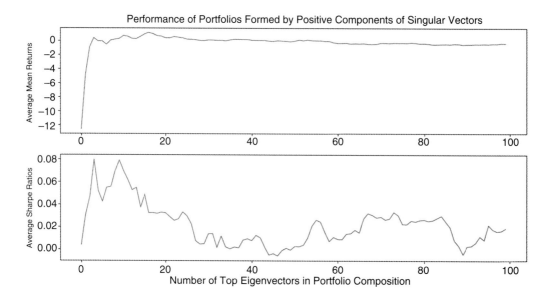

Figure 5.17 Average performance of 1,000 of positive-only components of 1–50 singular vectors. Portfolios consisting of only positive components around 40 singular vectors outperform as measured by mean Sharpe ratios.

correlations and removing some of the less important correlations allow us to overcome the dimensionality curse as well as produce stable results. As a result of such an application, the computational time required for trading, portfolio management, and risk management applications may be substantially reduced.

Principal Component Regression

Another application of dimensionality reduction is principal component regression, also known as eigenregression. In a principal component regression, the dependent variable is regressed not on other variables in the data set, but on linear combinations of these variables as determined by top eigenvalues and eigenvectors. This approach is particularly useful when the sample is short, relative to its number of features, that is, when the sample has a low rank. Traditional econometric modeling stumbles in this situation, but principal component analysis allows the key relationships in the features (columns of the data) to be condensed into a tightly packed wad of information.

Eigenvalues and eigenvectors can be thought of as the core representation of the data, or its most important characteristics. The motivation behind the principal component regression then is to elucidate the dependent variable's characteristics vis-à-vis these powerful eigenvalue-driven factors.

As an example of an application of the principal component regression, consider financial data analysis that covers the entire healthcare industry (665 stocks), but only over the past quarter (63 trading days). A traditional econometrician would insist that no such analysis can be performed on data with fewer than 665 daily observations. The principal component regression, however, allows us to intelligently compress the number

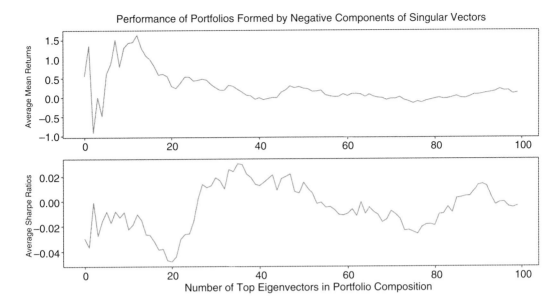

Figure 5.18   Average performance of 1,000 of negative-only components of 1–100 singular vectors. Portfolios consisting of only positive components around 40 singular vectors outperform as measured by mean Sharpe ratios.

of stocks into its most meaningful portfolios and analyze the latter over a much shorter time interval.

Key Big Data Tools: SVD and PCA in Detail

Singular value decomposition (SVD) was briefly introduced in the previous section. Here, we dive in depth into some of the key tools and techniques that will be used throughout much of the book. To showcase the usefulness of the tools, they are presented in the context of a meaningful application: dimensionality reduction.

The power of dimensionality reduction via SVD was graphically illustrated in the previous section. In non-graphical data, dimensionality reduction involves finding a new, smaller set of columns, all of which are some linear combination of the original columns, such that the new column set retains as much data variability and information from the original set as possible. Mathematically, dimensionality reduction is a projection of high-dimensional data onto lower-dimensional data. Given n data points $x_1, x_2, \ldots x_n$ in R^p, we would like to project the data onto a smaller data set of d dimensions, $d < p$. This is very useful when dealing with large unwieldy portfolios like the S&P 500 or Russell 3000. Our objective is to find a d-dimensional projection that preserves as much variance of $x_1, x_2, \ldots x_n$ as possible.

Most PCA- and SVD-based methods operate on the second-moment conditions: they seek to find the orthogonal axes that explain the most data variation.

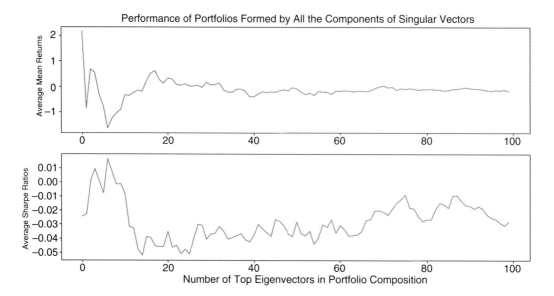

Figure 5.19   Average performance of 1,000 of positive and negative components of 1–100 singular vectors. Portfolios comprising securities weighted by the coefficients of 3 and 4 singular vectors outperform the rest as measured by both the average mean return and the mean Sharpe ratio of the 1,000 random portfolios under consideration. After the fourth singular vector, the portfolio performance drops off sharply in either the mean return, mean Sharpe ratio, or both.

SVD.   The SVD of a matrix A is the factorization of A into three matrices: $A = USV^T$ where the columns of U and V are orthonormal, and the matrix S is diagonal with positive real entries. The SVD is an important technique for the Big Data Science used extensively throughout this book.

The singular value decomposition (SVD) of a matrix A is the factorization of the matrix into the product of three matrices:

$$A = USV^T \qquad (5.3)$$

where all the columns of U and V are orthogonal to each other and normalized to be unit vectors, or *orthonormal* for short, and where the singular value matrix S is diagonal with real positive values (a diagonal matrix may have non-zero values only on its diagonal, and has zeros everywhere else). The columns of V are known as the right singular vectors of A and always form an orthogonal set with no assumptions on A. Similarly, the columns of V are known as the left singular vectors of A and also always form an orthogonal set with no assumptions on A. Due to the orthogonality of U and V, whenever the matrix A is square and invertible, the inverse of A is:

$$A^{-1} = VS^{-1}U^T$$

This property becomes very useful in finance applications dealing with matrix inverses, like portfolio management.

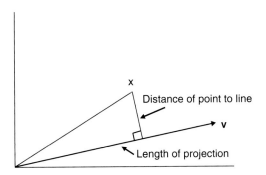

Figure 5.20 An illustration of the relationship between distance of point to line and length of the projection.

In general, however, the matrix A does not need to be square – unlike PCA that requires the input data to be strictly square, SVD happily takes on rectangular matrices. If A is $n \times d$, its rows are n points in a d-dimensional space. SVD then can be thought of as the algorithm finding the best k-dimensional ($k < d$) subspace with respect to the points of A. This can be done via *best least squares fit* by minimizing the sum of the squares of the perpendicular distances of the points to the subspace. An alternative is to find the function to minimize the y axis distance to the subspace of the x_i.

When $k = 1$, the subspace is a line through the origin. To project the point $x_i = [x_{i1} \ x_{i2} \ \dots \ x_{id}]$ onto the line via the best least squares fit, we need to minimize the perpendicular distance of point to line, shown in Figure 5.20. By Pythagoras Theorem,

$$(Distance \ of \ point \ to \ line)^2 = (x_{i1}^2 + x_{i2}^2 + \ \dots \ + x_{id}^2) - (length \ of \ projection)^2$$

Since $(x_{i1}^2 + x_{i2}^2 + \ \dots \ + x_{id}^2)$ is independent of the line, minimizing $(Distance \ of \ point \ to \ line)^2$ is equivalent to maximizing the $(length \ of \ projection)^2$.

The singular vectors of an $n \times d$ matrix A are unit vectors v on the lines through the origin that maximize the lengths of projection for different dimensions. If x_i is the ith row of A, a_i, then the length of the projection of a_i on v is $|a_i \cdot v|$. The sum of the lengths squared of all projections is then $|Av|^2$. The best fit line maximizes $|Av|^2$. The Greedy SVD algorithm then works as follows.

The *first singular vector*, v_1, of A is the best fit line through the origin for the n points in the d-dimensional space that are rows of A:

$$v_1 = arg \ max_{|v|=1}|Av|$$

The value of $\sigma_1(A) = |Av_1|$ is known as the first singular value of A; $\sigma_1^2(A)$ is the sum of the squares of the projections to the line determined by v_1.

The *second singular vector*, v_2, is defined by the best fit line perpendicular to the first singular vector, v_1:

$$v_2 = arg \ max_{v \perp v_1, |v|=1}|Av|$$

and the value $\sigma_2(A) = |Av_2|$ is known as the second singular value of A.

The *third singular vector*, v_3, is defined by the best fit line perpendicular to the first two singular vectors, v_1 and v_2:

$$v_2 = arg\ max_{v \perp v_1, v_2, |v|=1} |Av|$$

And the value $\sigma_3(A) = |Av_3|$ is known as the third singular value of A.

The process is repeated until the rth singular vector, v_r, is found. It can be shown that the number of orthogonal singular vectors of the matrix A equals the rank of A, r. Next, we can define the left singular vectors as $u_i = \frac{1}{\sigma_i} Av_i$, also orthogonal to each other for $i = 1, 2, \ldots, r$, and formalize the SVD as $A = \sum_{i=1}^{r} \sigma_i u_i v_i^T$. From now on, we'll refer to v_i as right-singular vector.

PCA. SVD is a close cousin of PCA. PCA was introduced well over 100 years ago by Pearson (1901). Given the data set $x_1, x_2, \ldots x_n$ with the sample mean, μ_n, and sample covariance, Σ_n shown in Eqs. (5.4) and (5.5), respectively:

$$\mu_n = \frac{1}{n} \sum_{k=1}^{n} x_k \tag{5.4}$$

$$\Sigma_n = \frac{1}{n-1} \sum_{k=1}^{n} (x_k - \mu_n)(x_k - \mu_n) \tag{5.5}$$

Even though the data set $x_1, x_2, \ldots x_n$ may only be a subset of some larger data distribution, if $x_1, x_2, \ldots x_n$ are sampled independently from that larger distribution, it can be shown that μ_n and Σ_n are unbiased estimators of the mean and covariance of the larger distribution.

Formally, PCA's objective is to find the d-dimensional orthonormal basis $V = [v_1, \ldots, v_d]$, $V^T V = I_{d \times d}$, such that the projection of $X = [x_1, \ldots x_n]$ on V has the most variance. This is equivalent to seeking the most variance for $V^T X$. Hence, our PCA optimization problem becomes:

$$max_{V^T V = I} \sum_{k=1}^{n} \left\| V^T x_k - \frac{1}{n} \sum_{r=1}^{n} V^T x_r \right\|^2 = max_{V^T V = I} \sum_{k=1}^{n} || V^T (x_k - \mu_n) ||^2 \tag{5.6}$$

$$= max_{V^T V = I} Tr(V^T \Sigma_n V) \tag{5.7}$$

$$= \sum_{i=1}^{d} v_i \lambda_i, \tag{5.8}$$

where λ_i are the leading eigenvalues of the sample covariance of $x_1, x_2, \ldots x_n$, Σ_n, and $V = [v_1, \ldots, v_d]$ are the associated eigenvectors.

PCA vs. SVD. PCA requires finding the eigenvalues of the covariance of data, Σ_n. To do PCA, therefore, one first needs to construct the covariance matrix Σ_n, which takes $\mathcal{O}(np^2)$ computational time, and then find the eigenvalues of the covariance matrix in $\mathcal{O}(p^3)$ time. The resulting computational complexity of the process is $\mathcal{O}(max\{np^2, p^3\})$ (see, e.g., Horn and Johnson (1985) and Golub (1996)).

SVD, on the other hand, seeks eigenvalues of demeaned data, instead of the covariance matrix. That is, SVD decomposes $X - \mu_n I^T$ into the Unitary vectors U, a diagonal matrix of singular values S, and singular vectors V, which are identical to the eigenvectors generated by PCA:

$$X - \mu_n I^T = USV^T \tag{5.9}$$

To convert from SVD to PCA is as easy as to observe that, by Eqs. (5.5) and (5.9), the covariance matrix of X is

$$\Sigma = \frac{1}{n-1}(X - \mu_n I^T)(X - \mu_n I^T)^T = \frac{1}{n-1}(USV^T)(USV^T)^T = \frac{1}{n-1}VSU^TUSV^T \tag{5.10}$$

$$= V\frac{S^2}{n-1}V^T = V\Lambda V^T$$

where Λ are the eigenvalues computed by PCA.

From Eq (5.10), eigenvalues computed by PCA are $\Lambda = \frac{S^2}{n-1}$.

While we obtain the same result with PCA and SVD, the computational load of SVD, $O(min(np^2, n^2p))$, is a lot lighter than PCA. An added advantage of SVD vs. PCA is the unitary matrix U, which describes how each row relates to each eigenvector – an added informational dimension.

In addition to being comparatively computationally complex, PCA may cause a loss of precision as well as the outright inability to compute the result. Classic examples like the Läuchli matrix (Läuchli 1967) showcases where PCA fails to converge altogether while SVD delivers solid computation.

Norms. Two important matrix norms, the Frobenius norm, $||A||_F$, and the 2-norm, $||A||_2$, are also often used throughout this book. The 2-norm, $||A||_2$, is formally defined as

$$||A||_2 = max_{|v|=1}|Av|$$

and is thus equal to the largest eigenvalue of A.

It can also be shown that the sum of squares of the singular values equals the Frobenius norm squared,

$$\sum_i \sigma_i^2(A) = ||A||_F^2$$

Computing PCA and SVD

Techniques like PCA and SVD are central to data science and help speed up processes and quickly infer meaning by retrieving the structure of the data. Even though PCA and SVD are critical to data scientists today, they originated in the twentieth century. Today, researchers are looking for ways to improve on the traditional PCA and SVD: (i) to speed up the computation further; (ii) to take advantage of the developments in other fields, like Random Matrix Theory, that did not exist when PCA and SVD were created; and (iii) to make PCA and SVD work even more efficiently with today's computational technology that has drastically improved since PCA and SVD first came to light.

Most off-the-shelf programming packages offered built-in PCA and SVD functionality at the time this book was written. However, in many cases, off-the-shelf PCA and SVD calculations take up a significant portion of the programming resources. In some programs, while still drastically outperforming traditional non–Big Data methods, PCA and SVD create bottlenecks, accounting for a disproportionately large calculation time compared to the rest of the data logic.

The computational efficiency of PCA and SVD can be measured by the speed of processing an arbitrarily large data set. After all, isn't this what Big Data is all about? However, in the current advanced, but still growing, power of computing technology, extremely large data sets may still be hard to process. Instead, researchers deploy stochastic techniques to randomly sample the data. These *online* methods grab a random slice of data, thereby creating a smaller data set that is still representative of the original big data set. Next, PCA or SVD is applied to the smaller data sample, and the sampling process is repeated until a certain stopping condition is met and the results are aggregated. In this approach, the algorithm may process the entire data set or only a portion thereof.

Another metric of the algorithm efficiency is the iteration complexity. Iteration complexity measures the number of loops taken by the algorithm; the fewer the loops, the more efficient the computation. Breaking up the sample and iterating over each piece generates a large number of loops, something that takes up potentially large computational time.

The computational time required to produce SVD estimates depends on the algorithm. The most popular algorithms for SVD over the years have been the power algorithm (Hotelling 1933) and the Lanczos algorithm (Lanczos 1958).

Over the years, researchers have strived to improve the efficiency of PCA and SVD calculations. As a result, several powerful "Golden standard" algorithms emerged and are presented in this section that may or may not be part of the off-the-shelf solutions and may warrant in-house implementation. These algorithms include the power algorithm and its extensions, including a range of Lanczos algorithms, various stochastic approaches, and Fast SVD, discussed in this chapter.

The Power Algorithm for SVD and PCA Estimation. The power algorithm is simple, yet robust and has been extended in many forms over the years and is the basis for many SVD and PCA algorithms. The name "power" refers to the process of self-multiplying matrices, or raising them to a power, in order to determine the singular values and vectors. Here, we first consider a sketch of the case of the power method applied to a square symmetric matrix, and then generalize the result to any $n \times m$ matrix.

When matrix A is square symmetric, under certain assumptions, it can be represented as it has the same right and left singular vectors v_i:

$$A = \sum_{i=1}^{m} \sigma_i v_i v_i^T$$

Next,

$$A^2 = \left(\sum_{i=1}^{m} \sigma_i v_i v_i^T \right) \left(\sum_{j=1}^{m} \sigma_j v_j v_j^T \right) = \sum_{i,j=1}^{m} \sigma_i \sigma_j v_i v_i^T v_j v_j^T$$

Since the inner product $v_i^T v_j = 0$ whenever $i \neq j$ by orthogonality (the outer product $v_i v_j^T$ is not 0),

$$A^2 = \sum_{i,j=1}^{m} \sigma_i \sigma_j v_i v_i^T v_j v_j^T = \sum_{i=1}^{m} \sigma_i^2 v_i v_i^T$$

In general, if we raised A to the power k,

$$A^k = \sum_{i=1}^{m} \sigma_i^k v_i v_i^T$$

With $\sigma_1 > \sigma_2 > \ldots > \sigma_k$,

$$\frac{1}{\sigma_1^k} A^k \to v_1 v_1^T$$

Since σ_1 is unknown at this point, we cannot compute A^k directly. However, dividing A^k by its Frobenius norm $||A^k||_F = \sqrt{\sum_{j=1}^{m} \sum_{i=1}^{m} |a_{i,j}|^2}$ results in matrix A converging to the rank 1 matrix $v_1 v_1^T$. From the latter, we can compute v_1.

In general, the assumption of a square and symmetric matrix A having the same left and right eigenvectors is too strong. However, we can always find $B = AA^T$ that satisfies our original assumptions. If A can be decomposed, say, via SVD, into $A = \sum_i \sigma_i u_i v_i^T$, then the spectral decomposition of B is:

$$B = AA^T = \left(\sum_i \sigma_i u_i v_i^T \right) \left(\sum_i \sigma_i u_i v_i^T \right) = \sum_{i,j} \sigma_i \sigma_j u_i v_i^T v_j u_j^T = \sum_{i,j} \sigma_i^2 u_i u_i^T$$

since $v_i^T v_j = 0$ for all $i \neq j$ due to orthogonality. Furthermore, powering up B produces

$$B^k = \sum_{i,j} \sigma_i^{2k} u_i u_i^T \text{ if } \sigma_i < \sigma_1$$

As k increases, for $i > 1$ and $\sigma_i(A) < \sigma_1(A)$, $\sigma_i^2 / \sigma_1^2 \to 0$, and so

$$B^k \to \sigma_i^{2k} u_i u_i^T$$

Thus, the power method involves powering up the data in order to determine the associated eigenvalues. The convergence of the power method can be shown to be achieved quickly if there is a significant gap Δ between the first and the second eigenvalues. Known as the *eigen-gap*, Δ is a common determinant of the speed of SVD and PCA algorithms as it determines the speed with which eigenvalues can be separated from each other. The higher the gap, the easier it is to separate the eigenvalues and reach decomposition.

Computing B^k costs k matrix multiplications, or $O(k)$, if matrices are multiplied by B once per iteration. To reduce the complexity, successively squaring B^k lowers the complexity to $O(log(k))$. Computing $B^k x$, where x is a randomly chosen unit vector, lowers the complexity further to $O(1/\Delta)$ iterations and can operate in a stochastic sample-driven fashion. The Lanczos method, due to Lanczos (1958), optimizes the power method in the direction of the extreme highest and lowest eigenvalues and typically takes $O(1/\sqrt{\Delta})$ iterations. Due to its directionality, the Lanczos method needs to work with a full sample, i.e., it cannot work in the online environment.

Optimization of the performance of PCA and SVD calculations was an active area of research at the time this book was written. The algorithm by Liberty, Woolfe, Martinsson, Rokhlin, and Tygert (2007), dubbed Fast SVD, uses Fast Fourier Transform to speed up the computation. Musco and Musco (2015) use bootstrapping via the block Krylov method to derive convergence independent of the eigen-gap Δ. Bhojanapalli, Jain, and Sanghavi (2015) use alternating minimization to achieve a low-complexity performance in sub-sampling of the matrix. Shamir (2016) proposes a stochastic variance-reduction PCA. Xu, He, De Sa, Mitliagkas, and Ré (2018) propose an extension of the power method, power iteration with momentum, that works online and achieves Lanczos performance of $O(1/\sqrt{\Delta})$ iterations.

Fast SVD. Fast SVD due to Liberty, Woolfe, Martinsson, Rokhlin, and Tygert (2007), discussed in this section, is one of the recent improvements of the technique. Liberty et al. apply the randomization and Fast Fourier Transform (FFT) to traditional SVD to dramatically increase its computational speed. Due to the application of FFT to randomization, their algorithm also has a finite probability of failure; however, Liberty et al. estimate that this probability is on the order of 10^{-17}.

To create the fast version of SVD, Liberty et al. first create interpolative decompositions (IDs), described in this section, and then convert IDs into SVD. An ID is an approximate decomposition of any matrix $A_{m \times n}$ of rank k into a product of two matrices:

- a subset of matrix A, $B_{m \times k}$, and
- matrix $P_{k \times n}$, such that, by Lemma (1) in Liberty et al. (2007):
    - Some set of the columns of P makes up an identity matrix $k \times k$.
    - The absolute values of all entries of P are less than or equal to 1
    - $||P_{k \times n}||_2 \le \sqrt{k(n-k)+1}$
    - The least, same as the kth greatest singular value of P is at least 1
    - When $k = m$ or $k = n$, $B_{m \times k} P_{k \times n} = A_{m \times n}$

- When $k < m$ or $k < n$, $||B_{m \times k} P_{k \times n} - A_{m \times n}||_2 \leq (\sqrt{k(n-k)+1})\sigma_{k+1}$, where σ_{k+1} is the $(k+1)$st greatest singular value of A.

The approximation $B_{m \times k} P_{k \times n} \approx A_{m \times n}$ is then numerically stable and is referred to as the interpolative decomposition (ID) of A.

At the core of Liberty et al.'s research is a speedy randomized Discrete Fourier Transform. The transform is a uniform random sampler S of a Discrete Fourier Transform F of diagonal matrices D to use in the fast computation of the IDs, following Ailon and Chazelle (2006):

- D is a diagonal $m \times m$ matrix with complex independent and identically distributed random-variable entries $d_1, d_2, \ldots, d_m$, distributed uniformly on the unit circle.
- F is the $m \times m$ Discrete Fourier Transform with $F_{i,j} = exp(-2\pi\sqrt{-1}\,(i-1)(j-1)/m)$.
- S is a real $l \times m$ matrix, an operator that uniformly randomly selects rows from the product of F and D. As such, all of the entries of S are 0 except for one 1 in the diagonal in each of the randomly selected columns j, with j uniformly drawn with replacement from $j = \{1, 2 \ldots m\}$.

The resulting speedy randomized Discrete Fourier Transform is an operator

$$\Phi_{l \times m} = S_{l \times m} F_{m \times m} D_{m \times m}$$

with the cost of applying Φ to any arbitrary vector via Sorrensen and Burrus (1993) being

$$C_{m,l} = O(m \, log(l))$$

Armed with the speedy randomized Discrete Fourier Transform, Liberty et al. (2007) describe two algorithms for Interpolative Decomposition (ID), followed by an algorithm of converting ID into SVD.

Conclusion

PCA and SVD are powerful techniques that allow researchers to distill the structure of the data, identifying key drivers. The drivers let the data speak for themselves, without requiring the researchers to provide traditional hypotheses. The techniques are potentially game-changers in modern finance.

These Big Data methods allow us to process large data sets quickly, without adding computing power, saving corporations millions of dollars by timely short-term identification of impending risk events. The Big Data Science hypothesis-less paradigm further allows more reliable and efficient conclusions to be drawn by removing researchers' subjectivity in posing the research question.

Appendix 5.A PCA and SVD in Python

Both PCA and SVD are easy to program in Python.

To obtain the first five principal components of a dataset X, all one needs to write is the following code:

```
from sklearn.decomposition import PCA
pca = PCA(n_components=5)
PCs = pca.fit_transform(X)
```

Of course, PCA is based on analyzing variance of the data, so it helps when all the columns of the data are standardized to approximate the $N(0,1)$ distribution. Luckily for us, the standardization of data is also taken care of in Python and is done with the following code:

```
from sklearn.preprocessing import StandardScaler
X = StandardScaler().fit_transform(X)
```

Such pre-processing of data is now a standard feature in many applications and produces better predictions than relying on raw data as inputs.

PCA's cousin, SVD, is equally easy to build in Python. The matrices U, S, and V of SVD decomposition of matrix X can be obtained with the following two lines of code:

```
from scipy import linalg
U, s, Vh = linalg.svd(X)
```

The simplicity and elegance of the Python code make the analysis fast, simple, and even very enjoyable!

For specific code examples, please visit https://www.BigDataFinanceBook.com, and register with password *SVD* (case-sensitive).

References

Ailon, N. and Chazelle, B. (2006). Approximate nearest neighbors and the fast Johnson-Lindenstrauss transform. In: *Proceedings of the Thirty-Eighth Annual ACM Symposium on the Theory of Computing, 557–563*. New York: ACM Press.

Aldridge, I. (2016). ETFs, high-frequency trading, and flash crashes. *The Journal of Portfolio Management* 43(1): 17–28.

Avellaneda, M. and Lee, J. (2010). Statistical arbitrage in the U.S. equities market. Quantitative Finance 10(7): 761–782.

Bhojanapalli, S., Jain, P., and Sanghavi, S. (2015). Tighter low-rank approximation via sampling the leveraged element. *SODA* 902–920.

Brown, S.J., Goetzmann, W., Ibbotson, R.G., and Ross, S.A. (1992). Survivorship bias in performance studies. *The Review of Financial Studies* 5(4): 553–580.

Fama, E. and French, K. (1992). The cross-section of expected stock returns. *Journal of Finance* 47: 427–465.

Fama, E. and French, K. (1993). Common risk factors in the returns on stocks and bonds. *Journal of Financial Economics* 33: 3–56.

Fan, J., Fan, Y., and Lv, J. (2008). High dimensional covariance matrix estimation using a factor model. *Journal of Econometrics* 147: 186–197.

Golub, G.H. (1996). *Matrix Computations*. 3rd ed. Baltimore, MD: Johns Hopkins University Press.

Horn, R.A. and Johnson, C.R. (1985). *Matrix Analysis*. Cambridge: Cambridge University Press.

Hotelling, H. (1933). Analysis of a complex of statistical variables into principal components. *Journal of Educational Psychology* 24(6): 417.

Johnstone, I.M. (2001). On the distribution of the largest eigenvalue in principal components analysis. *Annals of Statistics* 29: 295–327.

Lanczos, C. (1958). Linear systems in self-adjoint form. *American Mathematical Monthly* 65: 665–679.

Läuchli, P. (1961). Jordan-Elimination und Ausgleichung nach kleinsten Quadraten. *Numerical Mathematics* 3: 226. https://doi.org/10.1007/BF01386022.

Liberty, E., Woolfe, F., Martinsson, P., Rokhlin, V., and Tygert, M. (2007). Fast SVD. *PNAS* 104(51): 20167–20172.

Lintner, J. (1965). The valuation of risk assets and the selection of risky investments in stock portfolios and capital budgets. *Review of Economics and Statistics* 47(1): 13–37.

Musco, C. and Musco, C. (2015). Randomized block Krylov methods for stronger and faster approximate singular value decomposition. *NIPS* (2015): 1396–1404.

Pearson, K. (1901). On lines and planes of closest fit to systems of points in space. *Philosophical Magazine Series* 6, 2(11): 559–572.

Ross, S.A. (1976). The arbitrage theory of capital asset pricing. *Journal of Economic Theory* 13: 341–360.

Ross, S.A. (1977). The Capital Asset Pricing Model (CAPM), short-sale restrictions and related issues. *Journal of Finance* 32: 177–183.

Shamir, O. (2016). Fast stochastic algorithms for SVD and PCA: Convergence properties and convexity. In: *Proceedings of the 33rd International Conference on Machine Learning*, New York.

Sharpe, W.F. (1964). Capital asset prices: A theory of market equilibrium under conditions of risk. *Journal of Finance* 19(3): 425–442.

Sorrensen, H.V. and Burrus, C.S. (1993). Efficient computation of the DFT with only a subset of input or output points. *IEEE Transactions on Signal Processing* 41: 1184–1200.

Stewart, G. (1993). On the early history of the singular value decomposition. SIAM Review 35(4): 551–566.

Xu, P., He, B., De Sa, C., Mitliagkas, I., and Ré, C. (2018). Accelerated stochastic power iteration. In: *Proceedings of International Conference on Artificial Intelligence and Statistics* (AISTATS), *PMLR* 84: 58–67.

Chapter 6

Big Data Factor Models

A s shown in Chapter 5, unsupervised learning delivers essential cleansing of the data, separating "macro" signal components common to all the dataset elements from the idiosyncratic noise of individual data constituents. The singular vectors produced by SVD are orthogonal by design and also serve as data factors.

Factoring financial data has been widely accepted and practiced. Sharpe's (1964) and Lintner's (1965) Capital Asset Pricing Model (CAPM) factorizes returns of financial instruments vis-à-vis market returns. Ross's (1976; 1977) Arbitrage Pricing Theory (APT) factors financial returns over a wide spectrum of diverse explanatory variables. The famed Fama-French factors (Fama and French 1992) explain securities returns by stock characteristics. Harvey, Liu, and Zhu (2016) point out that, over the years, researchers in finance have come up with over 300 factors capable of explaining various aspects of financial returns, all published in the financial research literature. The sheer number of proposed financial factors led Cochrane (2011) to refer to the multitude of variables as a "factor zoo" and to question various factors' validity and relative importance.

As this chapter shows, unsupervised learning techniques deliver the optimal factorization. As such, SVD and PCA are also perfectly positioned to sort through the "zoo" in a fast and efficient manner, extracting most meaningful factors from the explanatory variables proposed to date.

Why PCA and SVD Deliver Optimal Factorization

Consider again our objective of finding a d-dimensional projection that preserves as much variance of $x_1, x_2, \ldots x_n$ as possible. Finance practitioners will quickly recognize the idea as factoring. Dating back to Ross's (1976; 1977) Arbitrage Pricing Theory, returns on assets were expressed as linear combinations of other, fewer, returns or macroeconomic variables. The key difference of Big Data dimensionality reduction versus traditional factor models of Finance is factor identification. In traditional Finance, all factors are well known in advance, while in Data Science, the projection process discerns the best factors available for the job to be done. In other words, in Finance, the factoring begins with factor selection by a researcher, and proceeds with the researcher validating or disputing his hypothesis. In Big Data, the factoring process itself uncovers the optimal factors from a large data set. This section mathematically shows how factoring of any data into the $d < n$ factors that capture the most variance is indeed PCA and, referencing Chapter 5, SVD.

Once again, given n data points $x_1, x_2, \ldots x_n$ in R^p, we would like to project the data onto a smaller dataset of d dimensions, $d < p$. Our data factorization problem then becomes:

$$x_k \approx \mu + \beta \sum_{i=1}^{d} (\beta_k)_i v_i \tag{6.1}$$

where we are trying to approximate each x_k with $d < n$ factors. Here, β_k are familiar factor coefficients of the d new factors, $v_1, v_2, \ldots v_d$. Ideally, the factors are not at all correlated, and thus form, once again, *an orthonormal basis for a d-dimensional subspace*. If the factors are indeed uncorrelated, that is, orthogonal to each other, they can be collectively represented by a vector $V = [v_1, v_2, \ldots v_d] \in R^{p \times d}$, such that

$$V^T V = I_{d \times d} \tag{6.2}$$

Then, Eq (6.1) becomes:

$$x_k \approx \mu + V\beta_k \tag{6.3}$$

To measure how well the factors V fit the data $x_1, x_2, \ldots x_n$ we can use least squares:

$$\min_{V, \mu, \beta_k} \sum_{k=1}^{n} \left\| x_k - (\mu + V\beta_k) \right\|_2^2 \tag{6.4}$$

To optimize for μ, we solve the first-order conditions with respect to μ to find the optimal value of μ, μ^*:

$$\sum_{k=1}^{n} (x_k - (\mu^* + V\beta_k)) = 0 \tag{6.5}$$

which expands into

$$\sum_{k=1}^{n}(x_k) - n\mu^* + V\sum_{k=1}^{n}(\beta_k) = 0 \tag{6.6}$$

Since $\sum_{k=1}^{n}(\beta_k) = 0$, we obtain that the optimal value of μ^* is the sample mean:

$$\mu^* = \frac{1}{n}\sum_{k=1}^{n}(x_k) = \mu_n \tag{6.7}$$

The optimization of Eq (6.4) can be decoupled for each k and becomes:

$$\min_{\beta_k}\left\|x_k - \mu_n - V\beta_k\right\|_2^2 = \min_{\beta_k}\left\|x_k - \mu_n - \sum_{i=1}^{d}(\beta_k)_i v_i\right\|_2^2 \tag{6.8}$$

Carrying on and optimizing the first-order condition of Eq (6.8) with respect to β_k we obtain:

$$(\beta_k)_i = v_i^T(x_k - \mu_n) \tag{6.9}$$

or, more generally:

$$\beta_k = V^T(x_k - \mu_n) \tag{6.10}$$

Now, the optimization of Eq (6.10) can be rewritten as:

$$\min_{V^TV=I}||(x_k - \mu_n) - VV^T(x_k - \mu_n)||_2^2 \tag{6.11}$$

which is equivalent to

$$\begin{aligned}
&\min_{V^TV=I}(x_k - \mu_n)^T(x_k - \mu_n) - 2(x_k - \mu_n)^TVV^T(x_k - \mu_n)\\
&+(x_k - \mu_n)^TV(V^TV)V^T(x_k - \mu_n)\\
&= \min_{V^TV=I}(x_k - \mu_n)^T(x_k - \mu_n) - (x_k - \mu_n)^TVV^T(x_k - \mu_n)\\
&= \max_{V^TV=I}(x_k - \mu_n)^TVV^T(x_k - \mu_n) \tag{6.12}
\end{aligned}$$

since $(x_k - \mu_n)^T(x_k - \mu_n)$ does not depend on V. Using properties of Tr, such as $Tr(A + B) = Tr(A) + Tr(B)$, the optimization of Eq (6.12) can be rewritten as

$$\begin{aligned}
&\max_{V^TV=I}\sum_{k=1}^{n}(x_k - \mu_n)^TVV^T(x_k - \mu_n)\\
&= \max_{V^TV=I}Tr\left[\sum_{k=1}^{n}(x_k - \mu_n)^TVV^T(x_k - \mu_n)\right]\\
&= \max_{V^TV=I}\sum_{k=1}^{n}Tr[(x_k - \mu_n)^TVV^T(x_k - \mu_n)]\\
&= \max_{V^TV=I}Tr[V^T(x_k - \mu_n)(x_k - \mu_n)^TV]\\
&= \max_{V^TV=I}(n-1)Tr[V^T\Sigma_nV]\\
&= \max_{V^TV=I}Tr[V^T\Sigma_nV] = \sum_{i=1}^{d}v_i\lambda_i \tag{6.13}
\end{aligned}$$

where λ_i are the leading eigenvalues of the sample covariance of $x_1, x_2, \ldots x_n$, Σ_n. The latter expression is, of course, PCA, showing that the optimal factoring is indeed PCA itself!

Eigenportfolios

While PCA delivers the optimal linear factor structure with given factors, the factors themselves may in principle be nonlinear functions of observed or latent variables outside of the scope of the original data set. For example, the best factors identified by PCA and SVD in the stock return data may be economic indicators outside of the scope of the original data set.

Following the optimal portfolio theory dating back to Markowitz (1952), the portfolio optimization problem further relies on the interaction of returns, factors, and other variables impacting the financial markets. The key idea of a successful portfolio composition is diversification. The diversification simply states that an optimal portfolio should withstand all states: the downturns, severe crises, and periods of sunny growth. To do so, the optimal portfolio should contain instruments, the returns of which may move in the opposite directions to offset losses on some with gains on others. The interaction between returns can be measured using covariances, and, in more detail, correlations. The more uncorrelated the returns in a portfolio, the higher is the portfolio's likelihood of withstanding potential shocks.

With the number of financial securities traded in the United States. easily hitting 8,000 at the time this book was written, the problem of portfolio selection becomes too big to manage in conventional ways. The Big Data analysis comes in extremely handy in managing portfolio optimization.

To determine the optimal factors of returns in portfolio composition, we observe that the first eigenvector is the solution of the variational problem

$$V^{(1)} = \text{argmax}\{ V^t R \; V; ||V|| = 1 \} \tag{6.14}$$

where N is the number of assets and $||\cdot||$ is the Euclidean norm in R^N. Various candidates for R have been proposed, as discussed throughout this chapter. Equation (6.14) shows that the principal eigenvector is the vector which captures the most variance of matrix R.

The principal eigenvector satisfies

$$R \; V^{(1)} = \lambda^{(1)} V^{(1)} \tag{6.15}$$

The other eigenvectors and eigenvalues are computed in the same way, but restricting the maximization over the sub-space of vectors which are orthogonal to the space spanned by the ones computed previously, i.e.,

$$V^{(k)} = \text{argmax}\{ V^t R \; V; ||V|| = 1, \;\; V \cdot V^l = 0, l < k \}, \tag{6.16}$$

$$R \; V^{(k)} = \lambda^{(k)} V^{(k)} \tag{6.17}$$

The eigenvalues satisfy $\lambda^{(1)} > \lambda^{(2)} \geq \ldots \geq \lambda^{(N)}$.

The Karhunen-Loève representation (see, for example, Watanabe 1965) of the standardized asset returns X_j is

$$X_j = \sum_{k=1}^{N} \sqrt{\lambda^{(k)}} \; V_j^{(k)} F^{(k)}$$

with

$$F^{(k)} = \frac{1}{\sqrt{\lambda^{(k)}}} \sum_{j=1}^{N} V_i^{(k)} X_i \tag{6.18}$$

By construction, $F^{(k)}$ are uncorrelated and have variance = 1. Since these random variables are linear combinations of the standardized returns of the assets, we call them "eigenportfolios" (Avellaneda and Lee 2010), with the caveat that the "weights" should be divided by the volatility of each asset, in order to convert to economic, portfolio-theoretic, units.

The PCA is a way of learning about the system of asset returns in terms of its variability and the determination of common factors affecting the returns. The first eigenportfolio, associated with the r.v. $F^{(1)}$, is a common factor which explains the maximum variability, and we have

$$X_j = \beta_j F^{(1)} + \varepsilon_j$$

where β_j is the regression coefficient of the standardized return on the first EP. The "residuals" ε_j are uncorrelated with $F^{(1)}$, which is nice, but they are generally correlated for two different stocks.

The second EP is extracted from the ε_j, j=1, ... ,N.

In the following discussions relating PCA factorization, we will often refer to factors and factor loadings. The factors, often referred to as eigenportfolios, are defined as

$$F^{(k)} = \frac{1}{\sqrt{\lambda^{(k)}}} \sum_{j=1}^{N} V_i^{(k)} X_i$$

Factor loadings β are the coefficients relating the dependent variable to the factors:

$$X_j = \beta_{j,k} F^{(k)} + \varepsilon_j$$

An important consideration is whether all EPS should be used in the Karhunen-Loève representation. In the case of economic data, which is noisy, the idea is to disregard EPs which correspond to low eigenvalues. In a celebrated paper, Laloux et al. (2000) proposed using RMT to model the standardized returns as:

$$X_j = \sum_{k=1}^{m} \beta_j^{(k)} F^{(k)} + \varepsilon_j$$

where $\beta_j^{(k)}$ are "factor loadings" and ε_j are uncorrelated, m is a cutoff which is to be determined from the context.

While the original Big Data factorization of market data, which has become known as the approximate factor model, is due to Connor and Korajczyk (1986; 1998), the ideas have been extended in many different directions. Despite the optimality of the spectral factorization shown in the previous section, some data and models require more management. Methodologies tweaking basic spectral analysis discussed in this Chapter include Fan, Fan, and Lv (2008), Doz, Giannone, and Reichlin (2011), Fan, Liao, and Mincheva (2013), and Avellaneda (2019).

Using Factors to Predict Returns

Stock and Watson (2002) consider a universe of known candidate predictors, an N-dimensional time series matrix X_t. The objective is to find the best predictors for future realizations of another time series y_{t+h}. Thus, X_t may represent economic variables and y_{t+h} forward-looking market returns, h steps ahead. Stock and Watson's (2002) method first decomposes the economic variable series into orthogonal factors using PCA, $X_t = \Lambda F_t + e_t$, where F_t are r latent factors common to the predictor set X_t. Next, Stock and Watson build a common-factor predictive regression for y_{t+h}, where the right-hand side includes factors F_t as well as autoregressive components $\{y_t, \ldots, y_{t+h}\}$:

$$y_{t+h} = \beta_F F_t + \gamma_1 y_{t+h-1} + \gamma_2 y_{t+h-2} + \ldots + \gamma_h y_t$$

Factor Discovery

While Stock and Watson's (2002) goal was successful prediction of y_{t+h}, in other situations, the main objective may be identification of the factors F_t themselves. To uniquely identify the factors, Bai and Ng (2013) point out that for the PCA-based factors to identify uniquely, the corresponding eigenvalues must be distinct.

In discussion of both methodologies below, we will follow the common notation. At the core of both Doz, Giannone, and Reichlin's (2011) and Fan, Liao, and Mincheva's (2013) methodologies is an approximate factor model that has been used by Chamberlain and Rothschild (1983), Fama and French (1993), Bai and Ng (2002), and others:

$$y_{it} = \beta_{i1} f_{t1} + \beta_{i2} f_{t2} + \ldots + \beta_{iK} f_{tK} + u_{it}$$

where y_{it} is the time-t return on the ith asset, or more generally, y_{it} is the time-t response of the ith variable, $t = 1, 2, \ldots, T$; β_{ij} is the factor loading corresponding to the jth factor and ith return, $i = i, 2, \ldots p, j = 1, 2, \ldots K$, and f_{tj} is the value of the jth factor or principal component at time t. The returns y_{it} depend only on the contemporaneous values of f_{tj}, and not the lagged values with t–1, t–2, etc. To accommodate large dimensionality, both p and T are assumed to diverge to infinity, but the number of factors K remains fixed. Furthermore, to model realistic data conditions, p is assumed to be potentially much larger than T, $p \gg T$.

In the model, only γ_{it} is observable. The reliability of inferring the unknown common factors increases as the number of variable increases, with $p \to \infty$. In matrix notation,

$$Y_t = BF_t + U_t$$

where $Y_t = (\gamma_{1t}, \gamma_{2t}, \ldots \gamma_{pt})'$, B is a $p \times K$ matrix of factor loadings for instruments Y_t, $F_t = (f_{1t}, f_{2t}, \ldots f_{Kt})$, and U_t is a vector of errors, $U_t = (u_{1t}, u_{2t}, \ldots u_{pt})'$.

Assuming that the $p \times p$ covariance matrix of returns Y_t, Σ, is time-invariant, we obtain

$$\Sigma = B \, cov(F_t) \, B' + \Sigma_U$$

where $\Sigma_U = (\sigma_{u,ij})_{p \times p}$ is the covariance of U_t.

Unknown Factors: Creating Factor Approximations

Traditional econometric modeling of the latent factors involves regressing the data on a set of potential factor candidates or even a vector of ones to proxy for the unknown factor. Stock and Watson (2006), Bai and Ng (2002; 2008; 2013), Ludvigson and Ng (2009), Onatski (2010, 2012), Doz, Giannone, and Reichlin (2011), Aït-Sahalia and Xiu (2017), and Lettau and Pelger (2018) consider factor estimation using PCA and its variants. Since the factors are not known and are constructed from PCA inferences, the models have become known as *approximate factor models*.

Doz, Giannone, and Reichlin (2011) approximate unknown factors in time series data with the following methodology:

1. Run Singular Value Decomposition (SVD) on the raw data, with dates in rows and features in columns.
2. Assume that the first K principal components are the true factors.
3. Run Ordinary Least Squares (OLS), regressing the raw data on the K principal components to find factor loadings.

The key idea here is that the observable variables Y_t can be decomposed into two orthogonal unobserved processes:

1. The common component driven by a few common shocks. The common component captures much of the covariation between the time series.
2. Idiosyncratic component driven by time-series-specific dynamics.

The first K principal components represent the common components or factors. To investigate the idiosyncratic components, Doz, Giannone, and Reichlin (2011) further apply Kalman filtering to the tail principal components.

Unknown Factors: The POET Method

Fan, Liao, and Mincheva (2013) account for the unobservable factors influencing the covariance structure.

The decomposition $Y_t = BF_t + U_t$ is considered to be asymptotically identified as $p \to \infty$ if all of the eigenvalues of Σ_U are bounded as $p \to \infty$ and the first K eigenvalues of $B \, cov(F_t) \, B'$ diverge at rate $O(p)$. Per Fan, Liao, and Mincheva (2013), the assumption holds whenever a considerable fraction of factor loadings are non-vanishing. Furthermore, Fan, Liao, and Mincheva (2013) assume that Σ_U is approximately sparse in the sense of Bickel and Levina (2008) and Rothman et al. (2009):

$$m_p = max_{i \leq p} \sum_{j \leq p} |\sigma_{u,ij}|^q \text{ for some } q \in [0, 1)$$

A condition $q = 0$ defines the exact sparsity assumption, under which the maximum number of non-zero elements in each row is $m_p = max_{i \leq p} \Sigma_{j \leq p} I_{\sigma_{u,ij} \neq 0}$.

When the factors are observable, one can use regression analysis to estimate $\{U_t\}_{t=1}^T$ following Fan, Liao, and Mincheva (2011).

When the factors are not observable, Fan, Liao, and Mincheva (2013) develop a thresholding optimization-free procedure for inferring the factors using only the data from the sample covariance matrix $\hat{\Sigma}_{sam}$ of Y_t.

The estimator, dubbed POET for Principal Orthogonal ComplEment Thresholding, is computed in the following steps:

1. Run the Singular Value Decomposition (SVD) on the sample covariance matrix $\hat{\Sigma}_{sam}$ of Y_t.
2. Keep the covariance matrix formed by the first K singular values (if K is unknown, it can be estimated from data).
3. Apply the thresholding procedure to the remaining covariance matrix.

The thresholding of the "rest" of the covariance matrix, not captured by the first K principal components, is applied following Rothman et al. (2009) and Cai and Liu (2011) and can be summarized as follows:

• If the elements of the sample covariance matrix not captured by the first K eigenvalues exceed a certain entry-dependent threshold $\tau_{ij} > 0$, then they remain intact.
• The elements of the sample covariance matrix not captured by the first K eigenvalues that fall below the threshold, however, are transformed. A common transformation is $s_{ij}()$, a generalized shrinkage function of Antoniadis and Fan (2001), employed by Rothman et al. (2009) and Cai and Liu (2011), and $\tau_{ij} > 0$ is an entry-dependent threshold. The simplest version of the shrinkage function is known as hard-thresholding and was used by Bickel and Levina (2008): $s_{ij}(x) = x \, I(|x| \geq \tau_{ij})$, whereby all entries the absolute values of which are not meeting the threshold are set to 0.

Fan, Liao, and Micheva (2013) show that the rate of convergence for the POET estimator for Σ_U achieves the optimal rate in Cai and Zhou (2012).

Following Fan, Liao, and Micheva (2013), we perform SVD on the covariance of returns of the S&P 500, then reconstruct the factor from the data by taking into account

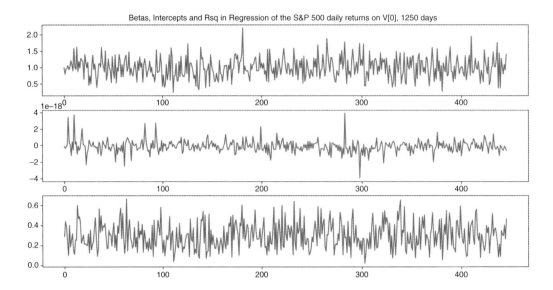

Figure 6.1 In-sample explanatory power of the first "eigenfactor" or principal component for the S&P 500 daily returns, 2013–2017.

only the first singular value and the associated eigenvector. Next, we perform a linear regression analysis to evaluate the explanatory performance of the factor on the S&P 500 returns in sample. Figure 6.1 shows the regression coefficient beta, the intercept, and the explanatory power, R^2, of the regression of returns of the stocks comprising the S&P 500 on the daily realizations of our newly created factor $R_{f0,t}$:

$$R_{i,t} = \alpha_i + \beta_i R_{f0,t} + \varepsilon_{i,t}$$

As Figure 6.1 shows, the first eigenfactor performs rather well. The betas tend to hover around 1, indicating a solid correspondence between the returns of the individual S&P 500 constituents and the eigenfactor. The intercept is practically nonexistent, registering on the scale of 10^{-18}. The explanatory power of the factor model is also quite high as measured by R^2: it often reaches 40% and above, indicating that a significant portion of daily returns find correspondence in the daily factor variation.

How does this factor perform relative to the established factor models, for example, the famed Capital Asset Pricing Model (CAPM)? To establish this frame of reference, we perform a similar factor analysis on the market "factor," which we take to be the average daily S&P 500 returns for the purpose of this exercise:

$$R_{i,t} = \alpha_i + \beta_i R_{M,t} + \varepsilon_{i,t}$$

$$R_{M,t} = \frac{1}{N} \sum_{i=1}^{N} R_{i,t}$$

Figure 6.2 shows the slope β_i, the intercept α_i, and the explanatory power R^2 of the regression.

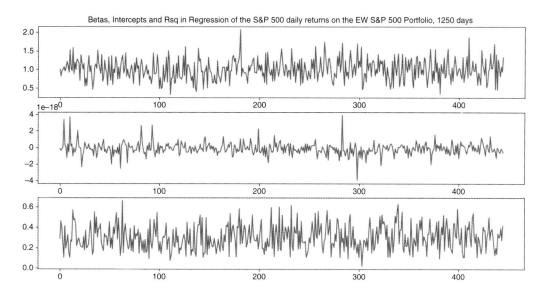

Figure 6.2 In-sample explanatory power of the market portfolio (here, the daily equally weighted average return of the S&P 500) for the S&P 500 daily returns, 2013–2017.

Comparing the performance of the first eigenfactor in Figure 6.1 and the market portfolio in Figure 6.2, we notice considerable similarities. The regression coefficients β_i, the intercept α_i, and even the explanatory power R^2 of the two models appear similar. To ascertain the relationship between the two models, we next plot the betas of the two models against each other. The results are shown in Figure 6.3.

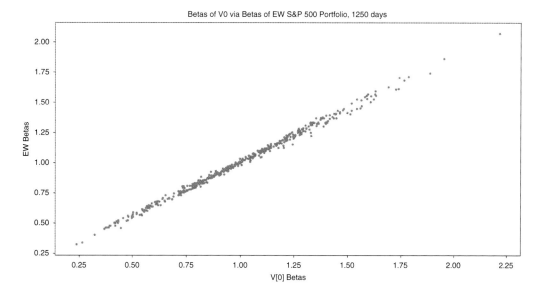

Figure 6.3 In-sample regression coefficients β_i of the Equally Weighted S&P 500 portfolio plotted versus those of the first eigenfactor for each of the S&P 500 constituents, 2013–2017.

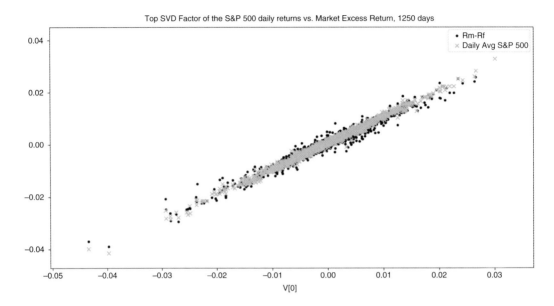

Figure 6.4 First principal component vs. daily average return on the S&P 500 and the excess market return, 2013–2017. The daily average return is proving to be a better fit for the first factor identified by the PCA than excess market returns.

What does this say about the first eigenfactor vis-à-vis the market portfolio? In Figure 6.4, the two time series are plotted against one another. As Figure 6.4 shows, the two produce nearly identical results. SVD says that the first and most important optimal factor for the S&P daily returns is market returns! In other words, CAPM still rules, but with a caveat: the "market" returns are best represented by the average returns on the S&P 500 portfolio, and not the traditional excess returns on the market.

To illustrate the point, Figure 6.4 compares the top eigenportfolio with the average returns on the S&P 500 portfolio and the traditional excess returns on the market obtained from the website of Kenneth French (https://mba.tuck.dartmouth.edu/pages/faculty/ken.french/data_library.html). As Figure 6.4 shows, the average daily S&P 500 returns provide a much tighter fit to the top eigenvector than does the excess market return.

Interestingly, the nice and orderly relationship shown in Figure 6.4 breaks down when the analysis is carried out on Russell 3000, approaching the results discussed in Chapter 5 instead.

Instrumented PCA

Kelly, Pruitt, and Su (2017) follow Connor, Hagmann, and Linton (2012) to produce Instrumented PCA to address typical time invariance of the factor loadings, a.k.a. eigenvalues or singular components generated by PCA or SVD. In their model, Kelly, Pruitt, and Su allow factor loadings $\beta'_{n,t-1}$ to vary with time by introducing time dependencies via instrumental variables $z'_{n,t-1}$ as follows:

$$y_{n,t} = \beta'_{n,t-1} f_t + \varepsilon_{n,t}$$

$$\beta'_{n,t-1} = z'_{n,t-1} \Gamma + v'_{n,t-1}$$

where K is the total number of latent factors f, L is the number of instruments z, Γ is an $L \times K$ mapping from instruments to loadings, and $v'_{n,t-1}$ allows for unobservable time variation of factor loadings, which may or may not capture the true variation. Whenever the number of instruments is greater than or equal to the number of latent factors, $L \geq K$, the Instrumented PCA applies PCA to a transformed problem where y depends on the observed instrumental variables z.

The Three-Pass Model

The three-pass model of Giglio and Xiu (2019) combines PCA with two-pass cross-sectional regressions to provide consistent estimates for risk premia for unobserved factors. To do so, Giglio and Xiu first run PCA on a large panel of return data to extract the optimal factors and their loadings. Next, the researchers find the risk premia of the principal components identified in the previous step by regressing the principal components on the returns. Finally, they regress candidate factors of interest, like economic indexes hypothesized to explain returns, on the principal components to find the identifiable traditional factors that best fit the PCA-discovered principal components.

Risk-Premium PCA

Lettau and Pelger (2019) argue that the traditional PCA is not adequate in factor identification as it only focuses on the second moments by seeking the dimensions that capture the most variation in the data. Instead, Lettau and Pelger propose a Risk-Premium PCA (RP-PCA) that takes into account and optimizes over the levels of returns and indexes in addition to their variability. Lettau and Pelger apply RP-PCA and show that the approach yields higher Sharpe ratios and lower pricing errors than traditional PCA factorization.

Nonlinear Factorization

While PCA delivers optimal linear factorization, it leaves some researchers questioning its true potential. These questions arise in particular with respect to the PCA/SVD performance versus machine learning techniques that can deliver a lot more nonlinear estimates. In response, a number of nonlinear PCA models have been developed.

Projected PCA

While PCA provides the optimal factorization for linear factoring problems, the variable relationships may not always be best approximated by linear models. Fan, Liao, and Wang (2016) develop a methodology whereby PCA can be applied to select the optimal underlying functional form, away from basic linear relation. Specifically, the researchers include B-spline, Fourier series, polynomial series, and wavelets in the set of feasible functionals, over which they subsequently optimize with PCA.

Fan, Liao, and Wang (2016) consider a situation where the factor loadings of the factorized data X are themselves functions of the underlying data X, specifically to determine the semi-parametric model

$$y_{it} = \sum_{k=1}^{K} g_k(X_i) f_{tk} + u_{it}$$

Fan, Liao, and Wang (2016) propose representing $g_k(X_i)$ as a projection

$$\beta_{ik} = g_k(X_i) + \gamma_{ik}, i = 1, \dots p, k = 1, \dots, K$$

where $E[\gamma_{ik}] = 0$, and γ_{ik} is independent of u_{it} and X_i. This technique is closely following the supervised singular value decomposition model of Li, Yang, Nobel, and Shen (2015).

Next, each component $g_k(X_i) = \sum_{l=1}^{d} g_{kl}(X_{il}), d = dim(X_i)$ is estimated by the sieve method (see, for example, Chen (2007)). We define a set of basic functions $\Phi = \{\phi_1, \phi_2, \dots \}$, that can comprise B-spline, Fourier series, polynomial series, and wavelets. Here, Φ spans a dense linear space of the functional space for g_{kl}. For each $l \leq d$,

$$g_{kl}(X_{il}) = \sum_{j=1}^{J} b_{j,kl} \phi_j(X_{il}) + R_{kl}(X_{il})$$

where $R(X)$ is the remainder function not captured by $\sum_{j=1}^{J} b_{j,kl} \phi_j(X_{il})$ and representing the approximation error, J is the number of sieve terms that grows slowly as $p \to \infty$ with $sup_x |R_{kl}(X)| \to 0$ as $J \to 0$.

In the special case of constant $\phi_j(X_{il})$, $g_k(X_i) = \beta$, the model reduces to the traditional factor model:

$$y_{it} = \sum_{k=1}^{K} g_k(X_i) f_{tk} + u_{it} = \sum_{k=1}^{K} [g_k(X_i) + \gamma_{ik}] f_{tk} + u_{it} = \beta f_t + \gamma_i f_t + u_{it}$$

The Projected PCA of Fan, Liao, and Wang (2016) allows us to determine the optimal nonlinear functional for the underlying data X, potentially enabling us to detect latent variables with nonlinear relationships where linear aggregation may fail.

Correlation-Based Factors

Laloux et al. (2000), Cizeau, Potters, and Bouchaud (2000), and Avellaneda and Lee (2010) show that the decomposition of the covariance of the returns results in potentially highly correlated covariance structure. Since all financial instruments gain volatility along with the market during high-risk events, covariance-based factors reflect common volatility and produce highly correlated residuals. In other words, when returns on the jth instrument, $R_j = \sum_{k=1}^{m} \beta_j^{(k)} F^{(k)} + \varepsilon_j$, where $F^{(k)}$ is the kth eigenportfolio based on the singular vector generated in the covariance decomposition, $E[\varepsilon_j \varepsilon_i] \neq 0$. To overcome this issue, Laloux et al. (2000), Cizeau, Potters, and Bouchaud (2000), and Avellaneda and Lee (2010) and Avellaneda (2019) use the returns correlation as the basis for portfolio weights calculation, instead of covariance.

How do correlation-based eigenportfolios stack up against covariance-based factorization in practice? Figures 6.5–6.10 show the performance of correlation-based and covariance-based factorization when the factor analysis is conducted within all U.S. traded stocks comprising individual industries. The correlation and covariance matrices for each month t are first decomposed into eigenfactors. Next, predictive factor loadings are determined by regressing returns of the month t+1 on the factors from month t. Subsequently, out-of-sample portfolios are formed at the end of month t+1, and the strategy performance for each industry is measured at the end of month t+2. Finally, the results of different intra-industry portfolios are aggregated using a simple average for each month and compared with the "naïve" equally weighted portfolio across all stocks. As Figures 6.5–6.10 show, correlation-based factorization outperforms covariance-based methodology for various numbers of top eigenvectors. Although volatile, the correlation-based methodology also outperforms the equally weighted portfolio of all the U.S.-traded stocks.

Interestingly, eigenportfolios of individual industries may not fare as well. Eigenportfolios of high-growth industries like biotechnology, in particular, appear to lag behind vanilla equally weighted industry portfolios, as shown in Figures 6.11–6.14. A possible explanation for this is that high-growth industries are followed by a large number of analysts who essentially raise awareness and, in a way, promote the industries to investors. In contrast, boring old industries toil in relative obscurity and that is where eigenportfolios strike gold.

Hierarchical PCA (HPCA)

To further reduce the correlation of the residuals of the factor models, Avellaneda (2019) proposes splitting the securities into their natural groups, industry sectors, with the two-fold intention:

1. Taking advantage of the fact that different sectors will have little inter-sector correlation outside of broad market influences, since different sectors face different business models, supply chains, and shocks.
2. Sectors form natural factors and can be used to factorize returns for all traded instruments.

The hierarchical PCA is designed to combine the power of PCA to select explanatory factors with the natural structure of a market, which is always divided into asset classes.

Consider first an abstract model, in which the data matrix of dimensions $T \times N$, can be partitioned into blocks $M_1, M_2, \ldots, M_b$. These blocks have dimensions $T \times N_i$ with $i = 1, 2, \ldots b$. For simplicity, we assume that the blocks are adjacent. The blocks represent the classification of the data into sectors, or sub-classes of the full universe of securities. There are two cases that we have in mind:

- The blocks represent data of industry sectors for equities in the same economy (e.g., GIC sectors associated with the 500 or so stocks in the S&P 500 index). In this case, the columns of a block M_i correspond to the historical standardized returns of one of the stocks in sector i, observed on T consecutive dates.
- Each block represents a stock or index and all of the derivatives written on it. In this case, the columns represent the returns of the stock, or the returns of options written on the stock with different strikes and tenors.[1]

The hierarchical PCA algorithm for the matrix consisting of b blocks is:

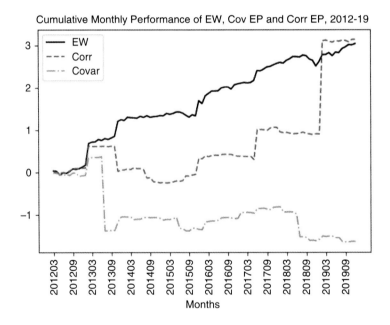

Figure 6.5 Comparison of aggregate industry-based portfolios constructed with correlation-based eigenportfolios, covariance-based eigenportfolios, and plain equally weighted portfolios, the first eigenvector only.

---

[1] In the case of options, one should consider a standardized set of strikes and tenors (usually in terms of Deltas and time to maturity). The returns of the corresponding implied volatilities and equities are observed. Based on these observations, one can deduct returns on select option contracts for each date and for a constant set of strikes/maturities. This information is then used to fill the columns of the corresponding block matrix.

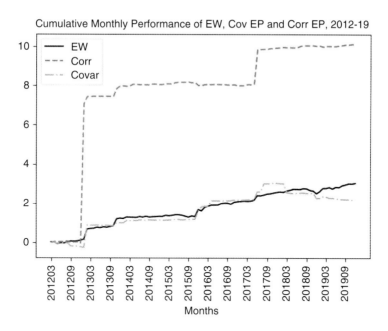

Figure 6.6 Comparison of aggregate industry-based portfolios constructed with correlation-based eigenportfolios, covariance-based eigenportfolios, and plain equally weighted portfolios, first two eigenvectors.

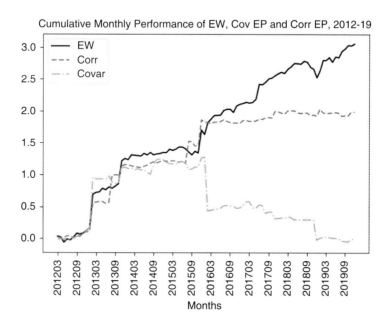

Figure 6.7 Comparison of aggregate industry-based portfolios constructed with correlation-based eigenportfolios, covariance-based eigenportfolios, and plain equally weighted portfolios, first three eigenvectors.

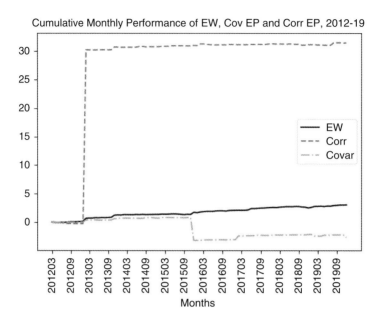

Figure 6.8　Comparison of aggregate industry-based portfolios constructed with correlation-based eigenportfolios, covariance-based eigenportfolios, and plain equally weighted portfolios, first four eigenvectors.

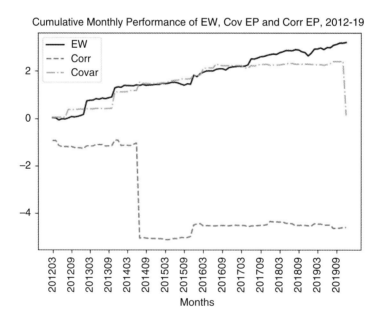

Figure 6.9　Comparison of aggregate industry-based portfolios constructed with correlation-based eigenportfolios, covariance-based eigenportfolios, and plain equally weighted portfolios, first five eigenvectors.

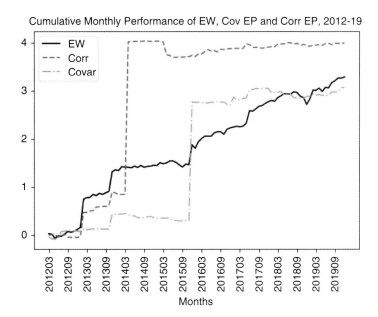

Figure 6.10   Comparison of aggregate industry-based portfolios constructed with correlation-based eigenportfolios, covariance-based eigenportfolios, and plain equally weighted portfolios, first six eigenvectors.

- Step 1: Perform PCA for the correlation matrix R_i for each block separately.
- Step 2: For each block, consider the normalized eigenportfolio $EP^{(1)}$ and the corresponding factor $F_i^{(1)}$, $i = 1, 2, \ldots, b$. The definition of the first factor is given in Eq (6.19).
- Step 3: Consider the $b \times b$ correlation matrix $\underline{R}$ of the factors, i.e.,

$$\underline{R}_{i\,i'} = \mathrm{Corr}(F_i^{(1)}, F_{i'}^{(1)}) \qquad (6.19)$$

- Step 4: Perform the PCA of the matrix $\underline{R}$ and extract the principal eigenvalue end EP.

Simplified correlation structure of hierarchical PCA
   Consider the function

$$I(j) = i \iff \text{asset } j \text{ is in block } i.$$

According to Eq (6.19) we can write, for each asset in the "big universe,"

$$X_j = \beta_{j,I(j)}\, F_{I(j)}^{(1)} + \varepsilon_j \qquad (6.20)$$

where $\beta_{j,I(j)}$ is the regression coefficient of the returns of asset j on the first factor of block $I(j)$ and ε_j is the residual – consisting of the additional terms in the KL decomposition of the block containing j.

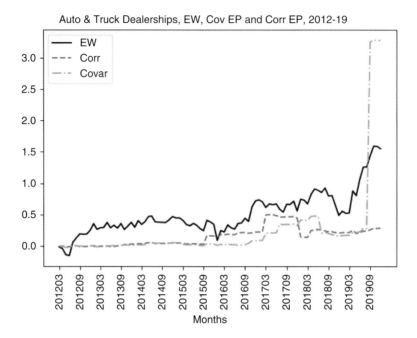

Figure 6.11   Auto and truck dealerships, industry eigenportfolios, first eigenvector.

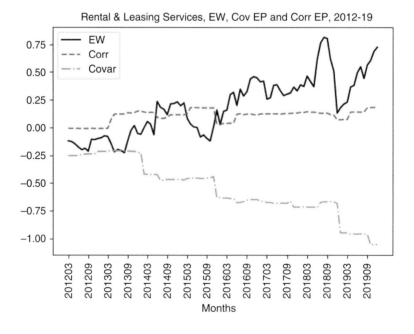

Figure 6.12   Rental and leasing, industry eigenportfolios, first three eigenvectors.

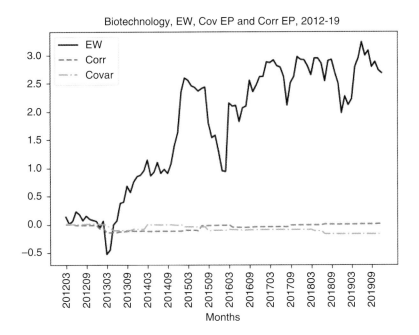

Figure 6.13 Biotechnology, industry eigenportfolios, first three eigenvectors.

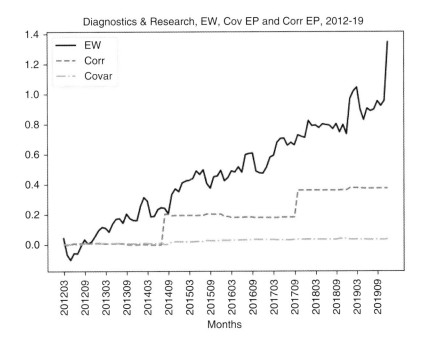

Figure 6.14 Diagnostics and research, industry eigenportfolios, first eigenvector.

Avellaneda (2019) makes the following assumption:

$$\text{If} \quad I(i) \neq I(j), \quad \text{then} \quad Corr(\varepsilon_i, \varepsilon_j) = 0$$

This assumption states that the residuals not explained by the first EPs are uncorrelated for assets in different sectors. Notice that this is a mathematically consistent model, because it is tantamount to postulating that Eq (6.20) defined the asset statistics in each block and the model is complete by specifying the joint statistics of the factors $F_i^{(1)}$, $i = 1, 2, \ldots, b$. If we restrict ourselves to second-order statistics, this means specifying the correlation structure of the factors.

This assumption can be called a "Level-1 model." A "Level-2 model" would correspond to using $F_i^{(1)}$ and $F_i^{(2)}$ in the KL representation and declaring that the residuals after removing 2 factors are uncorrelated, and so on. The "Level-m" where m is the largest number of columns that a block may have, is identical to the full model.

Notice that the assumptions say nothing regarding the intra-block correlations, which are set equal to the empirical correlations between asset returns within the same sector or block. Of course, the intra-block correlations could be further cleaned, using RMT if necessary.

Using the Level 1 simplification and the inter-factor correlation matrix we find that the proposed model corresponds to the following correlation structure:

$$Cor(X_j, X_{j'}) = R_{j\,j'} \qquad\qquad\qquad \text{if } I(j) = I(j')$$

$$Corr(X_j, X_{j'}) = \beta_{j,I(j)}\, \beta_{j',I(j')}\, \underline{R}_{I(j)\, I(j')} \qquad\qquad \text{if } I(j) \neq I(j') \qquad (6.21)$$

Avellaneda (2019) calls it a hierarchical model because it corresponds to a "tree structure."

- In the industry sector example, the tree structure consists of the market as top vertex, having 11 branches (corresponding to the GIC classification) and each branch having its branches corresponding to stocks.
- In the example with equity options, each "stock branch" gives rise to a lower level, namely, the options written on the stock (as well as the stock itself). In this case, the leaves of the tree correspond to option contracts and the low-level blocks to the correlation of delta-hedged options among themselves and with the stock return.
- Each of these blocks has a first-EP, corresponding to an "investment'" in the stock and options which explains the most variance for the group. The collection of these EPs can now be used to determine the correlation structure within the same industry sector. Going one more level up, we can calculate the EPs for each industry sector and the correlation matrix for it, arriving at a renormalized correlation for sectors, etc.
- A similar approach can be used to consider debt instruments and credit–default swaps. In this case, the issuer (company, sovereign) would constitute a sector or sub-block.

In summary, given a set of financial data for multiple instruments and multiple underlying assets, such as those used in real asset-management, Avellaneda (2019) considers a tree-like structure which corresponds to the classification of the asset as (sector,

Table 6.1 Results of the first stage of the HPCA analysis.

	Healthcare	Basic Materials	Industrials	Financial Services	Technology	Consumer Cyclical	Real Estate	Consumer Defensive	Energy	Utilities	Communication Services
Intercept	0.8802	0.0850	0.9751	0.1316	0.4151	0.2963	0.0745	0.049	0.3585	0.0310	0.0969
	(1.35)	(1.08)	(2.66)	(0.84)	(1.25)	(1.70)	(0.90)	(0.93)	(1.60)	(1.39)	(1.01)
F0	−241.4235	−1.8688	232.2829	705.5903	109.9657	−129.9175	−241.7586	−6.2144	213.3460	−48.3064	−6.3906
	(−2.57)	(−0.11)	(3.05)	(4.16)	(0.88)	(−3.09)	(−4.05)	(−0.42)	(9.56)	(3.88)	(−0.65)
F1	−164.6974	36.4079	46.0217	731.0591	−99.3723	197.4760	34.9561	−15.8554	29.6652	−112.8166	31.3266
	(−4.59)	(2.83)	(2.60)	(16.61)	(−2.72)	(7.69)	(1.52)	(−2.28)	(6.72)	(−21.74)	(7.77)
F2	−164.7381	26.5013	−91.2643	−25.8717	50.9290	21.2409	83.9814	−16.7242	48.1496	−8.9227	−38.1535
	(−6.96)	(5.93)	(−5.67)	(−0.48)	(3.54)	(1.19)	(5.61)	(−3.24)	(3.93)	(−2.18)	(−12.27)
F3	−62.3181	−19.1737	−111.1623	106.5968	−11.4743	−26.3030	40.7652	−4.3134	66.6766	22.9279	19.3820
	(−3.00)	(−4.91)	(−4.79)	(−3.94)	(−0.909)	(−2.52)	(3.81)	(−1.04)	(5.48)	(9.31)	(7.10)
F4	24.1889	17.5990	−20.5373	−15.5658	68.3160	−53.7733	56.4778	25.2631	42.0036	16.6108	17.6909
	(1.93)	(5.22)	(−1.44)	(−0.59)	(3.90)	(−3.52)	(7.09)	(6.84)	(6.89)	(6.74)	(3.18)
F5	−7.8210	−31.9622	−64.7140	−116.8665	42.7252	73.1057	70.6603	−11.4593	−48.2129	9.0183	26.6004
	(−0.31)	(−6.23)	(−3.58)	(−5.50)	(2.29)	(4.27)	(6.71)	(−3.61)	(−5.11)	(2.70)	(7.56)
F6	65.4992	14.6064	19.3985	−41.7389	−50.4022	−49.9090	35.2966	11.3922	−37.6872	9.0183	−9.3366
	(3.26)	(3.52)	(1.70)	(2.64)	(−2.44)	(−3.76)	(4.14)	(2.77)	(−5.95)	(0.55)	(−3.41)
F7	9.7958	−7.7734	−35.1914	86.3708	−35.6631	−23.4493	10.0887	20.0368	−29.6658	4.2486	32.0731
	(0.95)	(−2.46)	(−2.29)	(3.40)	(−1.29)	(−9.14)	(1.15)	(4.95)	(−5.11)	(1.44)	(7.21)
F8	−53.8676	24.4860	43.4272	70.9843	−4.9601	−36.5815	−1.9270	−4.6251	38.2474	16.4594	−24.6570
	(−3.14)	(−8.96)	(2.66)	(3.54)	(−0.39)	(−3.11)	(−0.18)	(−1.19)	(6.57)	(9.34)	(−6.35)
F9	27.1939	−27.8352	−20.1762	−109.4950	−13.6018	−105.5101	53.1448	−26.8894	30.8181	−13.9294	15.4918
	(2.64)	(−8.40)	(−2.01)	(−4.45)	(−0.75)	(−7.84)	(5.54)	(−7.90)	(10.15)	(−8.386)	(5.67)
Adj. R-sq (%)	31.2	86.6	31.0	85.7	61.2	75.6	69.3	61.1	87.4	86.3	86.8

stock, debt, options). The hierarchical approach to correlations modeling gives rise to a mathematically sound framework which combines the details of the security with the explanatory power of PCA.

Table 6.1 shows the results of the first stage of the HPCA analysis: the out-of-sample intra-sector regression of 2016 daily returns on the first ten eigenfactors generated from the correlation matrix of the 2016 daily returns in each industry. The t-statistic for each industry is shown in parentheses. As Table 6.1 shows, the factors offer tremendous explanatory power, often reaching 80 percent.

As shown in Table 6.1, the intercept is generally not statistically significant. This implies that the factors capture substantial variability of returns of individual securities. The vast majority of the industry factors based on the 2016 returns earn 99 percent statistical significance in-sample in each given industry (all t-ratios greater than 2 are shown in bold in Table 6.1). Finally, Adjusted R^2 of the intra-industry regressions is also extremely powerful, ranging from 31% to 87%. With the exception of Industrials, the sectors' intrinsic eigenportfolios explain the majority of return variation in the sectors. Similar in-sample results hold for 2017 and 2018.

Interestingly, the top eigenvalues representing the core structure of the data change little from one year to the next. Figures 6.15–6.25 show the annual changes in the top 10 eigenfactors across the industries.

Figures 6.26–6.36 show out-of-sample performance of annual in-sector returns computed with the previous year's top eigenfactors and factor loadings. In every year t, the top 10 eigenportfolios were calculated by performing the SVD on the return correlation matrix for all the stocks traded that were identified in the given sector. Next, factor loadings β were calculated by regressing the annual returns realized in year t of all the securities in a given sector on the top-10 eigenportfolios calculated in the year t. For the following year t+1, the portfolios were formed by matrix multiplying β and the top-10 eigenfactors

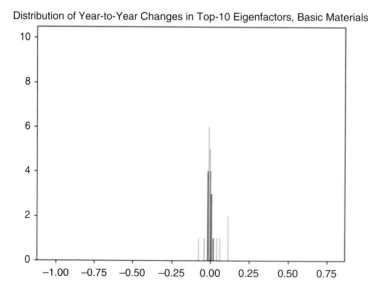

Figure 6.15   Distribution of year-to-year changes in top-10 eigenfactors, Basic Materials.

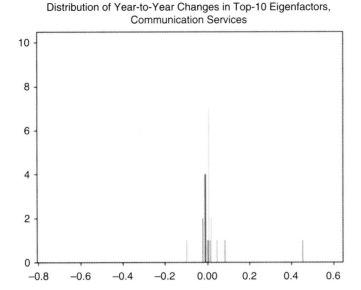

Figure 6.16   Distribution of year-to-year changes in top-10 eigenfactors, Communication Services.

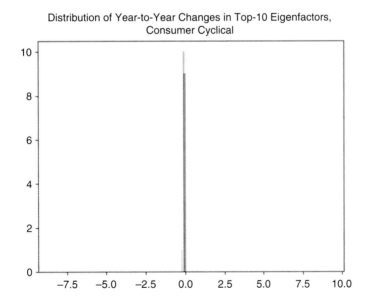

Figure 6.17   Distribution of year-to-year changes in top-10 eigenfactors, Communication Cyclical.

identified in year t. The resulting portfolio weights based on year t data can be positive (long) or negative (short). The out-of-sample results were next calculated by applying these portfolios to the annual returns for year t+1 of each stock in the sector. The eigenfactors and factor loadings were next recomputed for year t+1 to be applied for the out-of-sample return computation for year t+2 and so on in a rolling window fashion.

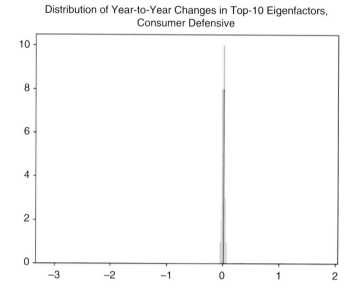

Figure 6.18   Distribution of year-to-year changes in top-10 eigenfactors, Consumer Defensive.

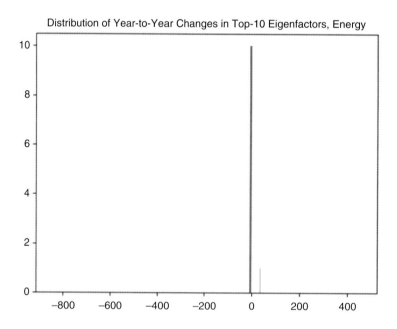

Figure 6.19   Distribution of year-to-year changes in top-10 eigenfactors, Energy.

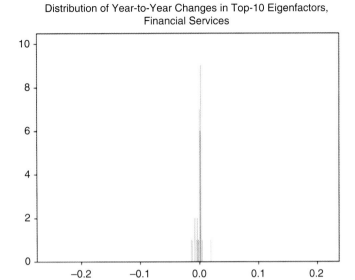

Figure 6.20   Distribution of year-to-year changes in top-10 eigenfactors, Financial Services.

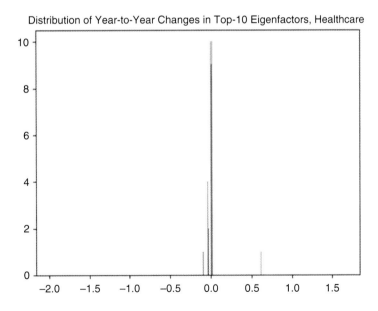

Figure 6.21   Distribution of year-to-year changes in top-10 eigenfactors, Healthcare.

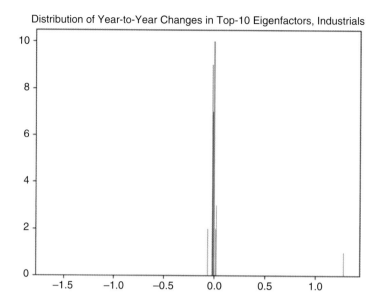

Figure 6.22   Distribution of year-to-year changes in top-10 eigenfactors, Industrials.

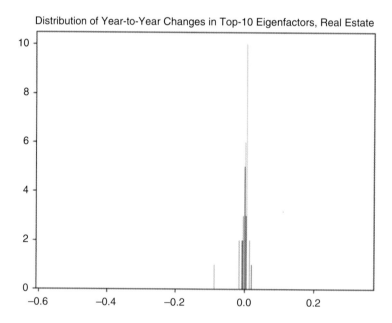

Figure 6.23   Distribution of year-to-year changes in top-10 eigenfactors, Real Estate.

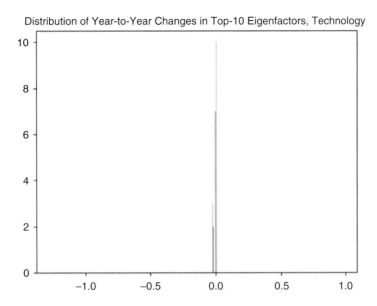

Figure 6.24 Distribution of year–to–year changes in top–10 eigenfactors, Technology.

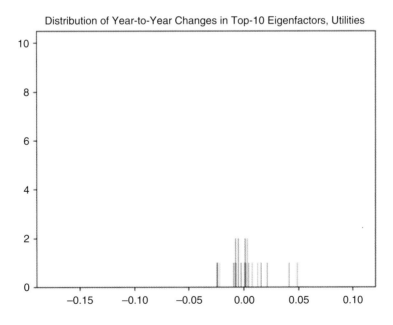

Figure 6.25 Distribution of year–to–year changes in top–10 eigenfactors, Utilities.

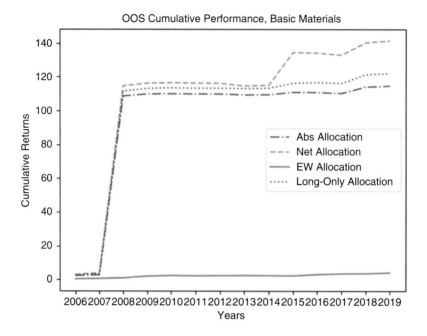

Figure 6.26   OOS cumulative performance, Basic Materials.

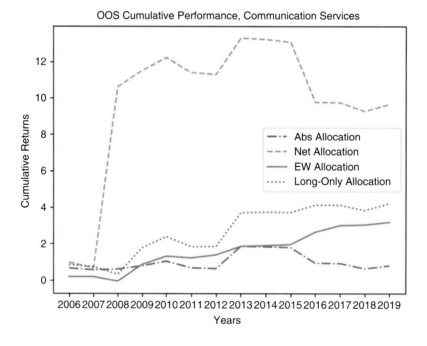

Figure 6.27   OOS cumulative performance, Communication Services.

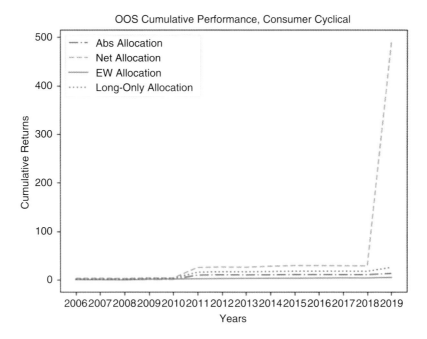

Figure 6.28   OOS cumulative performance, Consumer Cyclical.

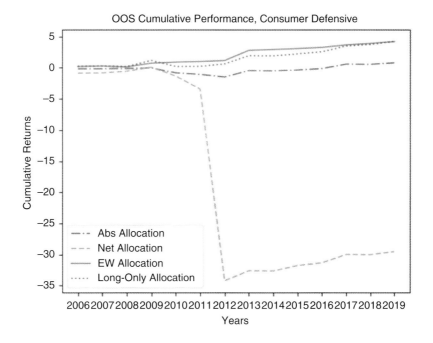

Figure 6.29   OOS cumulative performance, Consumer Defensive.

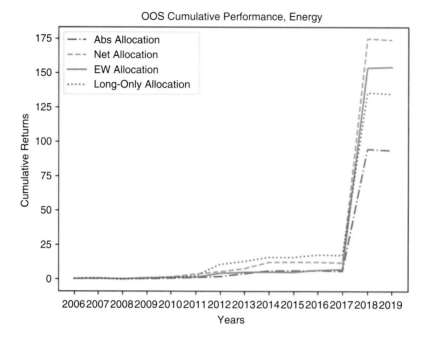

Figure 6.30   OOS cumulative performance, Energy.

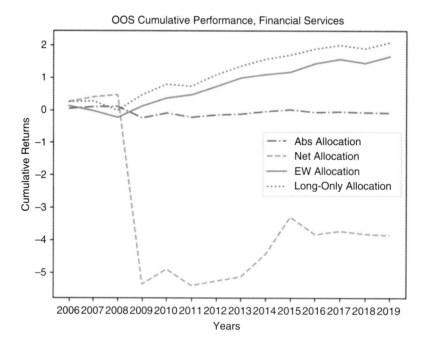

Figure 6.31   OOS cumulative performance, Financial Services.

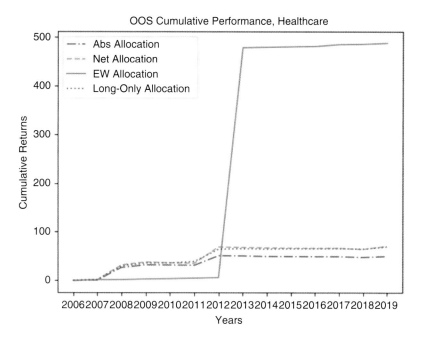

Figure 6.32   OOS cumulative performance, Healthcare.

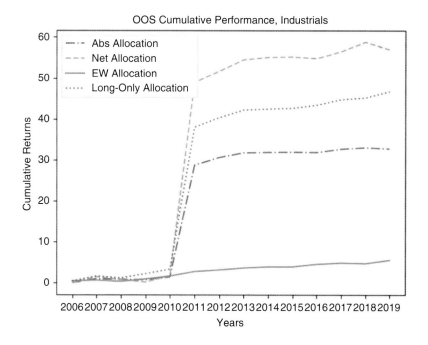

Figure 6.33   OOS cumulative performance, Industrials.

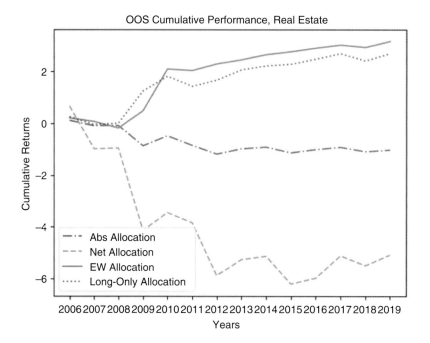

Figure 6.34   OOS cumulative performance, Real Estate.

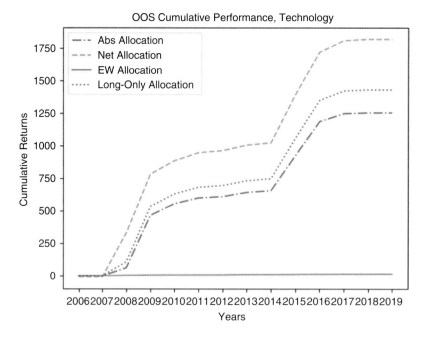

Figure 6.35   OOS cumulative performance, Technology.

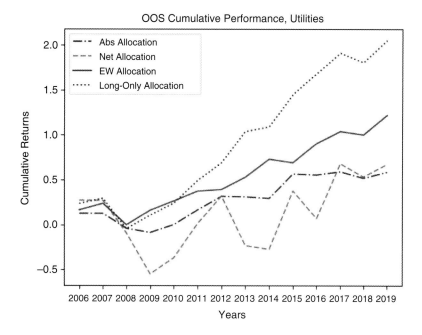

Figure 6.36 OOS cumulative performance, Utilities.

While the results shown in Table 6.1 are highly significant, they are not sufficient to predict out-of-sample returns, at least not on the year-ahead basis.

The out-of-sample results reported in Figures 6.26–6.36 contain several types of portfolio computations. The EW portfolio is a simple in-sector equally weighted return, a "baseline" scenario included for performance comparison.

The net portfolios are computed by netting out positive and negative portfolio allocations, effectively using the money from shorted portfolio positions to finance the long positions. Netting out portfolios reduces the total capital deployed and produces potentially higher overall returns, but may be misleading about the risk engaged in the portfolio.

Absolute portfolios, reported as "Abs Allocation" in Figures 6.26–6.36, compute the capital based as a total amount of portfolio funds deployed. Under the absolute allocation, negative (short) portfolio funds are calculated as cash-at-risk, just like the long portfolio funds. The resulting Absolute Allocation return is computed by dividing the obtained out-of-sample portfolio return by the total amount of funds used.

Long-only allocations ignore the negative portfolio positions altogether. The money is invested in the long (positive) portfolio positions only. As Figures 6.26–6.36 show, long-only allocations prove to be the winning intra-sector strategies based on eigenportfolios. The long-only allocations are also the most desired strategies for many institutional investors, like pension funds and insurance companies.

Disadvantages of PCA and SVD

The main disadvantage of PCA is that it makes no use of information that we have about assets and that is fundamental. Therefore, in many cases, we find that the PCA of financial correlation matrices gives us information we already expected. Most studies tend to justify the PCA approach by recognizing that it produces factors that have a "traditional" economic explanation, such as equating $EP^{(1)}$ with Sharpe's Market Portfolio, or assigning interpretations in terms of industry sectors for higher-order EPs. In the case of fixed income, the EPs are identified with parallel shifts of rates, long-term vs. short-term variations, i.e., changes in the slope of the yield curve, and so forth. Therefore, most papers in the field tend to focus on the identification of the factors $F^{(k)}$ and the corresponding eigenportfolios.

Interestingly enough, the PCA/RMT approach does not consider the nature of the securities that it examines or, if I can put it another way, it applies to relatively narrow sets of securities (like yield curves for a single credit) or, at the other end of the spectrum, runs into the problem of identification of the factors, and the worrisome question of the stability across different market regimes, such as recession, contraction, or different monetary regimes.

It could be argued that if the asset universe is broad, the correlations of assets which are not economically related (a tech stock and an energy stock, or a foreign stock) are probably difficult to measure precisely, due to the fact that prices are not sampled simultaneously. Only highly liquid instruments are available to trade in different time zones. The empirical correlation of the prices of out-of-the money options written on different underlying assets may not be reliable in practice.

All this suggests that a description of common factors affecting asset returns should recognize the economic function of the assets and perform PCA only on homogeneous groups, or sectors of the market. This analysis has the advantage that the systems to be analyzed are homogeneous and require less explanatory factors. In fact, it is very natural, if we pause to think that it is easier and more reasonable to perform small-scale variance-covariance analysis of small universes of assets. The question then becomes how to "integrate" them into the big picture. Techniques like HPCA allow researchers to retail the handle on the data and their economic interpretation.

Conclusion

Unsupervised learning produces optimal factorization. The resulting factors eliminate the guesswork of which factors are dominant and deliver superior performance in predicting future returns.

Appendix 6.A Python for Big Data Factor Models

To find the Karhunen-Loève eigenportfolio factorization, we can use the following code on standardized data X (code for data standardization was discussed in Appendix 5.A in Chapter 5):

```python
import numpy as np
corr = np.corrcoef(X)
s, V = np.linalg.eig(corr)
F0 = 1/(np.sqrt(s[0]))*np.dot(V[:,0], X)
```

Here, we decompose the correlation matrix of X with PCA using linalg.eig, and determine the first eigenportfolio F0 based on the first eigenvector.

Next, we can use the factor as an explanatory variable in a linear regression to explain variation in X as follows:

```python
from sklearn.linear_model import LinearRegression
regressor = LinearRegression()
regressor.fit(F0, X)
beta = regressor.coef_ #betas are portfolio factors
```

With a built-in LinearRegression library from scikit-learn, we obtain the portfolio factors as betas in the regression.

A POET model runs PCA on the covariance matrix of X, instead of its variance:

```python
import numpy as np
cov = np.cov(X)
```

Once again, the simplicity of the Python code delivers the easy optimization of data inferences.

For specific code examples, please visit https://www.BigDataFinanceBook.com, and register with password *DataFactors* (case-sensitive).

References

Aït-Sahalia, Y. and Xiu, D. (2017). Principal component estimation of a large covariance matrix with high-frequency data. *Journal of Econometrics* 201: 384–399.

Antoniadis, A. and Fan, J. (2001). Regularized wavelet approximations. *Journal of American Statistical Association* 96: 939–967.

Avellaneda, M. (2019). Hierarchical PCA. NYU Courant, working paper.

Avellaneda, M., and Lee, J.-H. (2010). Statistical arbitrage in the US equities market. Quantitative Finance 10(7): 761–782.

Bai, J. and Ng, S. (2002). Determining the number of factors in approximate factor models. *Econometrica* 70: 191–221.

Bai, J. and Ng, S. (2008). Forecasting economic time series using targeted predictors. *Journal of Econometrics* 146: 304–317.

Bai, J. and Ng, S. (2013). Principal components estimation and identification of static factors. *Journal of Econometrics* 17: 18–29.

Bickel, P. and Levina, E. (2008). Covariance regularization by thresholding. *The Annals of Statistics* 36: 2577–2604.

Cai, T. and Liu, W. (2011). Adaptive thresholding for sparse covariance matrix estimation. *Journal of American Statistical Association* 106: 672–684.

Cai, T. and Zhou, H. (2012). Optimal rates of convergence for sparse covariance matrix estimation. *The Annals of Statistics* 40: 2389–2420.

Chamberlain, G. and Rothschild, M. (1983). Arbitrage, factor structure and mean-variance analysis in large asset markets. *Econometrica* 51: 1305–1324.

Chen, X. (2007). Large sample sieve estimation of semi-nonparametric models. In: *Handbook of Econometrics*. Amsterdam: North Holland.

Cizeau, P., Potters, M., and Bouchaud, J-P. (2000). Correlation structure of extreme stock returns. *Quantitative Finance* 1(2): 217–222.

Cochrane, J.H. (2011). Presidential address: Discount rates. *Journal of Finance* 66: 1047–1108.

Connor, G., Hagmann, M., and Linton, O. (2012). Efficient semiparametric estimation of the Fama-French model and eExtensions. *Econometrica* 80(2): 713–754.

Connor, G. and Korajczyk, R.A. (1986). Performance measurement with the arbitrage pricing theory: A new framework for analysis. *Journal of Financial Economics* 15: 373–394.

Connor, G. and Korajczyk, R.A. (1988). Risk and return in an equilibrium apt: Application to a new test methodology. *Journal of Financial Economics* 21: 255–289.

Doz, C., Giannone, D., and Reichlin, L. (2011). A two-step estimator for large approximate dynamic factor models based on Kalman filtering. *Journal of Econometrics* 164: 188–205.

Fama, E. and French, K. (1992). The cross-section of expected stock returns. *Journal of Finance* 47: 427–465.

Fama, E. and French, K. (1993). Common risk factors in the returns on stocks and bonds. *Journal of Financial Economics* 33: 3–56.

Fan, J., Fan, Y., and Lv, J. (2008). High dimensional covariance matrix estimation using a factor model. *Journal of Econometrics* 147: 186-197.

Fan, J., Liao, Y., and Mincheva, M. (2011). High dimensional covariance matrix estimation in approximate factor models. *The Annals of Statistics* 39: 3320–3356.

Fan, J., Liao, Y., and Mincheva, M. (2013). Large covariance estimation by thresholding principal orthogonal complements. *Journal of the Royal Statistical Society, Series B, Statistical Methodology* 1: 75.

Fan, J., Liao, Y., and Wang, W. (2016). Projected principal component analysis in factor models. *The Annals of Statistics* 44: 219–254.

Giglio, S., and Xiu, D. (2019). Asset Pricing with Omitted Factors. Chicago Booth Research Paper No. 16-21.

Harvey, C.R., Liu, Y., and Zhu, H. (2016). … and the cross-section of expected returns. *Review of Financial Studies* 29: 5–68.

Kelly, B., Pruitt, S., and Su, Y. (2017). Instrumented principal component analysis. Working paper.

Laloux, L., Cizeau, P., Potters, M., and Boucheaud, J.-P. (2000). Random matrix theory and financial correlations. *Mathematical Methods in Applied Sciences* 1(2): 217–222.

Lettau, M. and Pelger, M. (2019). Factors that fit the time series and cross-section of stock returns. UCLA and Stanford University, working paper.

Li, G., Yang, D., Nobel, A.B., and Shen, H. (2015). Supervised singular value decomposition and its asymptotic properties. *Journal of Multivariate Analysis* 146: 7–17.

Lintner, J. (1965). The valuation of risk assets and the selection of risky investments in stock portfolios and capital budgets. *Review of Economics and Statistics* 47(1): 13–37.

Ludvigson, S. and Ng, S. (2009). Macro factors in bond risk premia. *Review of Financial Studies* 22(12): 5027–5067.

Onatski, A. (2010). Determining the number of factors from empirical distribution of eigenvalues. *The Review of Economics and Statistics* 9(4): 1004–1016.

Onatski, A. (2012). Asymptotics of the principal components estimator of large factor models with weakly influential factors. *Journal of Econometrics* 168(2): 244–258.

Ross, S.A. (1976). The arbitrage theory of capital asset pricing. *Journal of Economic Theory* 13: 341–360.

Ross, S.A. (1977). The Capital Asset Pricing Model (CAPM), short-sale restrictions and related issues. *Journal of Finance* 32: 177–183.

Rothman, A., Levina, E., and Zhu, J. (2009). Generalized thresholding of large covariance matrices. *Journal of American Statistical Association* 14: 177–186.

Sharpe, W.F. (1964). Capital asset prices: A theory of market equilibrium under conditions of risk. *Journal of Finance* 19(3): 425–442.

Stock, J.H. and Watson, M.W. (2002). Forecasting using principal components from a large number of predictors. *Journal of the American Statistical Association* 97: 1167–1179.

Watanabe, S. (1965). Karhunen-Loève expansion and factor analysis. In: *Transactions of the 4th Prague Conference on Information Theory*.

Chapter 7

Data as a Signal versus Noise

Introduction

A recent *Business Insider* article reported that the data spending by financial companies reached a record $7 billion, and is expected to grow further. Even so, the financial firms find themselves struggling to figure out what to do with this data, or even if the data they are buying has much meaning. To address the issue, firms like hedge funds and banks turn to pricey data scientists, employees, and consultants to help them figure out the value of data and data applications. Anecdotally, often the newly hired highly paid data scientist is handed a "bag of data stuff" the company has previously paid to acquire and is asked to tell the firm how to make money from all that.

To someone trained in classical econometrics, the question of "how to make money from all that" can be daunting. Econometrics teaches students how to select a proper distribution and estimation model for the yes/no questions the researcher may have. Econometrics does not, however, work well with open-ended questions of "how" and "why."

This is where data science comes in quite handy. In particular, Big Data techniques discussed in this chapter can help quickly answer if "the bag of data" is valuable or not.

Random Data Shows in Eigenvalue Distribution

To begin our examination of the data bag, we require several concepts. An n × n symmetric matrix A (i.e., a Hermitian matrix) with real independent, identically distributed (i.i.d.) elements X_{ij} satisfying

$$E[X_{ij}^2] < \infty, \quad 1 \leq j \leq i \leq \infty, \quad X_{ij} = X_{ji} \tag{7.1}$$

is known as the Wigner Matrix. Eugene Wigner originally developed Wigner matrices to model the nuclei of heavy atoms. A Wigner matrix with real Gaussian (0,1) entries is known as a Gaussian Orthogonal Ensemble (GOE), although GOEs in general do not need to be symmetric. Formally, GOEs are data tables containing i.i.d. Gaussian (0,1) data elements. Wigner matrices work well for modeling correlation matrices with random entries, while non-symmetric GOEs work well for representing normally distributed random Gaussian (0,1) returns and other data.

The interesting feature of the Wigner matrices and GOEs is that the distribution of eigenvalues of both, when scaled by the squared root of n, is a perfect semicircle! A sample semicircular distribution of eigenvalues is shown in Figure 7.1. This phenomenon is known as the Wigner Semicircle Law after Wigner (1955, 1958).

The Wigner Semicircle Law, the Central Limit Theorem for Wigner matrices, states that for all n × n Wigner matrices and GOEs, the distribution of eigenvalues is a semicircle. There are n random eigenvalues which we will denote by $\lambda_1 \leq \lambda_2 \leq \ldots \lambda_n$.

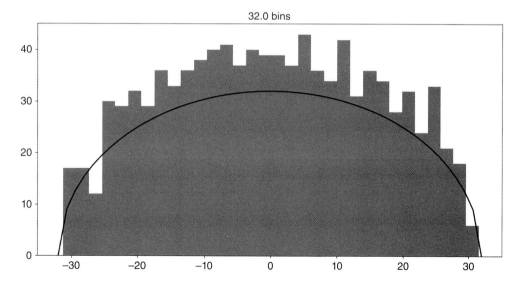

Figure 7.1   Wigner Semicircle Law: the distribution of eigenvalues of a Gaussian Orthogonal Ensemble (GOE) – a Wigner matrix with Gaussian (0,1) elements. The matrix in the image was generated by populating a 600×600 matrix with random numbers, then taking the covariance of the matrix, then finding the eigenvalues of the covariance, dividing each eigenvalue by the square root of n, and finally plotting the eigenvalue distribution.

The eigenvalues happen to be continuous functions of the n × n Wigner matrix M_n, hence they are random variables themselves. The empirical cumulative distribution of eigenvalues is

$$l(x):=\frac{1}{n}\sum_{i=1}^{n} \quad X(\lambda_i < x) \tag{7.2}$$

and the corresponding empirical density function is

$$l'(x):=\frac{1}{n}\sum_{i=1}^{n} \quad \delta(x - \lambda_i). \tag{7.3}$$

When the matrix is normalized to have all eigenvalues lie on [-1, 1], then the Wigner Semicircle Law says that with probability 1 as $n \to \infty$, the empirical density function of eigenvalues of any Wigner and GOE matrix converges to the function

$$l'(x) = \frac{1}{n}\sum_{i=1}^{n} \quad \delta\left(x - \frac{l_i}{2\sqrt{n}}\right) \to P(x) = \frac{2}{\pi}\sqrt{1 - x^2} \tag{7.4}$$

Technically, the Wigner Semicircle Law holds not just for real-valued matrices, but also for complex representations. In finance, all mathematics tend to work solely with real numbers, so we will focus our discussion solely on real numbers.

Application: What's in the Data Bag?

Both real Wigner matrices and GOEs, by definition, contain random data, also known as noise. The natural application of the Wigner Semicircle Law then is to test a data table to find out if the data elements contained within are pure random noise, or if some other structure, a signal, can be detected.

How would you go about testing your data? You may do it in two different ways, whichever closer matches your target application.

1. Normalize data to the required mean 0, variance 1 format: compute the mean and standard deviation of the data, subtract the mean from the data, then divide the data by the standard deviation.
2. Take the covariance of the data matrix.
3. Compute the eigenvalues of the covariance and divide them by the square root of n, the number of rows or columns in the matrix.
4. Plot the histogram of the resulting eigenvalues.

If you have a large number of eigenvalues (a prerequisite) and their distribution resembles the semicircle in Figure 7.1, then you have a high probability of data being simply random, a Gaussian noise, also known as white noise, or, less euphemistically, garbage.

If your histogram of eigenvalues is mostly a semicircle, but with a few histogram bins "spiking up" from the semicircle profile, you probably have a spike model on your hands, where the spike indicates a clear valuable data feature, also known as a signal. Such occurrences are tracked in the so-called "spike models."

However, for the data to look like a nice semicircle, it does have to be a Wigner matrix. What if your data is not? Luckily for us, the Marčenko-Pastur Theorem provides the answer.

The Marčenko-Pastur Theorem

The Marčenko-Pastur result, due to Marčenko and Pastur (1967), is a generalized version of the Wigner Semicircle Law. It applies to random data with any underlying distribution. For any such data, Marčenko and Pastur (1967) showed that the distribution of eigenvalues of sample covariances weakly converges to a specific distribution, now known as the Marčenko-Pastur function. If the data is not completely random, the "spike" signal breaking through the Marčenko-Pastur envelope can be seen on the eigenvalue distribution plot.

Formally, the empirical density function for the eigenvalue distribution of a sample covariance matrix S of an $n \times p$ matrix with independent identically distributed (i.i.d.) entries $\{X\}$ with mean 0 and variance 1, $S = \frac{1}{n}X'X$, when $p, n \to \infty$ in such a way that $p/n \to \gamma \in [0, 1]$, is

$$l'(x) := \frac{1}{n} \sum_{i=1}^{n} \delta\left(x - \frac{\lambda_i}{2\sqrt{n}}\right) \to G'(x) = \frac{1}{2\pi x\gamma}\sqrt{(b-x)(x-a)}, b \leq x \leq a \quad (7.5)$$

The convergence occurs almost certainly as $\frac{p}{n} \to \gamma$, with the smallest eigenvalue a and the largest eigenvalue b satisfying

$$a = (1 - \gamma^{1/2})^2 \quad (7.6)$$

$$b = (1 + \gamma^{1/2})^2 \quad (7.7)$$

For a proof of Marčenko-Pastur, the reader may refer to Bai (1999), among many other sources.

Just like the Wigner Semicircle Law, the Marčenko-Pastur theorem describes the distribution of the eigenvalues of a covariance matrix of normalized data (with the mean subtracted and divided by the standard deviation of the data set to present the i.i.d. entries with mean 0 and variance 1). Unlike the Wigner Semicircle Law, the Marčenko-Pastur theorem relaxes the assumptions on the size and the actual distribution of data. Under the Marčenko-Pastur theorem, the matrices can be rectangular $n \times p$, and no longer have to be square $n \times n$ as in the Wigner Semicircle Law. Equally, if not more, importantly, the underlying distribution of data under the Marčenko-Pastur theorem no longer has to be Gaussian – it can be anything, as long as it is i.i.d.

Figures 7.2–7.5 show the distribution of eigenvalues for covariances of random matrices normalized to have mean 0 and variance of 1 and the associated Marčenko-Pastur distributions for matrices of different sizes.

If $\gamma > 1$, as in the case when the return covariance is estimated on a much smaller number of sequential data points than the number of instruments, given the rank of the

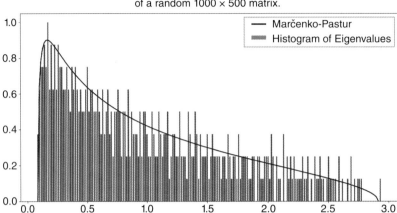

Figure 7.2 Distribution of eigenvalues of covariance of a randomly generated 1000×500 matrix ($\gamma = 0.5$). The data matrix was normalized to have mean 0 and variance 1.

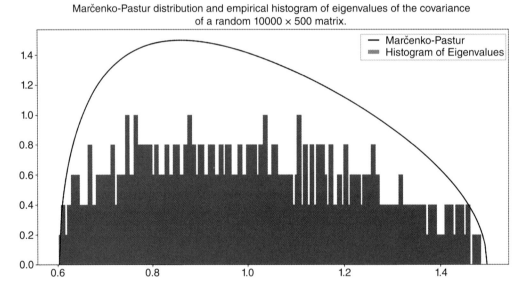

Figure 7.3 Distribution of eigenvalues of covariance of a randomly generated 10000×500 matrix ($\gamma = 0.05$). The data matrix was normalized to have mean 0 and variance 1.

covariance matrix $rank(S) = p \wedge n$, approximately $n(1 - \gamma)$ eigenvalues will be zero. The resulting eigenvalue distribution of the sample covariance will have a mass of $(1 - \gamma^{-1})$ at 0 and a Marčenko-Pastur set of eigenvalues as shown in Figure 7.4.

When n = p, $\gamma = 1$, $a = 0$ and $b = 4$. Thus,

$$G'(x) = \frac{1}{2\pi x \gamma} \sqrt{(4 - x)x}, 4 \leq x \leq 0 \tag{7.8}$$

as shown in Figure 7.5.

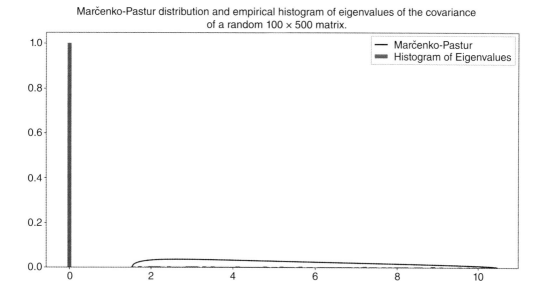

Figure 7.4 Distribution of eigenvalues of covariance of a randomly generated 100×500 matrix ($\gamma = 5$). The data matrix was normalized to have mean 0 and variance 1. The figure shows a large mass at 0 corresponding to the zero-eigenvalues resulting from a reduced rank of the matrix.

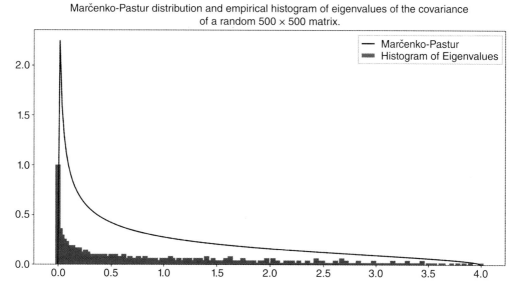

Figure 7.5 Theoretical and empirical distribution of eigenvalues of the covariance of a randomly generated 500×500 matrix ($\gamma = 1$). The resulting eigenvalues are distributed between 0 and 4. The underlying random data matrix was normalized to have mean 0 and variance 1.

Spike Model: Which Value to Pick on the "Elbow"?

Eigenvalue distributions play an important role in Data Science. Identifying the signal in the data via distribution outliers known as spikes is a useful tool. In addition, spike models can be used to pinpoint the optimal number of significant eigenvalues to be retained in models involving dimensionality reduction, optimal factorization like POET, discussed in Chapter 5, and many others.

To determine the optimal number of significant eigenvalues, one needs to pinpoint the optimal "elbow" cut-off in the corresponding scree plot – the plot of sorted eigenvalues. Doing so by eyeballing the data can be challenging and, more importantly, difficult to objectively justify the results. Why not let Big Data handle this aspect of modeling as well?

Several ideas have been put forth over the years to automate the "eyeballing" of the scree plot. Researchers following Kaiser (1960) choose to fix the number of significant values used in analysis before commencing the analysis. The scree test, first developed by Cattell (1966), seeks a gap between significant and insignificant eigenvalues on the scree plot. Horn (1965), Buja and Eyuboglu (1992), Dobriban and Owen (2019), and others explore *parallel analysis*, whereby the given distribution of eigenvalues is compared to a randomly generated distribution with the same variances, but 0 covariances. Then, the eigenvalues in the original sample distribution are deemed significant if they exceed a certain threshold, say, 95 percentile of all the eigenvalues of the generated random distribution. In the finance literature, Connor and Korajczyk (1993) propose an alternative method based on finding the $k+1$ factor that explains asymptotically zero cross-sectional asset variability.

A method based on Marčenko-Pastur (1967), which has become the standard in the statistical literature and is discussed here, considers the eigenvalues significant if they lie above the theoretical Marčenko-Pastur eigenvalue distribution support $[a, b]$, where a and b are given by Eqs. (7.6) and (7.7). To determine the significant eigenvalues, consider the eigenvalue distribution. The spikes in the histogram represent the signal–driven outliers that are the significant eigenvalues. Counting the outlier spikes falling outside of the parameterized eigenvalue distribution envelope delivers the answer for the optimal eigenvalue cut-off.

While "eyeballing" the distribution has been a traditional process to determine the "elbow" cut-off for many years, Marčenko-Pastur gifts us a fully automated ability to do the same, ensuring maximum transparency and objectivity in the model-selection process. To find the elbow, one may use the key property of Marčenko-Pastur: discerning the signal from the noise. A signal immersed in the otherwise noisy data corresponds to a "spike" that "pops out" of the Marčenko-Pastur support of the eigenvalue distribution (Figures 7.6a and 7.6b).

To understand the power of the concept better, consider the following example. We create a data set X with vectors $\{x_1, x_2, \ldots, x_n\}$ to be a mixture of two distributions: a pure Gaussian noise $g \sim N(0, 1)$ and a signal s. The signal consists of a diagonal M × M

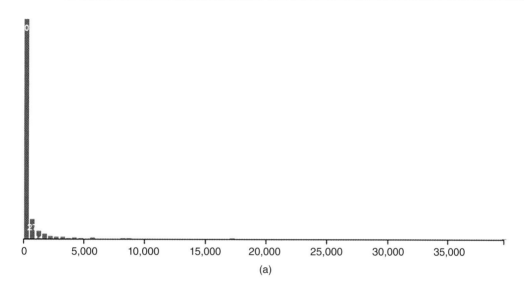

Figure 7.6a   These eigenvalues "pop out" from the Marčenko–Pastur distribution.

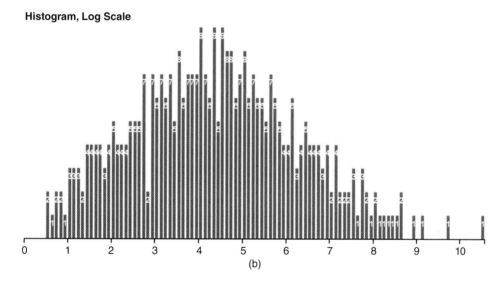

Figure 7.6b   Log scale of the histogram in Figure 7.6. Here, the log scale shows the spiked eigenvalues more clearly.

matrix with diagonal elements represented by a Gaussian variation $g_0 \sim N(0, \beta)$, with g_0 being independent of g $(E[gg_0] = 0)$. The data elements x then are

$$x = g + s = g + \sqrt{\beta}v \tag{7.9}$$

with distribution

$$x \sim N(0, I + \beta v v^T) \tag{7.10}$$

Can Marčenko-Pastur help us to separate the signal part of x? Different signal-versus-noise properties have a varying ability to separate the signal from the noise, as illustrated in Figures 7.7 and 7.8.

What is the "critical" value of β that allows us to separate the noise from the signal? The β above which eigenvalues pop up from the distribution support, and below which

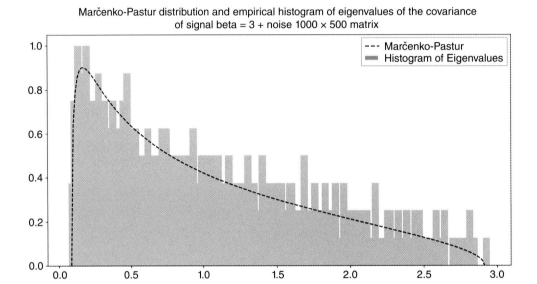

Figure 7.7   Marčenko-Pastur for a signal of Eq (7.10) with $\boldsymbol{\beta = 3.0}$ for N $=$ 1000 and M $=$ 500 matrix ($\boldsymbol{\gamma = 0.70711, 1/\gamma = 1.41421}$), $\boldsymbol{\beta > 1/\gamma}$. The signal "pops out" from the distribution.

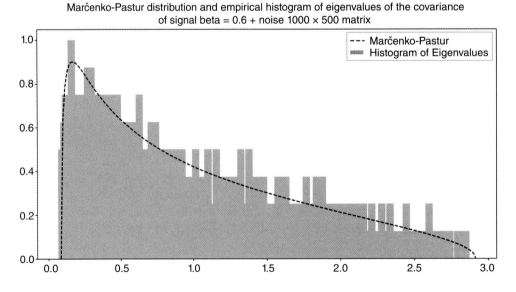

Figure 7.8   Marčenko-Pastur for a signal of Eq (7.10) with $\boldsymbol{\beta = 0.6}$ for N $=$ 1000 and M $=$ 500 matrix ($\boldsymbol{\gamma = 0.70711, 1/\gamma = 1.41421}$), $\boldsymbol{\beta < 1/\gamma}$. The signal is "lost" in the noise distribution.

the noise absorbs the signal, is known as the *BBP transition* after Baik, Ben-Arous, and Peche (2005). It is possible to show that

$$\beta = 1/\sqrt{\gamma} \qquad (7.11)$$

where $\gamma = p/n$, is such a transition point.

For derivation and related inferences, see Johnstone (2001), Baik, Ben-Arous, and Peche (2005), Karoui (2005), Baik and Silverstein (2005), Paul (2007), Benaych-Georges and Nadakuditi (2011), and Benaych-Georges and Nadakuditi (2012).

The BBP transition delineates the break between no significant eigenvalues outside of Marčenko-Pastur support and at least one significant eigenvalue ("spike") in the eigenvalue distribution past the Marčenko-Pastur maximum. As a result, the stream of literature studying spikes is known as the "spike modeling" or "spiked covariance models."

Spiked covariance models aid our ability to predict the location of significant eigenvalues based on the data shape. Typically, the data considered has to be voluminous as the models are studying the asymptotic properties of eigenvalues, true to a large data population. In general, spiked covariance models involve covariance matrices of the type

$$\Sigma = diag(s_1, s_2, \ldots, s_k, 1, 1, \ldots 1) \qquad (7.12)$$

with $s_1 \geq s_2 \geq \ldots \geq s_k > 1$ for some $1 \leq k < p$.

In other words, the data under consideration is uncorrelated. In contrast, most of the daily, monthly, quarterly, and annual data in finance exhibits high correlation, with daily stock time series often correlating as much as 50 percent and higher. The spiked covariance matrices are not suitable for such data examination. The intraday data, however, is mostly uncorrelated. Epps (1979) was the first to notice that securities correlations broke down as the data frequency increased from daily to hourly, to minutes to seconds and milliseconds. The intraday market data are also massive in comparison with daily or lower frequency data, both in length and breadth. The length of the data is driven by how frequently the data are sampled: in just one trading day, there are 390 1-minute data rows during the "regular" trading hours from 9:30 AM ET to 4 PM ET, which can be sampled as 23,400 1-second data rows, 23,400,000 1-millisecond data rows, or 23,400,000,000 1-microsecond data rows. Some financial instruments like Foreign Exchange and selected futures trade around the clock, generating a lot more observations. The breadth of intraday data is also unparalleled. The data for just one security includes the traditional Open, High, Low, and Close prices for each time period, in addition to a multitude of limit orders of different sizes placed at different price levels, limit order revisions, and limit order cancellations. Due to the highly asynchronous nature of intraday trading, most of the trading data is largely uncorrelated among different securities and, in a larger context, financial instruments. For the intraday data, the spiked covariance model is very relevant and is discussed next.

A well-known property of eigenvalue decomposition in the uncorrelated data is that the eigenvalues of data with a diagonal matrix are the diagonal elements themselves while the eigenvectors are the unit vectors. In other words, a diagonal matrix $C = diag(c_{11}, c_{22}, \ldots, c_{pp})$ (where off-diagonal elements $c_{ij} = 0$ for all $i \neq j$) satisfies:

$$CE = \Lambda E \qquad (7.13)$$

where Λ is a vector of eigenvalues $\Lambda = [\lambda_1, \lambda_2, \ldots , \lambda_p]$ and E is the matrix of eigenvectors with

$$\lambda_1 = c_{11}, \, e_1 = [1, 0, 0 \ldots 0]^T$$
$$\lambda_2 = c_{22}, \, e_2 = [0, 1, 0 \ldots 0]^T$$

$$\ldots$$

$$\lambda_p = c_{pp}, \, e_p = [0, 0, 0 \ldots 1]^T$$

However, Ahn, Marron, Muller, and Chi (2007), among others, have shown that as dimensionality (number of features or columns) in the data increases relative to the number of observations, the eigenvalues estimated by PCA are likely to blur and become indistinguishable from those of an identity covariance matrix. In other words, as the number of columns in the data increases or the number of observations decreases, the signal disappears in the noise entirely. However, Johnstone (2001) and Ahn, Marron, Muller, and Chi (2007) also show that the first eigenvalue can still be estimated by PCA reliably in uncorrelated or weakly correlated data when the signal is dominant. In this case, the covariance is said to be "extremely spiked," that is,

$$\Sigma = diag(p^\alpha, 1, 1, \ldots 1), \alpha > 1 \tag{7.14}$$

where p is the dimension of data, i.e., the number of columns.

In this extremely spiked setup, Ahn, Marron, Muller, and Chi (2007) show that the first eigenvalue of the data, λ_1, is indeed $\lambda_1 = p^\alpha$, with the rest of the eigenvalues $\lambda_2 = \lambda_2 = \ldots = \lambda_p = 1$, and eigenvectors being the p-dimensional unit vectors. Jung and Marron (2009) showed that in data with a diagonal covariance matrix, the largest k eigenvalues can also be reliably estimated under specific conditions.

Dealing with Highly Correlated Data

While the Marčenko-Pastur and spike models apply to the largely uncorrelated intraday data, they are not well suited to daily and longer-term financial returns that are known to exhibit high correlations since Marčenko-Pastur assumes the underlying data to be i.i.d. To address the issue, we apply PCA to correlation instead of covariance of correlated data. While the process is identical except that PCA is performed on normalized correlation data, it is known then as the Karhunen-Loève Transform (KLT).

The KLT premise is that PCA performed on the correlation matrix, instead of a covariance matrix, factors out a lot of variation in the correlation structure into the singular values. Indeed, the largest eigenvalue of the correlation matrix always happens to be the average correlation of the data while the other singular values capture the other dimensions of the largest correlation variability in decreasing order. Reconstructing the correlation matrix under Karhunen-Loève follows an identical process to that under PCA. Marčenko-Pastur cut-offs now apply even when the data are highly correlated because PCA on the correlation data decoupled or defactored the correlations into orthogonal components.

In portfolio management applications, the use of Karhunen-Loève is readily apparent. The portfolios with reduced dimensions are constructed with the principal components of the correlation matrix. Marčenko-Pastur applies and delivers sound results.

Deconstructing the Mona Lisa

To illustrate the concepts discussed in this chapter, consider once again the image of the Mona Lisa, repeated for convenience in Figure 7.9.

The image measures 250 pixels across and 360 pixels vertically. As before, each pixel in grayscale is actually represented by a number in [0,255], with 0 rendering as black, 255 as white, and everything else in darker or whiter shades of gray. The colors of the image change slowly with many columns showing similar coloring. As a result, the image data are highly correlated. The histogram of the Mona Lisa's correlation is shown in Figure 7.10.

As Figure 7.10 shows, the Mona Lisa correlation mass is well in excess of the 50 percent reached by the daily returns of the U.S. S&P 500 stocks. From this perspective, it is interesting to demonstrate the techniques discussed in this chapter on the Mona Lisa image.

If we detrend and descale the image data column-by-column, and then run Marčenko-Pastur, the Mona Lisa scree plot shows only 6 significant eigenvalues (Figure 7.11). This number is close to what a human researcher is likely to pick as the "elbow" of the scree plot just by eyeballing the plot. While the result delivers a compact

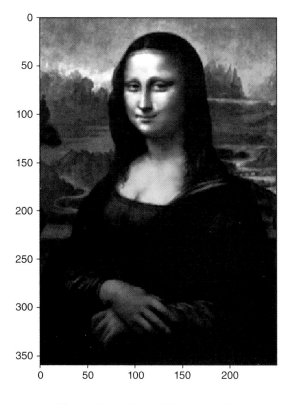

Figure 7.9 Mona Lisa, grayscale.

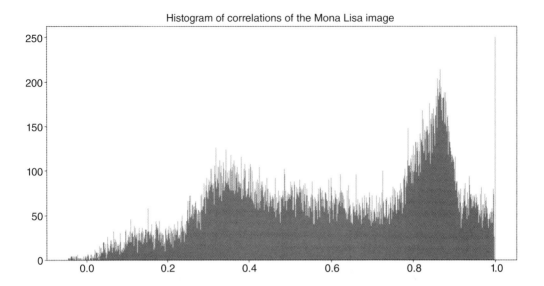

Figure 7.10   Histogram of correlations of the Mona Lisa's columns.

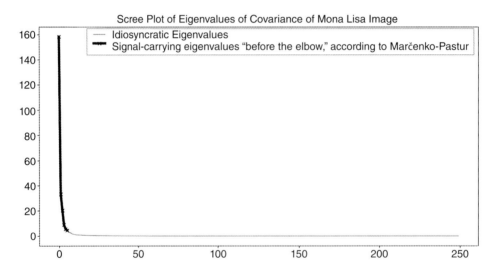

Figure 7.11   The Marčenko-Pastur "elbow" of the detrended and descaled covariance of the columns of the Mona Lisa image.

representation of the image – we just reduced 250 columns down to 6 – the image reconstruction with just six eigenvalues may not be fully satisfying to a human viewer, as shown in Figure 7.12.

In contrast, applying Marčenko-Pastur to the covariance of the unnormalized, raw image produces a much higher significant eigenvalue cut-off value, 120 (Figure 7.13). This in turn delivers a much clearer image reconstruction, shown in Figure 7.14.

Mona Lisa reconstruction with 6 most significant eigenvalues, selected by Marčenko-Pastur

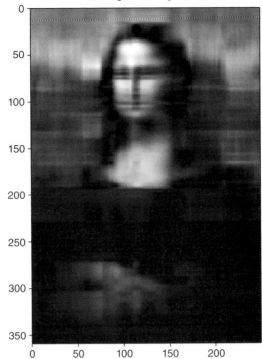

Figure 7.12 Mona Lisa reconstruction with just six significant eigenvalues.

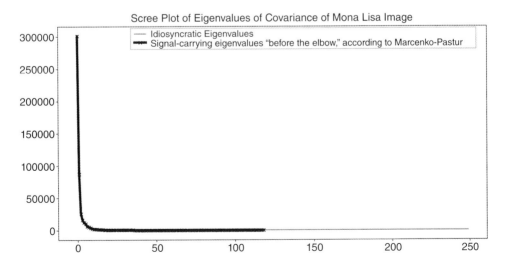

Figure 7.13 Marčenko–Pastur cut-off on the unnormalized (raw) Mona Lisa image. The Marčenko-Pastur value comes in at 120.

Mona Lisa reconstruction with 119 most significant eigenvalues, selected by Marčenko-Pastur

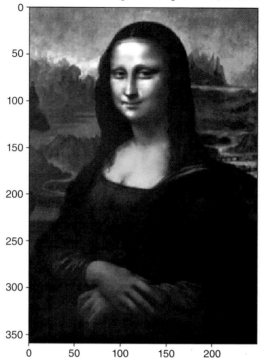

Figure 7.14 Subsequent SVD reconstruction of the image with 120 significant eigenvalues delivers the image nearly identical to the original from a human eye perspective.

What's in the Data Bag?

We have constructed the data distribution and identified the number of eigenvalues to keep via Marčenko-Pastur. What kind of inferences can we make from the data?

Applications

1. Determining the "Cut-off" of Significant Eigenvalues in i.i.d. Processes

While theoretical exercises involving random matrices are very informative, the focus of this book is on financial applications of the Big Data models. Application of Marčenko-Pastur to the actual S&P 500 returns is shown in Figures 7.15–7.22. Indeed, the financial returns differ considerably from the random data dynamics shown in Figures 7.2–7.5.

Figure 7.15 shows the distribution of eigenvalues of covariances of daily returns of the S&P 500 computed over 750 trading days spanning 2013–2015. The narrower shape of the distribution is driven by the significant outliers of the eigenvalue distribution. The largest theoretical eigenvalue of the covariance of pure noise (Marčenko-Pastur) is

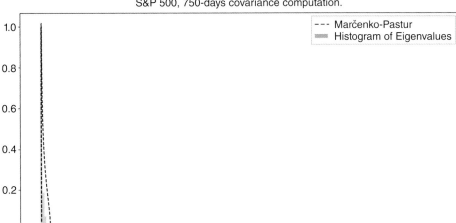

Figure 7.15 Marčenko-Pastur and the empirical distribution of the eigenvalues of the covariances of the daily normalized S&P 500 returns. 750 trading day returns (three trading years) were used in the computation shown.

$b = 3.13695$ computed for $\gamma = 1.5$ ($\gamma = p/n, n = 750, p = 500$). In the empirical eigenvalue distribution of the covariance of the 750 daily S&P 500 returns for 2013–2015, 18 eigenvalues exceed the "b threshold." These "popping-out of the distribution" or "spiking" eigenvalues are: 137.62393, 20.36657, 13.07877, 9.12688, 6.05041, 5.83210, 5.33807, 4.73916, 4.64517, 4.53902, 4.30116, 4.02740, 3.83986, 3.70290, 3.50262, 3.31965, 3.19999, and 3.14793.

A cut-off in the eigenvalues is the elbow in the scree plot first discussed in Chapter 5 of this book. The original approach to dealing with the selection of significant eigenvalues involved a researcher's subjective judgment to discern the tilting point of the elbow in the scree plot. Needless to say, such an approach was fraught with instability, error, and complications in replication. Marčenko-Pastur provides us a relief from subjectivity by delivering a cut-off of eigenvalues where they fall outside of the support of Marčenko-Pastur distribution. Specifically, we are interested in the largest eigenvalues that exceed the largest eigenvalue considered to be random by Marčenko-Pastur, b in Eq (7.7), repeated here for convenience:

$$b = (1 + \gamma^{1/2})^2 \tag{7.15}$$

where γ is the ratio of the number of columns to the number of rows in the underlying data matrix, $\gamma = p/n$. Additionally, more precise tools for determining the distribution of the largest eigenvalue of random data are discussed in Chapter 4.

Figure 7.16 shows the Marčenko-Pastur cut-off of the significant eigenvalues on a scree plot. As Figure 7.16 illustrates, the "elbow" chosen by Marčenko-Pastur falls lower, that is, includes more significant eigenvalues, than one may naively pick by eyeballing the scree plot. Figures 7.18, 7.20, 7.22, 7.24, 7.26, and 7.28 similarly show the significant eigenvalues picked by Marčenko-Pastur for various numbers of daily S&P 500

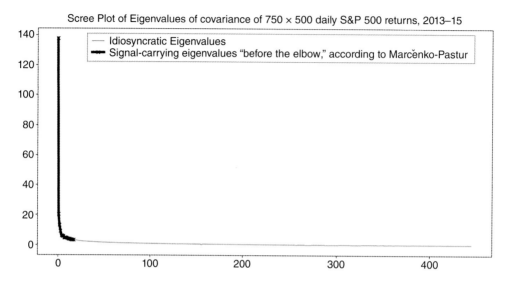

Figure 7.16 The scree plot of the singular values corresponding to the data shown in Figure 7.15 delineating eigenvalues greater than the largest Marčenko-Pastur eigenvalue. 18 eigenvalues "spiked" after the Marčenko-Pastur cut-off.

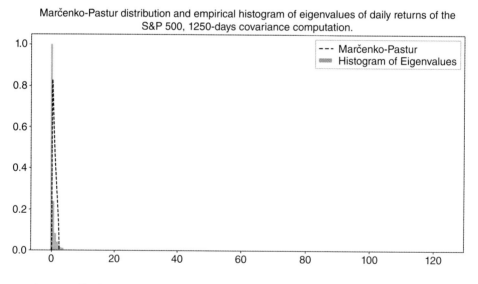

Figure 7.17 Marčenko-Pastur and the empirical distribution of the eigenvalues of the covariances of the daily normalized S&P 500 returns. 1,250 trading day returns (five trading years) were used in the computation shown.

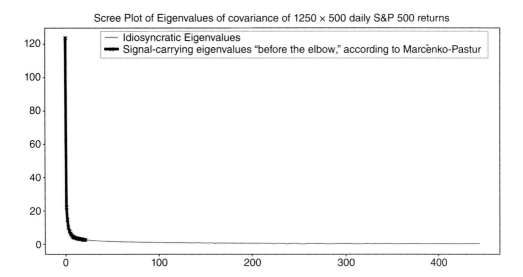

Figure 7.18   The scree plot of the singular values corresponding to the data shown in Figure 7.17 delineating eigenvalues greater than the largest Marčenko-Pastur eigenvalue. 22 eigenvalues "spiked" after the Marčenko-Pastur cut-off.

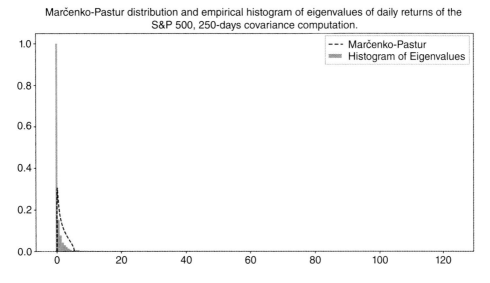

Figure 7.19   Marčenko-Pastur and the empirical distribution of the eigenvalues of the covariances of the normalized S&P 500 returns. 250 trading day returns (one trading year) were used in the computation shown.

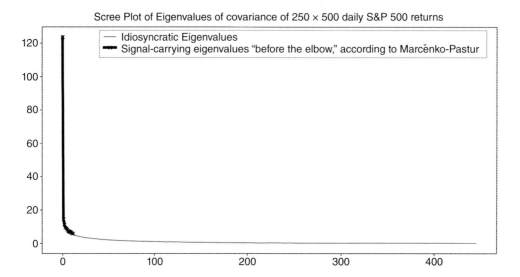

Figure 7.20   The scree plot of the singular values corresponding to the data shown in Figure 7.19 delineating eigenvalues greater than the largest Marčenko-Pastur eigenvalue. Only 12 eigenvalues "spiked" after the Marčenko-Pastur cut-off.

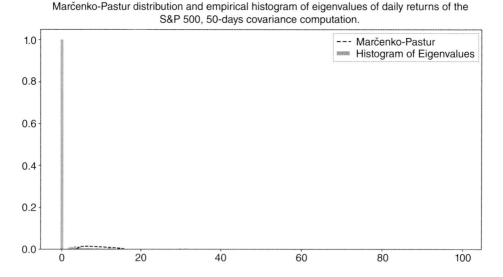

Figure 7.21   Marčenko-Pastur and the empirical distribution of the eigenvalues of the covariances of the daily normalized S&P 500 returns. 50 trading day returns were used in the computation shown.

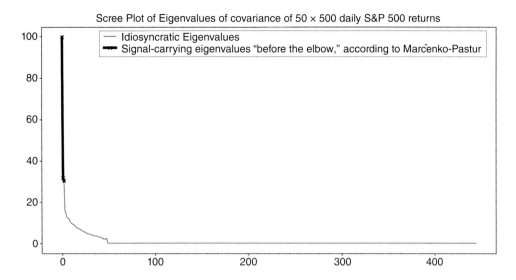

Figure 7.22 The scree plot of the singular values corresponding to the data shown in Figure 7.21 delineating eigenvalues greater than the largest Marčenko-Pastur eigenvalue. Only three eigenvalues "spiked" after the Marčenko-Pastur cut-off.

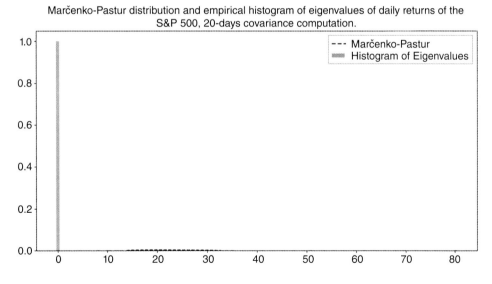

Figure 7.23 Marčenko-Pastur and the empirical distribution of the eigenvalues of the covariances of the normalized S&P 500 returns. Twenty trading day returns were used in the computation shown.

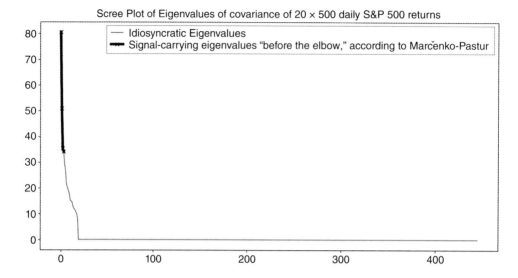

Figure 7.24   The scree plot of the singular values corresponding to the data shown in Figure 7.23 delineating eigenvalues greater than the largest Marčenko-Pastur eigenvalue. Four eigenvalues "spiked" after the Marčenko-Pastur cut-off.

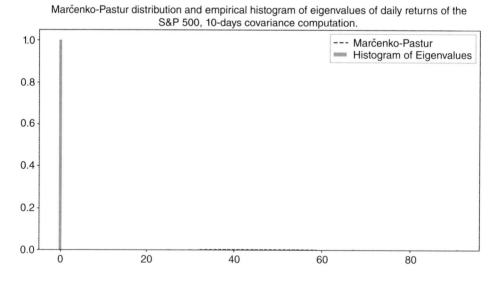

Figure 7.25   Marčenko-Pastur and the empirical distribution of the eigenvalues of the covariances of the normalized S&P 500 returns. Ten trading day returns were used in the computation shown.

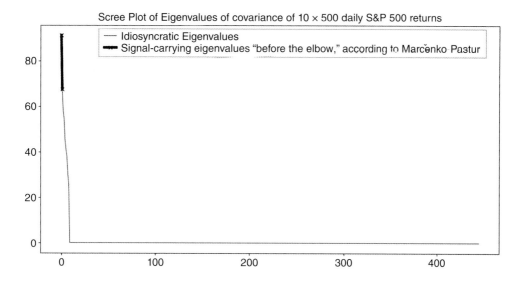

Figure 7.26   The scree plot of the singular values corresponding to the data shown in Figure 7.25 delineating eigenvalues greater than the largest Marčenko-Pastur eigenvalue. Just two eigenvalues "spiked" after the Marčenko-Pastur cut-off.

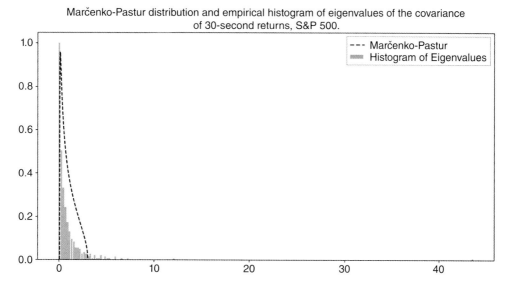

Figure 7.27   Marčenko-Pastur and the empirical distribution of the eigenvalues of the covariances of the 30-second normalized S&P 500 returns recorded on March 31, 2017, 780 × 500 matrix.

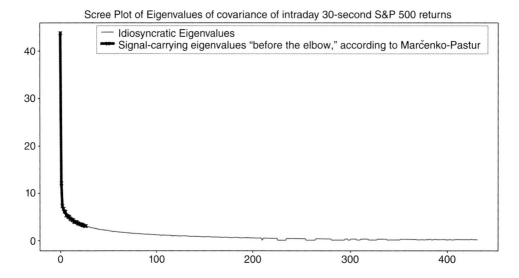

Figure 7.28   The scree plot of the singular values corresponding to the data shown in Figure 7.27 delineating eigenvalues greater than the largest Marčenko-Pastur eigenvalue. Twenty-eight eigenvalues "spiked" after the Marčenko-Pastur cut-off.

returns. Figures 7.17, 7.19, 7.21, 7.23. 7.25, and 7.27 show the Marčenko-Pastur and the empirical distribution of the eigenvalues of the covariances of the normalized S&P 500 returns for various daily returns. A trend appears: fewer rows in matrices result in fewer significant eigenvalues picked out by Marčenko-Pastur.

While a few eigenvalues "pop out" of the Marčenko-Pastur distributions when the S&P 500 is considered, on an intraday basis, the number of eigenvalues exceeding the Marčenko-Pastur envelope is a lot more numerous, as shown in Figures 7.27 and 7.28. According to the Marčenko-Pastur interpretation, the more outliers outside the Marčenko-Pastur envelope, the stronger and more varied the signal the eigenvalue/principal component framework is picking up.

2. Determining the "Cut-off" of Significant Eigenvalues in Non-i.i.d. Heteroscedastic Processes

In many cases, the assumption of independent identically distributed processes is just too strong. Figure 7.29 shows the histogram of correlations of the daily S&P 500 returns, computed over the 2013–2017 period. As shown in Figures 7.29–7.31, the S&P 500 daily return data are highly correlated. In addition, stock returns, in particular those computed over several years, are subject to changing market environments and other structural changes that may drastically affect their distribution. Regime switches from high market volatility periods to low volatility and back are all too common and have a significant impact on the underlying stock distributions. This section discusses determination of the optimal number of significant eigenvalues when the underlying processes X are non-i.i.d.

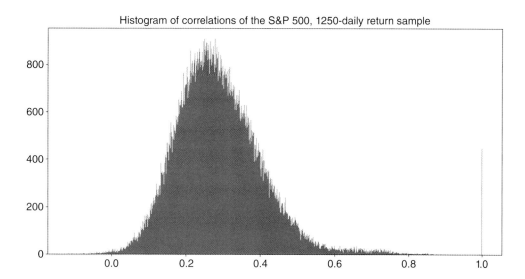

Figure 7.29 Histogram of correlations of daily returns of the S&P 500, 1,250 observations, 2013–2017.

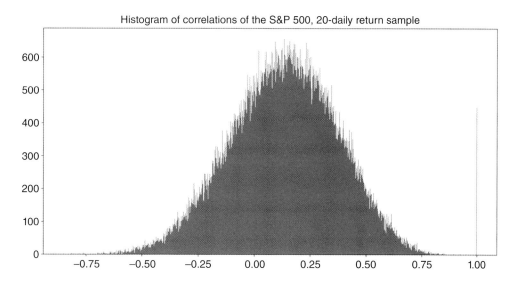

Figure 7.30 Histogram of correlations of daily returns of the S&P 500, $T = 20$ days.

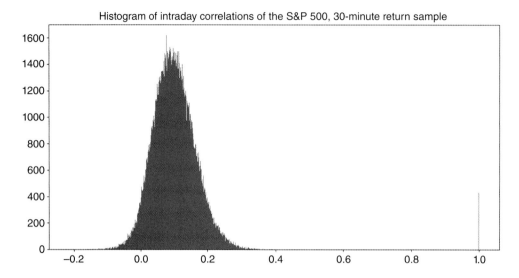

Figure 7.31 Histogram of correlations of intraday 30-minute returns of the S&P 500, 1 day corresponds to $T = 780$ 30-minute observations.

and have variance that changes over time. Such processes X are known in econometrics as the heteroscedastic processes.

The Karhunen-Loève Transform

The Karhunen-Loève Transform (KLT) is often used to draw inferences from highly correlated data, like the long-term U.S. stock market returns. Marčenko-Pastur on PCA assumes that the underlying data is independent identically distributed (i.i.d.), implying that the correlations of the data studies are all 0. In practice, however, this is often not the case and is seldom the case in finance, in particular.

The Karhunen-Loève Transform takes care of the correlations by extracting the correlation variance into the eigenvalues (see, for example, Friedman and Weisberg, 1981). Projecting the data onto the eigenvectors produces "decoupled" data with diminished correlation structure. This data can then be assumed to approximate the no-correlation data required by many models (Figures 7.32–7.35).

A method proposed by Laloux, Cizeau, Bouchaud, and Potters (1999) performs eigenvalue decomposition on the correlation matrix instead of the covariance. In this setup, the variances are removed from consideration altogether. Eigenvalue decomposition of the correlation coefficients on the intraday data corresponding to Figures 7.34 and 7.35 is shown in Figures 7.36 and 7.37. The correlation method produces fewer significant eigenvalues than the covariance method: 20 significant eigenvalues in the correlation coefficients of the intraday data versus 28 in the covariance. Similarly, Figures 7.38 and 7.39 show eigenvalues of the correlation matrix of 750 daily returns on the S&P 500 corresponding to the eigenvalues of covariances shown in Figures 7.38 and 7.39 Marčenko-Pastur produced only 11 significant eigenvalues in the correlation matrix,

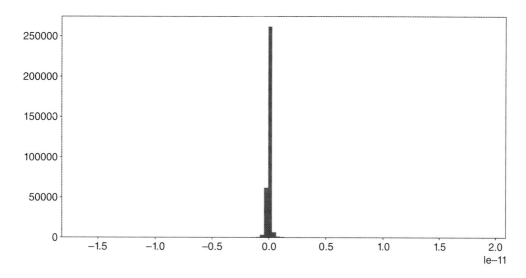

Figure 7.32   Histogram of errors of intraday returns and predicted returns decomposed and then reconstructed by KLT.

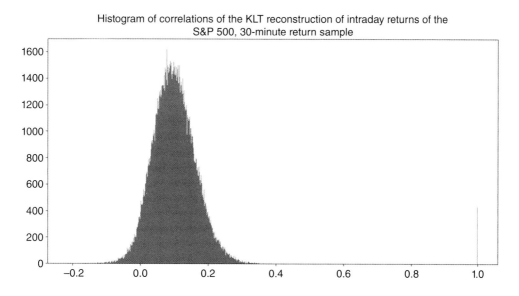

Figure 7.33   Histogram of correlations of KLT prediction, all eigenvectors present in KLT reconstruction.

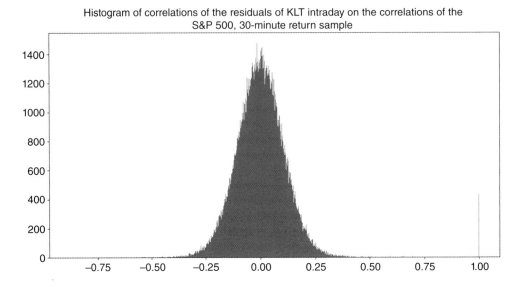

Figure 7.34   Histogram of correlations of residuals, all eigenvectors present in KLT reconstruction.

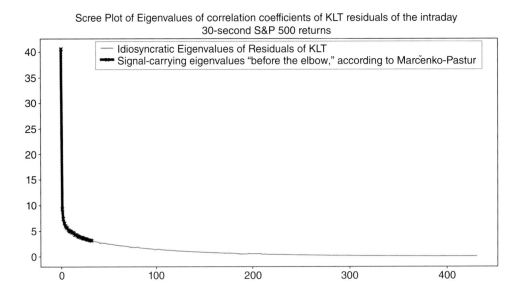

Figure 7.35   Scree plot of errors between the intraday 30–second S&P 500 returns and the KLT reconstruction of those returns.

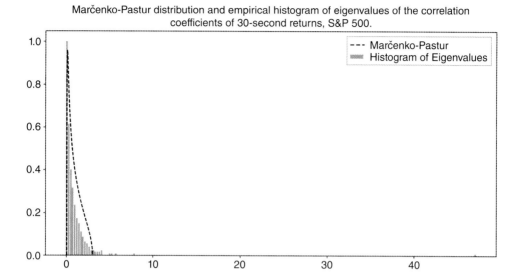

Figure 7.36 Marčenko-Pastur and the empirical distribution of the eigenvalues of the correlations of the 30-second normalized S&P 500 returns recorded on March 31, 2017, 780 × 500 matrix.

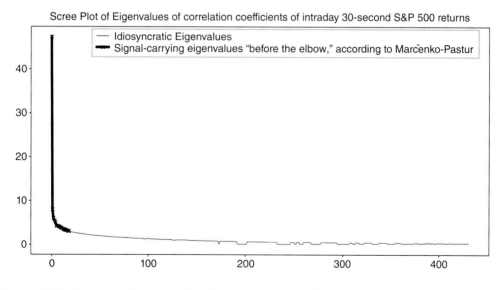

Figure 7.37 The scree plot of the singular values corresponding to the correlation data shown in Figure 7.35 delineating eigenvalues greater than the largest Marčenko-Pastur eigenvalue. 20 eigenvalues "spiked" after the Marčenko-Pastur cut-off.

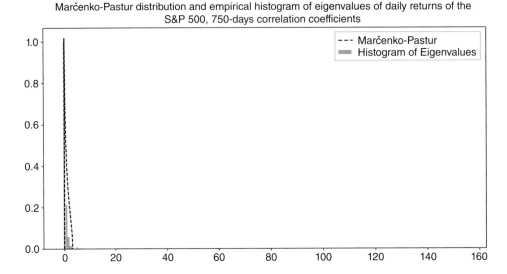

Figure 7.38 Marčenko–Pastur and the empirical distribution of the eigenvalues of the correlation coefficients of the daily normalized S&P 500 returns. 750 trading day returns (three trading years, 2013–2015) were used in the computation shown.

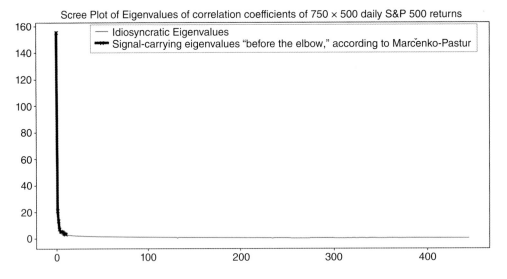

Figure 7.39 The scree plot of the singular values corresponding to the data shown in Figure 7.38 delineating eigenvalues greater than the largest Marčenko–Pastur eigenvalue. 11 eigenvalues "spiked" after the Marčenko–Pastur cut-off.

as compared to the 18 significant eigenvalues in covariance decomposition shown in Figure 7.35.

The Laloux, Cizeau, Bouchaud, and Potters (1999) method goes even further than the correlation analysis. In order to find a reliable cut-off, the researchers propose taking off the most significant individual eigenvalues one by one until the remaining data fits into the Marčenko-Pastur distribution:

1. Distribution of eigenvalues of Gaussian (0,1) noise (Wigner) (Figure 7.40).
2. Identifying signal: spike models (Figure 7.41).

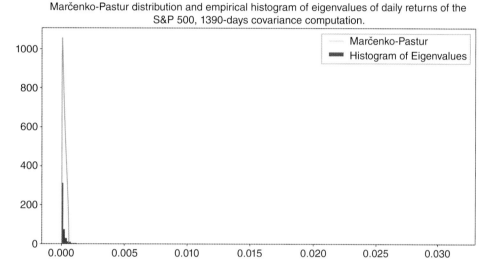

Figure 7.40   Theoretical Marčenko-Pastur distribution for the eigenvalues of the covariance of daily S&P 500 returns 2013–2018 and the realized distribution.

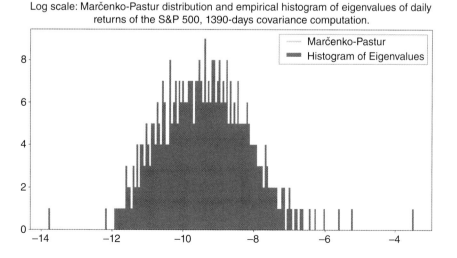

Figure 7.41   Log scale of the distribution of the eigenvalues of the covariance of daily S&P 500 returns 2013–2018 shows "spikes" or outliers more clearly.

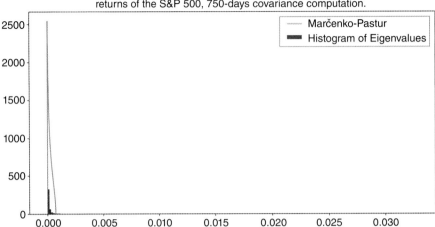

Figure 7.42   Theoretical Marčenko-Pastur distribution for the eigenvalues of the covariance of daily S&P 500 returns 2013–2015 and the realized distribution.

3. Distribution of eigenvalues of i.i.d. (0,1) noise (Marčenko-Pastur).
4. Signal identification in the presence of i.i.d. noise.

Changing the number of daily observations that feeds into the covariance matrix computation changes the distribution of eigenvalues (Figure 7.42).

Data Imputation

Financial data have traditionally suffered from biases and computational complications that arose from missing or small-sample data. The rigidity of econometrics has demanded that all the data be perfect, aligned in precisely spaced intervals in neat rows and columns with all the i's dotted and the t's crossed.

The main idea behind the Data Science approach is that very large quantities of imperfect data allow for much stronger population inferences than the perfectly structured and scrubbed, yet comparatively small, samples of econometric data. To compare scales, Data Science observations number in billions and trillions while econometric models survive on data points often numbering in just hundreds.

And financial data numbering in billions and larger quantities is widely available: exchanges alone generate trillions of data points every second. More and more exchanges are gearing to stay open 24 hours a day, 5 days a week, following the successes of around-the-clock trading in foreign exchange and futures. Most U.S. equity exchanges offer extended trading hours that begin at 4 AM ET and end at 8 PM. With trading approaching the true 24×5 model, the amount of data from trading alone is extremely large.

In many financial data applications, the problem of limited data arises. For example, many financial instruments, such as small stocks, options, and futures with far-out maturities, are highly illiquid. The challenge of correctly estimating their true price is, therefore, critical in these applications. Knowing the true price may directly lead to profitable trading decisions. The ability to accurately price illiquid securities potentially expands the investing and trading universe. The possibly superior mark-to-market techniques may enable extra profitability in fixed income and options spaces.

Another set of applications of imputation of missing data is in intraday and real-time data streaming. A large share of today's data quotations is conducted over the public Internet networks. As such, the data are prone to bottlenecks, missing information, and more. Furthermore, the majority of real-time quote data are presently distributed in a way to lighten the network load and, therefore, avoid data receipt confirmation and resubmission. Unlike trade executions data that are delivered like email with a guarantee and resubmission using the TCP/IP protocol, quote data are streamed like video data with the so-called UDP protocol. The idea of the UDP is that a new quote rapidly replaces the lost quote, just like a new movie frame takes the place of the missing frame without sacrificing the viewer's quality. However, traders, market makers, and execution managers relying on the accurate and timely quotes to run on-the-go data analysis may be at a disadvantage as the data they relied on in the backtest to build their models failed to materialize. Sophisticated data imputation may once again come to the rescue and accurately fill in the data lost en route.

Of course, intraday trading and quote data are also notoriously asynchronous, which presents potential estimation problems to the classically trained finance empiricists. Data imputation may once again usefully estimate the missing data, thus providing researchers with an accurate data set to draw inferences.

One of the key advantages of the powerful Big Data imputation models is their speed. A fair amount of research in the space was developed in real-time image recognition, for example, with the aim of joining several poor-quality video cameras to obtain a decent image of the perpetrators. Also, state-of-the-art research into data imputation has been developed in cryogenic microscopy, where the researchers determine the shape of a molecule by freezing it to limit its movement and then combine various angles to attain the 3-D shape of the molecule. Data imputation has also been extensively developed and used in genomics, where it helps to estimate genetic sequences.

Naturally, Data Science concerns itself with missing data values. Unlike econometrics, the discipline that rigorously discards data points with partially missing values in most models, Data Science attempts to utilize all available data. With that, Data Science distinguishes among several categories of missing data:

1. *Missing at random*: the likelihood of a data point being missing may be related to the observed (non-missing) data, but is not related to the missing data themselves. Thus, an illiquid security may be missing a trade, even though the security's intrinsic value has changed along with the price fluctuations of the market or other liquid securities.

2. *Missing completely at random*: the likelihood of a data point being missing is independent of the values of both the missing data and the observed data. An example of a variable missing completely at random may be an event announcement that may go completely unnoticed and not make it into the researchers' databases.

3. *Missing not at random*: the missing data are related to the value of the missing data, a phenomenon well known as self-selection in econometrics. Examples of self-selection in financial data may include hedge fund performance numbers that are reported only when the hedge fund beats the benchmark, and omitted when the performance of the hedge fund is less appealing.

Traditional econometric removal of the data points does not distort the first two models, but will produce severely biased results in the third case. Instead of econometric deletion, Data Science aims for *imputation*: utilization of all available data. Even though tossing partially missing data may be possible, it can be undesirable, particularly in cases when the remaining sample is just too small to create meaningful inferences. This chapter examines the methods created to circumvent the missing data dilemma and utilize as much of available data (missing or not) as possible.

Imputation techniques have evolved largely in Computer Science, outside of Finance and econometrics. Imputation methods come from both statistics and machine learning. The machine learning imputation, known as semi-supervised learning discussed in Chapter 4, trains an algorithm to assign values and data labels where they are missing. Statistical approaches utilize data properties to create distributions of possible locations of the missing variables. Both approaches can be complementary to one another.

Both Data Science and machine learning approaches are highly technical, but manageable with the right researchers and tools in place. Data are the key ingredient: large raw data samples are required to create solid inferences. Large amounts of data call for advanced data storage and efficient processing software. Thanks to social media companies, both data storage and software costs can be negligible due to cloud technologies. Python and other efficient and highly popular statistical software packages are free and open-sourced, ensuring software stability and fast elimination of defects, known as "bugs."

In today's world of Internet-of-Things (IoT) and razor-thin margins, imputation becomes a competitive advantage. Suppose a sensor of truck traffic is sending you a continuous data stream that all of a sudden goes blank for 30 minutes due to an Internet outage. While your competitors and traditional econometricians may completely forget about the missing data, you can boost your profits by statistically and algorithmically reconstructing the missing data sample. The same ideas apply to illiquid trading data, whether in intraday, daily, monthly, or even quarterly time scales – correctly imputed values provide a strong advantage for investors, risk managers, and traders over the competition. For example, imputing the missing daily prices for illiquid securities can significantly broaden a hedge fund's investing universe. Similarly, imputing intraday prices during quiet or illiquid times helps execution managers and traders make better decisions about short-term actions.

Missing values can be imputed using techniques from supervised, semi-supervised, and unsupervised learning. Bertsimas, Pawlowski, and Zhou (2018) provide a convenient summary of references for existing methodologies. Repeated here for the reader's convenience, the methodologies highlighted by Bertsimas, Pawlowski, and Zhou (2018) are:

- Mean impute due to Little and Rubin (1987).
- Expectation Maximization (EM) by Dempster, Laird, and Rubin (1977).
- EM with mixture of Gaussians and multinomials (Ghahramani and Jordan 1994).
- EM with bootstrapping (Honaker et al. 2011).
- K-Nearest Neighbors (KNN) K-NN impute (Troyanskaya et al. 2001).
- Sequential K-Nearest Neighbors (K-NN) (Kim et al. 2005).
- Iterative K-Nearest Neighbors (K-NN) (Caruana 2001; Bras and Menezes 2007).
- Support Vector Regression (SVR) (Wang et al. 2006).
- Predictive-Mean Matching (PMM) LS MICE (Buuren and Groothuis-Oudshoorn 2011).
- Least Squares (LS) (Bø et al. 2004).
- Sequential Regression Multivariate Imputation LS (Raghunathan et al. 2001).
- Local-Least Squares (LS) (Kim et al. 2005).
- Sequential Local-Least Squares (LS) (Zhang et al. 2008).
- Iterative Local-Least Squares (LS) (Cai et al. 2006).
- Sequential Regression Trees Tree MICE (Burgette and Reiter 2010).
- Sequential Random Forest Tree miss (Stekhoven and Bühlmann 2012).
- Singular Value Decomposition (SVD) (Troyanskaya et al. 2001).
- Bayesian Principal Component Analysis (SVD PCA) Methods (Oba et al. 2003; Mohamed et al. 2009).
- Factor Analysis Model for Mixed Data (FA) (Khan et al. 2010).

Supervised learning can be used for data imputation, but the available data typically needs to be perfectly precise. Figure 7.43 illustrates the famous example of the imputation of faces under different supervised learning models. The model is trained on the database known as Olivetti faces. The bottom half of each true face is erased and then reconstructed using extra trees, K-NN, linear regression, and ridge regression from the top portion of the face relative to the Olivetti training set.

As Figure 7.43 shows, the models do an okay job in predicting the missing portion of the faces. Ridge regression appears to perform the best. Figures 7.44 and 7.45 do the same for the Mona Lisa.

The Mona Lisa image is first altered in the following way: black dots replace randomly-chosen pixels in the original image. In the grayscale world, the color black is denoted as 0. Blacking-out random points in the image is, therefore, equivalent to setting random elements of the matrix to 0.

The eigenvalues of the resulting image are analyzed and compared with those of the original, non-edited, picture. Notably, the eigenvalues of the original and the edited images remain the same whenever 200 or fewer image pixels are replaced at random. The original image contained 460 rows and 318 columns, or $460 \times 318 = 146,280$ matrix elements. Blacking out 200 pixels out of 146,280 represents an effective white out of just over 0.1% of the dataset.

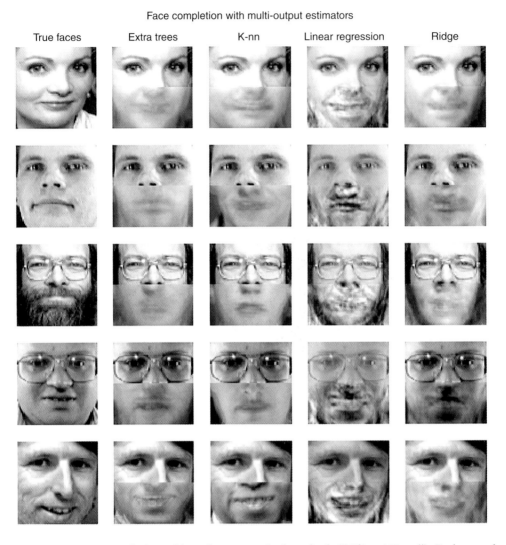

Figure 7.43   Face completion with various supervised methods ("Olivetti Faces"). Python code source: https://ndownloader.figshare.com/files/5976027.

Figure 7.45 shows the distribution of the eigenvalues for levels of blackout ranging from 0 to 200 pixels. As the Figure shows, the eigenvalues hardly move. Figure 7.47 confirms this finding by displaying the top eigenvalues side-by-side for different levels of data blackout.

Similar findings are obtained whenever a random sample of the image pixels were replaced with white color, that is assigned the value of 255. Figures 7.46 and 7.48 show that the eigenvalues hardly moved from one level of whiteout to the next. The eigenvalue comparisons illustrate an important fact: the eigenvalues do not move even when a small portion of the data is corrupted or missing at random, regardless of the point replacement values.

The Marčenko-Pastur cut-off of Karhunen-Loève Transform remains fixed at 7 with varying degrees of blackout up to 200 data points (Figures 7.45 and 7.47).

A very close look at the differences in the eigenvalues, however, shows that very small discrepancies between eigenvalues do in fact exist, as shown in Figures 7.49 and 7.53.

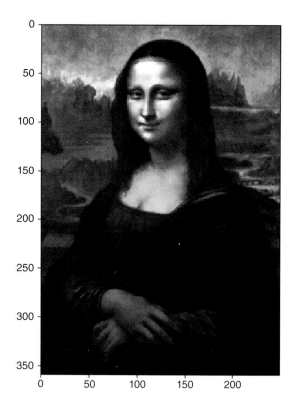

Figure 7.44   Original Mona Lisa image.

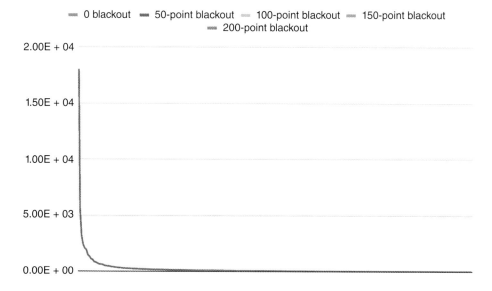

Figure 7.45   Distribution of eigenvalues for Mona Lisa with 0, 50, 100, and 200 data points set to 0 at random.

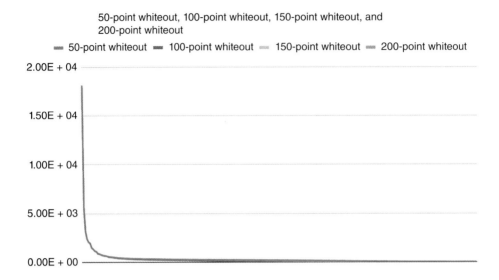

Figure 7.46   Eigenvalue changes for various whiteout regimes. Eigenvalues hardly change.

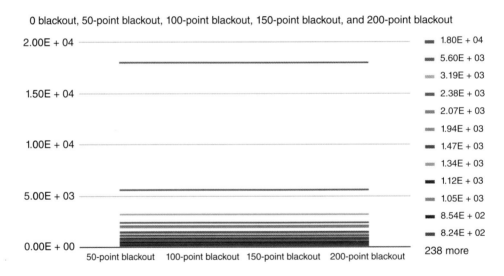

Figure 7.47   Distribution of eigenvalues for Mona Lisa with 0, 50, 100, and 200 data points set to 0 at random.

Figure 7.49 shows absolute differences in corresponding eigenvalues for different levels of black out. Figure 7.50 shows the relative change in the eigenvalues among different blackout levels. Figure 7.51 shows the relative eigenvalue changes for for different level of whiteout, and Figure 7.52 evaluates the relative changes in eigenvalues following introduction of random [0,255] values to the randomly selected pixels. Figure 7.53 displays the impact of noise sampled from [0,127].

As Figures 7.50–7.53 show, the most variation in eigenvalues occurs not in the dominant (top) set, and not in the idiosyncratic tail, but in the middle of the eigenvalue spectrum.

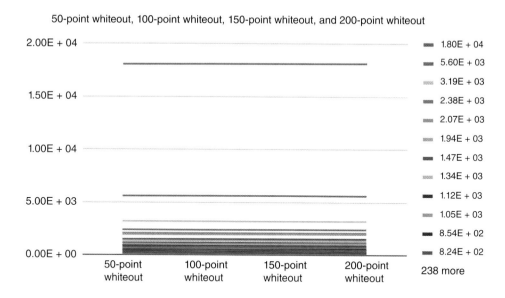

Figure 7.48   Eigenvalues for different whiteout regimes. The eigenvalues hardly change.

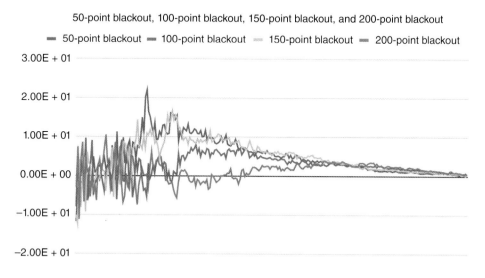

Figure 7.49   Absolute differences in eigenvalues between 50-point blackout and the original image, 100-point blackout and the original image, 150-point blackout and the original image, and 200-point blackout and the original image.

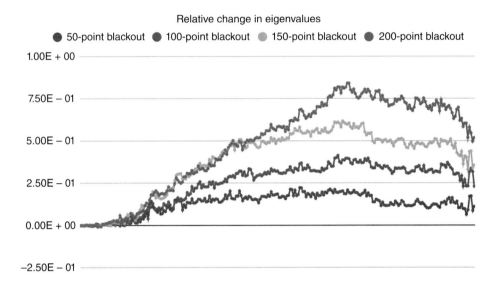

Figure 7.50   Relative changes in the eigenvalues for different blackout levels of the Mona Lisa image.

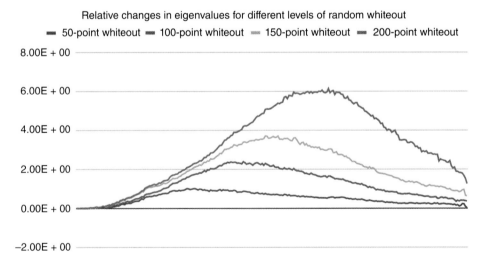

Figure 7.51   Differences in sequential eigenvalues between whiteout Mona Lisa image and the original image for different levels of random whiteout.

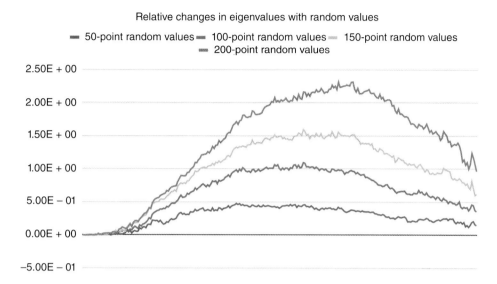

Figure 7.52 Relative changes in eigenvalues from random data replacement in the original Mona Lisa image. The random values inserted in the original Mona Lisa image are in the range [0,255].

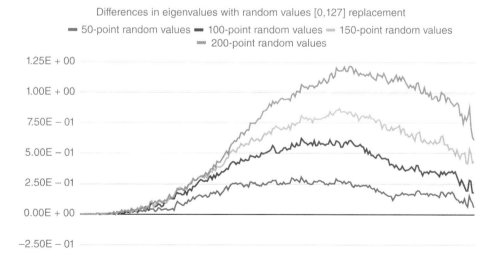

Figure 7.53 Relative changes in eigenvalues from random data replacement in the original Mona Lisa image. The random values inserted in the original Mona Lisa image are in the range [0,127].

Furthermore, a closer comparison of images in Figures 7.49–7.53 shows that the change in the mid-range eigenvalues is proportional to the following:

1. The number of data points replaced.
2. The mean of the replacement distribution.

From the perspective of unsupervised learning, where the objective is to retain the top eigenvalues, the key eigenvalues hardly move when the data is missing at random. Even when the objective is to retain the most idiosyncratic components at the tail of the eigenvalue spectrum, noise again does not cause much distortion.

In the context of financial modeling, these observations lead to an interesting perspective in financial data analysis: even when a healthy proportion of the financial data set is missing at random, the unsupervised learning inferences remain strong. Figures 7.54 and 7.55 show the eigenvalues of the S&P 500 in the original daily data and when 20% of the data were set to 0 at random. As Figures 7.55 and 7.55 illustrate, the eigenvalues of the data barely changed from Figure 7.54 to Figure 7.55, indicating that the structure of data is preserved even when a fair proportion of data is lost. These findings are very different from the expectations of the traditional econometric analysis where rows with partially missing data would simply be discarded. Unsupervised learning can be useful to take advantage of every small morsel of data.

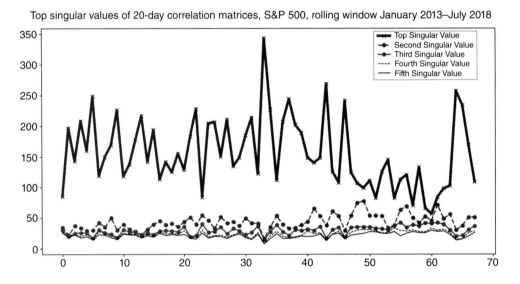

Figure 7.54   Top 5 eigenvalues of the S&P 500 correlation matrix (20-day non-overlapping rolling windows, 2013–2018).

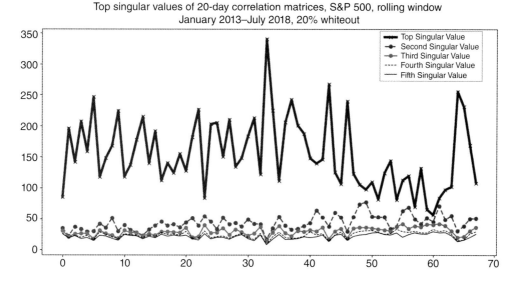

Figure 7.55 Top 5 eigenvalues of the S&P 500 correlation matrix (20-day non-overlapping rolling windows, 2013–2018) where 20% of the underlying returns were randomly set to 0 in each time period.

Missing Eigenvalues

When computing eigenvalues via PCA or SVD is too time-consuming or plain difficult due to missing data, the Tracy-Widom distribution discussed in detail in the next section provides a numerical alternative.

The problem of missing values can particularly cause portfolio managers to stumble when the securities under consideration are not liquid enough to generate the required data for the sample return covariance matrix. The Tracy-Widom distribution comes to the rescue then (Figure 7.56).

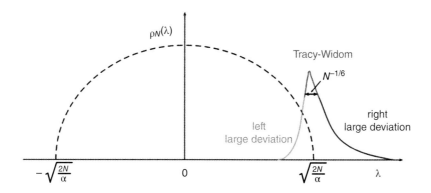

Figure 7.56 Relationship between Wigner and Tracy-Widom distributions. Source: Nadal and Majumdar (2011).

Implementing the Tracy-Widom distribution in code can be difficult. Tracy and Widom derived the distribution based on the theory of Fredholm determinants. Nadal and Majumdar (2011), for example, derive the distribution as the partition function of a two-dimensional Coulomb gas constrained to a line and placed in a harmonic trap.

Bai, Yin, and Krishnaiah (1986) showed that the largest eigenvalue of an $n \times p$ covariance matrix of the form $\left(\frac{1}{n}XX'\right)$ with $p/n \to \gamma \in (0, \infty)$ tends almost surely to $(1 + \sqrt{\gamma})^2$ as $n \to \infty$. Subsequently, Bai and Yin (1993) showed that the smallest eigenvalue of the same matrix tends almost surely to $(1 - \sqrt{\gamma})^2$ as $n \to \infty$.

Johnstone (2001) showed that Tracy-Widom applies to Gaussian covariance $\left(\frac{1}{n}XX'\right)$ matrices of $n \times p$ sizes, when the data are centered by $\mu_p = (\sqrt{n-1} + \sqrt{p})^2$ and scaled by $\sigma_p = (\sqrt{n-1} + \sqrt{p})(1/\sqrt{n-1} + 1/\sqrt{p})^{1/3}$.

Lee and Schnelli (2014) examined the Tracy-Widom distribution of the covariance matrices. Lee and Schnelli (2014) show that for any mean-zero random variable $y = (y_1, \ldots, y_M)' \in \mathcal{R}^M$ with the population covariance $\Sigma = Eyy'$, the Tracy-Widom distribution works under the following conditions. Given sample N independent measurements $(y_1, \ldots, y_N)$ with sample covariance $\frac{1}{N}\sum_{i=1}^{N} y_i y_i'$, and representing $y_i = (N\Sigma)^{1/2}x_i$, $Q := (\Sigma^{1/2}X)(\Sigma^{1/2}X)^*$, where $X = (x_1, \ldots, x_N)$, Q almost surely converges to Σ as N tends to infinity. Per Lee and Schnelli (2014), the Tracy-Widom distribution of eigenvalues of Q then holds if either of the following holds:

1. The entries of X are independent identically distributed Gaussians, or
2. The general population's covariance matrix Σ is diagonal and the entries of X have heavy tails, further validating applicability to financial time series.

In general, Tracy-Widom has found applications in:

1. Speedy computation of eigenvalues of covariance matrices. Johnstone (2001) lists Value-at-Risk computation via covariance decomposition as an application of Tracy-Widom.
2. Portfolio management of illiquid securities.
3. Portfolio management at high frequencies.

Thus, even when there are gaps in trading that induce sample correlations to be potentially "out-of-tune" due to the partially missing return data, the Tracy-Widom distribution can provide eigenvalues that can be used in portfolio optimization. The results apply not only to the infrequently traded securities, but also to all financial instruments on the intraday basis when the trading is asynchronous and correlations break down, a phenomenon known as the Epps Effect, first documented by Epps (1979).

While Tracy-Widom does not enable us to reconstruct missing values y_i in the data sample, it does allow us to find the missing eigenvalues. The missing eigenvalues are then used as inputs into a portfolio optimization framework. For empirical applications of Tracy-Widom to portfolio optimization, see Chapter 3.

The Tracy-Widom Distribution

The Tracy-Widom distribution is developed for various cases of real and complex data. As in Chapter 2, we hereby restrict the discussion to Gaussian Orthogonal Ensembles (GOE). A GOE is a random matrix model (RMM) that is a probability space $(\Omega, \mathbb{P}, \mathcal{F})$ where the sample space Ω is a set of $N \times N$ real symmetric matrices, and $\mathbb{P}$ is a unique (up to a choice of the mean and variance) measure that is invariant under orthogonal transformations and the algebraically independent matrix elements are i.i.d. random variables.

For the largest eigenvalues of such a data set, the distribution function of the largest eigenvalue can be defined as:

$$F_N(t):=\mathbb{P}_N(\lambda_{max} < t)$$

Then, per Tracy and Widom (1993, 1994, 1996), the limit of $N \to \infty$ exists,

$$F(x):=lim_{N\to\infty} F_N\left(2\sigma\sqrt{N} + \frac{\sigma x}{N^{1/6}}\right)$$

where σ is the standard deviation of the Gaussian distribution of the off-diagonal matrix elements. $F(x)$ can be derived for GOEs explicitly as a unique solution to the Painlevé II equation:

$$F(x) = exp\left(-\frac{1}{2}\int_x^\infty q(\gamma)d\gamma\right)\left(exp\left(-\int_x^\infty (\gamma-x)q^2(\gamma)d\gamma\right)\right)^{1/2}$$

Tracy and Widom (2002) report distributional statistics for $F(x)$ for GOEs, shown in Table 7.1.

Tracy and Widom (2002) also describe tail asymptotics for the largest eigenvalue density, $F(x)$. As $x \to +\infty$,

$$F(x) = \left[1 - \frac{exp(-\frac{4}{3}x^{3/2})}{32\pi x^{3/2}}\left(1 + O\left(x^{-3/2}\right)\right)\right]\left[1 - \frac{exp\left(-\frac{2}{3}x^{3/2}\right)}{4\sqrt{\pi}x^{3/2}}\left(1 + O\left(x^{-3/2}\right)\right)\right]$$

Table 7.1 The high-precision mean (μ), variance (σ^2), skewness (S), and kurtosis (K) of the distribution function of the largest eigenvalue $F(x)$ for GOEs reported in Tracy and Widom (2002) for Gaussian zero-mean data normalized with standard deviation of the off-diagonal elements $\sigma = \frac{1}{\sqrt{2}}$.

μ	−1.206533574
σ^2	1.607781034
S	0.293464524
K	0.165242938

As $x \to -\infty$, Baik, Buckingham, and Di Franco (2008) showed that for GOE:

$$F(x) = \tau |x|^{-1/16} \left(exp \left(-\frac{1}{24}|x|^3 - \frac{1}{3\sqrt{2}}|x|^{3/2} \right) \right) \left(1 - \frac{1}{24\sqrt{2}|x|^{3/2}} + O(|x|^{-3}) \right)$$

where the constant $\tau = 2^{-11/48} exp \left(\frac{1}{2}\zeta'(-1) \right)$ and $\zeta'(-1)$ is the derivative of the Riemann zeta function evaluated at -1, $\zeta'(-1) = -0.1654211437$.

The above results were developed for distributions of the largest eigenvalue, λ_N, and for GOEs only. Dieng (2005) developed distribution functions for the next largest, next-next largest, etc. eigenvalues λ_{N-1}, λ_{N-2}, …. Tracy and Widom (2002) look to relax the restrictions on the data properties.

Identifying (and Replacing) Missing Values in Streaming Data (the Johnson–Lindenstrauss Lemma)

The innovation of unsupervised learning extends well beyond the applications discussed in this book up to now. Its intelligent sampling is extremely useful in all applications involving lots of data: take multi-asset portfolios with the number of instruments in excess of Russell 1500, or something like high-frequency trading where the number of intraday data points reaches billions for one instrument in just one day. All the data points are typically not equal in their information content: some are packed with value, whereas others are just place fillers. Strategic Big Data sampling allows us to discriminate between content and noise on the fly, and estimate the price trends and distributions with high speed and without processing every possible byte of information.

An important result in Big Data is the Johnson-Lindenstrauss Lemma. The Lemma says that any n data points in high-dimensional Euclidean space can be mapped onto k dimensions with $k \geq O(\log n / \varepsilon^2)$ without distorting the Euclidean distances between the points by more than $1 \pm \varepsilon$. Furthermore, the probability of the distance between a pair of data points falling out of the $1 \pm \varepsilon$ boundary during a mapping to the k dimensions is $P(E) \leq 1 - \frac{1}{n}$. For proof and additional applications, see Berry, Drmac, and Jessup (2001), Achlioptas (2003), and Dasgupta and Gupta (2003).

When data are streaming, as in the case of high-frequency exchange data, a natural question arises as to how to capture and make the most use of it in real time. The Johnson-Lindenstrauss Lemma has answers for this as well. In the streaming data model, we assume that we can only capture the data as they arrive and have no time to search for the data on a storage medium. In the process, we may miss some data. An interpretation of the Johnson-Lindenstrauss Lemma assures us that the main structure of the data up to a small perturbation.

How often do data go missing? In the intraday setting, the data may be missing repeatedly. Some data may disappear due to the Internet issues: the bottlenecks and outages in the computer networks may physically inhibit data delivery. Other issues with streaming financial data may include the data architecture itself.

All financial message traffic today floats through two underlying communication protocols: TCP/IP (Transmission Control Protocol/Internet Protocol) or UDP (User Datagram Protocol). The TCP/IP protocol, also used for much of email, counts the number of message packets sent and resends the message stream if the entire package did not reach its destination. TCP/IP guarantees delivery of a message, making it a must in areas like order communication and confirmations. However, the reliability of TCP/IP makes it sacrifice its speed, as every resend takes up time.

TCP/IP itself runs on a protocol known as UDP. UDP is one of the most basic communication tools in the Internet domain. UDP broadcasts messages, and if some are lost, it does not retransmit them. By its function, UDP is most suitable to applications such as quote dissemination – lost market quotes are immediately rendered stale by new quotes, so losing a packet of data occasionally does not deprive the receiving party of observing the current market dynamics. As a result, data losses are quite common.

A natural solution to data loss from UDP is positioning the data receiving and processing servers as close to the exchange data-distributing servers as possible, and, optimally avoiding UDP altogether by relying on direct exchange cable connection instead. The practice of direct data acquisition is known as co-location; many exchanges enable co-location by subletting portions of their server hangars to those interested in the best data quality possible.

Still, Big Data solutions also exist and may work just as well for many applications. In the Big Data solution, the received data is acquired and processed in samples – batches of data – with the explicit understanding that some of the data could potentially have been lost.

Treating streaming data formally as an exercise in sampling allows us to develop and keep track of statistics of the likelihood of captured data elements reflecting the true values. The probabilities in turn allow us to perform complicated mathematical operations, such as matrix multiplication, on the fly, all the time taking into account data probabilities.

For example, suppose we are receiving streaming tick data and collecting the values in vectors: vector $A = \{a_i\}$ captures the best offer quotes or asks of the financial instrument i, vector $B = \{b_i\}$ captures the best bid quotes of the financial instrument i, and other similarly constructed vectors capture other relevant information, such as prices, trade sizes, limit orders away from the market, and, possibly, much more. Suppose further that in the sample we are observing, the value for a particular quote item is stored in a vector $X = \{x_i\}$. We are interested in finding out the probability that the value x_i

we are observing while reading the sample is indeed the true value x_i^*. According to Drineas, Kannan, and Mahoney (2006), the probability of a data item pertaining to a financial instrument i^* appearing in the sample decreases with the number of times n that x_i appears in the sample, particularly if all financial instruments are assumed to appear in the data uniformly:

$$P(i = i^*) = x_{i,n} / \left(\sum_{\gamma=1}^{n} x_{i,\gamma} \right)$$

In other words, while we take the last arriving value for variable x_i to be the true value x_i^*, the probability of observing another data point x belonging to the financial instrument i decreases as the number of past observations within the sample increases.

Why is this interesting? For two reasons:

1. We may need to predict the probability of near-term arrival of a specific data point for a particular financial instrument.
2. The probability $P(i = i^*)$ helps us perform matrix multiplication on the fly.

When the data arrives in a two-dimensional matrix format x_{ij}, perhaps like options with expiration dates indexed by j, the on-the-fly probability of seeing another observation is determined using the Frobenius norm:

$$P(\{i,j\} = \{i^*, j^*\}) = x_{ij,n} / ||X||_F$$

where

$$||A||_F = \sqrt{\sum_{i=1}^{n} \sum_{j=1}^{m} A_{ij}^2}$$

If we are receiving data for two vectors A and B, and we sample c rows from vector A and c columns from vector B, thn the probabilities are deployed in determining a fast matrix product from the respective samples of A and B:

- Sample of A, $L_t = A_{i,t} / \sqrt{cP_{i,t}}$
- Sample of B, $R_t = B_{i,t} / \sqrt{cP_{i,t}}$

And the matrix multiplication of the samples of A and B is:

$$LR = \sum_{t=1}^{c} L_t R_t = \sum_{t=1}^{c} (A_{i,t} / \sqrt{cP_{i,t}})(B_{i,t} / \sqrt{cP_{i,t}}) = \sum_{t=1}^{c} \frac{A_{i,t} B_{i,t}}{cP_{i,t}} \approx \sum_{t=1}^{n} A_t P_t$$

At the core, the streaming data sampling process works as follows:

1. Input a sample of data.
2. Return output based on the sample of data.
3. When all the data are similar, uniform random sampling should suffice.
4. When the data are not similar, non–uniform sampling is required.

5. To ensure that we receive the desired results, we need to keep comparative performance statistics to determine how the uniform and non-uniform sampling stack up against each other as well as against the solution involving the full data sample.

Conclusion

Big Data reframes data analysis into utilizing every piece of information, no matter how fractured or incomplete. In doing so, Big Data techniques produce stronger, more aware inferences than those based on extensively cleaned subsamples.

Appendix 7 Finding the Optimal Number of Eigenvectors in Python

The Python implementation of the Karhunen-Loève Transform is discussed in the Appendix to Chapter 6 of this book. Here, we cover the code for the Marčenko-Pastur cut-off – an approach to determine the optimal number of eigenvectors of data X to consider in a model.

The native Python attribute shape returns the number of rows N and columns M in the data X:

```
[N, M] = X.shape
```

The Marčenko-Pastur cut-offs are next determined as follows, rounded to the next integer value:

```
#compute Marcenko-Pastur
y = M/N
a = (1-y**(0.5))**2
b = (1+y**(0.5))**2
```

For specific code examples, please visit https://www.BigDataFinanceBook.com, and register with password *MP* (case-sensitive).

References

Achlioptas, D. (2003). Database-friendly random projections: Johnson-Lindenstrauss with binary coins. *Journal of Computer and System Sciences* 66(4): 671–687.

Ahn, J., Marron, J.S., Muller, K.M., and Chi, Y-Y. (2007). The high-dimension, low-sample-size geometric representation holds under mild conditions. *Biometrika* 94(3): 760–766.

Bai, Z.D. (1999). Methodologies in spectral analysis of large dimensional random matrices: a review. *Statistica Sinica* 9: 611–677.

Bai, Z.D. and Yin, Y.Q. (1993). Limit of the smallest eigenvalue of a large-dimensional sample covariance matrix. *The Annals of Probability* 21(3): 1275–1294.

Bai, Z.D., Yin, Y.Q., and Krishnaiah, P.R. (1986). On limiting spectral distribution of product of two random matrices when the underlying distribution is isotropic. *Journal of Multivariate Analysis* 19: 189–200.

Baik, J., Ben-Arous, G., and Peche, S. (2005). Phase transition of the largest eigenvalue for nonnull complex sample covariance matrices. *The Annals of Probability* 33(5): 1643–1697.

Baik, J., Buckingham,, R., and DiFranco, J. (2008). Asymptotics of the Tracy-Widom distributions and the total integral of a Painlevé II function, *Communications in Mathematical Physics* 280: 463–497.

Baik, J. and Silverstein, J.W. (2005). Eigenvalues of large sample covariance matrices of spiked population models. *Journal of Multivariate Analysis* 97(6): 1382–1408.

Benaych-Georges, F. and Nadakuditi, R.R. (2011). The eigenvalues and eigenvectors of finite, low rank perturbations of large random matrices. *Advances in Mathematics* 227(1): 494–521.

Benaych-Georges, F. and Nadakuditi, R.R. (2012). The singular values and vectors of low rank perturbations of large rectangular random matrices. *Journal of Multivariate Analysis* 111: 120–135.

Berry, M.W., Drmac, Z., and Jessup, E.R. (2001). Matrices, vector spaces, and information retrieval. *SIAM Review* 41(2): 335–362.

Bertsimas, D., Pawlowski, C., and Zhou, Y.D. (2018). From predictive methods to missing data imputation: an optimization approach. *Journal of Machine Learning Research* 18: 1–39.

Bø, T.H., Dysvik, B., and Jonassen, I. (2004). LSimpute: Accurate estimation of missing values in microarray data with least squares methods. *Nucleic Acids Research* 32(3): e34–e34.

Bras, L.P. and Menezes, J.C. (2007). Improving cluster-based missing value estimation of DNA microarray data. *Biomolecular Engineering* 24(2): 273–282.

Buja, A. and Eyuboglu, N. (1992). Remarks on parallel analysis. *Multivariate Behavioral Research* 27: 509–540.

Burgette, L.F. and Reiter, J.P. (2010). Multiple imputation for missing data via sequential regression trees. *American Journal of Epidemiology* 172: 1070–1076.

Buuren, S. and Groothuis-Oudshoorn, K. (2011). MICE: Multivariate imputation by chained equations in R. *Journal of Statistical Software* 45(3).

Cai, Z., Heydari, M. and Lin, G. (2006). Iterated local least squares microarray missing value imputation. *Journal of Bioinformatics and Computational Biology* 4(05): 935–957.

Caruana, R. (2001). A non-parametric EM-style algorithm for imputing missing values. *AISTATS*. Corpus ID: 46622803.

Cattell, R.B. (1966). The scree test for the number of factors. *Multivariate Behavioral Research* 1: 629–637.

Connor, G. and Korajczyk, R. (1993). A test for the number of factors in an approximate factor model, *Journal of Finance* 58: 1263–1291.

Dasgupta, S. and Gupta, A. (2003). An elementary proof of a theorem of Johnson and Lindenstrauss. *Random Structures and Algorithms* 22(1): 60–65.

Dempster, A.P., Laird, N.M., and Rubin, D.B. (1977). Maximum likelihood from incomplete data via the EM algorithm. *Journal of the Royal Statistical Society. Series B (methodological)* 39: 1–38.

Dieng, M. (2005). Distribution functions for edge eigenvalues in orthogonal and symplectic ensembles: Painlevé representations, *International Mathematics Research Notices* 37: 2263–2287.

Dobriban, E. and Owen, A.B. (2019). Deterministic parallel analysis: An improved method for selecting factors and principal components. *Journal of the Royal Statistical Society: Series B (Statistical Methodology)* 81(1): 163–183.

Drineas, K. and Mahoney, P. (2006). Fast Monte Carlo algorithms for matrices I: Approximating matrix multiplication, *SIAM Journal of Computing* 36(1): 132–157.

Epps, T.W. (1979). Comovements in stock prices in the very short run. *Journal of the American Statistical Association* 74: 291–298.

Friedman, S. and Weisberg, H. (1981). Interpreting the first eigenvalue of a correlation matrix. *Educational and Psychological Measurement* 41(1): 11–21.

Ghahramani, Z. and Jordan, M.I. (1994). Supervised learning from incomplete data via an EM approach. In: Cowan, J.D., Tesauro, G., and Alspector, J. (Eds.) *Advances in Neural Information Processing Systems 6*. Cambridge, MA: MIT Press.

Honaker, J., King, G., Blackwell, M. et al. (2011). Amelia II: A program for missing data. *Journal of Statistical Software* 45(7): 1–47.

Horn, J.L. (1965). A rationale and test for the number of factors in factor analysis. *Psychometrika* 30: 179–185.

Johnstone, I.M. (2001). On the distribution of the largest eigenvalue in principal components analysis. *The Annals of Statistics* 29: 295–327.

Jung, S. and Marron, J.S. (2009). PCA consistency in high dimension, low sample size context. *The Annals of Statistics* 37: 4104–4130.

Kaiser, H.F. (1960). The application of electronic computers to factor analysis. *Educational and Psychological Measurement* 20: 141–151.

Karoui, N.E. (2005). Recent results about the largest eigenvalue of random covariance matrices and statistical application. *Acta Physica Polonica B* 36(9).

Khan, M.E., Marlin, B.M., Bouchard, G., and Murphy, K.P. (2010). Variational bounds for mixed-data factor analysis. *Advances in Neural Information Processing Systems* 23: 1–9.

Kim, H., Golub, G.H., and Park, H. (2005). Missing value estimation for DNA microarray gene expression data: Local least squares imputation. *Bioinformatics* 21(2): 187–198.

Kim, K.-Y., Kim, B. J., and Yi, G.-S. (2011). Reuse of imputed data in microarray analysis increases imputation efficiency. *BMC Bioinformatics* 5(1): 160.

Laloux, L., Cizeau, P., Bouchaud, J.-P., and Potters, M. (1999). Noise dressing of financial correlation matrices. *Physical Review Letters* 83: 1467–1470.

Lee, J.O. and Schnelli, K. (2014). Tracy-Widom distribution for the largest eigenvalue of real sample covariance matrices with general population. *The Annals of Applied Probability* 26(6): 3786–3839.

Little, R.J.A. and Rubin, D.B. (1987). *Statistical Analysis with Missing Data*. New York: John Wiley & Sons, Inc.

Marčenko, V.A. and Pastur, L.A. (1967). Distribution of eigenvalues for some sets of random matrices. *Mathematics of the USSR-Sbornik* (N.S.) 1(4): 457–483.

Mohamed, S., Ghahramani, Z., and Heller, K.A. (2009). Bayesian exponential family PCA. In: *Advances in Neural Information Processing Systems*. Cambridge, MA: MIT Press, pp. 1089–1096.

Nadal, C. and Majumdar, S. (2011). A simple derivation of the Tracy-Widom distribution of the maximal eigenvalue of a Gaussian unitary random matrix. *Journal of Statistical Mechanics: Theory and Experiment* 2011 April.

Oba, S., Sato, M, Takemasa, I, Monden, M., Matsubara, K., and Ishii, S. (2003). A Bayesian missing value estimation method for gene expression profile data. *Bioinformatics* 19: 2088–2096.

Paul, D. (2007). Asymptotics of the leading sample eigenvalues for a spiked covariance model. *Statistica Sinica* 17: 1617–1642.

Raghunathan T.E., Lepkowski J.M., van Hoewyk J., and Solenberger, P. (2001). A multivariate technique for multiply imputing missing values using a sequence of regression models. *Survey Methodology* 27: 85–95.

Stekhoven, D.J. and Bühlmann, P. (2012). Missforest: Non-parametric missing value imputation for mixed-type data. *Bioinformatics* 28(1): 112–118.

Tracy, C.A. and Widom, H. (1993). Level-spacing distribution and the Airy kernel. *Physics Letters B* 305: 115–118.

Tracy, C.A. and Widom, H. (1994). Level-spacing distribution and the Airy kernel. *Communications in Mathematical Physics* 159: 151–174.

Tracy, C.A. and Widom, H. (1996). On orthogonal and symplectic matrix ensembles. *Communications in Mathematical Physics* 177: 727–754.

Tracy, C.A. and Widom, H. (2002). Distribution functions for largest eigenvalues and their applications. In: *Proceedings of the International Congress of Mathematicians*, Vol. I. Beijing: Higher Education Press, pp. 587–596.

Troyanskaya, O., Cantor, M., Sherlock, G. et al. (2001). Missing value estimation methods for DNA microarrays. *Bioinformatics* 17(6): 520–525.

Wang, X., Li, A., Jiang, Z., and Feng, H. (2006). Missing value estimation for DNA microarray gene expression data by support vector regression imputation and orthogonal coding scheme. *BMC Bioinformatics* 7(1): 1. DOI:10.1186/1471-2105-7-32.

Wigner, E. (1955). Characteristic vectors of bordered matrices with infinite dimensions. *Annals of Mathematics* 62, 548–564.

Wigner, E. (1958). On the distribution of the roots of certain symmetric matrices. *Annals of Mathematics* 67: 325–328.

Zhang, X., Song, X., Wang, H., and Zhang, H. (2008). Sequential local least squares imputation estimating missing value of microarray data. *Computers in Biology and Medicine* 38(10): 1112–1120.

Chapter 8

Applications: Unsupervised Learning in Option Pricing and Stochastic Modeling

Introduction

This chapter presents two applications for unsupervised learning: optimization of option pricing and, separately, optimization of Markov Chains. Perhaps two of the most popular financial applications, both inferences of options pricing and various Markov Chains components, can be dramatically sped up and improved with unsupervised learning, as this chapter illustrates.

Application 1: Unsupervised Learning in Options Pricing

The options data comprise trillions of data points per day. The options on the U.S. stocks alone number in millions, each with a different strike price, expiration, and action. In addition to the U.S. securities, there are options on commodity futures, currencies, and fixed income. All of the options have the capacity to be traded and, thus, convey public information about someone's belief about the markets.

Despite the richness of the options data, traditionally, these data have been aggregated into a handful of indicators, like

- call-put implied volatility spread (Bali and Hovakimian 2009; Cremers and Weinbaum 2010; and Yan 2011).
- risk-neutral skewness (Xing, Zhang, and Zhao 2010; Rehman and Vilkov 2012; Conrad, Dittmar, and Ghysels 2013; Stilger, Kostakis, and Poon 2016; and Bali, Hu, and Murray 2016).
- option to stock volume ratio (Roll, Schwartz, and Subrahmanyam 2010; and Johnson and So 2012).
- volatility of implied volatility (Baltussen, Van Bekkum, and Van der Grient 2018).

Most of the indicators are related to the famous Black-Scholes model (Black and Scholes 1972; 1973; Merton 1973), which allows the researchers to backtrack the unobserved volatility σ "implied" by the Black-Scholes equations for call and put options:

$$C(s, t) = S \, N(d_1) - K \, exp(-r(T - t)) \, N(d_2)$$

$$P(s, t) = K \, \exp(-r(T - t)) \, N(-d_2) - S \, N(-d_1) \tag{8.1}$$

where S is the current price of the instrument on which the option is written (the *underlying*), K is the option exercise price, N is the cumulative distribution function of the standard normal $(0,1)$, r is the prevailing risk-free interest rate, T is the option expiration date, and d_1 and d_2 are defined as follows:

$$d_1 = [ln(S/E) + (r + \sigma^2/2)(T - t)]/(\sigma \sqrt{T - t})$$

$$d_2 = d_1 - \sigma \sqrt{T - t} \tag{8.2}$$

The implied volatility is computed numerically from the Black-Scholes formula given realized put and call option prices observed in the market with different expiration dates and exercise prices.

The implied volatility changes with strike prices and times to expiration, forming what has become known as *volatility surface*, a function $\sigma_t(K, T)$. An implied volatility surface for call options on SPX for December 12, 2008, is shown in Figure 8.1.

The volatility surface continuously changes with time, directly depending on the prevailing market option prices, which in turn reflect economic regimes and other variables (Xu and Taylor 1994; Campa and Chang 1995). Figure 8.2 shows the implied volatility surface for options on SPX computed for several days in December 2008–2012 from Avellaneda and Dobi (2014).

As Figure 8.2 illustrates, the volatility surface is not flat, instead possessing a smile or a skew, and highlighting the market inefficiency at pricing options vis-à-vis Black-Scholes. The time instability and a high degree of nonlinearity make the volatility surface estimation and, especially, out-of-sample prediction into very much of a Big Data problem, as shown in Avellaneda and Cont (2002).

Even options data aggregated into indicators like implied volatilities are numerous. For example, Muravyev, Vasquez, and Wang (2018) study the entire set of optionable

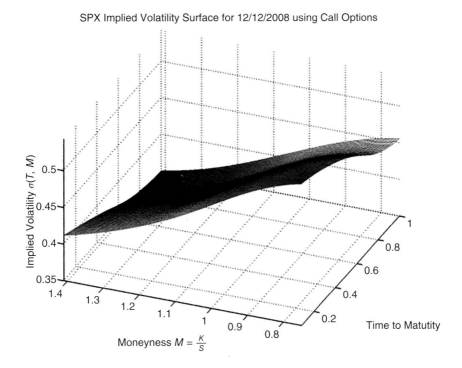

Figure 8.1   Implied volatility surface for SPX using call options, December 12 2008.

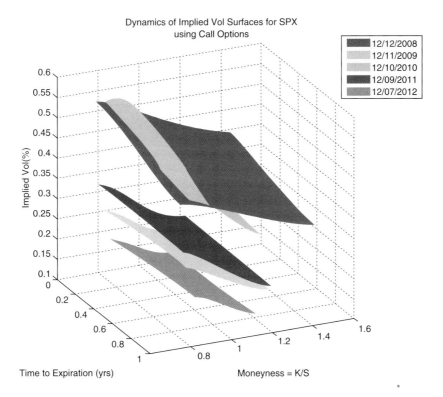

Figure 8.2   Implied volatility surfaces for call options on SPX computed on sequential days using OptionMetrics data in December 2008–2012. Source: Avellaneda and Dobi (2014).

U.S. stocks for the 1996–2014 period. They find that daily data for each stock comprise 112 implied volatilities for each stock. These volatilities vary across puts and calls, option maturities of 30–365 days, and different moneyness, i.e., deltas, from 0.2–0.8. The implied volatilities alone make the option data a Big Data problem across 6,000–8,000 publicly traded U.S. stocks per year, especially in comparison with just five daily data points available for each underlying security: Open, High, Low, and Closing prices and daily volume.

Historically, the volatility surface has been modeled in various ways: stochastic volatility, deterministic volatility functions, mean-reverting diffusion, data fit using parametric and nonparametric regressions, and more. Many models not mentioned here are discussed in Gatheral and Taleb (2011).

Stochastic volatility model due to Hull and White (1987) treats volatility as a random variable. While such an approach reflects the fact that volatility changes with time, the approach fails to model the actual dynamics inherent in volatility fluctuations. Furthermore, the approach depends on calibrating the volatility distribution parameters to the price of volatility risk, which cannot be readily observed in the market. Heston (1993) developed a now classic, improved stochastic volatility model that varies with moneyness of the option, or absolute value of delta, the derivative of the option price relative to the price of the underlying, $| \Delta |=| ln(S \exp(r(T - t))/K)/\sqrt{T - t} |$. Heston's (1993) model was verified empirically by Derman, Miller, and Park (1996). However, factors other than moneyness may dominate the volatility parameters and are not included in the model.

The deterministic volatility functions (Dupire 1994; Derman and Kani 1998) assume that the volatility function is entirely predictable from time to expiration. Dumas, Fleming, and Whaley (1998), among others, have shown that these approaches fail to accurately price derivatives out-of-sample as the functional dependencies of the implied volatility also change continuously.

Cont, Fonseca, and Durrleman (2002) and others model implied volatility as a mean-reverting Ornstein-Uhlenbeck process, which also requires fitting of parameters to the arbitrage bounds of Lee (2004). Carmona and Nadtochiy (2008) consider the volatility surface as a mixture of several processes, each parameterized locally. Schweizer and Wissel (2008) also argue for local volatility parameterization. Stable parameterization, however, may be difficult to accomplish in the ever-changing environment.

Empirical data fitting using parametric and nonparametric regressions is the most popular approach to modeling implied volatility surface, see, for example, Cont and Fonseca (2002). The use of implied volatility differentials is frequent in the options literature. Mixon (2007) and Vasquez (2017) use IV differentials to determine term structure slopes. Bates (2000) and Hafner and Wallmeiery (2000) use IV differentials to quantify shapes of the smiles. The empirical fit approach suffers from poor out-of-sample predictability, given the ever-changing nature of the volatility.

An additional issue in modeling options is the discrete nature of expiration dates. In order to achieve a smooth implied volatility surface ripe for functional analysis, some researchers approximate the expiration date–induced discontinuities in the volatility surface. Carr and Wu (2008), for example, propose a multivariate interpolation approach to compute daily IV values at any given maturity or moneyness level.

The Big Data approach has also been on the radar of the options researchers and traders (Skiadopoulos, Hodges, and Clewlow 1999; Avellaneda and Cont 2002; Bouchaud, Laloux, and Potters 2005; Bouchaud and Potters 2009; Avellaneda and Dobi 2014; Dobi 2014). The advantage of the Big Data method is that it helps discern the main factors of the changes in the volatility surface structure, regardless of whether the data are discrete or what functional form may fit the data best. The structural data factors may prove to be more persistent over time than functions formed by pure data mining and fitting. Skiadopoulos, Hodges, and Clewlow (1999) decompose volatility surface and extend it to principal components using GARCH (Bollerslev 1986) to predict future realizations.

Big Data Options Factors

Whereas traditional finance scholars attempt to identify the factors a priori to examine their effect and influence on the data, the Big Data approach is, as usual, to tease out the factors from the data themselves. The key advantage of the traditional factors is immediate human interpretability. For example, Benzoni, Collin-Dufresne, and Goldstein (2011) use a general equilibrium framework to show that when a threat of an abnormally low economic growth (or economic expansion) is present, the implied volatility of out-of-the-money put options becomes higher (or lower) than that of at-the-money and in-the-money puts. Bollen and Whaley (2004) find that the supply and demand for options significantly influence the skew of the implied volatility.

The ability of the factors to foretell the variables under consideration is known as the explanatory power of the factors. The explanatory power for each principal component is the corresponding eigenvalue. Each eigenvalue measures the proportion of the variation in the variable explained by the associated principal component.

The Big Data analysis is proactive and precise on delivering factors driving the structural changes in the data. The SVD/PCA framework delivers ready recipes for the orthogonal factors ranked sequentially from the critically important to fully idiosyncratic. As always, however, challenges arise as to the interpretation of Big Data factors in human terms. Solutions have been developed, however, to account for maturity and moneyness by analyzing the structure of the options data by different maturity-moneyness categories. For example, Skiadopoulos, Hodges, and Clewlow (1999) perform PCA on the options data separated by maturity and find that the first three principal components explain the majority of variance for the shortest-expiry options, while just the first principal component explains most variation in the longer-expiry options data.

Christoffersen, Fournier, and Jacobs (2017) run PCA on the levels of the implied volatility and its slope vis-à-vis moneyness and, separately, term structure measured by days to maturity, *DTM*. To do so, they first run the following regression on the cross-section of options on the U.S. equities as follows:

$$IV_{j,l,t} = a_{j,t} + b_{j,t} \cdot (S_t^j / K_{j,l}) + c_{j,t} \cdot (DTM_{j,l}) + \varepsilon_{j,l,t} \tag{8.3}$$

where l is an option available on day t for firm j. In PCA on the levels of implied volatility, $a_{j,t}$, Christoffersen, Fournier, and Jacobs report that the first principal component explains 77% of variation in implied volatilities and is 92% correlated with the implied volatility levels of the options on the S&P 500 Index. The explanatory power of the second principal component of $a_{j,t}$ drops to 13%. The first principal component of the moneyness slope $b_{j,t}$ explains 77% of variation and has 64% correlation with the moneyness slope of the S&P 500 index. Finally, the term structure slope $c_{j,t}$ captures just 60% of the variation in $c_{j,t}$ and displays 80% correlation with the term slope of the S&P 500 Index options. By doing so, Christoffersen, Fournier, and Jacobs further confirm that the results of the principal component analysis are consistent with the traditional finance literature that stipulates that the market drives much of the variation in the financial securities.

Muravyev, Vasquez, and Wang (2018) use the entire set of optionable U.S. stocks for the 1996–2014 period to study demeaned daily correlations of implied volatility surfaces using PCA. They first reduce the data set to weekly, by taking a Tuesday to Monday average for each stock and week to obtain a weekly volatility surface. This results in 936 weekly periods from 1996–2014. Furthermore, the authors remove stocks that traded fewer than 50 calls and 50 puts on any given day, potentially introducing a large stock bias into the analysis. Still, even with the imposed restrictions, their sample results in 936 weeks and 1,982 unique firms that tally up to 1,897,536 firm-week observations. Muravyev, Vasquez, and Wang next compute a correlation matrix of the 112 demeaned implied volatilities for the 1,982 securities, and perform PCA on the resulting correlations.

Muravyev, Vasquez, and Wang find that the first five principal components capture 78% of variation in the volatility surfaces, allowing a substantial dimensionality reduction from 112 to 5 linear combinations of the 112 columns. The first principal component alone explains only 32% of data variation, with the second through the fifth explaining 21%, 13%, 8%, and 4%, respectively.

The researchers note that the first principal component can be interpreted in the framework of established finance literature. Specifically, they find that the first principal component has a 66% correlation with the call–put volatility spread defined in Cremers and Weinbaum (2010). They also find that the first principal component has a –39% correlation with the option skew defined in Xing, Zhang, and Zhao (2010). In this sense, Muravyev, Vasquez, and Wang (2018) interpret the first principal component as an index combining the put–call volatility spread and the option skew.

Muravyev, Vasquez, and Wang (2018) further find that the second principal component is not significantly correlated with any established variables, but changes sign with the option maturity: the second principal component is positively correlated with shorter-maturity put and call options, and negatively correlated with those with longer maturity. The researchers estimate that the sign changes at maturity of about 150 days to expiration.

Finally, Muravyev, Vasquez, and Wang examine the third, fourth, and fifth principal components. They find that the third principal component has 28% correlation with the option skew and a correlation of -22% with risk-neutral skewness. The fourth principal component is –15% correlated with risk-neutral skewness. The fifth principal component is –26% correlated with the implied volatility spread.

The correlation of principal components with existing indicators humanizes Big Data analysis and introduces a certain degree of comfort with the technology. At the same time, the technique presents new challenges, such as creating an intuitive explanation for the maturity-sensitive second principal component discussed above.

To assess the predictive power of the principal components on the future stock returns, Muravyev, Vasquez, and Wang recompute weekly and monthly principal components and perform tried-and-true Fama and MacBeth (1973) regressions on step-ahead weekly and monthly stock returns:

$$r_{i,t+1} = \alpha_t + \beta_{1,t}\, PC1_{i,t} + \beta_{2,t}\, PC2_{i,t} + \beta_{3,t}\, PC3_{i,t}$$
$$+ \beta_{4,t}\, PC4_{i,t} + \beta_{5,t}\, PC5_{i,t} + \varphi_t Z_{i,t} + e_{i,t+1} \qquad (8.4)$$

where $Z_{i,t}$ is a vector of characteristics observed for the firm i at the end of week or month t. Muravyev, Vasquez, and Wang (2018) find that the first three components predict future stock returns with 99% confidence. When traditional variables like implied volatility skew and spread are included in the regression, the principal components dominate and retain their 99% significance while the traditional factors appear non-significant in comparison. Muravyev, Vasquez, and Wang (2018) also report that the principal components predict returns as far ahead as 15 weeks, all the while driving out traditional indicators like the option smirk and skew.

In a nutshell, the Big Data factors deliver a better, more precise factorization, yet related to the factors previously known to researchers. More work can be done to explain the factors in traditional terms to deepen our understanding of the options-underlying dynamics. The Big Data analysis inverts the traditional research process: instead of researchers first hypothesizing the factors and then testing their performance, the Big Data approach delivers the factors which are to be related to the real-world observations by the researchers. Since the Big Data factors are typically optimal, as shown in Chapter 5 of this book, the Big Data process in turn optimizes the research process by saving researchers a lot of time on finding the factors, instead focusing their time on factor interpretation.

The Optimal Number of Principal Components

Muravyev, Vasquez, and Wang (2018) hand-pick the first five principal components based on the variation the components explain. Many studies (Litterman and Scheinkman 1991; Cont and Fonseca 2002; Bouchaud, Laloux, and Potters 2005; and Bouchaud and Potters 2009) have considered the optimal number of top principal components to retain in the financial analysis. Litterman and Scheinkman (1991) analyze returns on Treasury bonds and find that 82% of variation can be explained with only three factors that are principal components. Cont and Fonseca (2002) study the returns correlation matrix of the DAX options and find that the variance can be explained with just three principal components.

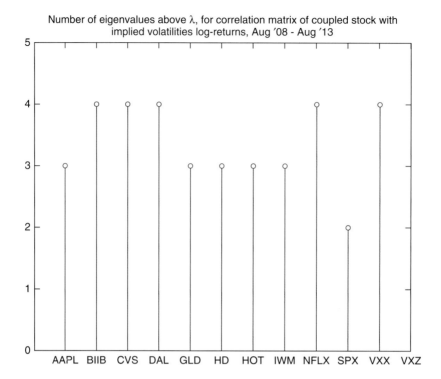

Figure 8.3   The number of significant top eigenvalues as determined by the Marcenko-Pastur threshold $\lambda+$ for selected stocks. By projecting along these corresponding eigenvectors we may distinguish signal from noise in the correlation matrix.

Avellaneda and Dobi (2014) apply the Marcenko-Pastur framework to determine the optimal number of factors in the implied volatility surfaces for the U.S. equities. They find that the optimal number of principal components to be retained varies by security. Thus, according to Marcenko-Pastur, implied volatility data for AAPL, GLD, and HD, among others, can be explained by the three top principal components, while the data for BIIB, CVS, and NFLX require four principal components, as shown in Figure 8.3. SPX can be summarized with only two principal components.

For the options on the top-20 most liquid ETFs, Avellaneda and Dobi (2014) find that the top-three principal components often explain over 90% of variation in the implied volatility surface (Figure 8.4). The first principal component alone explains as much as 70–90% of variance for those ETFs, as shown in Figure 8.5.

Estimating Systematic Risk

Avellaneda and Dobi (2014) propose using Big Data analysis to measure the financial instruments' systematic and idiosyncratic risks. To do so, the researchers take into consideration the top eigenvalue as a measure of the level of systemic risk exposure. The higher the first eigenvalue, the stronger the shift in the implied volatility surface across

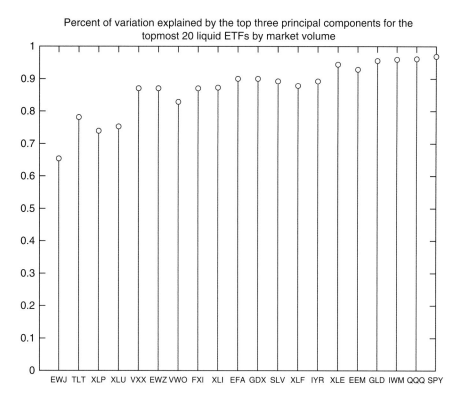

Figure 8.4   Percent of variation explained by the first three components for the 20 most liquid ETFs by market volume. Data from August 2004 (or creation of asset) until August 2013. Source: Avellaneda and Dobi (2014).

all the options for a given underlying, indicating systematic risk. Avellaneda and Dobi argue that the second and the third eigenvalues correspond to the variation in time-skew and delta-skew, and, therefore, are the metrics of idiosyncratic risk of each underlying.

When considering the options on all the constituents of the S&P 500, Avellaneda and Dobi find that, when sorted by the top eigenvalue, the stocks with the highest first eigenvalues of the implied volatility surfaces are the largest widely held stocks (Table 8.1). At the same time, the stocks with the smallest eigenvalues were the small-size stocks. The largest 15 stocks indeed exhibit the most systematic risk, displaying 63% correlation with the market, the average daily volatility of 2.8%, and the average Marcenko-Pastur cut-off at 3 eigenvalues. The smallest 15 stocks show the least systematic risk and the most idiosyncratic risk instead, with market correlation of 47%, average daily volatility of just 1.5% and the average Marcenko-Pastur cut-off at 7.3 eigenvalues. For comparison, within the entire S&P 500, the average correlation with the market is 60%, the average daily volatility is 2.3%, and the average Marcenko-Pastur cut-off is at 4.3 eigenvalues. Thus, the first eigenvalue of the implied volatility surface is inversely correlated with the idiosyncratic risk of an instrument.

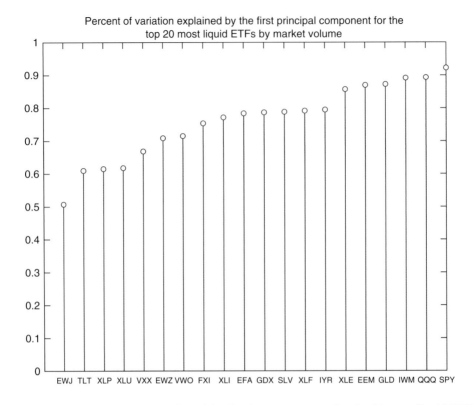

Figure 8.5   Percent of variation explained by the first component for the 20 most liquid ETFs by market volume. Data from August 2004 (or creation of asset) until August 2013 in order of increasing systemic risk. Source: Avellaneda and Dobi (2014, p. 14).

Table 8.1   Top 15 underlying constituents and bottom 15 underlying constituents by first eigenvalue.

Bottom 15 constituents	EV1	Top 15 constituents	EV1
KMI	0.27272	GS	0.87176
POM	0.31406	JPM	0.87092
WEC	0.34958	BAC	0.85115
PNW	0.35611	SLB	0.84669
HCBK	0.35995	CAT	0.84219
NLSN	0.36338	AAPL	0.84126
TE	0.36342	XOM	0.84109
NU	0.3667	NOV	0.83737
BMS	0.37675	CME	0.83639
XEL	0.3828	MA	0.8358
WIN	0.38664	MS	0.83471
RSG	0.39779	APA	0.83081
FTR	0.40043	GOOG	0.83011
MKC	0.40475	HIG	0.8301
XYL	0.40596	HES	0.82965

Source: Avellaneda and Dobi (2014).

Next, Avellaneda and Dobi (2014) test their findings on the entire OptionMetrics universe of 3,300 optionable stocks. To do so, they separate the top 1% and the bottom 1% of stocks by volume traded and estimate the following eigenvalue (EV) statistics:

- average EV1, EV2, EV3 and EV4
- number of eigenvalues above the Marcenko-Pastur cut-off
- average daily volatility
- average correlation with the market
- average volume traded

The results are presented in Table 8.2.

Avellaneda and Dobi (2014) also find that the top eigenvalues of implied volatility surfaces of the entire cross-section of stocks tend to increase in times of crises and high market volatility, such as Lehman Brothers' bankruptcy (October 2008), the Flash Crash of May 6, 2010, and the U.S. federal government credit rating downgrades in November 2011. The universal increase in the top eigenvalue corresponds to the rise in systematic risk across all equities, whereby all stocks exhibit rising correlation with the market when the market collapses, as documented by Ang, Chen, and Xing (2006).

The top eigenvalue of a correlation matrix indeed approximates the average correlation $\bar{\rho}$ in the correlation matrix under consideration. To prove this, consider the correlation matrix C with the eigenvectors V generated by spectral decomposition

$$C = V \Lambda V^T \tag{8.5}$$

where Λ is a diagonal matrix of eigenvalues. Considering the first eigenvalue λ_1 and the first eigenvector V^1, the first column of the matrix V, we can rewrite Eq (8.5) as follows:

$$\lambda_1 = (V^1)^T C V^1 = \sum_{i=1}^{N} (V_i^1)^2 + \sum_{i \neq j} V_i^1 V_j^1 \rho_{ij} \tag{8.6}$$

Table 8.2 Average values across all remaining assets (around 3,300) and those of the bottom and top 1 percent.

	EV1	EV2	EV3	EV4	# EVs > MP	Vol.	Corr.	Volume
Top 1%	0.921	0.031	0.017	0.012	1.617		0.030	0.208	168M
Bottom 1%	0.322	0.166	0.114	0.074	7.30		0.023	0.159	.65M
Mrkt Avg.	0.590	0.115	0.077	0.042	5.08		0.031	0.278	4.5M

Source: Avellaneda and Dobi (2014).

Since

$$V_i^1 \approx \frac{1}{\sqrt{N}} \tag{8.7}$$

$$\sum_{i=1}^{N} (V_i^1)^2 \approx 1 \tag{8.8}$$

$$\sum_{i \neq j} V_i^1 V_j^1 \approx N(N-1)/N = N-1 \tag{8.9}$$

and Eq (8.6) can be rewritten as follows:

$$\lambda_1 = 1 + \sum_{i \neq j} V_i^1 V_j^1 \left[\left(\sum_{i \neq j} V_i^1 V_j^1 \rho_{ij} \right) \Big/ \left(\sum_{i \neq j} V_i^1 V_j^1 \right) \right] \tag{8.10}$$

then, rearranging Eq (8.10), we obtain:

$$(\lambda_1 - 1) \Big/ \left(\sum_{i \neq j} V_i^1 V_j^1 \right) = \left(\sum_{i \neq j} V_i^1 V_j^1 \rho_{ij} \right) \Big/ \left(\sum_{i \neq j} V_i^1 V_j^1 \right) \tag{8.11}$$

Hence, $(\lambda_1 - 1)/(N-1) \approx \rho$ and

$$\underline{\rho} \approx \frac{\lambda_1}{N} \tag{8.12}$$

Avellaneda and Dobi (2014) next use the magnitude of the top-three eigenvalues as a basis for classification of securities into two classes, those carrying a higher proportion of systematic risk and those dominated by the idiosyncratic risk. The stocks with large first eigenvalue are deemed the ones carrying the systematic risk. The stocks dominated by the systematic risk may warrant a different risk management treatment compared to the idiosyncratic-risk stocks.

Extracting Granular Data from Dimensionally Reduced Matrices

The Big Data techniques allow us to significantly compress the voluminous options data at hand. In the case of options, for example, Avellaneda and Dobi (2014) and Muravyev, Vasquez, and Wang (2018), among others, show that three to five principal components are sufficient to represent the universe of as many as 130 eigenvectors. In other words, the size of the options data sets can be reduced by a factor of 30 or 40 via PCA, an operation that can be performed almost instantaneously on a reasonably powerful computer.

   One of the key questions that arises relative to the dimensionality reduction is the ability to retrieve highly granular data from the PCA-compressed data set. Avellaneda and Dobi (2014) show that a linear smoothing kernel that interpolates the available data points that surround the location of the sought data works well in the case of options' implied volatility surfaces.

Application 2: Optimizing Markov Chains with the Perron-Frobenius Theorem

The application of Big Data to stochastic modeling is the cornerstone of success of many social media companies. The ability to predict the changes in browsing patterns, shifts in interests and associates has helped companies like Google and Facebook to accurately assess advertising responses and much more.

An application of a fast Big Data steady-state inference technique, known as the Perron-Frobenius Theorem and discussed in this chapter, launched Google founders into their present circle of billionaire unicorns. By sampling the paths of the Internet and then applying Perron-Frobenius to the sample matrices, Sergey Brin and Larry Page were able to generalize the distribution of the Internet links and select the most popular links in each category in record-breaking time and attract billions of advertising revenue dollars to Google's search engine. The underlying sampling technology, on which Google founders Sergey Brin and Larry Page were working during their PhD studies at Stanford, is directly applicable to many traditionally time-consuming financial applications.

Google's approach to automatically and efficiently rank the web content works as follows: Google web spider starts at a random web page, from where it scans all the links to other web pages and randomly selects one to follow. Once on the next page, the Google web spider repeats its activity, identifying and randomly following additional links until it reaches a page with no outbound links, and goes back "home" to start the process from the beginning. There, the Google web spider once again selects a new web page at random, identifies all the links presented on the page, selects one link at random, follows it and repeats the process until another "dead-end" web page is reached. While the spider crawls the Internet, it records and transmits its activity back to Google databases.

By randomly sampling the links, Google imitates the web-surfing activity of random individuals surfing at their leisure or for another purpose. Once Google performs the surfing operation a sufficient number of times, Google creates the "transition probabilities" of the web universe. In general, such transitions are known as Markov Chains. From the sample Markov Chain transitions, Google perfected a fast Big Data technique for extrapolating the transitions for the entire web-browsing population, allowing Google to efficiently rank the entire universe of websites in a very short space of time.

What does any of this has to do with Finance? Markov Chains occur quite often. The most obvious application is transitions among credit ratings of a borrower. Here, the borrower may stay in the same rating bucket, as well as move up or move down the ladder. Markov Chains are also the foundation of the Poisson process, a model that is used to approximate information diffusion in the markets (e.g., Babus and Kondor 2018), the long memory of disruptive events like economic crises and news announcements (e.g., Schennach 2018), jumps in prices of instruments underlying derivatives (e.g., Glasserman and Kou 2003), and other applications. The traditional approach to dealing with Markov Chains calls for lengthy and computationally expensive multiplication of matrices. The Big Data approach, on the other hand, provides a speedy and computationally efficient solution discussed in this chapter that makes Markov Chain estimation a breeze. Another application of Markov Chains discussed in this chapter is optimization of option pricing.

The innovation of the Google method, however, extends even further. Its intelligent sampling is extremely useful in all applications involving lots of data: take multi-asset portfolios with the number of instruments in excess of Russell 1500, or something like high-frequency trading where the number of intraday data points reaches billions for one instrument in just one day. All the data points are typically not equal in their information content: some are packed with value, whereas others are just place fillers. Strategic Big Data sampling allows us to discriminate between content and noise on the fly, and estimate the price trends and distributions with high speed and without processing every possible byte of information.

Fast Steady-State Inferences with the Perron–Frobenius Theorem. The Perron-Frobenius Theorem was proved for strictly positive matrices in 1907 by Oskar Perron (1880–1975), and was extended in 1912 for non-negative irreducible matrices by Ferdinand Georg Frobenius (1849–1917) in Frobenius (1912). Despite its age, Perron-Frobenius is a theorem that keeps giving, literally, improvements in asset pricing, including that of options, intraday trading dynamics, investment methodologies, and many other topics in Finance involving Markov Chains and Poisson processes.

Any non-negative irreducible $n \times n$ matrix A has a positive real eigenvalue λ_{max}, such that all other eigenvalues λ of A satisfy

$$|\lambda| \leq \lambda_{max} \tag{8.13}$$

Furthermore, if elements of another non-negative irreducible matrix B are smaller than those of A, $0 \leq B \leq A$, $B \neq A$, then every eigenvalue ν of B satisfies

$$|\nu| < \lambda_{max} \tag{8.14}$$

λ_{max} is known as Perron-Frobenius eigenvalue.

A review of the proof of the Perron-Frobenius Theorem can be found in MacCluer (2020).

The Perron-Frobenius eigenvalue's λ_{max} has associated nonnegative (left and right) eigenvectors that are called (left and right) Perron-Frobenius eigenvectors. The Perron-Frobenius eigenvectors need not be unique or positive.

Markov Chains

Markov Chains occur in multiple financial applications ranging from loan pricing to market microstructure to options pricing. The most inconvenient part of Markov Chains is their computational complexity. Computations of potential outcomes of loan default scenarios or prices of the instruments underlying the options contracts often take days. The computational delays in turn slow down trading and risk management functions, often causing practitioners to react too late to critical events. As a result, investors leave billions of dollars on the table every year. The Perron-Frobenius Theorem comes to the rescue and helps speed up the required computations by a significant margin.

A Markov Chain is a probabilistic model of switching among many deterministic outcomes. It is often described by an $n \times n$ matrix of transition probabilities between n states. A corporate credit default matrix is a perfect example of a Markov Chain: all borrowers are assigned a rating from a set of 27 states, ranging from AAA (most sound) to D (in default). From the creditor's perspective, borrowers transition between various credit ratings every so often, depending on the borrower's financial stability and prevailing market conditions. The credit rating is estimated by credit rating agencies like Moody's, S&P, and Fitch. Transition from one credit rating to the next occurs with certain probabilities that may depend on the borrower's industry, contemporary market conditions, and the rating agency's methodology.

Figures 8.6–e show the distribution of ratings of corporate and sovereign debt generated by Egan-Jones Ratings Company, Morningstar Credit Ratings, LLC, Fitch Ratings, Japan Credit Rating Agency, Ltd., and Standard & Poor's Ratings Services, as reported in the open credit rating database.[1] As Figures 8.6a–e show, different rating agencies have structurally different approaches to credit ratings. The samples of credit ratings include millions of observations, yet different credit rating firms choose their own credit metrics. Egan-Jones, for instance, conservatively errs on ranking issues on the lower end of A. At the same time, Fitch and Morningstar's ratings more resemble a bimodal distribution with lots of AAA and D ratings. Japan Credit Rating Agency, Ltd. also gives out quite a few D's, but few, if any, B's and C's. Perhaps S&P strives for a balanced approach with a significant mass of ratings from C to AAA-, in addition to spikes at D and AAA.

A popular approach to estimating credit risk involves determining steady-state transition probabilities from one rating to another. A steady-state transition probability answers the question of what is the likelihood of an issuer changing its credit rating from the present to the next assessment, and which way is the rating most likely to go?

Table 8.3 shows realized transition probabilities determined from Morningstar credit rating data. The dataset covers 2010–2016 and contains 19,749 credit ratings for over 108 companies. To find the probabilities, Morningstar ratings for each entity were lined up in ascending order and then counted. For every transition, the corresponding cell in the transition matrix was incremented. A transition from A to AA, for example, incremented cell (21, 24), with the 21st row being the starting point of the transition and the 24th row representing the end point. Once all the transitions were accounted for, each row of the matrix was divided by the sum of all the transitions in that row to find the statistical distribution of the transitions.

The result, the transition probability matrix, is a rule book for determining possible moves between credit ratings. While it is often assumed that the ratings upgrade or downgrade only to their closest neighbors (e.g., AA to either AA- or AA+), in reality, the ratings can jump all over the place. As Table 8.3 shows, an issue rated by Morningstar

---

[1] See   https://public.opendatasoft.com/explore/dataset/ratings-history/table/?sort=par_valuehttps://
public.opendatasoft.com/explore/dataset/ratings-history/table/?sort=par_value

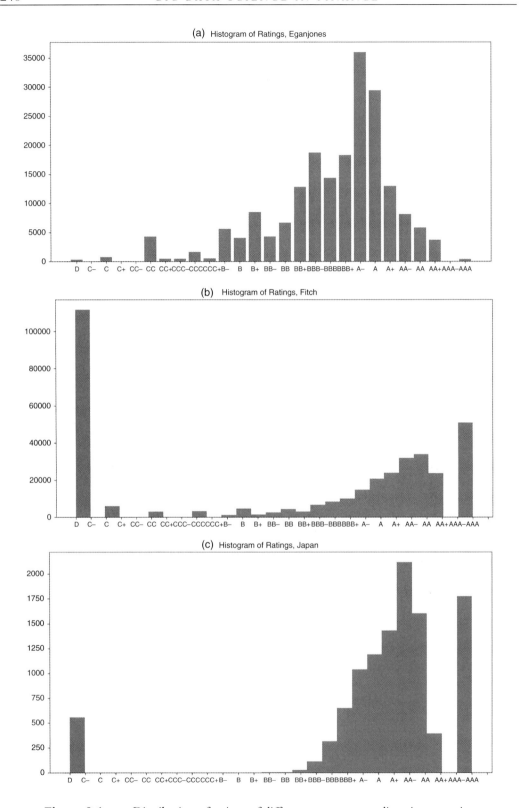

Figure 8.6a–e   Distribution of ratings of different corporate credit rating agencies.

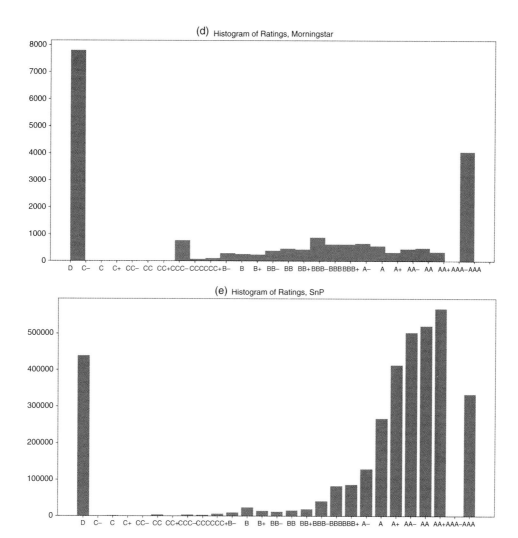

Figure 8.6a–e   (*Continued*)

Table 8.3 Morningstar realized transition probabilities, 2010–2016.

	D	C-	C	C+	CC-	CC	CC+	CCC-	CCC	CCC+	B-	B	B+	BB-	BB	BB+	BBB-	BBB	BBB+	A-	A	A+	AA-	AA	AA+	AAA-	AAA
D	50	0	0	0	0	0	0	15	0	0	0	0	0	0	0	0	0	0	0	0	0	0	0	0	0	0	6
C-	0	0	0	0	0	0	0	0	0	0	0	0	0	0	0	0	0	0	0	0	0	0	0	0	0	0	0
C	0	0	0	0	0	0	0	0	0	0	0	0	0	0	0	0	0	0	0	0	0	0	0	0	0	0	0
C+	0	0	0	0	0	0	0	0	0	0	0	0	0	0	0	0	0	0	0	0	0	0	0	0	0	0	0
CC-	0	0	0	0	0	0	0	0	0	0	0	0	0	0	0	0	0	0	0	0	0	0	0	0	0	0	0
CC	0	0	0	0	0	0	0	0	0	0	0	0	0	0	0	0	0	0	0	0	0	0	0	0	0	0	0
CC+	0%	0%	0%	0%	0%	0%	0%	0%	0%	0%	0%	0%	0%	0%	0%	0%	0%	0%	0%	0%	0%	0%	0%	0%	0%	0%	0%
CCC-	32%	0%	0%	0%	0%	0%	1%	25%	1%	3%	3%	2%	2%	3%	3%	2%	2%	1%	0%	3%	2%	0%	0%	0%	3%	0%	5%
CCC	27%	0%	0%	0%	0%	0%	8%	2%	8%	6%	8%	2%	8%	6%	6%	2%	4%	0%	0%	0%	0%	6%	0%	0%	0%	0%	12%
CCC+	16%	0%	0%	0%	0%	0%	1%	18%	1%	3%	2%	3%	4%	5%	4%	2%	7%	2%	1%	3%	3%	2%	4%	1%	2%	0%	4%
B-	18%	0%	0%	0%	0%	0%	2%	9%	0%	5%	1%	2%	2%	4%	4%	5%	2%	4%	1%	4%	2%	6%	1%	3%	2%	0%	21%
B	7%	0%	0%	0%	0%	0%	2%	6%	1%	2%	8%	1%	6%	5%	3%	4%	3%	5%	1%	4%	4%	5%	1%	4%	3%	0%	26%
B+	9%	0%	0%	0%	0%	0%	2%	11%	2%	5%	1%	10%	4%	5%	5%	2%	5%	2%	2%	4%	2%	5%	2%	0%	4%	0%	27%
BB-	8%	0%	0%	0%	0%	0%	0%	4%	0%	8%	4%	1%	3%	3%	5%	3%	6%	4%	2%	3%	1%	6%	2%	4%	0%	0%	25%
BB	10%	0%	0%	0%	0%	0%	1%	8%	1%	1%	3%	2%	5%	7%	3%	2%	4%	3%	2%	4%	1%	4%	3%	1%	0%	0%	32%
BB+	14%	0%	0%	0%	0%	0%	2%	10%	2%	2%	2%	2%	5%	3%	10%	4%	4%	2%	1%	4%	1%	3%	3%	0%	0%	0%	18%
BBB-	10%	0%	0%	0%	0%	0%	1%	4%	1%	1%	2%	2%	2%	3%	2%	3%	5%	5%	2%	5%	2%	5%	2%	0%	0%	0%	30%
BBB	7%	0%	0%	0%	0%	0%	1%	5%	1%	3%	2%	1%	8%	6%	4%	3%	8%	2%	3%	5%	4%	9%	4%	0%	0%	0%	23%
BBB+	10%	0%	0%	0%	0%	0%	0%	4%	0%	1%	2%	1%	4%	9%	3%	3%	3%	5%	4%	3%	4%	5%	4%	0%	0%	0%	29%
A-	4%	0%	0%	0%	0%	0%	0%	3%	0%	3%	2%	2%	5%	8%	4%	1%	9%	2%	2%	7%	1%	4%	1%	0%	0%	0%	38%
A	9%	0%	0%	0%	0%	0%	0%	3%	0%	1%	1%	2%	8%	6%	4%	4%	2%	12%	2%	2%	4%	9%	2%	0%	0%	0%	28%
A+	8%	0%	0%	0%	0%	0%	1%	4%	0%	1%	1%	2%	7%	3%	3%	6%	6%	4%	9%	2%	5%	9%	0%	0%	0%	0%	23%
AA-	10%	0%	0%	0%	0%	0%	0%	2%	0%	3%	2%	2%	4%	6%	4%	5%	7%	2%	0%	10%	1%	2%	0%	0%	0%	0%	34%
AA	10%	0%	0%	0%	0%	0%	0%	5%	0%	1%	2%	1%	5%	5%	5%	6%	4%	8%	2%	1%	11%	2%	0%	0%	0%	0%	28%
AA+	15%	0%	0%	0%	0%	0%	1%	6%	1%	2%	2%	0%	2%	3%	3%	4%	2%	4%	5%	2%	4%	14%	0%	0%	0%	0%	25%
AAA-	0%	0%	0%	0%	0%	0%	0%	0%	0%	0%	0%	0%	0%	0%	0%	0%	0%	0%	0%	0%	0%	0%	0%	0%	0%	0%	0%
AAA	2%	0%	0%	0%	0%	0%	0%	1%	0%	0%	1%	1%	2%	2%	1%	2%	4%	3%	2%	4%	3%	2%	3%	2%	0%	0%	61

Source: https:// public.opendatasoft.com/explore/dataset/ratings-history/table/?sort=par_value

248

as B- has a 21% chance of ending up as a AAA, a 3% chance moving to AA+, 2% to AA, 4% to AA-, 1% to A+, 2% to A, 6% to A-, 2% to BBB+, 2% to BBB, 5% to BBB-, 4% to BB+, 4% to BB, 5% to BB-, 2% to B+, 1% to B, 5% remaining at B-, 2% moving to CCC+, 9% moving to CCC-, and 18% of defaulting (obtaining rating D). Also, contrary to many academic studies, the default state is not absorbing; that is, once in default, an entity has a 50% chance of getting back on track, including the 15% chance of landing on CCC-, and even a 6% chance landing on AAA, as shown in Table 8.3.

The credit-rating matrix contains probabilities of moving from one credit rating to another in one period, say, one month or one year, but most typically, until the next credit review. In practice, most credit rating agencies review corporate and sovereign debt at least once a year, and often seek to incorporate changes to corporate outlook every quarter. Consumer credit, on the other hand, is evaluated more frequently, once a month or even more often. Amazon is said to measure its customers' credit score in near real time based on their cell phone usage and shopping activity, opening new credit accounts to previously underserved markets that were traditionally difficult to rank for companies like Equifax.

In Table 8.3, the probability of staying in D (default) state for one period is the element (1,1) – the probability of moving from state 1 to state 1. According to Morningstar rating, the probability of remaining in default is 50%. The probability of moving from D to CCC- is 15%, as shown in the element (1,8). The probability of moving from D to AAA is a surprising 6%. In general, the row defines the "origin" state, and the column represents the "destination" state.

By matrix construction, the sum of elements in each row is necessarily 1: a borrower starting in any state will necessarily end in the same or another state with 100% probability. Since the borrower may only end up in one state at a time, the transition probabilities are additive.

The objective of a lender is to estimate the probability of default of the borrower over the lifetime of the loan. The price of the loan, the spread between the risk-free rate, and the rate charged by the borrower are then estimated on the basis of the said long-term probability of default.

The transition probabilities in Table 8.3 address a specific number of "states": the credit ratings can migrate only within these states. While the credit ratings may move around randomly, or *stochastically*, their motion from one state or rating to another is guided by the transition probability matrix. The literal definition of "stochastic" in the *Oxford English Dictionary* is "randomly determined; having a random probability distribution or pattern that may be analyzed statistically but may not be predicted precisely." Thus, a company starting in the AA+ rating may have its rating change at random from the data point of view, but still be five times more likely to end up in the AAA rating (transition probability from AA+ to AAA of 25% in Table 8.3) than A+ rating (transition probability from AA+ to A+ is 5% in Table 8.3).

Overall, the states in the rating system and the transition probabilities form a Markov Chain. A Markov Chain, first devised by Andrey Markov in 1903, is a stochastic process where the given state of a variable is only dependent on its previous state. Since the process is independent of its earlier realizations, it is said to be *memoryless*.

When dealing with a basket of loans, it is common to find the *steady-state probability distribution* of the entire loan portfolio. The steady-state probability distribution is effectively the steady-state histogram of distribution of ratings of a portfolio of loans, developed from the transition probability matrix. This steady-state histogram is similar to those shown in Figures 8.6a–e, but only in format: the actual steady-state "end states" of the loans can be quite different from their historical realizations depicted in Figures 8.6a–e. In Markov Chain notation, a probability distribution π contains steady-state probabilities and is called a stationary distribution of the Markov Chain with transition matrix P and state space Ω if π satisfies $\pi = \pi P$.

The steady-state distribution estimates the probability of ending up in each given state after countless steps through the Markov Chain, independent of the start. As with any Markov process, we can compute steady-state ratings probabilities by multiplying the rating transition matrix by itself enough times to reach the end of the loan lives. Each round of transition matrix multiplication extends transition probabilities by one time period. Thus, if credit rating changes quarterly (4 times per year), and the loan under consideration is extended for 25 years, then the lifetime default probabilities are computed as a product of the credit rating transition matrix with itself taken $25 \times 4 = 100$ times. In standard notation, if matrix P is the one-transition probability matrix, and the total estimation horizon is n periods, the long-term transition probability matrix π is computed as

$$\pi = (P)^n \tag{8.15}$$

While it may appear that π is quite similar to P, a simple test shows otherwise. Consider a primitive 2×2 sample probability transition matrix P:

$$P = \begin{bmatrix} 0.8 & 0.2 \\ 0.4 & 0.6 \end{bmatrix} \tag{8.16}$$

Multiplying the matrix P by itself results in matrices increasingly converging to the matrix's steady state of P_{ss}, quite different from the original matrix:

$$P_{ss} = \begin{bmatrix} 0.66 & 0.33 \\ 0.66 & 0.33 \end{bmatrix} \tag{8.17}$$

Figure 8.7 shows the convergence of the matrix elements to their steady state. While a 2×2 matrix convergence is quite fast, the convergence of a larger transition probability matrix can take many more iterations and the multiplication itself takes a lot of computational time.

The challenge with estimating π is that as the number of elements of P grows, the matrix multiplication of P takes too long, even with superior computing power. In some cases, the estimation procedure takes so long that when the results are obtained, they are no longer useful from the business point of view. Once again, the Big Data approach comes to the rescue. Specifically, the Perron-Frobenius Theorem allows us to estimate the steady-state probabilities fast.

By the Perron-Frobenius Theorem, the right-hand eigenvector of the 1-period transition probability matrix happens to be the steady-state transition probability matrix.

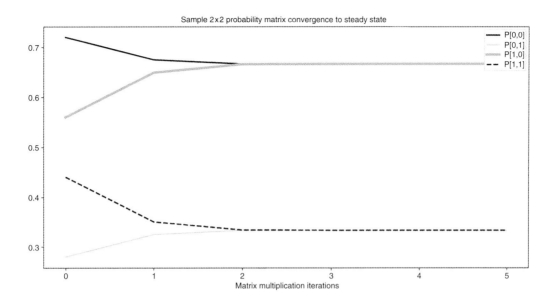

Figure 8.7   Convergence of a sample 2×2 transition probability matrix.

More rigorously, for all Markovian transition probability matrices A, with $x>0$ being the right-handed eigenvector corresponding to the A's eigenvalue r, $Ax = rx$, we choose a row vector $y>0$ with $Ay = ry$ so that $y \cdot x = 1$. The rank one matrix $H := x \otimes y^T$ has image space R, the one-dimensional space spanned by x and $H^2 = H$, so H is a projection. The operator $I - H$ is then also a projection whose image is the null space N of H. Also, $AH = Ax \otimes y = rx \otimes y = x \otimes ry = HA$. This is a direct sum decomposition of our space as $R \oplus N$ which is invariant under A.

The restriction of A to N has all its eigenvalues λ slightly less than r in absolute value: $|\lambda| < r$. The restriction of A to the one-dimensional space R is multiplication by r.

If we set $P := \frac{1}{r}A$, then the restriction of P to N has all its eigenvalues less than one in absolute values. The above decomposition is invariant under all powers of P and the restriction of P^k to N tends to 0 as $k \to \infty$. The restriction of P to R is the identity. Hence,

$$lim_{k \to \infty} \left(\frac{1}{r}A\right)^k = H$$

Going back to the toy 2×2 matrix example of Eq (8.16) and convergence shown in Figure 8.7, the Big Data technique produces the desired results quickly and reliably. The first eigenvector of the matrix of Eq (8.16), once normalized, delivers the exact [0.6666 0.3334] convergence values. In general, Big Data calculations produce a fast and efficient way to find the steady-state default probabilities and more. Using PCA on the Morningstar realized transition probabilities shown in Table 8.3, and examining the first resulting singular vector, we obtain the normalized steady-state ratings probabilities shown in Figure 8.8.

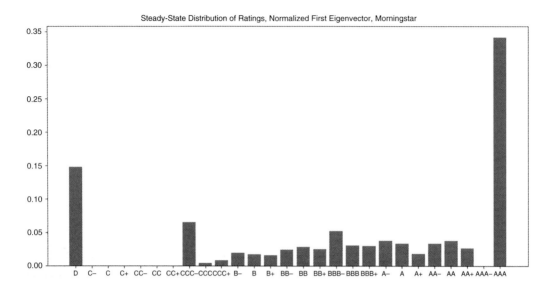

Figure 8.8   Steady-state ratings distribution in Morningstar ratings as predicted by Perron-Frobenius Theorem.

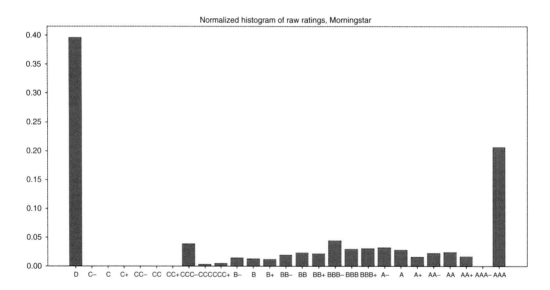

Figure 8.9   Normalized empirical distribution of actual Morningstar ratings. This is a normalized version of the distribution appearing in Figure 8.6d.

It is interesting to compare the steady-state distribution of credit ratings shown in Figure 8.6d with the normalized empirical sample distribution of credit scores for Morningstar shown in Figure 8.9. The empirical distribution of Figure 8.9 projects a large number of defaulting borrowers and a relatively small number of AAA-borrowers. In contrast, the steady-state distribution shown in Figure 8.9 has a much lower rate of default and a much higher incidence of AAA rating vis-à-vis the original layout in Figure 8.6d.

How do these models help us measure credit risk in practice? Being able to quickly compute the percentage of borrowers in default allows us to more reliably estimate the expected loss. In the case of Morningstar, the steady-state number of borrowers in default is significantly smaller than that in the empirical distribution. As a result, the reduced default values diminish the expected loss. This can be particularly useful in calculation of risk capital as required by Basel I, II, and III regulations. Specifically, Basel requires that all financial institutions proactively manage their *Expected Loss* (EL), defined as the product of *Probability of Default* (PD), *Loss Given Default* (LGD), and *Exposure at Default* (EAD):

$$EL = LGD \times PD \times EAD \tag{8.18}$$

LGD measures the portion of the loan that is not recoverable in the event of a borrower's default; e.g., loans secured by collateral, such as mortgages, have a higher default recovery rate (lower loss given default) than unsecured loans such as credit card debt and working capital loans. EAD refers to the total loan amount outstanding at the time of default. PD is the probability of default – the expected steady-state rate of collapse of loan agreements. It is the PD metric that can be more accurately estimated using the Big Data methodology, often leading to the lower rates of default and lower EL computations as a result. In turn, lower expected rate of default means lower risk capital requirements, and the lower the cash the institution is required to keep on hand, allowing for higher reinvested amounts and higher returns.

In addition to the statistics contained in the top eigenvector, the top several eigenvalues are also of importance to data scientists. The largest eigenvalue is known as the Perron-Frobenius eigenvalue, $\lambda_{pf} \geq |\lambda|$ for any eigenvalue λ. For any real and nonnegative matrix $A \in R^{n \times n}$, the Perron-Frobenius eigenvalue λ_{pf} is real and nonnegative. For a special case of any Markov Chain transition probability matrix, the respective λ_{pf} is dominant and always 1. In other applications considered in Chapter 9, λ_{pf} delivers the overall rate at which the transition matrix converges to the steady-state values. In the Markov Chain transition probability matrices, it is the top eigenvalue by magnitude with λ_{pf} removed, $\mu = max\{|\lambda_2|, |\lambda_3|, \ldots |\lambda_n|\}$, that indicates the convergence rate to steady state. Specifically, the approximate number of time periods, T, over which the transition probability matrix approaches convergence is:

$$T = 1/\log(1/\mu) \tag{8.19}$$

In the traditional Markov Chain literature, T is often referred to as a *mixing time*.

For the Morningstar example, the sorted raw and absolute eigenvalues are plotted in Figure 8.10. The largest eigenvalue by magnitude with the top eigenvalue removed is $\mu =$

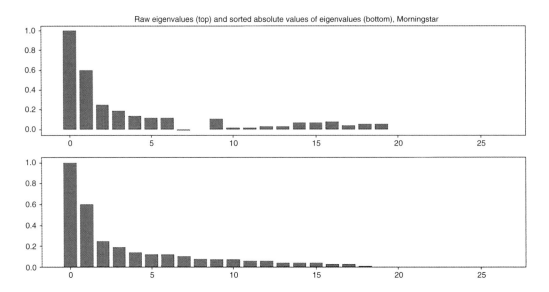

Figure 8.10   The raw eigenvalues of the Morningstar empirical credit rating transition probabilities (top panel) and the sorted absolute values of those eigenvalues (bottom panel).

0.6011. This asymptotic convergence rate indicates that the ratings converge monotonically to their steady-state values in approximately $T = 1/\log(1/\mu) = 1.9611 \sim 2$ time periods.

In addition to examining the Perron-Frobenius eigenvalue and associated eigenvector, the latter known as the right eigenvector in SVD, the researchers may be interested in considering the left eigenvectors generated by SVD. The left eigenvectors, u_i, show the relative values of ratings i to the steady-state computation. As such, they may be interesting to researchers looking to quantitatively analyze and improve the accuracy of the rankings.

Aside from the regulatory capital, how does the model help predict near-term credit ratings? The Markovian model delivers the steady-state probability of default for all the ratings within a given group of borrowers, given a specific rating methodology. Thus, all borrowers rated by Morningstar, in the steady state many periods ahead, may expect to end up in the 15% default pool as predicted by the Markov model and optimized by Perron-Frobenius.

The accuracy of the Markov Chain credit rating result is questionable, particularly on long-term horizons. By construction, the Markovian model assumes that future transition probabilities remain the same as they are today – possibly an unrealistic assumption. For example, Figures 8.11a–f show Markov-Perron-Frobenius predicted and realized Morningstar ratings for different years. As Figures 8.11a–f illustrate, in some years, the model comes close to realized out-of-sample ratings, whereas in other years, the past ratings serve as much better predictors of the next year's rating distribution.

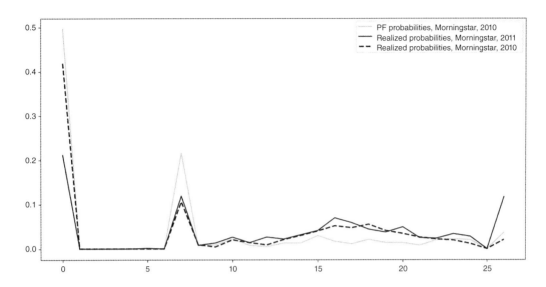

Figure 8.11a   2010 prediction of 2011 Morningstar ratings distribution and realized 2011 distribution.

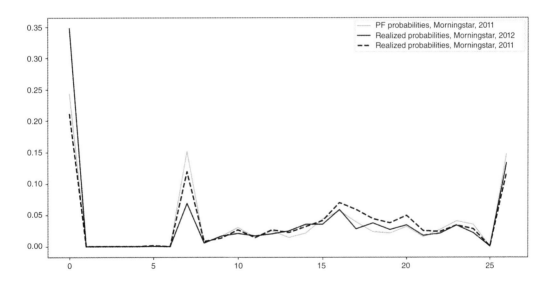

Figure 8.11b   2011 prediction of 2012 Morningstar ratings distribution and realized 2012 distribution.

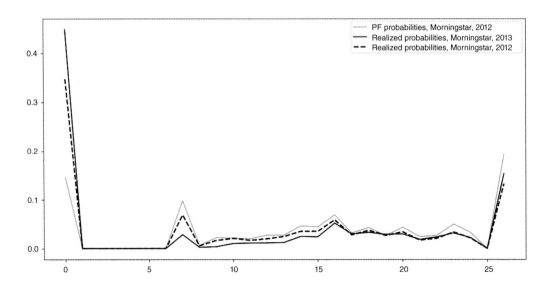

Figure 8.11c   2012 prediction of 2013 Morningstar ratings distribution and realized 2013 distribution.

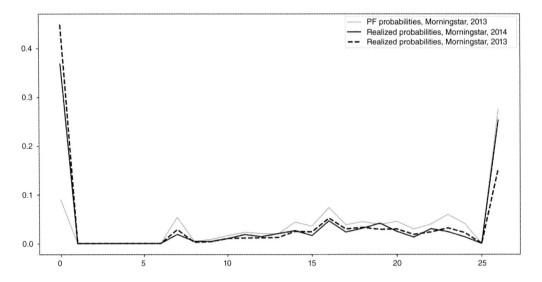

Figure 8.11d   2013 prediction of 2014 Morningstar ratings distribution and realized 2014 distribution.

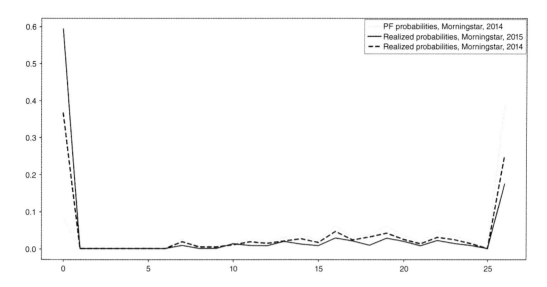

Figure 8.11e   2014 prediction of 2015 Morningstar ratings distribution and realized 2015 distribution.

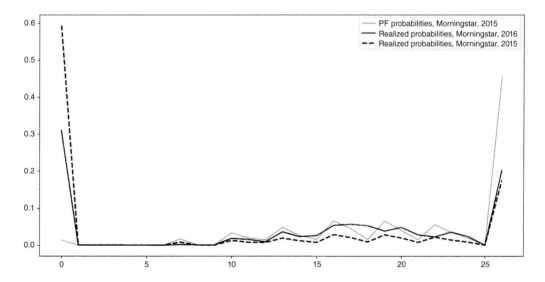

Figure 8.11f   2015 prediction of 2016 Morningstar ratings distribution and realized 2016 distribution.

Conclusion

The Big Data technique provides concise approaches to estimation of voluminous stochastic data, such as options data. The Perron-Frobenius Theorem dramatically improves computational speed in many Markov Chain applications.

Appendix 8.A Determining the Percentage of Variation Explained by the Top Principal Components in Python

Even though the Marcenko-Pastur Theorem provides a ready out-of-the-box approach to estimate the number of significant principal components, researchers may still be interested in assessing the percent of variation captured by the vectors. Once again, Python provides a handy way to extract this information.

For a standardized matrix X (see Appendix 5.A in Chapter 5 in this book for Python data standardization methods), finding the proportion of variation explained by the top-three eigenvalues is as easy as calling the PCA method e">explained_variance_ratio_:

```
from sklearn.decomposition import PCA
pca = PCA(n_components=2)
principalComponents = pca.fit_transform(x)
explained_variation = pca.explained_variance_ratio_
```

For specific code examples, please visit https://www.BigDataFinanceBook.com, and register with password explained_variance (case-sensitive).

References

Ang, A., Chen, J., and Xing, Y. (2006). Downside risk. *Review of Financial Studies* 19(4): 1191–1239.

Avellaneda, M. and Cont, R. (2002). Special issue on volatility modeling. *Quantitative Finance* 2.

Avellaneda, M. and Dobi, D. (2014). Modeling volatility risk in equity options market: a statistical approach. NYU Courant, working paper.

Babus, A. and Kondor, P. (2018). Trading and information diffusion in over-the-counter markets. *Econometrica* 86(5): 1727–1769.

Bali, T.G., and Hovakimian, A. (2009). Volatility spreads and expected stock returns. *Management Science* 55: 1797–1812.

Bali, T.G., Hu, J., and Murray, S. (2016). Option implied volatility, skewness, and kurtosis and the cross-section of expected stock returns. Working paper.

Baltussen, G., Van Bekkum, S., and Van der Grient, B. (2018). Unknown unknowns: Vol-of-vol and the cross-section of stock returns. *Journal of Financial and Quantitative Analysis* 53(4): 1615–1651.

Bates, D.S. (2000). Post-'87 crash fears in the S&P 500 futures option market. *Journal of Econometrics* 94(1–2): 181–238.

Benzoni, L., Collin-Dufresne, P., and Goldstein, R.S. (2011). Explaining asset pricing puzzles associated with the 1987 market crash. *Journal of Financial Economics* 101(3): 552–573.

Besag, J. (1974). Spatial interaction and the statistical analysis of lattice systems. *Journal of the Royal Statistical Association Series B* 36: 192–236.

Bishop, C. (2006). 11.4: Slice sampling. In: *Pattern Recognition and Machine Learning*. New York: Springer.

Black, F.S. and Scholes, M.S. (1972). The valuation of option contracts and a test of market efficiency. *Journal of Finance* 27(2): 399–417.

Black, F.S. and Scholes, M.S. (1973). The pricing of options and corporate liabilities. *Journal of Political Economy* 81(3): 637–654.

Bollen, N.P. and Whaley, R.E. (2004). Does net buying pressure affect the shape of implied volatility functions? *The Journal of Finance* 59(2): 711–753.

Bollerslev, T. (1986). Generalized autoregressive conditional heteroskedasticity. *Journal of Econometrics* 31: 307–327.

Bouchaud, J-P., Laloux, L., and Potters, M. (2005). Financial applications of random matrix theory: Old laces and new pieces. *Finance and Stochastics*, arXiv.physics/0507111.

Bouchaud, J-P. and Potters, M. (2009). Financial application of random matrix theory: A short review. *Finance and Stochastics*. arXiv.org.

Boyd, S., Diaconis, P., and Xiao, L. (2004). Fastest mixing Markov Chain on a graph. *SIAM Review* 46: 667–689.

Campa, J.M. and Chang, P.K. (1995). Testing the expectations hypothesis on the term structure of volatilities in foreign exchange options. *The Journal of Finance* 50(2): 529–547.

Carmona, R. and Nadtochiy, S. (2008). Local volatility dynamic models. *Finance and Stochastics* 13: 1–48.

Carr, P. and Wu, L. (2008). Variance risk premiums. *The Review of Financial Studies* 22(3): 1311–1341.

Christoffersen, P., Fournier, M., and Jacobs, K. (2017). The factor structure in equity options. *Review of Financial Studies* 31(2): 595–637.

Conrad, J., Dittmar, R.F., and Ghysels, E. (2013). Ex-ante skewness and expected stock returns, *Journal of Finance* 68: 85–124.

Cont, R. and Fonseca, J. (2002). Dynamics of implied volatility surfaces. *Quantitative Finance* 2: 45–60.

Cont, R., Fonseca, J., and Durrleman, V. (2002). Stochastic models of implied volatility surfaces. *Economic Notes* 31: 361–377.

Cremers, M. and Weinbaum, D. (2010). Deviations from put–call parity and stock return predictability. Journal of Financial and Quantitative Analysis 45: 335–367.

Damlen, P., Wakefield, J., and Walker, S. (1999). Gibbs sampling for Bayesian non-conjugate and hierarchical models by using auxiliary variables. *Journal of the Royal Statistical Society, Series B (Statistical Methodology)* 61(2): 331–344.

Derman, E. and Kani, I. (1998). Stochastic implied trees: arbitrage pricing with stochastic term and strike structure of volatility. *International Journal of Theoretical and Applied Finance* 1: 4–53.

Derman, E., Miller, M., and Park, D. (2016). *The Volatility Smile*. Hoboken, NJ: Wiley Finance Editions.

Dobi, D. (2014). Modeling systemic risk in the options market. PhD thesis, NYU Courant.

Duffie, D. (1996). State-space models of the term structure of interest rates. In: *Stochastic Analysis and Related Topics V: The Silivri Workshop* (ed. H. Körezlioglu, B. Øksendal, and A. Üstünel). Boston: Birkhauser.

Dumas, B., Fleming, J., and Whaley, R.E. (1998). Implied volatility functions: empirical tests. *Journal of Finance* 53(6): 2059–2106.

Dupire, B. (1994). Pricing with a smile. *RISK*. Available at: www.cmap.polytechnique.fr/~rama/dea/dupire.pdf.

Fama, E. and MacBeth, M.J. (1973). Risk, return, and equilibrium: Empirical tests. *Journal of Political Economy* 81: 607–636.

Frobenius, G. (1912). Uber Matrizen aus nicht negativen Elementen. Available at: www .bookdepository.com/Uber-Matrizen-Aus-Nicht.

Gatheral, J. and Taleb, N. (2011). *The Volatility Surface: A Practitioner's Guide*. Hoboken, NJ: Wiley Finance.

Geman, S. and Geman, D. (1984). Stochastic relaxation, Gibbs distributions and the Bayesian restoration of images. *IEEE Transactions on Pattern Analysis and Machine Intelligence* 6: 721–741.

Glasserman, P. and Kou, S.G. (2003). The term structure of simple forward rates with jump risk. *Mathematical Finance* 13(3): 383–410.

Hafner, R. and Wallmeiery, M. (2000). The dynamics of DAX implied volatilities. *International Quarterly Journal of Finance* 59: 1–27.

Hammersley, J. and Clifford, P. (1970). Markov fields on finite graphs and lattices. Unpublished manuscript.

Hastings, W.K. (1970). Monte Carlo sampling methods using Markov Chains and their applications. *Biometrika* 57(1).

Heston, S. (1993). A closed-form solution for options with stochastic volatility with applications to bond and currency options. *Review of Financial Studies* 6(2): 327–343.

Hornand, R.A. and Johnson, C.R. (1985). *Matrix Analysis*. Cambridge: Cambridge University Press.

Hull, J. and White, A. (1987). The pricing of options on assets with stochastic volatilities. *Journal of Finance* 42(2): 281–300.

Johannes, M. and Polson, N. (2010). MCMC methods for continuous time financial econometrics. In: *Handbook of Financial Econometrics: Applications*. 1–72. Oxford: Elsevier.

Johnson, T.L. and So, E.C. (2012). The option to stock volume ratio and future returns. *Journal of Financial Economics* 106: 262–286.

Lee, R. (2004). Implied volatility: Statics, dynamics, and probabilistic interpretation. In: *Recent Advances in Applied Probability*. New York: Springer.

Litterman, R. and Scheinkman, J. (1991). Common factors affecting bond returns. *The Journal of Fixed Income* 1(1): 54–61.

Merton, R.C. (1973). Theory of rational option pricing. *The Bell Journal of Economics and Management Science* 4(1): 141–183.

Metropolis, N., Rosenbluth, A.W., Rosenbluth, M.N., Teller, A.H., and Teller, E. (1953). Equations of state calculations by fast computing machines. *Journal of Chemical Physics* 2: 1087–1091.

Mixon, S. (2007). The implied volatility term structure of stock index options. *Journal of Empirical Finance* 14(3): 333–354.

Muravyev, D., Vasquez, A., and Wang, W. (2018). Making better use of option prices to predict stock returns. Boston College, working paper.

Neal, R.M. (2003). Slice sampling. *Annals of Statistics* 31(3): 705–767.

Rehman, Z. and Vilkov, G. (2012). Risk-neutral skewness: Return predictability and its sources. BlackRock and Goethe University, working paper.

Ritter, C. and Tanner, M. (1991). Facilitating the Gibbs sampler: The Gibbs stopper and the Griddy-Gibbs sampler. *Journal of the American Statistical Association* 87: 861–868.

Robert, C. and Casella, G. (1999). *Monte Carlo Statistical Methods*. New York: Springer.

Roberts, G. and Tweedie, R. (1996). Geometric convergence and central limit theorems for multidimensional Hastings and Metropolis algorithms. *Biometrika* 83: 95–110.

Roll, R., Schwartz, E., and Subrahmanyam, A. (2010). O/S: The relative trading activity in options and stock. *Journal of Financial Economics* 96: 1–17.

Schennach, S.M. (2018). Long memory via networking. *Econometrica* 86(6): 2221–2248.

Schweizer, M. and Wissel, J. (2008). Arbitrage-free market models for option prices: The multi-strike case. *Finance and Stochastics* 12: 469–505.

Skiadopoulos, G., Hodges, S., and Clewlow, L. (1999). The dynamics of the S&P 500 implied volatility surface. *Review of Derivative Research* 3: 263–282.

Stilger, P.S., Kostakis, A., and Poon, S.H. (2016). What does risk-neutral skewness tell us about future stock returns? *Management Science* 63: 1814–1834.

Vasquez, A. (2017). Equity volatility term structures and the cross-section of option returns. *Journal of Financial and Quantitative Analysis*, 52(6): 2727–2754.

Xing, Y., Zhang, X., and Zhao, R. (2010). What does the individual option volatility smirk tell us about future equity returns? *Journal of Financial and Quantitative Analysis* 45: 641–662.

Xu, X. and Taylor, S.J. (1994). The term structure of volatility implied by foreign exchange options. *Journal of Financial and Quantitative Analysis* 29(1): 57–74.

Yan, S. (2011). Jump risk, stock returns, and slope of implied volatility smile. *Journal of Financial Economics* 99: 216–233.

Chapter 9

Data Clustering

Introduction

Data clustering has long preoccupied researchers determined to categorize data sets using observable characteristics that can drive investment decisions. One may argue that the idea behind traditional portfolio analysis is a form of clustering as it answers the question of how to compose baskets of securities for optimal global portfolio performance. Today's Data Science delivers advanced methods for classifying data based on distributional characteristics, geometry, and other factors. In fact, data clustering is one of the prominent aspects of today's Data Science and is poised to make a deep impact in finance in the near future.

Data clustering is just beginning to take root in Finance; current applications are few and far between. However, the potential of clustering is enormous as these applications to solve open problems illustrate:

- Pre-hedging in execution: find the most similar instrument.
- Selling in crisis: again, sell the most similar liquid instrument.
- Loan ratings: have ratings for public companies, quickly find most similar ones for target private loans.
- Consumer ratings: based on online behavior, match consumers into credit buckets with known credit ratings.

In this chapter, we will consider clustering in a novel context for portfolio management to create sound portfolios with illiquid instruments, alleviating traditional hurdles for illiquid instruments and expanding the range of instruments used in investments. We show that the results apply to cryptocurrencies, commodities, and equities.

Here, clustering produces very useful results that are different from traditional Markowitz portfolio optimization or established techniques like eigenportfolio construction. While the well-established science of eigenportfolios focuses on finding the optimal combination of financial instruments that best describes the core of a given large portfolio, the eigenportfolio theory may cast aside illiquid financial instruments. Portfolio allocation using clustering incorporates all of the financial instruments under consideration. In doing so, clustered portfolios produce better results than eigenportfolios through higher risk premia of assets typically discarded during eigenportfolio construction.

Illiquid financial instruments tend to trade infrequently, resulting in sparse returns and muted correlation structures. These less prominent correlations often fail to show up in the main eigenvectors of eigenportfolios, and are ignored by portfolio managers, as a result. However, many illiquid instruments carry higher returns to compensate investors for the risk of illiquidity, and can be desirable additions to investor portfolios.

Clustering overcomes the challenges of illiquid instruments by reconstructing their full correlations. Correlation reconstruction is achieved by matching the illiquid instruments with their closest neighbors via graph theory. As this chapter shows, when armed with a full cluster-based correlation picture, investors are able to incorporate the full correlation information in their portfolios and achieve excess returns on their investments.

Clustering Methodology

Formally, data clustering refers to organizing the data into meaningful groups, according to their similarities. In the Big Data context, clustering allows for grouping of data, some of which may be missing, making the inferences all that much more powerful and harder to obtain with traditional econometric analysis.

The clustering techniques discussed are cousins of Gaussian mixtures, a traditional econometric clustering technique. The Gaussian mixtures technique is one of the simplest and most established examples of clustering, which works by separating the data into Gaussian clusters. A mixture of two Gaussians, for example, can be separated by identifying the points forming one Gaussian cluster, removing one Gaussian cluster, and then ending up with the second Gaussian cluster. This algorithm is well known in econometrics as maximum likelihood estimation (MLE).

While MLE is widely accepted and used in Economics and Finance, it is considerably limited. The technique seeks to find the minimum-distance vertex from each data point. When the number of clusters exceeds two or three, the problem becomes NP hard and difficult to solve in polynomial time. The application of MLE, therefore, has been limited to well-defined mixtures of two or three distributions.

As the range of available information explodes, so is the necessity to process multiple sources of data at once, the task that proves too complex for traditional econometric techniques. This is where the Big Data technique comes to the rescue.

The two most popular Big Data clustering techniques are K-means clustering and spectral clustering. Here, we consider the techniques in the context of portfolio construction with potentially illiquid instruments.

Generic K-Means Clustering

K-means is perhaps the most popular and widely used clustering algorithm in unsupervised learning. The K-means algorithm breaks the data set into K clusters, each containing points in maximum proximity to each respective cluster's mean.

An algorithm for K-means clustering takes three variables as inputs:

1. k, the number of clusters;
2. the set of starting centers for each of the k clusters, cj;
3. the algorithm stopping condition.

At the heart of the K-means algorithm is the observation that the K-means criterion based on centroids presents the most optimal cluster centers.

Formally:

$$Minimize\ d\ (S_1, S_2, \ldots, S_k) = \sum_{j=1}^{k} \sum_{a_i \in S_j} (c_j - a_i)^2$$

where c_j is the center of cluster j.

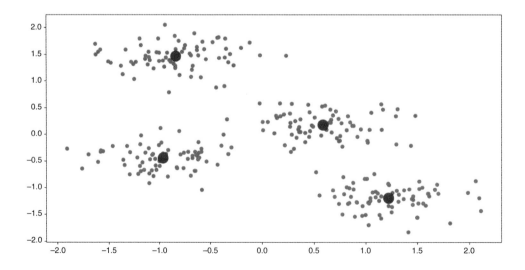

Figure 9.1   An illustration of K-means algorithm with K-4 on four convex data sets.

Lloyd's Algorithm for K-means

Generic K-means is NP-hard to solve and does not recognize patterns. Specifically, non-convex patterns like circles are divided among vertices, not clustered as a whole object. The performance of K-means is limited by two factors:

1. The K-means' objective function is non-convex and makes it computationally difficult to find the actual minimum.
2. K-means assumes the clusters to be convex and have similar properties along all dimensions, a condition known as *isotropy*.

Lloyd's algorithm (Lloyd 1982), also known as Voronoi iteration or relaxation, does not help with pattern recognition, but tends to make the computation more efficient, mitigating factor 1 above, the non-convexity of the K-means' objective function. Lloyd's algorithm tends to converge to a computational minimum, although the obtained minimum is most often local, not global.

Lloyd's algorithm starts with a random set of cluster "centers" or means, finds the points closest to these centers, then recomputes the new cluster centers. The algorithm next iterates K-means computation with a recomputed set of starting cluster centers, known as *centroids*, as follows:

1. Guess cluster centers.
2. Run K-means.
3. Recompute cluster centers as the means of all points belonging to the cluster.
4. Repeat steps 2–4 using cluster centers computed in step 3 above as a starting condition for step 2.

K-means clustering does not distinguish between "more" and "less" important clusters, separating the data set into proximity-based groups. While such separation is fast, its efficiency varies from application to application. In a statistical arbitrage sense where the objective is to identify clusters of securities to buy versus clusters to sell, K-means produces groups that are not uniquely identified as buy vs. sell. Figure 9.2, for example, shows K-means clustering of the lower left part of the correlation matrix of the 2017 S&P 500 stock returns based on correlation proximity with just two clusters (K = 2). The correlations of all the S&P 500 stocks are computed using daily returns, and then the correlations are broken into two groups, each with the highest inter-cluster correlations.

Spectral Clustering

To resolve the second problem with K-means, the algorithm's failure to recognize non-convex clusters, the researchers have devised a methodology known as spectral clustering. The original spectral clustering models date back to Donath and Hoffman (1973) and Fiedler (1973), and, more recently, to Ng, Jordan, and Weiss (2002), Belkin and Niyogi (2003), among others. Spectral clustering allows researchers to identify

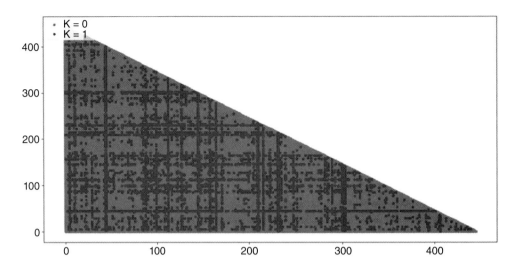

Figure 9.2   Clustering of the lower-left triangular correlation matrix of the S&P 500 returns. The correlations are computed using daily data over a 1-year span.

non-convex sets of data, for example, concentric circles and other complex data structures. In general, it has become a go-to technique for identifying clusters that are not convex or directionally dependent, also known as anisotropic.

The challenge with non-convex clusters is that they often are a result of low-dimensional data embedded on a high-dimensional data structure. Think of a thinly bordered circle with hollow center, instead of a fully shaded circle: the data structure, a two-dimensional table in this case, can support a lot of shading inside the circle, but instead contains just the empty space.

Spectral clustering is based on matrix perturbation theory, and the Davis-Kahan theorem in particular (Davis and Kahan 1970; Yu, Wang, and Samworth 2014). The Davis-Kahan theorem posits that if a sample matrix is representative of the population at large, then the eigenvectors of the sample matrix lie within a certain distance of the population vectors. The idea of clustering then seeks to isolate clusters by seeking eigenvectors that lie sufficiently far from one another.

Data as a Graph. At the core of any clustering algorithm is the idea that any data set can be represented as a graph. A graph is a set of vertices and edges connecting the vertices. Each vertex in a dataset is a data point, and each edge is a relationship between two data points.

In a black-and-white grayscale image, a matrix where all data points range from 0 (black) to 255 (white) of rank n, each data point i, j can be thought of as a weight of an edge between vertices i and j. In financial data, a correlation matrix can be used to measure the relationships between returns of any two instruments. Each data point i, j within the return correlation matrix can then measure a strength of the relationship between financial instruments i and j.

An adjacency matrix describes the "firmness" of connections or the number of paths between any two data points or nodes. The stronger the bond between any two data points i and j, the larger is the element A_{ij} in the adjacency matrix A.

A data graph can further be directed or undirected. In directed graphs, the path from element i to element j may only exist in one direction, or may be stronger in one direction than in the other direction. The direction is reflected in the adjacency matrix: in a directed graph, $A_{ij} \neq A_{ji}$. When the path from element i to element j is only one-way (there is no direct way to access data point i from point j), the corresponding adjacency matrix element $A_{ji} = 0$. An adjacency matrix can also be referred to as a weight matrix W with elements $w_{ij} \geq 0$. In financial data, the correlation matrix is symmetric, so the resulting graph will always be undirected.

An adjacency matrix is often normalized with a kernel for each edge weight w_{ij}. A popular kernel is a Gaussian:

$$w_{ij} = exp(-\|v_i - v_j\|^2/\sigma^2)$$

where

$$0 \leq w_{\min} \leq w_{ij} \leq w_{\max} \leq 1$$

Such a weighting system encodes the complex geometric structure of the data in a fairly simple way.

In the case of applications related to financial data and specifically those using correlation matrices, the correlation function itself may be thought of as a kernel transforming the data into a weight graph.

In addition to the adjacency matrices, graph theory uses *degree matrices*. A degree matrix D is a matrix of the cumulative weight of each data point. Specifically, the degree of a vertex $v_i \in V$ is defined as

$$deg_i = \sum_j w_{ij} \tag{9.1}$$

$w_{ij} = 0$ for all vertices non-adjacent to vertex i.

What Is a Spectral Cluster? There are many different variations of the meaning of a cluster. However, some common characteristics apply to most clusters. For example, the points within the clusters are typically connected, i.e., there is a path from one point belonging to a given cluster to any other point within the same cluster. On the other hand, when any two points are not connected, they should most likely not be clustered together. Schaeffer (2007) measures the "goodness" of a cluster by comparing *cluster densities*, defined as the sum of the number of edges the points within a given cluster share with each other:

$$\delta_{int}(C) = \frac{1}{|C|(|C| - 1)} \sum_{v \in C} deg_{int}(v, C) \tag{9.2}$$

To measure the overall clustering process, we can further define the average inter-cluster density as:

$$\delta_{int}(G|C_1,\ldots,C_k) = \frac{1}{k}\sum_{i=1}^{k}\delta_{int}(C_i) \qquad (9.3)$$

The intra-cluster densities for different clusters can then be compared with each other and with the inter-cluster density, the sum of the edges shared between clusters. The K-means clustering algorithm is based essentially on this approach.

In addition to numerical comparisons based on respective cluster densities, the clusters can be further divided into well-defined and somewhat fuzzy, based on the definition of their respective "borders." Well-defined and isolated clusters are known as *hard* and those overlapping with other clusters are referred to as *soft*.

The clusters can also be split according to their structure. Clusters that have no particular structure are referred to as *flat*. Clusters that contain other clusters within are known as *hierarchical*. The hierarchical clustering most often arises when the cluster structure is not known in advance. Flat clustering produces a clearer definition of clusters and is therefore preferred to hierarchical clustering.

In any clustering approach, we need to break up the clusters based on a specific variable. Clustering approaches include:

- Finding sub-clusters based on the highest density of edges within each cluster, known as density-based clustering.
- Finding the lowest edge density boundaries between clusters, known as cut-based clustering.
- Finding the edge density that exceeds that of a random graph, known as modularity clustering.

The degree distribution of edges in a random graph can be modeled as a Poisson process, as shown by Erdos and Renyi ([1960] 2011). In practice, degree distribution of edges has been shown to be heavy-tailed, violating Poisson assumptions. Based on this observation, Sorensen (2016) proposes power law modeling for the distribution of edges.

The partitions between clusters are known as *graph cuts*. The clusters are partitioned by graph cuts in the graph's adjacency/similarity matrix (see, for example, Ling and Strohmer, 2018). In many financial applications, it is preferable to find the clusters of equal size. For example, in stat-arb, it may be advantageous to create baskets of comparable sizes to mitigate potential liquidity shortages in any small cluster of instruments.[1]

A stream of literature known as normalized cuts or minimal ratio cuts focuses on the creation of balanced clusters in the data. Minimal ratio cuts were well described by Hagen and Kahng (1992) and von Luxburg (2007) while notable research on normalized cuts includes Dhillon, Guan, and Kulis (2004) and Shi and Malik (2000).

Spectral clustering seeks to separate the clusters based on their intrinsic densities, using eigenvalues of the adjacency matrix of the data. The results are accomplished with the Davis-Kahan theorem applied to data Laplacians, discussed in the following sections.

---

[1] A trader may encounter liquidity shortage when executing a stat-arb position, as some stocks may simply not be available to trade, i.e., not have enough liquidity or market depth.

Distance between Eigenvectors: The Davis-Kahan Theorem. The Davis-Kahan theorem states that the eigenvalues of the sample matrix differ from the eigenvalues of the population by a number with a well-defined maximum. In other words, the divergence between the eigenvalues of the sample and the eigenvalues of the true population can only be so great, and the sample eigenvalues may well be used to proxy the eigenvalues of the population.

The divergence between the eigenvectors of the sample and the population is measured by the angle a projection of the matrix makes on the population subspace and the sample subspace. The angle created by the eigenvectors of the sample and the population is known as the *canonical angle*.

Formally, if E and F are d–dimensional linear subspaces in R^p (d is the smaller dimension), then for 1-dimensional E and F that are spanned by respective eigenvectors v_E and $v_F \in S^{p-1}$, the distance between E and F can be measured by the angle between v_E and v_F:

$$\angle(v_E, v_F) = \cos^{-1}(|v_E, v_F|) \tag{9.4}$$

The angle is normalized to the unit norm and contains the absolute value since we are only interested in the acute angles.

For general $p \times d$ matrices E and F, P_E and P_F are orthogonal projection matrices onto E and F, respectively:

$$P_E = EE^T \tag{9.5}$$

$$P_F = FF^T \tag{9.6}$$

The kth canonical angle between E and F for $k = 1,\ldots, d$ is then defined as:

$$\cos^{-1}(\max_{x\in E,\|x\|=1} \max_{y\in F,\|y\|=1}) = \cos^{-1}(|x_k^T y_k|), x_i^T x_i = y_i^T y_i = 0, i = 1,\ldots, k-1 \tag{9.7}$$

Furthermore, if $\sigma_1 \geq \sigma_2 \ldots \geq \sigma_d \in [0,1]$ are the singular values of $E^T F = F^T E$ obtained with SVD, the canonical angles between E and F are:

$$\theta_1 = \cos^{-1}(\sigma_1), \ldots \theta_d = \cos^{-1}(\sigma_d) \tag{9.8}$$

Knowing $\theta_1,\ldots, \theta_d$, we can express singular values of $E^T F$ or $F^T E$ as:

$$s_i = \cos(\theta_i) \tag{9.9}$$

and

$$E^T F = F^T E = USv^T = U \cos\Theta \, v^T \tag{9.10}$$

where

$$\Theta = \theta_1 \, 0 \, \ldots \, 0$$

$$0 \quad \theta_2 \, 0 \, \ldots \tag{9.11}$$

$$0 \quad 0 \, \ldots \, \theta_d$$

Alternatively, canonical angles can be defined as:

$$\theta_k = \sin^{-1}(s_k), k = 1, \ldots, d \tag{9.12}$$

where s_k is the kth singular value of $P_E(1 - P_F) = U \sin\Theta \, v^T$ (see Stewart and Sun 1990).

The actual distance between E and F is then defined as a metric between d-dimensional subspaces, known as the Frobenius measure: $\|\sin\Theta \, (E, F)\|_F$.

The Davis-Kahan Sinθ Theorem. Let Σ and $\hat{\Sigma}$ be $p \times p$ symmetric matrices with eigenvalues $\lambda 1 \geq \lambda 2 \geq \cdots \geq \lambda p$ and $\hat{\lambda} \, 1 \geq \hat{\lambda} \, 2 \geq \cdots \geq \hat{\lambda} \, p$ respectively. Let $1 \leq r < s \leq p$ and $d = s - r + 1$. Let V and $\hat{V}$ be $p \times d$ matrices with columns given by eigenvectors of Σ and $\hat{\Sigma}$ corresponding to λj and $\hat{\lambda} \, j$, $j = r, \cdots, s$. By construction, V and $\hat{V}$ have orthonormal columns.

Let $\delta = \{\inf |\lambda\hat{\lambda}|, \lambda \in [\lambda_s, \lambda_r], \hat{\lambda} \in (-\infty, \hat{\lambda}_{s+1}] \cup [\hat{\lambda}_{r-1}, \infty)\}$ $\hat{\lambda}_0 = -\infty, \hat{\lambda}_{p+1} = \infty$ by convention. If $\delta > 0$ (meaning there is an eigengap), then:

$$\|\sin\Theta \, (E, F)\|_F \leq \frac{\|\Sigma^\wedge - \Sigma\|_F}{\delta} \tag{9.13}$$

where $E = \text{range}(v)$, and $F = \text{range}(\hat{V})$.

The Davis-Kahan inequality holds for the operator norm $\| \cdot \|_{op}$ as well as for any unitarily invariant matrix norm: $|||A||| = |||OAU^T|||$.

To use Davis-Kahan, assume that $\|\Sigma - \hat{\Sigma}\|_{op} \leq \gamma n$ with high probability and:

$$|\lambda^\wedge_{s+1} - \lambda_s| \geq \lambda_s - \lambda_{s+1} - \gamma n > 0$$

$$|\lambda^\wedge_{r-1} - \lambda_r| \geq \lambda_{r-1} - \lambda_r - \gamma n > 0$$

Then, by Davis-Kahan:

$$\|\sin\Theta\| \leq \|\Sigma - \Sigma^\wedge\|/(\delta^* - \gamma n) \tag{9.14}$$

where $\delta^* = \min\{\lambda_s - \lambda_{s+1}, \lambda_{r-1} - \lambda_r\}$. Typically, $r = 1$, $s = d < p$, which gives the eigengap:

$$\delta^* = \lambda_d - \lambda_{d+1} \tag{9.15}$$

λ_{d+1} is the first eigenvalue we are not interested in. If it is too close to the ones we are interested in, it will contaminate them and we cannot tell them apart.

Furthermore, if $\gamma n \to 0$, $\delta^* - \gamma n \geq \delta/2$ for large n. Yu, Wang, and Samworth (2014) developed an improvement over Davis-Kahan that removes eigengap dependency on the sample population:

$$\|\sin\Theta \, (E, F)\|_F \leq 2\min\{\sqrt{d}\|\Sigma^\wedge - \Sigma\|_{op}, \|\Sigma^\wedge - \Sigma\|_F\} / \min\{\lambda_s - \lambda_{s+1}, \lambda_{r-1} - \lambda_r\} \tag{9.16}$$

Determining the Structure of the Data with Laplacians. Laplacians have long been deployed in graph theory to create discrete approximations to a local neighborhood structure of graphs. In spectral clustering, a Laplacian is used to synthesize neighborhood data relationships. After a Laplacian is created, its eigenvectors indicate the location of clusters, based on the distance between vectors per the Davis-Kahan theorem discussed in the previous section. The resulting eigenmapping thus makes it more transparent for the subsequent K-means processing, which finishes the job by delineating the distinct clusters.

Clustering comes in very useful in financial data. In addition to applications such as determination of clusters of similar assets in stat-arb cluster trading, the data clustering helps with compressing and speeding up processing of data. It has been shown that any sort of data, financial or otherwise, are non-uniform (Belkin and Niyogi 2003). In other words, when we look at a table of data, say, that of financial asset correlations, the data are not distributed in a uniform way. Instead, we see concentrations of data points along several major clusters with fewer dimensions than the original number of data columns, often referred to as features.

Laplace operator is a fundamental geometric object that helps us identify smooth functions in the data, like the relationships of data points:

$$\Delta f = -\sum_{i=1}^{k} \frac{\partial^2 f}{\partial x_i^2} \tag{9.17}$$

A Laplace operator is also the only operator that is invariant under translations and rotations. It is used in heat, wave, or Schroedinger equations, as well as Fourier analysis.

Using a Laplacian, we substantially reduce the dimensionality of the entire data set while preserving the local characteristics of the data. This in turn allows us to make the subsequent K-means processing much more efficient, as follows: (1) Laplacian eigenmaps: construct a similarity graph from the data and the eigenvectors of the associated graph Laplacian are used to embed the data set into the feature space; (2) rounding procedure: K-means is applied to the embedded data set to obtain the clustering:

a. The data set is embedded in the eigenvectors of the associated Laplacian.
b. K-means clustering is applied to the data set in (a) to retrieve the labels.

Spectral clustering of data comprises three main steps:

1. Compute a similarity graph among the data points to cluster;
   - A simple similarity graph of n financial instruments can be a correlation matrix, with similarities represented by correlations.
2. Compute the Laplacian of 1 (next page).
3. Compute the first k eigenvectors of its Laplacian matrix to define a feature vector of each object:
   - Select k based on the "elbow" in the eigenvalues or spike model.
4. Run K-means algorithm to separate objects into k classes.

Computing Laplacians. While Eq (9.17) looks elegant and simple, its application to the discrete data requires approximations. Several computational solutions have been deployed to compute Laplacians in practice. Most computational approximations are derived from the heat equation. In R^n, Eq (9.18) describes the heat distribution at time t, $u(x, t)$, with initial distribution $u(x, 0) = f(x), x \in R^n, t \in R$:

$$\Delta_{R^n} u(x, t) = \frac{du}{dt}(x, t) \tag{9.18}$$

The solution is convolution with the *heat kernel*:

$$u(x, t) = (4\pi t)^{-n/2} \int_{R^n} f(y)\, e^{-(||x-y||^2)/4t} dy \tag{9.19}$$

The solution presented in Eq (9.19) can in turn be approximated with the following functional (Eq (9.20)) and empirical (Eq (9.21)) results. To obtain a functional result, we differentiate Eq (9.19) in the limit of $t \to 0$:

$$\Delta_{R^n} f(x) = \frac{d}{dt}\left[(4\pi t)^{-n/2} \int_{R^n} f(y)\, e^{-(||x-y||^2)/4t} dy \right]_0$$

$$\Delta_{R^n} f(x) \approx -\frac{1}{t}\, (4\pi t)^{-n/2} \left(f(x) - \int_{R^n} f(y)\, e^{-(||x-y||^2)/4t} dy \right) \tag{9.20}$$

An empirical approximation is then obtained by discretizing Eq (9.20) and applying it to the data:

$$\Delta_{R^n} f(x) \approx -\frac{1}{t}\, (4\pi t)^{-n/2} \left(f(x) - \sum_{x_i} f(x_i)\, e^{-(||x-x_i||^2)/4t} \right) \tag{9.21}$$

The main idea of clustering is to separate data points based on some similarity criteria. The points with similar properties fall into clusters separated from other, dissimilar, points. A tool used in spectral clustering is a map of local similarities, known as a similarity graph or similarity matrix. A similarity graph S comprises a set of data points referred to as vertices and a matrix of relationships between the data points, referred to as a weighted *adjacency matrix* $W = (w_{ij})_{i,j=1,..,N}$, $w_{ij} \geq 0$. When $w_{ij} = 0$, the elements i and j are not connected.

The similarity matrix identifies regions of points within a certain neighborhood and considers whether the points are similar or dissimilar. The neighborhood or vicinity can be defined in several ways:

- The k nearest neighbors graph identifies similarities among the closest k points. The nearest-k methodology may create non-symmetric similarity graphs, where similarity from i to j is not the same as similarity from j to i, depending on the k closest neighbors of each element.

- The ε-neighborhood graph considers similarities among all points that lie within ε distance from each other.
- The kernel graphs deploy a non-negative even kernel function $\Phi_\sigma(x, y)$ where σ is the size of the neighborhood, also known as bandwidth. Two common kernel functions are:
  - $\Phi(t) = 1_{\{|t| \leq 1\}}$ connects points if the distance between them is less than σ; this function produces the ε-neighborhood graph.
  - $\Phi(t) = e^{-t^2/2}$ is known as the *heat kernel* or Gaussian kernel.

The heat or Gaussian kernel is presently the most popular similarity graph construction methodology deployed in spectral clustering (per Ling and Strohmer, 2018) and we will primarily focus on it in going forward.

Given N data points with certain properties measured by x, the similarity graph constructed using the heat kernel is an $n \times n$ matrix S with elements of the adjacency matrix W specified as:

$$w_{ij} = s(x_i, x_j) = e^{-(||x_i - x_j||)^2/(2\sigma^2)}, W \in R^{N \times N} \tag{9.22}$$

From the similarity graph adjacency matrix W, we compute a *degree matrix D*, where the degree of each element or vertex i is determined as follows:

$$d_i = \sum_{i=1}^{N} w_{ij} \tag{9.23}$$

The associated degree matrix D is then an $N \times N$ diagonal matrix with $\{d_i\}_{i=1}^{N}$ on the diagonal:

$$D := diag(W 1_N) \tag{9.24}$$

Next, we are ready to compute Laplacians required for spectral clustering.

Algorithms for Laplacian Approximations. Various researchers identify different approximations to Laplacians, comprising their own field of study known as spectral graph theory. A Laplacian is computed from the similarity matrix of a graph discussed above. Here, we consider three categories of Laplacians: unnormalized, normalized for symmetric similarity graphs, and random-walk Laplacians for special computation cases. In all cases, the underlying similarity graphs used in the analysis are created with all the weights non-negative, $w_{ij} \geq 0$. Either unnormalized or normalized Laplacian is sufficient for spectral clustering, but leads to slightly different algorithms discussed below.

The unnormalized Laplacian is computed as follows:

$$L := D - W \tag{9.25}$$

Per Chung (1997), the symmetric normalized Laplacian is computed as:

$$L_{sym} := I_n - D^{-1/2}WD^{-1/2} \tag{9.26}$$

Since D is diagonal and positive, its reciprocal square root $D^{-1/2}$ is a diagonal matrix with diagonal entries comprising the reciprocal square roots of the diagonal entries of D.

L is real symmetric and positive semidefinite, and, therefore, diagonalizable:

L = USU', where S is the diagonal matrix containing L's sorted eigenvalues.

Another type of Laplacian is a *random-walk Laplacian*, L_{rw}, that embeds the probability $P_{ij} = \frac{w_{ij}}{d_i}$ of a random walk starting from vertex i and moving to the vertex j in the next step:

$$L_{rw} := I_n - P, \text{where } P := D^{-1}W \tag{9.27}$$

Von Luxburg (2006, pp. 5–6) proposes the following algorithm for unnormalized spectral clustering:

Unnormalized Spectral Clustering

Inputs: Similarity graph adjacency matrix $W \in R^{N \times N}$, number k of clusters to construct

- Construct a similarity graph by one of the ways described above.
  Let W be its weighted adjacency matrix.
- Compute the unnormalized Laplacian $L := D - W$
- Compute the first k eigenvectors $v_1, \dots, v_k$ of L.
- Let $V \in R^{n \times k}$ be the matrix containing the vectors $v_1, \dots v_k$ as columns.
- For i = 1, …, n, let $y_i \in R^k$ be the vector corresponding to the ith row of V.
- Cluster the points (y_i), i = 1, … ,n in R^k with the K-means algorithm into clusters $C_1, \dots, C_k$. Output: Clusters $A_1, \dots, A_k$ with $A_i = \{j \mid y_j \in C_i\}$.

Shi and Malik (2000) develop an alternative Normalized Spectral Clustering algorithm:

Normalized Spectral Clustering

Input: Similarity matrix $S \in R^{n \times n}$, number k of clusters to construct

- Construct a similarity graph by one of the ways described above.
  Let W be its weighted adjacency matrix.
- Compute the unnormalized Laplacian L.
- Compute the first k eigenvectors $v_1, \dots, v_k$ of the generalized eigenproblem $Lv = \lambda Dv$.
- Let $V \in R^{n \times k}$ be the matrix containing the vectors $v_1, \dots, v_k$ as columns.
- For i = 1, …, n, let $y_i \in R^k$ be the vector corresponding to the *i*th row of V.
- Cluster the points (y_i), i = 1, … ,n in R^k with the k-means algorithm into clusters $C_1, \dots ,C_k$. Output: Clusters $A_1, \dots ,A_k$ with $A_i = \{j \mid y_j \in C_i\}$.

Still alternative spectral clustering variations were developed by Ng, Jordan and Weiss (2002) and Ling and Strohmer (2018).

Spectral Clustering with Stochastic Block Models

When the adjacency matrix is readily observable, the spectral clustering classification models are referred to as *discriminative*. As such, they create relationship maps conditional on existing data. An alternative to discriminative models is the field of *generative* models, where the adjacency matrix is not observable, but is instead probabilistically developed and derived from conditional relationships between individual network elements.

One of the most popular generative models, known as the Stochastic Block Model, was first introduced by Holland, Laskey, and Leinhardt (1983). Rohe, Chatterjee, and Yu (2011) outline the classification methodology and Lei and Rinaldo (2015) derive the performance bounds, including misclassification rates, for the procedure.

Spectral clustering with stochastic block modeling is one of the "state-of-the-art" areas of active research. Among the latest directions of the stochastic block models is the research into how the models allow relaxation of convexity requirement in the K-means clustering (see Abbe, Bandeira, and Hall 2016; Abbe 2017; Agarwal et al. 2017; and Bandeira 2018).

Clustering Financial Data

Clustering in financial data has been studied since at least Boginski, Butenko, and Pardalos (2003). Boginski, Butenko, and Pardalos proposed clustering financial data based on their correlation structures. The highest-correlated instruments are thought to fall into the same cluster.

In Finance, how does one create an adjacency from the sample covariance or correlation matrix? One approach can be thresholding. In a manner similar to that of Principal Orthogonal ComplEment Thresholding (a.k.a., POET) by Fan, Liao, and Micheva (2013), the adjacency matrix can be created on the basis of a threshold. In a thresholding example, the covariance or correlation values that fall below the threshold can be set to 0 while the other values remain intact. Alternative solutions may include a shrinkage function of Antoniadis and Fan (2001), employed by Rothman et al. (2009) and Cai and Liu (2011). The hard-thresholding shrinkage by Bickel and Levina (2008), for example, is $s_{ij}(x) = x\, I(|x| \geq \tau_{ij})$.

Spectral clustering with stochastic models may be the new exciting frontier in modeling of financial applications, such as microstructure activity, options pricing, and beyond.

Clustering Illiquid Instruments

Most of the clustering research in Finance to date preconditioned the data by eliminating irregularly traded names, known as illiquid instruments. In this chapter, we specifically include illiquid instruments in our clustering analysis to show an efficient application of clustering in financial data.

While illiquid instruments may not trade often, they still possess intrinsic value that changes with the ebbs and flows in the market environment. The intrinsic value is not publicly discoverable, however, until the instrument changes hands in a market. On the days when an illiquid instrument trades, returns are generated. On the days when it does not, the returns are recorded as zeros, even though the instrument's intrinsic value may still change.

Clustering helps uncover the true intrinsic values of illiquid instruments in a portfolio setting. Since their return data are sparse, the correlations produced by illiquid instruments may or may not be meaningful. When an illiquid instrument is correlated with a frequently traded instrument, their correlation may reflect some of the true co-movement of the instrument returns. When an illiquid instrument is correlated with another illiquid instrument, however, the times when the two instruments trade at the same time may be limited, and the resulting correlation may be approximately zero. Clustering liquid and illiquid instruments into joint baskets establishes correlation links between liquid and illiquid names, and helps relate illiquid instruments to each other.

The resulting clusters are highly correlated within, but weakly correlated with each other. The clusters can then be aggregated into diversified portfolios, producing sizable investment gains, as this section illustrates.

In a nutshell, our algorithm works as follows:

1. Cluster liquid and illiquid instruments based on their correlations. The clustering process implicitly matches illiquid instruments with their closest liquid cousins. This in turn creates groups of instruments that may show no explicit correlation due to illiquidity.

2. Within each cluster, form an equally weighted intra-cluster portfolio from the highly correlated instruments within each cluster:

$$R_{\text{intra},C} = \frac{1}{N_C} \sum_i R_{i \in C} \qquad (9.28)$$

3. Form equally weighted inter-cluster portfolios from the weakly correlated intra-cluster portfolios created in step 2 above:

$$R_{\text{inter}} = \frac{1}{C} \sum_C R_{\text{intra},C}$$

Step 2 above averages the returns of the highly correlated returns in each portfolio. Step 3 takes advantage of the weak correlations between every two clusters, delivered by the clustering algorithm. Equally weighing weakly correlated intra-cluster portfolios results in diversified frameworks consistent with Markowitz seminal ideas of allocation.

Empirical Results

Here, we apply spectral clustering portfolio formation to the returns of cryptocurrencies and, separately, commodities. Using data for the January 2017–April 2020 period, we cluster the crypto and commodities returns on all traded instruments into different numbers of clusters. We show that as the number of clusters increases, the resulting portfolios created from the clusters become increasingly diversified and better performing.

Crypto Spectral Cluster Portfolios

Cryptocurrencies have become popular instruments for many investors. And while many investors have put their money into individual cryptocurrencies, few have thought about managing portfolios of cryptocurrencies to improve returns and diversify risks. At the time this book was written, much of the advice for portfolio management in cryptocurrencies amounted to selecting a threshold of one's total investment portfolio to allocate to cryptocurrencies and related instruments. An October 17, 2019, article in *Coin Telegraph*, for example, recommended that investors allocate between 2–10% of their total portfolio to cryptocurrencies: "2% for everyday investors, rising to 5% to 10% for enthusiasts."[2] The article made no mention of potential diversification within the crypto portfolios themselves.

However, cryptocurrencies have been extremely volatile instruments that could certainly benefit from portfolio diversification techniques. As the same *Coin Telegraph* article noted, 2017 saw a 4,500% increase in the market capitalization of digital currencies. In the first 8 months of 2018, however, crypto markets lost 80% of their value.

The digital currency markets are, of course, very new. Only 21 cryptocurrencies have history dating to 2017: ARDR, BTC, BTS, DASH, DCR, DGB, DGD, DOGE, ETC, ETH, LTC, MCO, MONA, REP, SC, STEEM, XMR, XRP, XVG, XZC, and ZEC. Their cumulative returns over the 2017–2020 period are shown in Figure 9.3. In an equally weighted portfolio, over the January 2017–May 2020 period, the cryptocurrencies would have together returned 679.5%, with average annualized return of

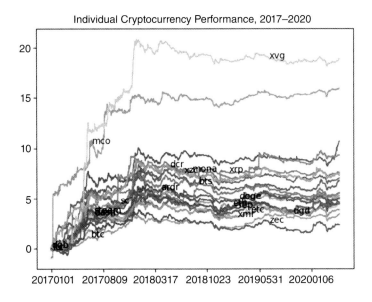

Figure 9.3   Cumulative January 2017–May 2020 returns per cryptocurrency trading on or before January 1, 2017.

---

[2] Source: https://cointelegraph.com/news/how-to-manage-and-understand-risk-tolerance-in-crypto-investing.

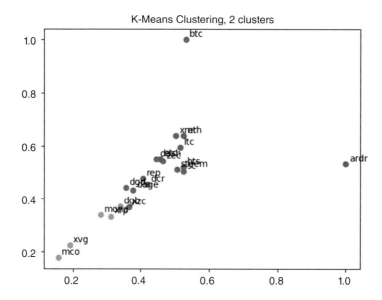

Figure 9.4   K-means clustering of cryptocurrency returns, January 2017–May 2020, number of clusters K = 2.

139.6%, but high volatility resulting in a Sharpe ratio of 0.89. As Figure 9.3 shows, the cryptocurrencies delivered outstanding returns in 2017, but thereafter their performance slowed, in part due to many new cryptocurrencies coming online and diluting the overall pool of offerings.

Intra-Cluster Portfolios

To construct the intra-cluster portfolios, we first create correlation matrices. In this section, we only cover the highly liquid cryptocurrencies that were trading on or before January 1, 2017, and continued trading through April 2020. The K-means and spectral clustering of the correlation matrix of returns of these instruments for the entire 2017–2020 period are shown in Figures 9.4–9.9. In the case of two clusters, highly correlated instruments are clustered into one cluster while low-correlation instruments separate into another cluster. This complexity increases with the number of clusters.

Results shown are for clustering into 2, 3, and 4 clusters. Table 9.1 shows in-sample returns for each cluster, computed as equally weighted returns within each cluster. As Table 9.1 shows, in the case of cryptocurrency clustering, both K-means and spectral approaches produce comparable results. As Figures 9.4–9.9 show, both K-means and spectral clustering produce comparable results.

Table 9.1 shows portfolio returns formed by the clusters, and Figures 9.10 and 9.11 show the cumulative portfolio returns of individual clusters versus an equally weighted portfolio for K-means and spectral clustering, respectively. Again, K-means and spectral

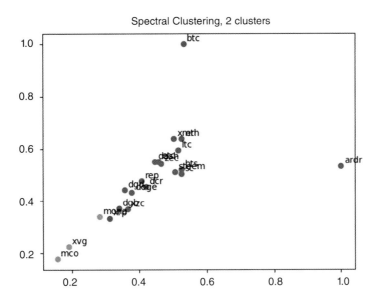

Figure 9.5 Spectral clustering of cryptocurrency returns, January 2017–May 2020, number of clusters K = 2.

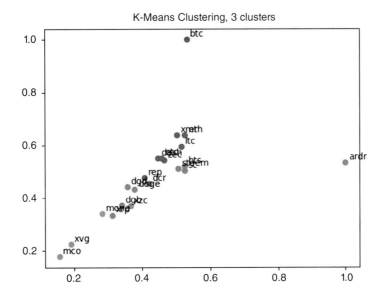

Figure 9.6 K-means clustering of cryptocurrency returns, January 2017–May 2020, number of clusters K = 3.

clustering produce similar in-sample performance. The equally weighted portfolio out-performs individual clusters when 2017 is taken into account. When 2017 is removed, the equally weighted portfolio reflects the sharp turmoil in the crypto markets and its performance suffers considerably while the cluster portfolios manage to hang on.

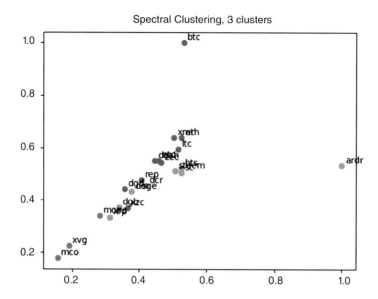

Figure 9.7 Spectral clustering of cryptocurrency returns, January 2017–May 2020, number of clusters K = 3.

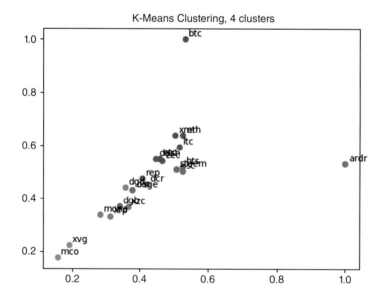

Figure 9.8 K-means clustering of cryptocurrency returns, January 2017–May 2020, number of clusters K = 4.

Table 9.1 summarizes the average (equally weighted) returns within each cluster observed in the highly liquid crypto market. As Table 9.1 and Figure 9.9 show, K-means and spectral clustering may or may not deliver different returns, depending on the cluster allocation. What Figure 9.9 also shows is that each of the clusters individually underperform the simple equally weighted allocation in the liquid crypto market.

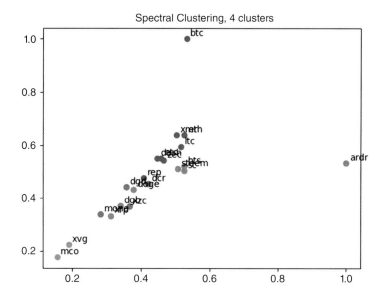

Figure 9.9 Spectral clustering of cryptocurrency returns, January 2017–May 2020, number of clusters K = 4.

Table 9.1 In-sample highly liquid January 2017–May 2020 returns for various cluster portfolios for cryptocurrencies that were trading in January 2017.

	K-means clustering	**Spectral clustering**
Two clusters		
Cluster 1	0.16779904582780514	0.13051036897718177
Cluster 2	1.0691191322957037	6.301072430346291
Three clusters		
Cluster 1	0.293648330198659	0.234918664158927
Cluster 2	6.301072430346291	6.301072430346291
Cluster 3	0.7483833926069926	0.9492149396563305
Four clusters		
Cluster 1	0.293648330198659	0.293648330198659
Cluster 2	9.451608645519435	9.451608645519435
Cluster 3	1.8709584815174816	1.8709584815174816
Cluster 4	0.6576028751218467	1.0848170738929492

The clusters individually underperformed the EW portfolio during the crypto boom of 2017. Subsequently, however, the clusters held up much better during the 2018–2019 crypto crash, as Figure 9.10 illustrates.

Inter-Cluster Portfolios and Out-of-Sample Results

To create aggregate inter-cluster portfolios, we average the intra-cluster results for each number of clusters. We measure the performance of these equally weighted global cluster portfolios out-of-sample monthly on all the cryptocurrencies trading in a given

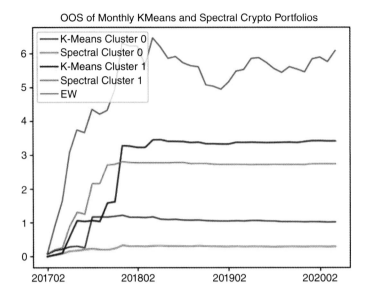

Figure 9.10   Spectral clustering of cryptocurrency returns, January 2017-May 2020, number of clusters K = 2.

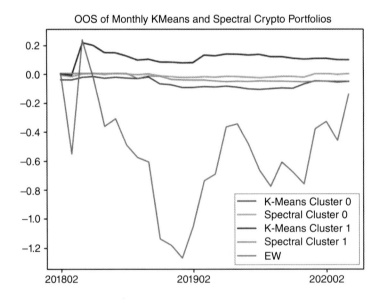

Figure 9.11   Spectral clustering of cryptocurrency returns, detail, January 2018–May 2020, number of clusters K = 2.

month, and not just on the major names. For example, to measure the performance of the cluster portfolios in April 2018, we examine returns of all the cryptocurrencies in March 2018. We assume the return of 0 if no trades were recorded on a given day for a specific cryptocurrency. After computing the daily returns for each cryptocurrency

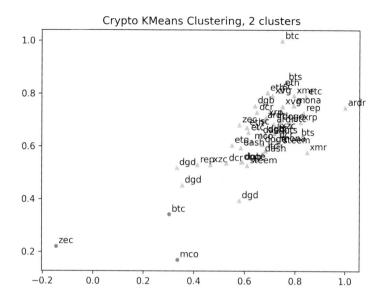

Figure 9.12   K-means clustering of cryptocurrencies, 2 clusters.

trading in March 2018, we create a return correlation matrix. We next apply K-means and, separately, spectral clustering to the correlation matrix. Subsequently, we form equally weighted portfolios from the cryptocurrencies in each cluster. Next, we compute out-of-sample returns of each cluster averaging April 2018 returns for each cryptocurrency in its respective cluster. Finally, we average the resulting out-of-sample intra-cluster returns into a global cluster portfolio.

Figures 9.12–9.25 show K-means and spectral cryptocurrency clustering for different numbers of clusters for March 2018. As Figures 9.12–9.25 show, the separation for a low number of clusters is easy to perform even visually. As the number of clusters increases, however, the clustering process becomes more complex.

As a result of the selected allocation scheme, the final allocation to each instrument is always positive or long. Its exact value for each cryptocurrency is:

$$x_i = \frac{1}{C}\frac{1}{N_{Ci}}$$

where C is the number of clusters and N_{Ci} is the number of instruments falling into the same cluster as the cryptocurrency i. The bigger the cluster, the lower the allocation to an individual instrument within the cluster.

Table 9.2 shows out-of-sample performance comparison; it includes all cryptocurrencies traded in a given month, with missing returns replaced by zeros. As Table 9.2 shows, when the number of clusters increases, so does the performance of the resulting strategies. Figures 9.26–9.32 show the out-of-sample K-means and spectral clustering for cryptocurrency portfolios monthly, with different clusters.

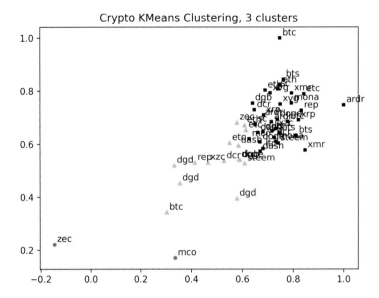

Figure 9.13 K-means clustering of cryptocurrencies, 3 clusters, March 2018.

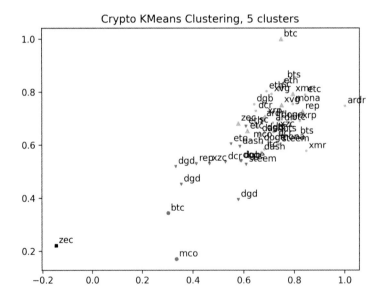

Figure 9.14 K-means clustering of cryptocurrencies, 5 clusters, March 2018.

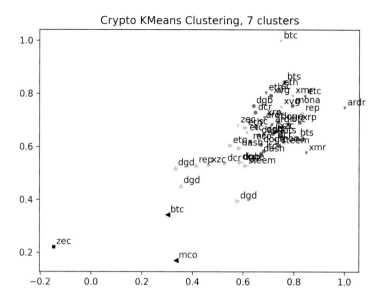

Figure 9.15 K-means clustering of cryptocurrencies, 7 clusters, March 2018.

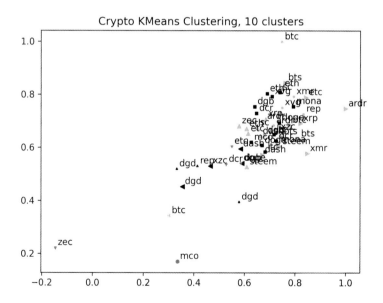

Figure 9.16 K-means clustering of cryptocurrencies, 10 clusters, March 2018.

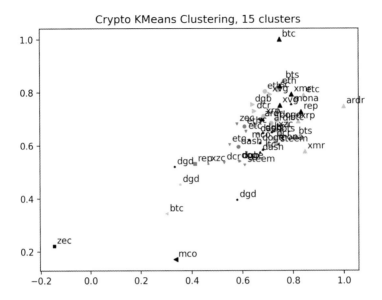

Figure 9.17   K-means clustering of cryptocurrencies, 15 clusters, March 2018.

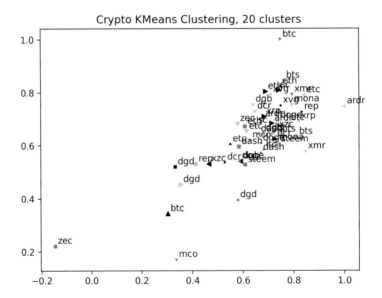

Figure 9.18   K-means clustering of cryptocurrencies, 20 clusters.

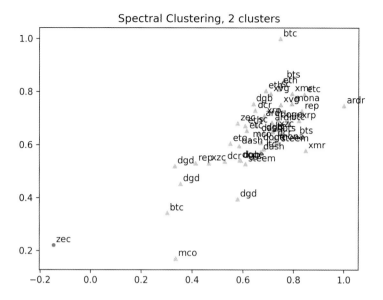

Figure 9.19   Spectral clustering of cryptocurrencies, 2 clusters.

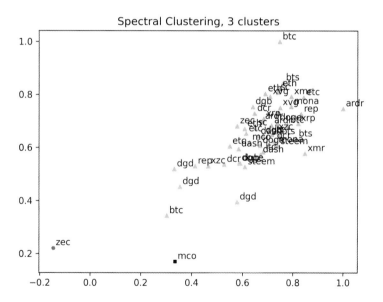

Figure 9.20   Spectral clustering of cryptocurrencies, 3 clusters.

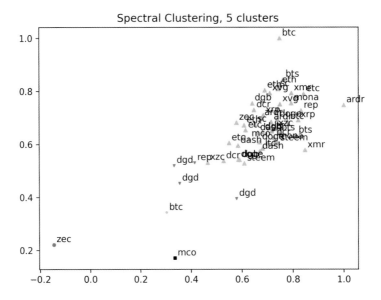

Figure 9.21   Spectral clustering of cryptocurrencies, 5 clusters, March 2018.

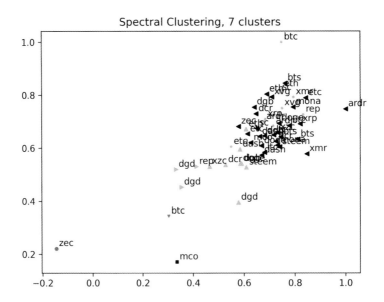

Figure 9.22   Spectral clustering of cryptocurrencies, 7 clusters.

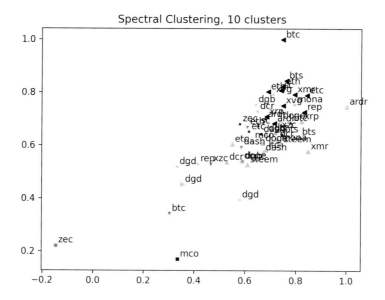

Figure 9.23   Spectral clustering of cryptocurrencies, 10 clusters, March 2018.

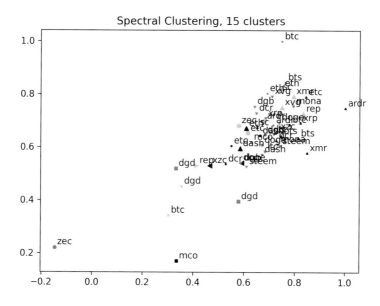

Figure 9.24   Spectral clustering of cryptocurrencies, 15 clusters.

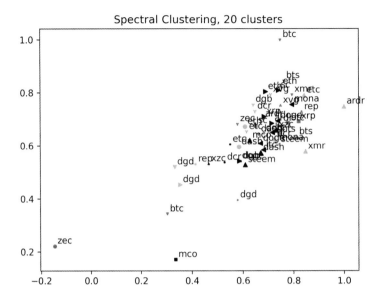

Figure 9.25   Spectral clustering of cryptocurrencies, 20 clusters.

Table 9.2   Annualized mean returns and Sharpe ratios of out-of-sample performance of investment strategies based on monthly clustering, cryptocurrencies, January 2017–April 2020.

Instrument Class	Number of Clusters	K-Means Annual Return	K-Means Sharpe Ratio	Spectral Annual Return	Spectral Sharpe Ratio	EW Annual Return	EW Sharpe Ratio
Crypto	2	0.7074	1.2489	0.4643	1.2861	1.8752	1.2269
Crypto	3	0.6811	1.2042	0.9623	0.9267	1.8752	1.2269
Crypto	5	1.3089	1.2315	0.9546	1.1663	1.8752	1.2269
Crypto	7	1.2955	1.3104	0.9732	1.1855	1.8752	1.2269
Crypto	10	1.4108	1.4070	1.2426	1.4186	1.8752	1.2269
Crypto	15	1.4613	1.2959	1.4744	1.3356	1.8752	1.2269
Crypto	20	1.7249	1.2944	1.8961	1.4525	1.8752	1.2269

Strategy Robustness

To check the versatility of the strategy, we perform a similar out-of-sample analysis on commodities. Utilizing all commodities trading in a given month, we follow the same portfolio formation process as in the preceding cryptocurrency analysis:

1. Compute daily returns; assign returns of 0 to days where no trades occur or information is unavailable.
2. In each month, create return correlation matrix for the month's daily returns.
3. Cluster returns based on their correlations.
4. Average the following month's returns within each cluster.
5. Average the clusters' returns into a global portfolio.

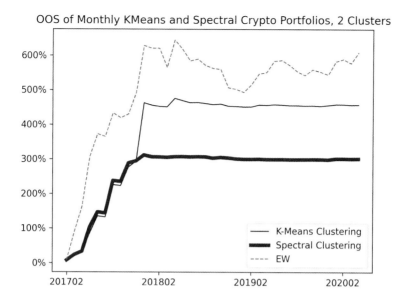

Figure 9.26 Monthly out-of-sample K-means and spectral clustering for cryptocurrency portfolios, 2 clusters.

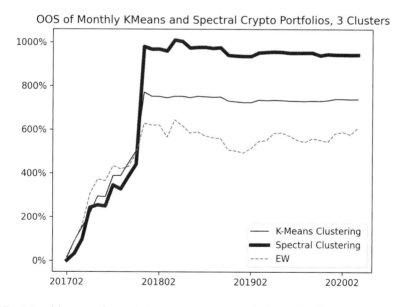

Figure 9.27 Monthly out-of-sample K-means and spectral clustering for cryptocurrency portfolios, 3 clusters.

Figures 9.33–9.52 show commodities clustering for March 2018. Table 9.3 summarizes the performance of commodity clustering. Figures 9.33–9.52 show cumulative out-of-sample returns. As Table 9.3 shows, commodity clustering significantly outperforms plain equally weighted portfolios. While spectral and K-means clustering produced nearly identical results in cryptocurrencies, in commodities, spectral clustering further outperforms K-means results.

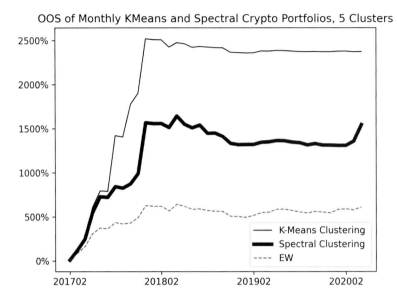

Figure 9.28 Monthly out-of-sample K-means and spectral clustering for cryptocurrency portfolios, 5 clusters.

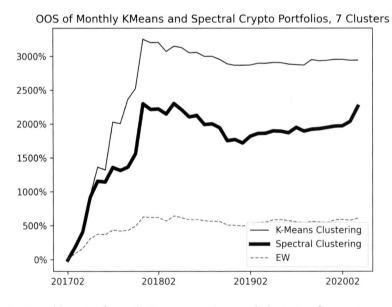

Figure 9.29 Monthly out-of-sample K-means and spectral clustering for cryptocurrency portfolios, 7 clusters.

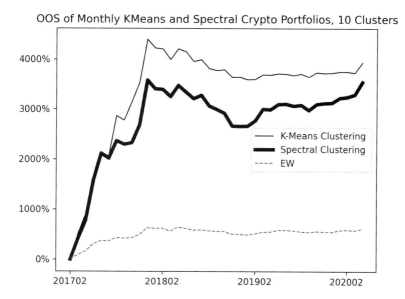

Figure 9.30 Monthly out-of-sample K-means and spectral clustering for cryptocurrency portfolios, 10 clusters.

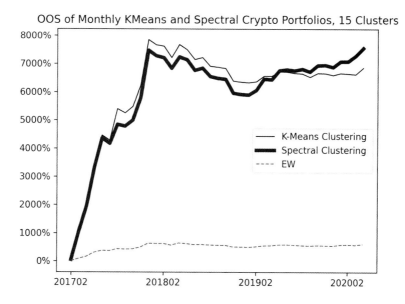

Figure 9.31 Monthly out-of-sample K-means and spectral clustering for cryptocurrency portfolios, 15 clusters.

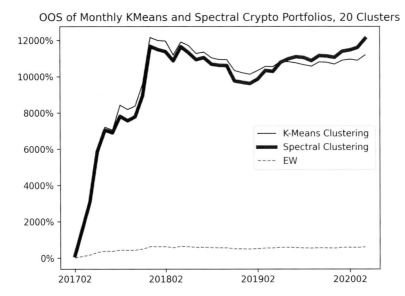

Figure 9.32 Monthly out-of-sample K-means and spectral clustering for cryptocurrency portfolios, 20 clusters.

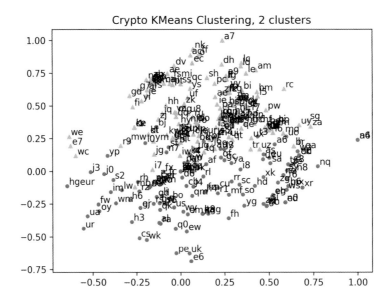

Figure 9.33 K-means clustering for commodities, 2 clusters.

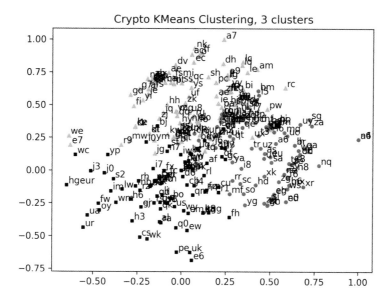

Figure 9.34 K-means clustering for commodities, 3 clusters.

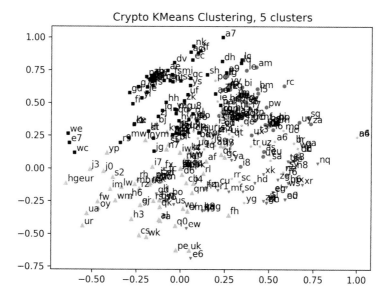

Figure 9.35 K-means clustering for commodities, 5 clusters.

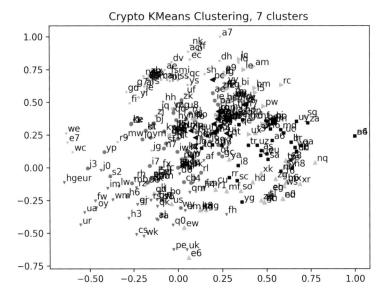

Figure 9.36   K-means clustering for commodities, 7 clusters.

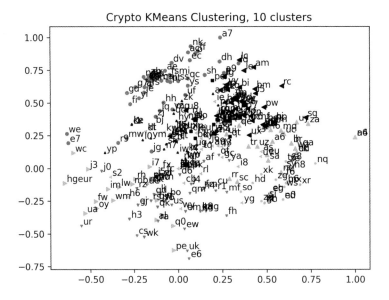

Figure 9.37   K-means clustering for commodities, 10 clusters.

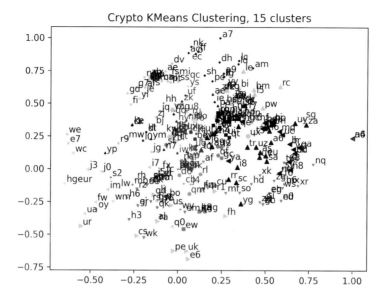

Figure 9.38 K-means clustering for commodities, 15 clusters.

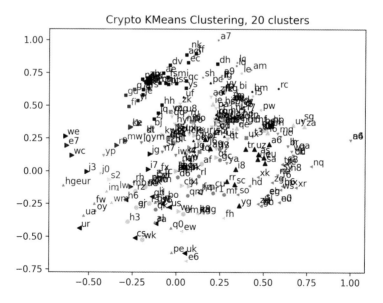

Figure 9.39 K-means clustering for commodities, 20 clusters.

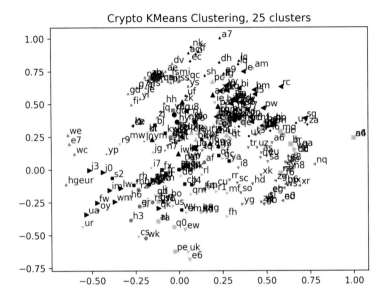

Figure 9.40 K-means clustering for commodities, 25 clusters.

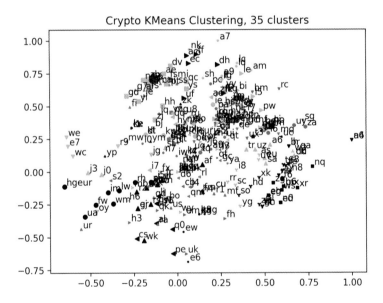

Figure 9.41 K-means clustering for commodities, 35 clusters.

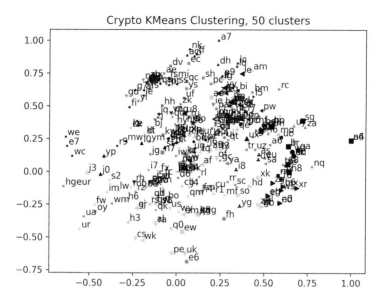

Figure 9.42   K-means clustering for commodities, 50 clusters.

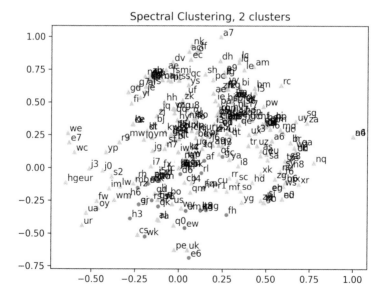

Figure 9.43   Spectral clustering for commodities, 2 clusters.

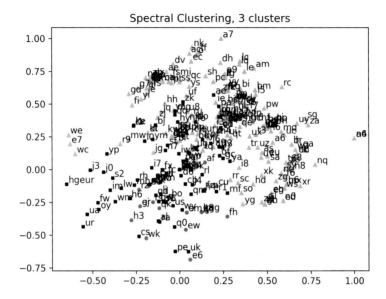

Figure 9.44   Spectral clustering for commodities, 3 clusters.

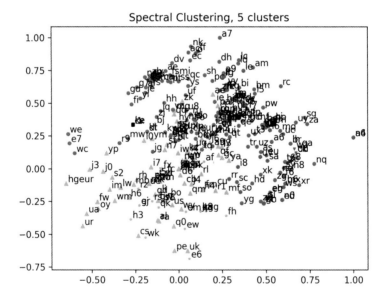

Figure 9.45   Spectral clustering for commodities, 5 clusters.

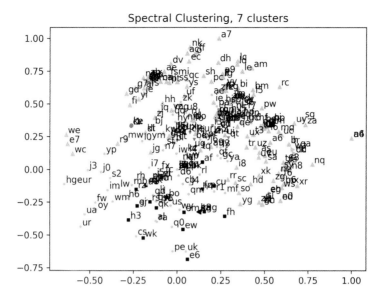

Figure 9.46   Spectral clustering for commodities, 7 clusters.

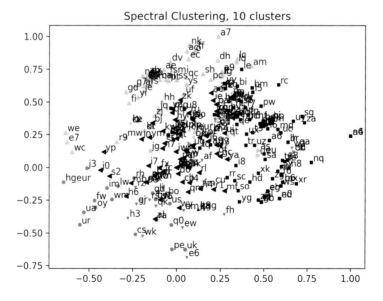

Figure 9.47   Spectral clustering for commodities, 10 clusters.

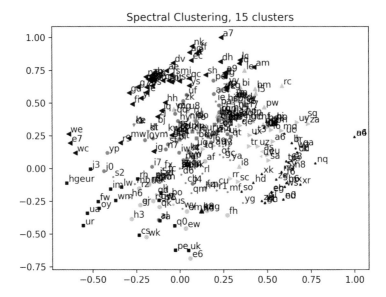

Figure 9.48   Spectral clustering for commodities, 15 clusters.

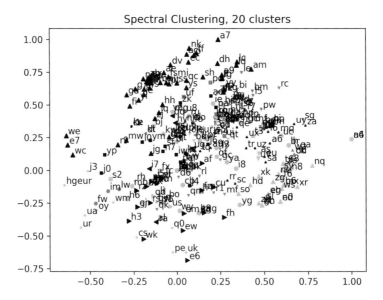

Figure 9.49   Spectral clustering for commodities, 20 clusters.

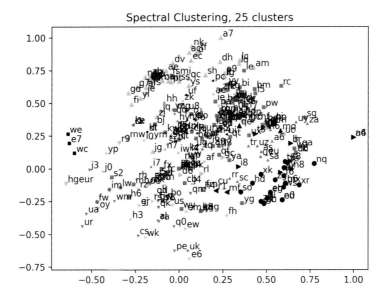

Figure 9.50 Spectral clustering for commodities, 25 clusters.

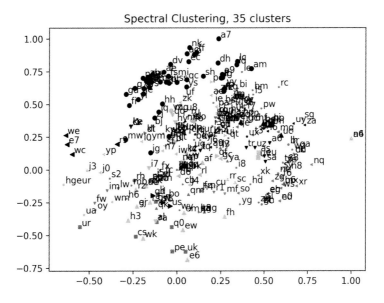

Figure 9.51 Spectral clustering for commodities, 35 clusters.

Figures 9.53–9.62 show the monthly out-of-sample K-means and spectral clustering for commodities portfolios for different clusters.

The clustering policy increases the returns, increasing the Sharpe ratios as well. The policy can, therefore, be used to up the returns without increasing the risks or leverage. Instead of borrowing large sums of money to invest, the investors can turn to clustering and obtain the same performance as a levered portfolio without taking on additional

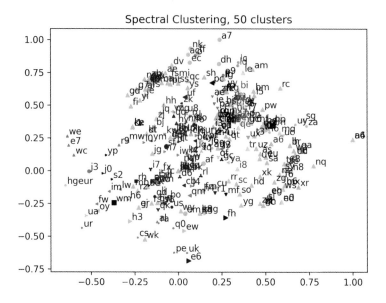

Figure 9.52   Spectral clustering for commodities, 50 clusters.

Table 9.3   Annualized mean returns and Sharpe ratios of out-of-sample performance of investment strategies based on monthly clustering, commodities, January 2017–April 2020.

Instrument Class	Number of Clusters	K-Means Annual Return	K-Means Sharpe Ratio	Spectral Annual Return	Spectral Sharpe Ratio	EW Annual Return	EW Sharpe Ratio
Commodities	2	0.00028	0.46985	−0.01836	−0.54710	0.00513	0.06385
Commodities	3	−0.00009	−0.06592	−0.02252	−0.94430	0.00513	0.06385
Commodities	5	−0.00227	−0.69594	−0.00948	−0.55252	0.00513	0.06385
Commodities	7	−0.00042	−0.11691	−0.00341	−0.19283	0.00513	0.06385
Commodities	10	−0.00022	−0.05245	0.00116	0.06255	0.00513	0.06385
Commodities	15	0.00059	0.10457	0.00759	0.43387	0.00513	0.06385
Commodities	20	0.00379	0.51757	0.02038	0.83556	0.00513	0.06385
Commodities	25	0.00230	0.22629	0.01726	0.74049	0.00513	0.06385
Commodities	35	0.00615	0.62358	0.03237	1.37612	0.00513	0.06385
Commodities	50	0.01238	0.87829	0.02334	0.89600	0.00513	0.06385

capital. This can prove to be a real benefit to investors who have obtained their target risk allocations and are seeking to maximize returns without additional credit risk exposure.

How does this method work? The clusters are created based on their correlations. The graph theory gives us the ability to connect financial instruments that are indirectly correlated. For instance, when one financial instrument is correlated with the second financial instrument, and the second financial instrument is correlated with the first and third financial instrument, the traditional correlation matrix may or may not show a correlation between the first and third instruments. This is especially the case whenever

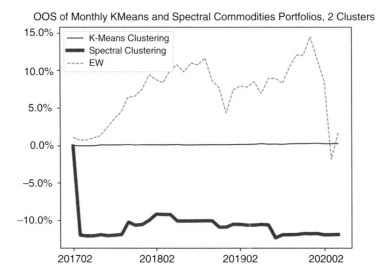

Figure 9.53   Monthly out-of-sample K-means and spectral clustering for commodities portfolios, 2 clusters.

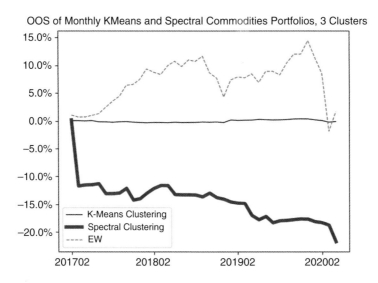

Figure 9.54   Monthly out-of-sample K-means and spectral clustering for commodities portfolios, 3 clusters.

the first and the third instruments are illiquid, i.e., trade infrequently. Clustering allows a different view of the correlation matrix, where the correlation matrix is filled in for instruments whose regular trading values are missing.

Because the returns of cluster portfolios are uncorrelated or weakly correlated with each other, the resulting global portfolio is diversified. The more clusters there are in the

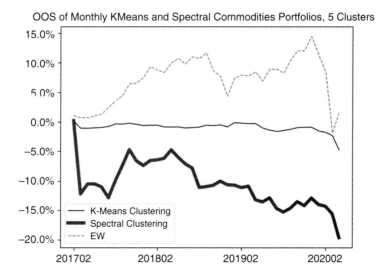

Figure 9.55 Monthly out-of-sample K-means and spectral clustering for commodities portfolios, 5 clusters.

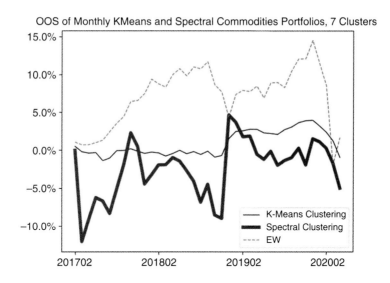

Figure 9.56 Monthly out-of-sample K-means and spectral clustering for commodities portfolios, 7 clusters.

system design, the more uncorrelated cluster portfolios are in the global portfolio, the higher is the achieved diversification of the global portfolio.

A high number of highly correlated instruments in an equally weighted portfolio reduces to just one cluster-portfolio component in the final portfolio. For portfolio managers charged with a specific stock selection, for example, as part of an ESG mandate, the strategy allows incorporation of all the issues. At the same time, the portfolio manager

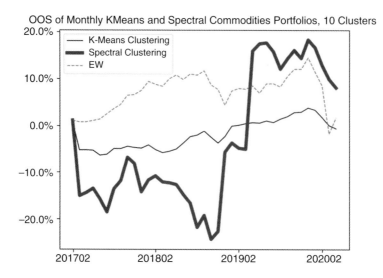

Figure 9.57 Monthly out-of-sample K-means and spectral clustering for commodities portfolios, 10 clusters.

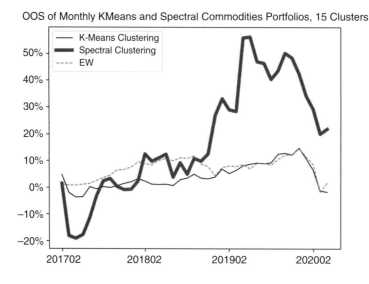

Figure 9.58 Monthly out-of-sample K-means and spectral clustering for commodities portfolios, 15 clusters

increases returns on his strategy without significantly affecting the Sharpe ratio, all with the original capital base.

Optimal Number of Clusters

As the out-of-sample performance shows, the higher number of clusters delivers more precision and produces better results out-of-sample. The number of clusters, is, of

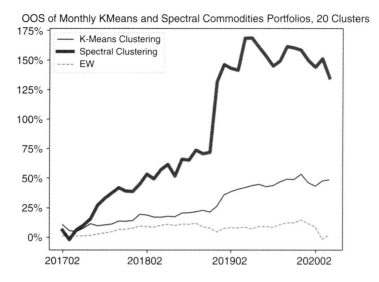

Figure 9.59   Monthly out-of-sample K-means and spectral clustering for commodities portfolios, 20 clusters.

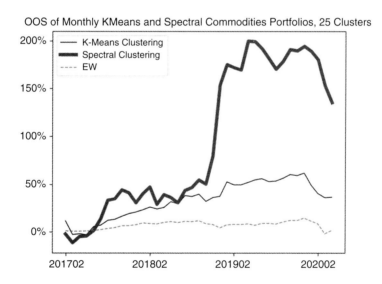

Figure 9.60   Monthly out-of-sample K-means and spectral clustering for commodities portfolios, 25 clusters

course, constrained by the number of financial instruments in the portfolio. As soon as the number of instruments increases past its optimal point, the clusters contain fewer and fewer instruments and the portfolio begins to approximate the equally weighted portfolio.

OOS of Monthly KMeans and Spectral Commodities Portfolios, 35 Clusters

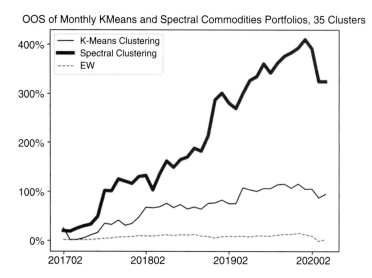

Figure 9.61 Monthly out-of-sample K-means and spectral clustering for commodities portfolios, 35 clusters.

OOS of Monthly KMeans and Spectral Commodities Portfolios, 50 Clusters

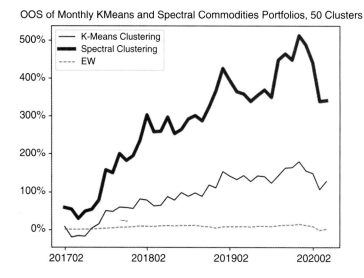

Figure 9.62 Monthly out-of-sample K-means and spectral clustering for commodities portfolios, 50 clusters

Beyond Equally Weighted Portfolios

Instead of equally weighing intra-cluster and inter-cluster portfolios, researchers may choose to deploy various existing portfolio construction methodologies to fine-tune the weights of the individual clusters. For example, mean-variance portfolio optimization

may produce even more tailored results. Another alternative is eigenportfolios, applied to intra-cluster portfolios by Akansu, Avellaneda, and Xiong (2020). As Akansu, Avellaneda, and Xiong state, fine-tuning cluster portfolios via eigenportfolio selection further increases intra-cluster portfolio performance. Better intra-cluster performance will invariably turn into better global portfolios.

Conclusion

Clustering presents a powerful new way of thinking about portfolio allocation, all fitting nicely into the traditional Markowitz diversification model. Delivering significant performance improvements over vanilla portfolios, clustering can add benefit to portfolio managers across a wide spectrum of mandates, including cryptocurrencies, commodities and beyond.

Appendix 9.A Clustering with Python

To program the K-means clustering algorithm in Python, we can use the built-in scikit-learn K-means library, aptly named *kmeans*. With that, in two lines of code, we have an iterative prediction for which cluster each variable of X should fall into:

```
from sklearn.cluster import KMeans
kmeans = KMeans(n_clusters=5, init='k-means++', max_iter=500, n_init=10,
random_state=0)
pred_y = kmeans.fit_predict(X)
```

The above example separates elements of X into five clusters, iterating at most 500 times (or fewer, if convergence is reached earlier) over the data.

Similarly, spectral clustering in Python can be performed in a few lines of code, with a built-in parameter label, delivering the cluster enumeration:

```
from sklearn.cluster import SpectralClustering
clustering = SpectralClustering(n_clusters=2,
        assign_labels="discretize",
        random_state=0).fit(X)
output_clusters = clustering.labels_
```

For specific code examples, please visit https://www.BigDataFinanceBook.com, and register with password *clustering* (case-sensitive).

References

Abbe, E. (2017). Community detection and stochastic block models: Recent developments, arXiv preprint arXiv:1703.10146.

Abbe, E., Bandeira, A.S., and Hall, G. (2016). Exact recovery in the stochastic block model. *IEEE Transactions on Information Theory* 62(1): 471–487.

Agarwal, N., Bandeira, A.S., Koiliaris, K., and Kolla, A. (2017). Multisection in the stochastic block model using semidefinite programming. In: *Compressed Sensing and its Applications*. New York: Springer, 125–162.

Akansu, A., Avellaneda, M., and Xiong, A. (2020). Quant investing in cluster portfolios. NJ Institute of Technology and Courant Institute for Mathematical Sciences, NYU, working paper.

Antoniadis, A. and Fan, J. (2001). Regularized wavelet approximations. *Journal of the American Statistical Association* 96: 939–967.

Bandeira, A.S. (2018). Random Laplacian matrices and convex relaxations. *Foundations of Computational Mathematics* 18(2): 345–379.

Belkin, M. and Niyogi, P. (2003). Laplacian eigenmaps for dimensionality reduction and data representation. *Neural Computation* 15(6): 1373–1396.

Bickel, P. and Levina, E. (2008). Covariance regularization by thresholding. *The Annals of Statistics* 36: 2577–2604.

Boginski, V., Butenko, S., and Pardalos, P.M. (2003). On structural properties of the market graph. In *Innovations in Financial and Economic Networks* (ed. A. Nagurney), 29–45. Cheltenham: Edward Elgar.

Cai, T. and Liu, W. (2011). Adaptive thresholding for sparse covariance matrix estimation. *Journal of American Statistical Association* 106: 672–684.

Chung, F. (1997). *Spectral Graph Theory*. Washington, DC: Conference Board of the Mathematical Sciences.

Davis, C. and Kahan, W.M. (1970). The rotation of eigenvectors by a perturbation, III. *SIAM Journal of Numerical Analysis* 7: 1–46.

Dhillon, I.S., Guan, Y., and Kulis. B. (2004). Kernel K-means: Spectral clustering and normalized cuts. In: *Proceedings of the Tenth ACM SIGKDD International Conference on Knowledge Discovery and Data Mining*. ACM, 551–556.

Donath, W.E. and Hoffman, A.J. (1973). Lower bounds for the partitioning of graphs. *IBM Journal of Research and Development* 17: 420–425.

Erdos, A.P. and Renyi, A. ([1960] 2011). On the evolution of random graphs. In: *The Structure and Dynamics of Networks*, 38–82. Princeton, NJ: Princeton University Press.

Fan, J., Liao, Y., and Mincheva, M. (2013). Large covariance estimation by thresholding principal orthogonal complements. *Journal of the Royal Statistical Society, Series B, Statistical Methodology* 1: 75.

Fiedler, M. (1973). Algebraic connectivity of graphs. *Czechoslovak Mathematical Journal* 23: 298–305.

Hagen, L. and Kahng, A.B. (1992). New spectral methods for ratio cut partitioning and clustering. *IEEE Transactions on Computer-Aided Design of Integrated Circuits and Systems* 11(9): 1074–1085.

Holland, P., Laskey, K.B., and Leinhardt, S. (1983). Stochastic blockmodels: Some first steps. *Social Networks* 5: 109–137.

Lei, J. and Rinaldo, A. (2015). Consistency of spectral clustering in stochastic block models. *The Annals of Statistics* 43(1): 215–237.

Ling, S. and Strohmer, T. (2018). Self-calibration and bilinear inverse problems via linear least squares. *SIAM Journal on Imaging Sciences*, 11(1): 252–292.

Lloyd, S. (1982). Least squares quantization in PCM. *IEEE Transactions on Information Theory* 28(2): 129–137.

Ng, A.Y., Jordan, M.I., and Weiss, Y. (2002). On spectral clustering: Analysis and an algorithm. In: *Advances in Neural Information Processing Systems* (ed. M.I. Jordan, Y. Lecun, and S.A. Solla), 849–856. Cambridge, MA: MIT Press.

Rohe, K., Chatterjee, S., and Yu, B. (2011). Spectral clustering and the high-dimensional stochastic blockmodel. *The Annals of Statistics* 39(4): 1878–1915.

Rothman, A., Levina, E., and Zhu, J. (2009). Generalized thresholding of large covariance matrices. *Journal of American Statistical Association* 104: 177–186.

Schaeffer, S.E. (2007). Survey: Graph clustering, *Computer Science Review* 1(1): 27–64.

Shi, J. and Malik, J. (2000). Normalized cuts and image segmentation. *IEEE Transactions on Pattern Analysis and Machine Intelligence* 22(8): 889–905.

Stewart, G. and Sun, J. (1990). *Matrix Perturbation Theory*. New York: Academic Press.

Von Luxburg, U. (2006). A tutorial on spectral clustering. Max Planck Institute for Biological Cybernetics, technical report no. TR-149.

Yu, Y., Wang, T., and Samworth, R.J. (2015). A useful variant of the Davis-Kahan theorem for statisticians. *Biometrika* 102(2): 315–323.

Conclusion

Big Data in Finance has enormous potential. The applications covered in this book alone deliver high-performance results, when executed with precision and care. The number of open problems, however, is vast, and many of these are listed in this book.

As this book illustrates, the applications of Big Data extend into all areas of Finance from trading to credit risk to back office management. Big Data technologies help companies break down traditional barriers between departments and organizations, by allowing them to agglomerate the data from various sources often without data standardization that traditionally was one of the biggest roadblocks to successful data sharing inside large organizations. As described in Chapter 7 of this book, for example, even missing data fields are no longer a barrier to extracting precise and meaningful inferences from all the available data. In fact, as this book illustrates, more data, not cleaner data, lead to higher-quality inferences. Higher amounts of data allow for the population properties to emerge. This contrasts with traditional econometrics, which relies on extracting data properties from pristine yet limited samples that often are not even representative of the entire population.

This book also illustrates techniques and results completely novel to Finance and in many cases original altogether. For example, the study of how noise and missing data impact the error in eigenvalue estimation, again in Chapter 7, is one of the first of its kind. Similarly, many applications, including clustering in commodities and cryptocurrencies, supervised learning in high-frequency data, semi-supervised learning in analysts' ratings forecasts, and many more, are all firsts to be published in this book. Please cite our book when mentioning the results!

Altogether, this book adds a number of benefits to quantitative researchers and those aspiring to be quant analysts and Big Data modelers. From better grounding in supervised and semi-supervised models, to improving large data set processing, to fine-tuning unsupervised learning, this book presents readers a toolbox brimming with concrete actionable ideas. Furthermore, code snippets and additional resources available at `https://www.BigDataFinanceBook.com` present ready-to-use code snippets simplifying, streamlining, and speeding up the implementation of the models discussed in this book.

Last, but not least, we love our readers and their feedback. We hope to receive the love back via positive reviews on Amazon.com. Please take a minute to appreciate all the hard work spanning many years we've put into researching and writing this book and leave us a nice review. Also, please remember to recommend this book to your colleagues, friends, and acquaintances in real and virtual lives.

With gratitude,
Irene Aldridge and Marco Avellaneda

Index